Toshiaki Iwashiro

Thank you all for sticking with me all this time. Bye for now.

The *Psyren* manga ends here, but you can enjoy the continuation of the story in the novelization by SOW.

Toshiaki Iwashiro was born December 11, 1977, in Tokyo and has the blood type of A. His debut manga was the popular *Mieru Hito*, which ran from 2005 to 2007 in Japan in *Weekly Shonen Jump*, where *Psyren* was also serialized.

PSYREN VOL. 16
SHONEN JUMP Manga Edition

STORY AND ART BY TOSHIAKI IWASHIRO

Translation/Camellia Nieh
Lettering/Annaliese Christman
Design/Matt Hinrichs
Editor/Erica Yee

PSYREN © 2007 by Toshiaki Iwashiro
All rights reserved.
First published in Japan in 2007 by SHUEISHA Inc., Tokyo.
English translation rights arranged by SHUEISHA Inc.

Printed in the U.S.A.

Published by VIZ Media, LLC
P.O. Box 77010
San Francisco, CA 94107

10 9 8 7 6 5 4 3 2 1
First printing, May 2014

THE WORLD'S
MOST POPULAR MANGA
www.shonenjump.com

www.viz.com

SHONEN JUMP MANGA EDITION

PSYREN

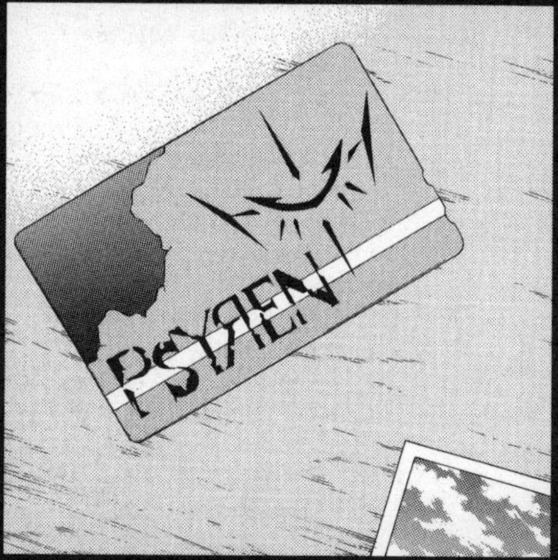
PSYREN

16

CONNECTED WORLD

Story and Art by
Toshiaki Iwashiro

AGEHA YOSHINA

SAKURAKO AMAMIYA

HIRYU ASAGA

OBORO MOCHIZUKI

KABUTO KIRISAKI

Characters

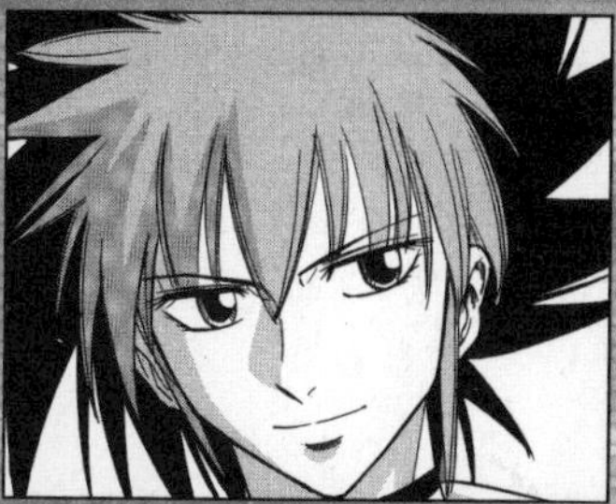

MATSURI YAGUMO

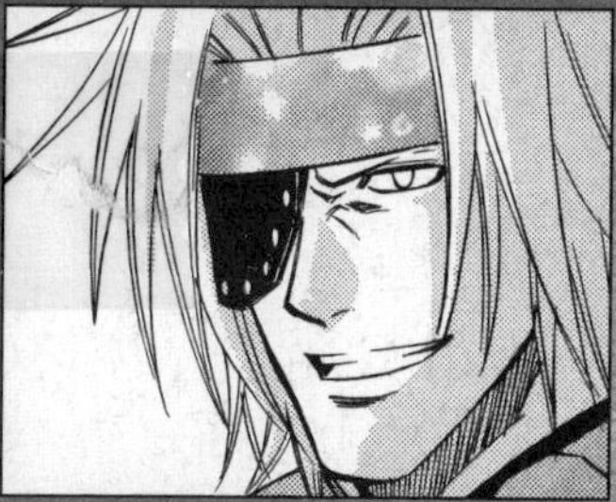

GRANAR

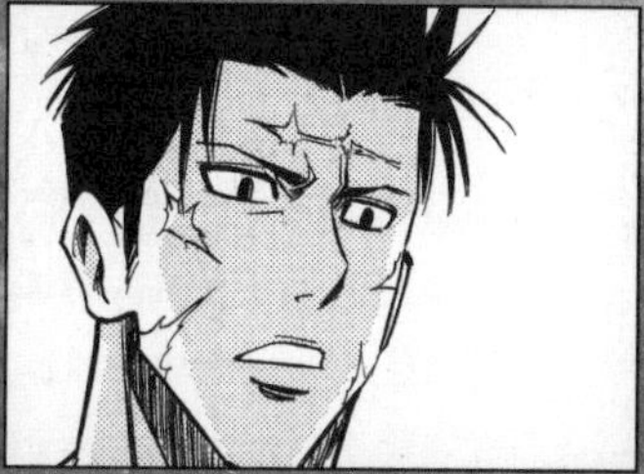

KAGETORA HYODO

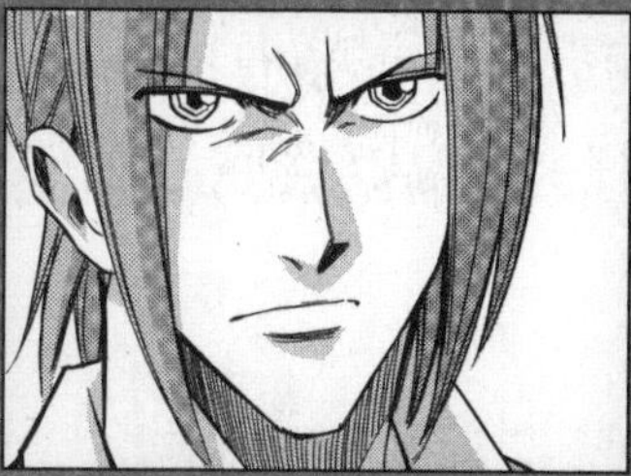

MIROKU AMAGI

Story

THIS IS THE STORY OF A GROUP OF TEENAGERS CAUGHT UP IN A LIFE-OR-DEATH GAME THAT HAS THEM TRAVELING BACK AND FORTH BETWEEN THE PRESENT AND THE FUTURE, IN A DESPERATE BATTLE TO AVERT THE END OF THE WORLD AS THEY KNOW IT.

WHEN AGEHA'S FRIENDS AND THE ELMORE WOOD GANG ATTACK W.I.S.E'S CAPITAL TO RESCUE THEIR FRIENDS, KYLE AND THE OTHERS FIND THEMSELVES IN A DESPERATE STRUGGLE FOR THEIR LIVES AGAINST THE STAR COMMANDERS. FORTUNATELY, THE LONG LOST OBORO APPEARS JUST IN TIME, AS DO MATSURI AND KAGETORA, WHO HAVE FINALLY MADE IT TO PSYREN. AS THE MELEE INTENSIFIES, AGEHA CONFRONTS MIROKU AMAGI ALONE TO SETTLE THE SCORE ONCE AND FOR ALL.

VOL. 16
CONNECTED WORLD
CONTENTS

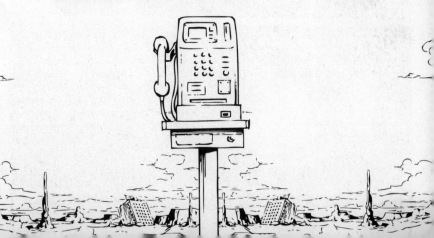

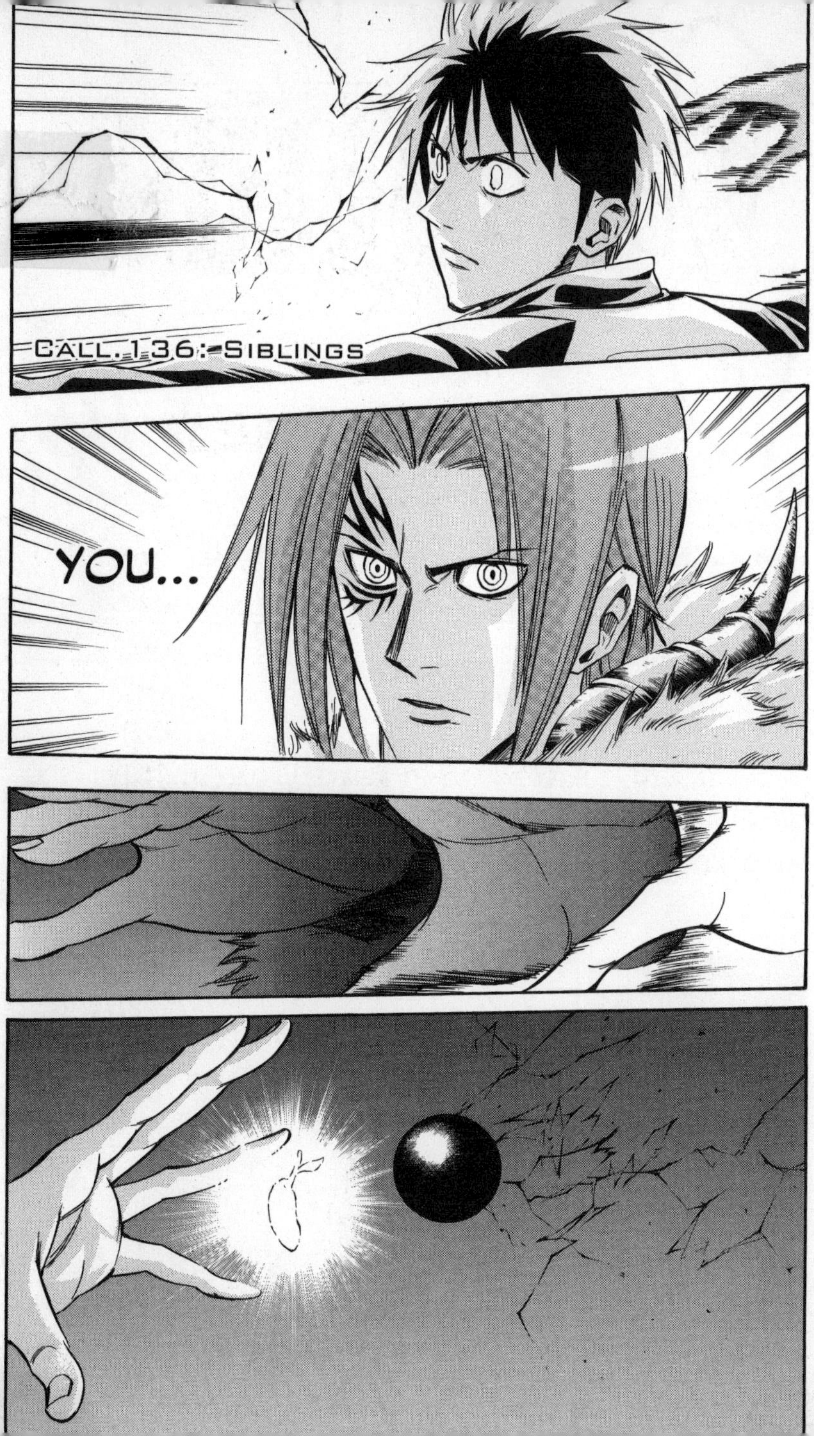
CALL. 136: SIBLINGS
YOU...

BWO
OSH
THERE ARE COUNTLESS STARS IN THE SKY.
ONLY DESTINY COULD CAUSE A REPEAT ENCOUNTER WITH THE SAME ONE.
WE MEET AGAIN, BOY.

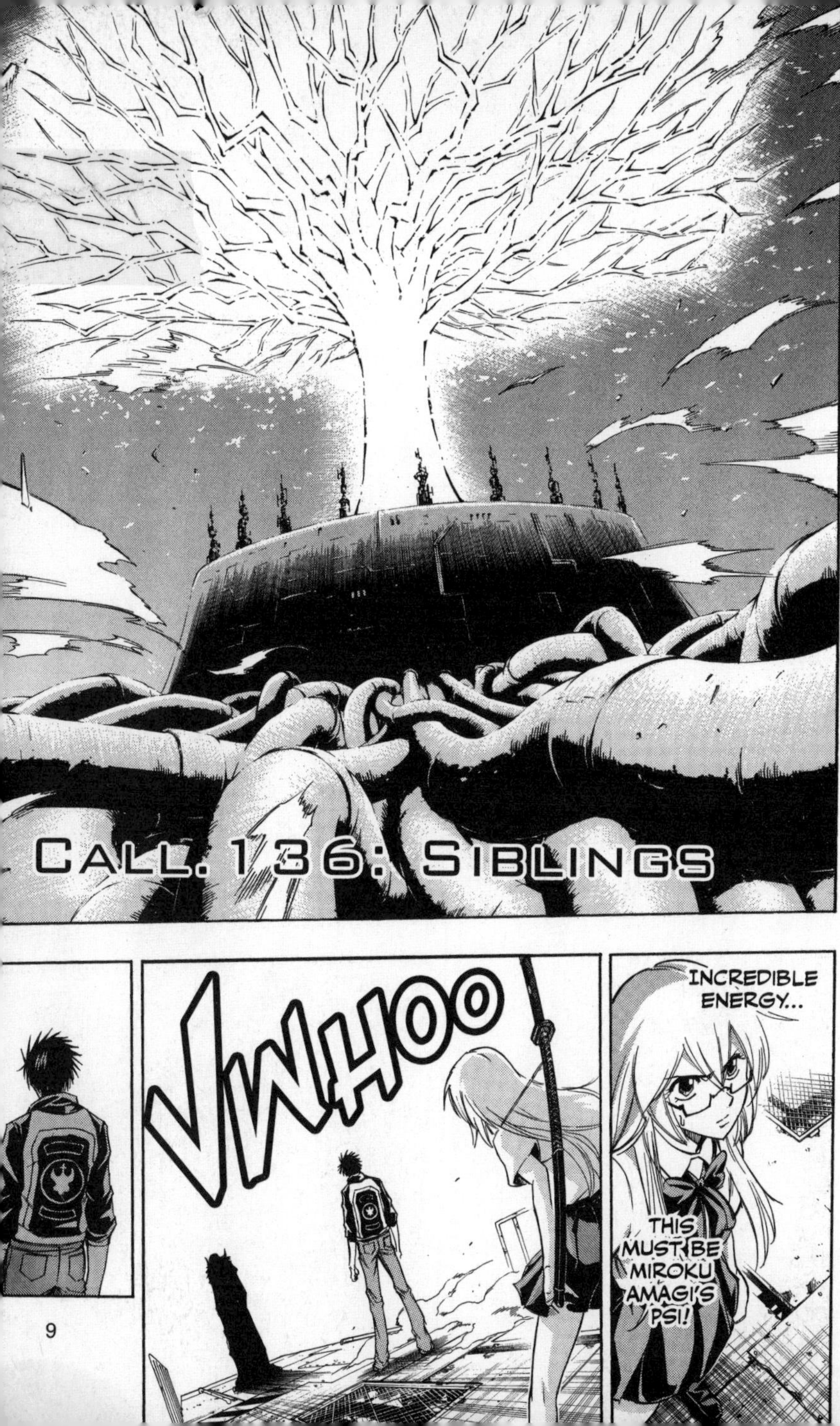
CALL. 136: SIBLINGS
INCREDIBLE ENERGY...
THIS MUST BE MIROKU AMAGI'S PSI!
VWHOO

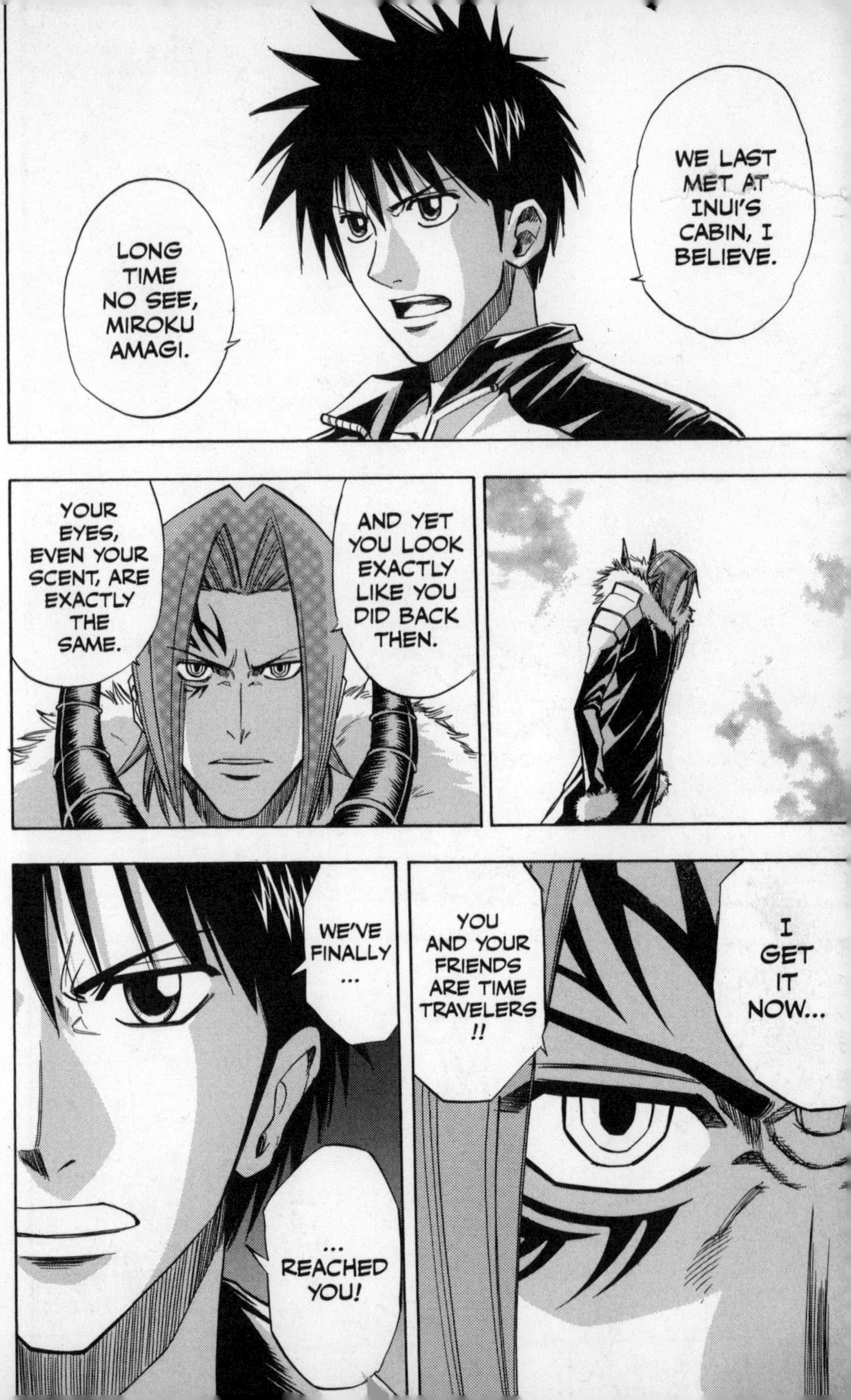
WE LAST MET AT INUI'S CABIN, I BELIEVE.
LONG TIME NO SEE, MIROKU AMAGI.
AND YET YOU LOOK EXACTLY LIKE YOU DID BACK THEN.
YOUR EYES, EVEN YOUR SCENT, ARE EXACTLY THE SAME.
I GET IT NOW...
YOU AND YOUR FRIENDS ARE TIME TRAVELERS !!
WE'VE FINALLY ...
... REACHED YOU!

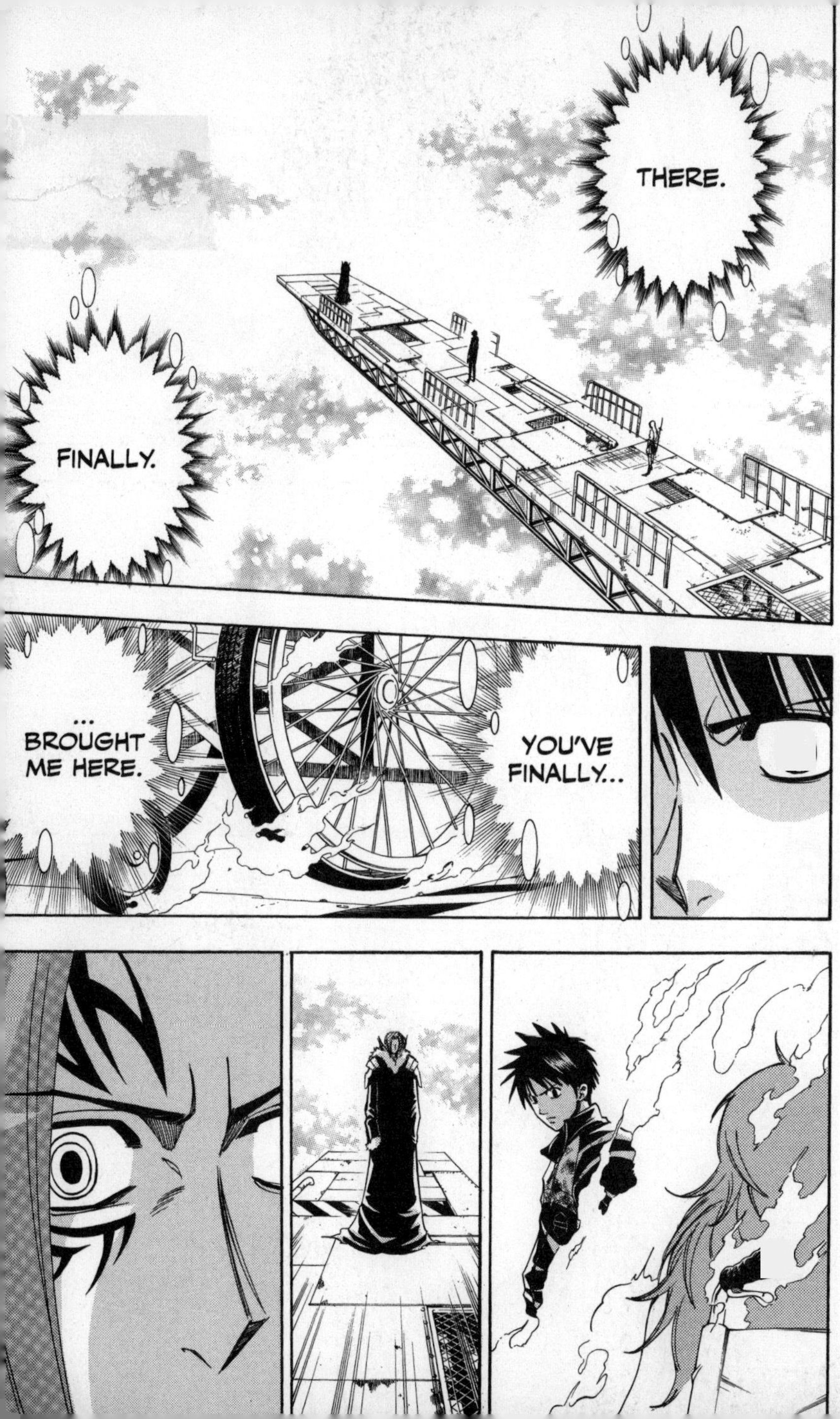
THERE.
FINALLY.
YOU'VE FINALLY...
... BROUGHT ME HERE.

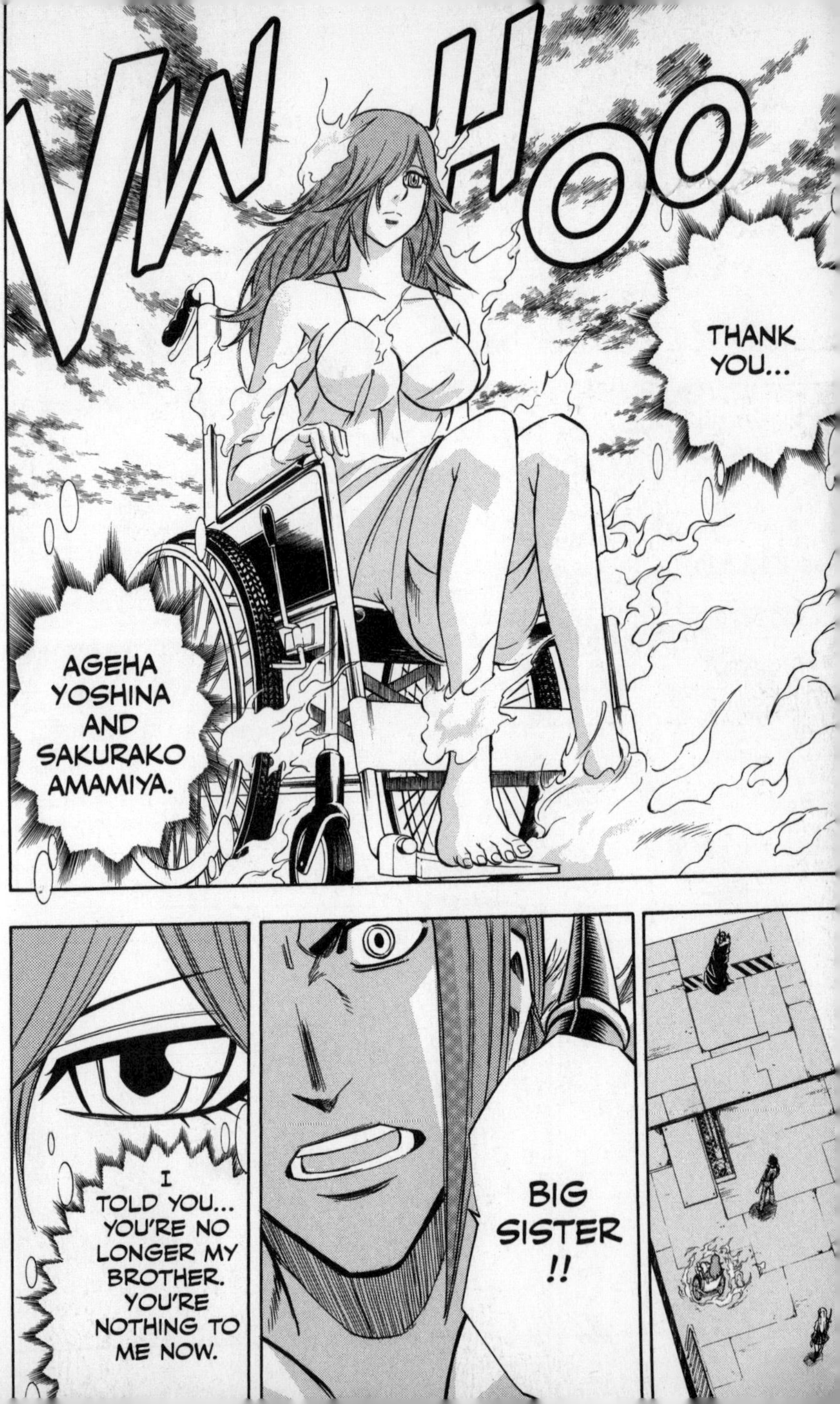
VWHOO
THANK YOU...
AGEHA YOSHINA AND SAKURAKO AMAMIYA.
BIG SISTER !!
I TOLD YOU... YOU'RE NO LONGER MY BROTHER. YOU'RE NOTHING TO ME NOW.

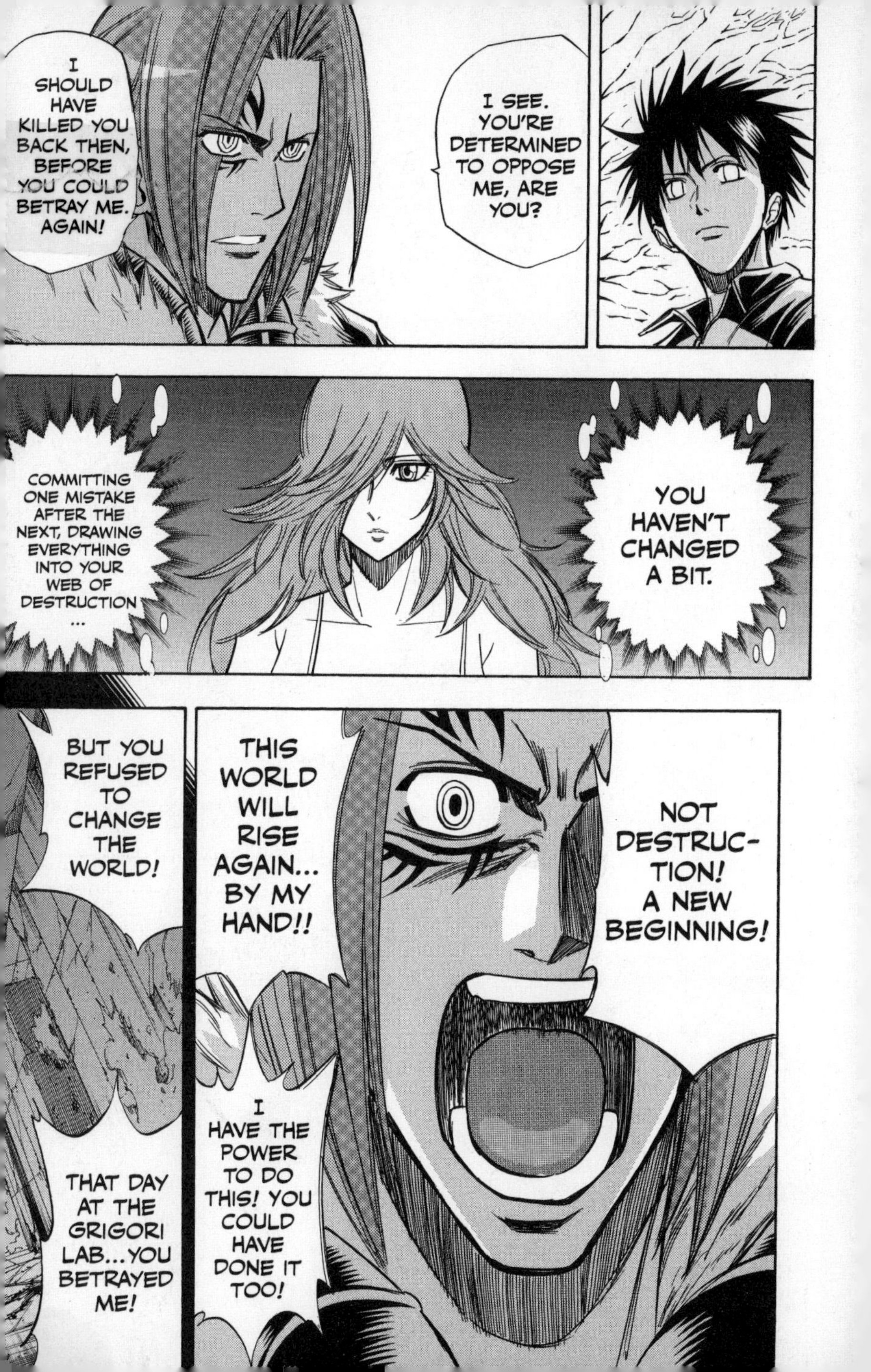
I SEE. YOU'RE DETERMINED TO OPPOSE ME, ARE YOU?
I SHOULD HAVE KILLED YOU BACK THEN, BEFORE YOU COULD BETRAY ME. AGAIN!
YOU HAVEN'T CHANGED A BIT.
COMMITTING ONE MISTAKE AFTER THE NEXT, DRAWING EVERYTHING INTO YOUR WEB OF DESTRUCTION...
NOT DESTRUC-TION! A NEW BEGINNING!
THIS WORLD WILL RISE AGAIN... BY MY HAND!!
I HAVE THE POWER TO DO THIS! YOU COULD HAVE DONE IT TOO!
BUT YOU REFUSED TO CHANGE THE WORLD!
THAT DAY AT THE GRIGORI LAB...YOU BETRAYED ME!

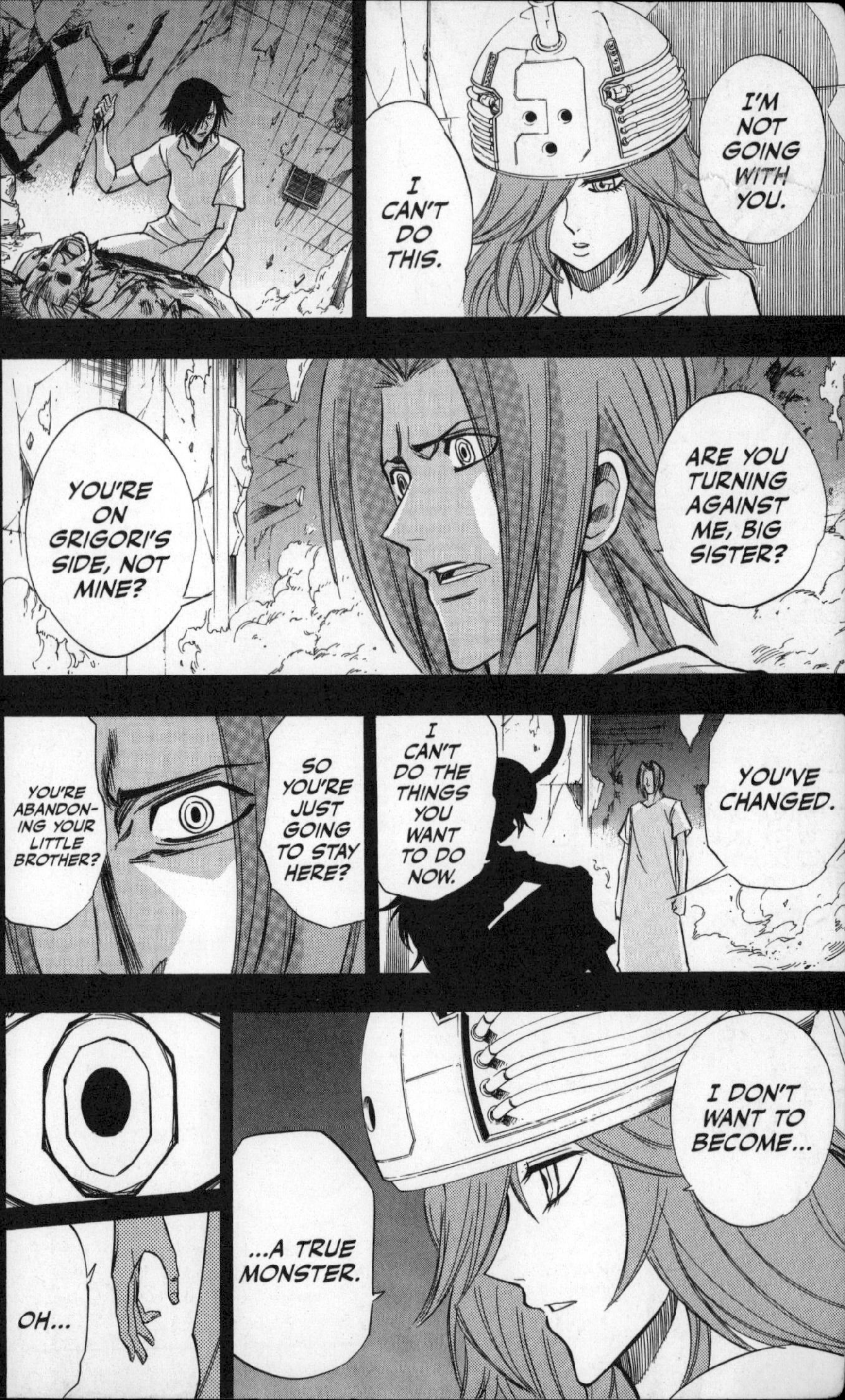
I'M NOT GOING WITH YOU.
I CAN'T DO THIS.
ARE YOU TURNING AGAINST ME, BIG SISTER?
YOU'RE ON GRIGORI'S SIDE, NOT MINE?
YOU'VE CHANGED.
I CAN'T DO THE THINGS YOU WANT TO DO NOW.
SO YOU'RE JUST GOING TO STAY HERE?
YOU'RE ABANDONING YOUR LITTLE BROTHER?
I DON'T WANT TO BECOME...
...A TRUE MONSTER.
OH...

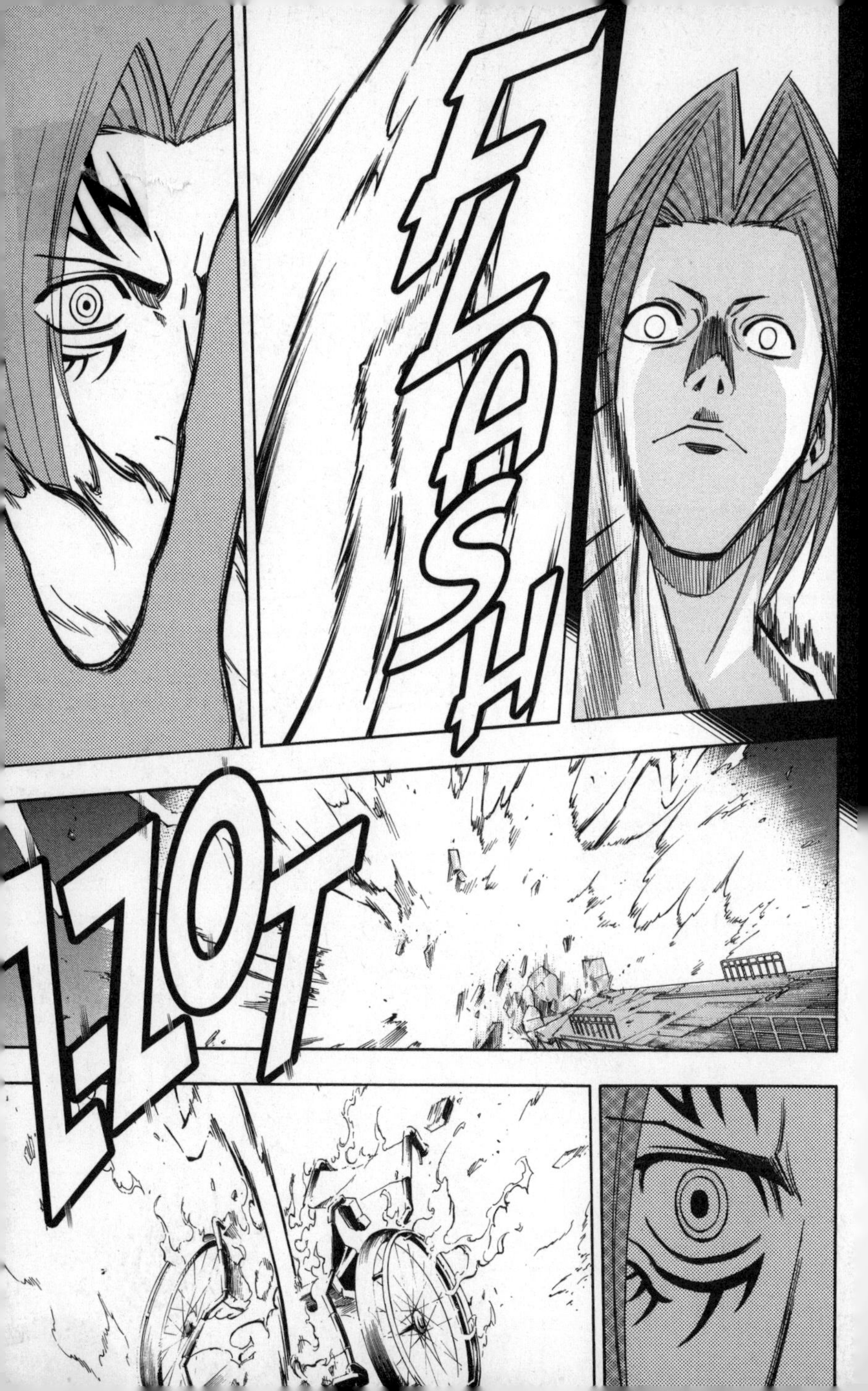
FLASH
ZZOT

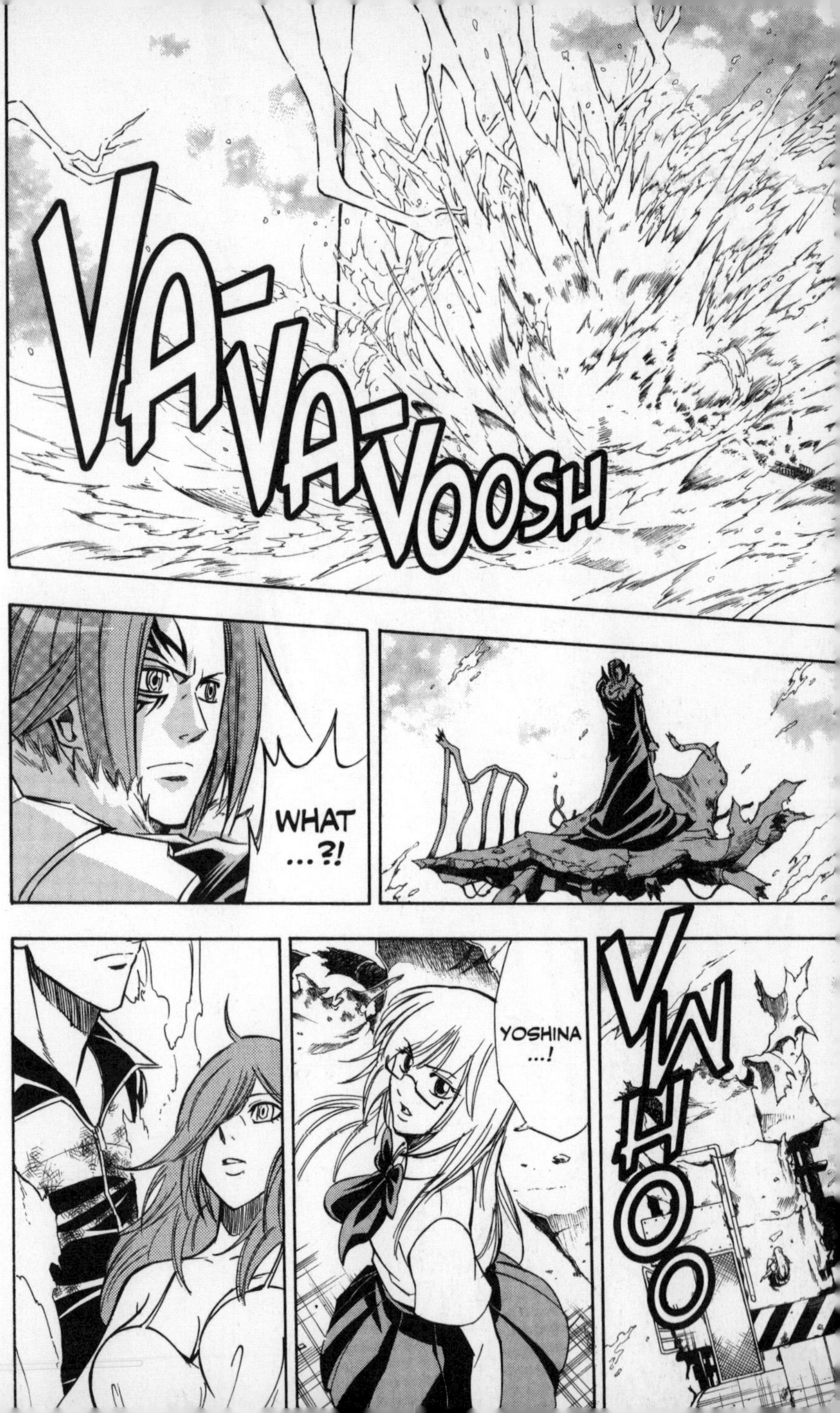
VA-VA-VOOSH
WHAT ...?!
VWHOO
YOSHINA ...!

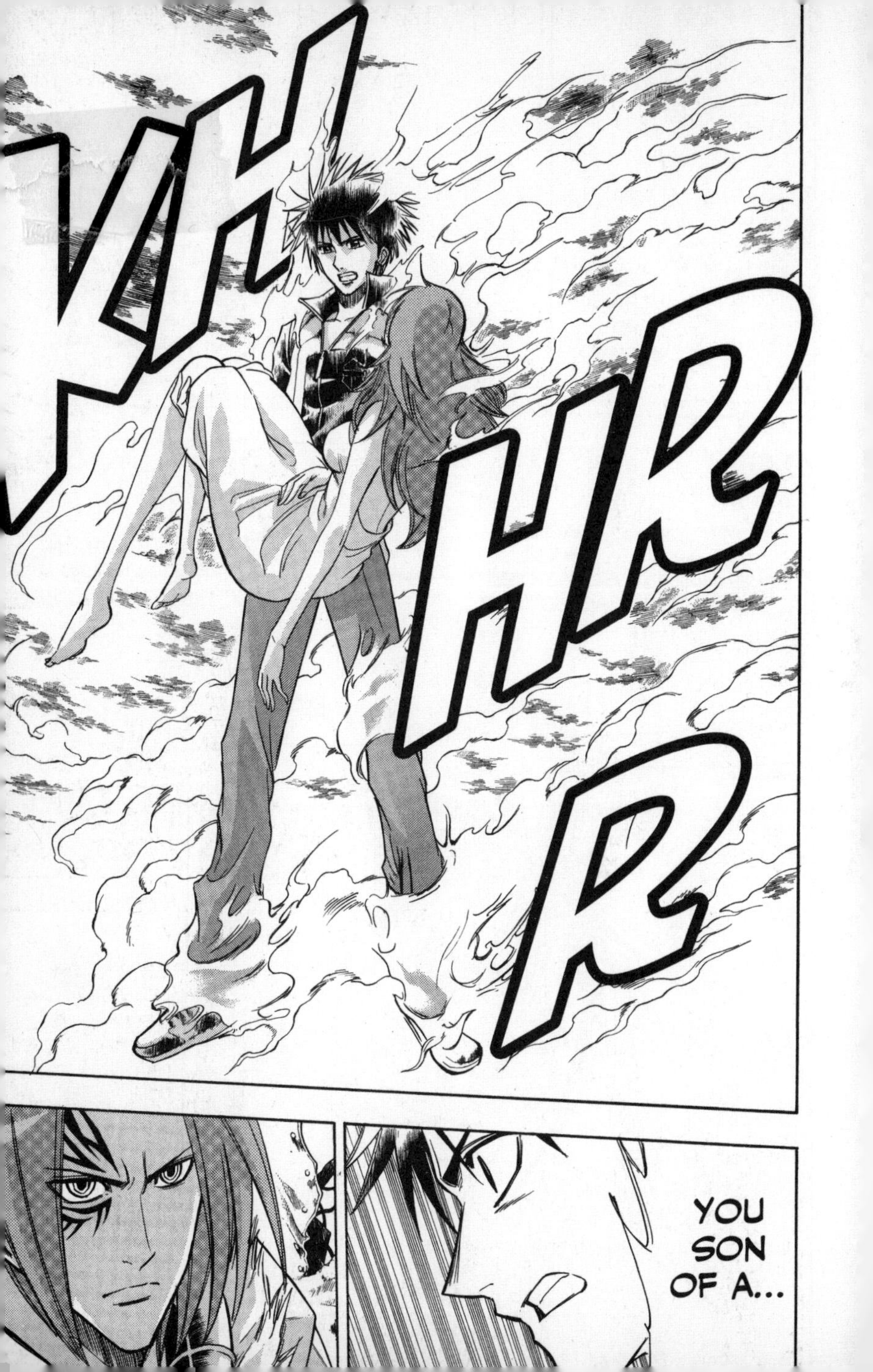
YOU SON OF A...

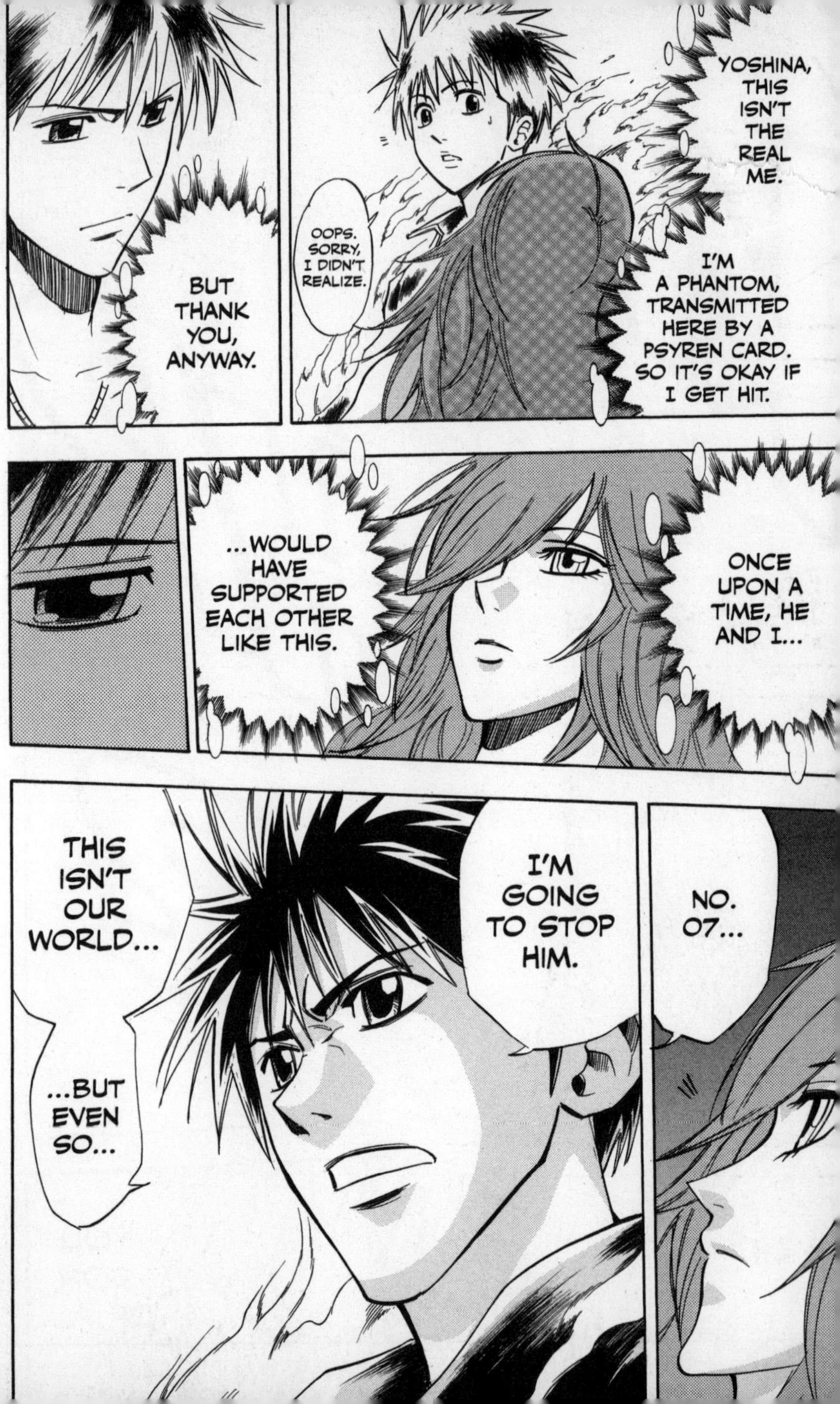
YOSHINA, THIS ISN'T THE REAL ME.
I'M A PHANTOM, TRANSMITTED HERE BY A PSYREN CARD. SO IT'S OKAY IF I GET HIT.
OOPS. SORRY, I DIDN'T REALIZE.
BUT THANK YOU, ANYWAY.
ONCE UPON A TIME, HE AND I...
...WOULD HAVE SUPPORTED EACH OTHER LIKE THIS.
NO. 07...
I'M GOING TO STOP HIM.
THIS ISN'T OUR WORLD...
...BUT EVEN SO...

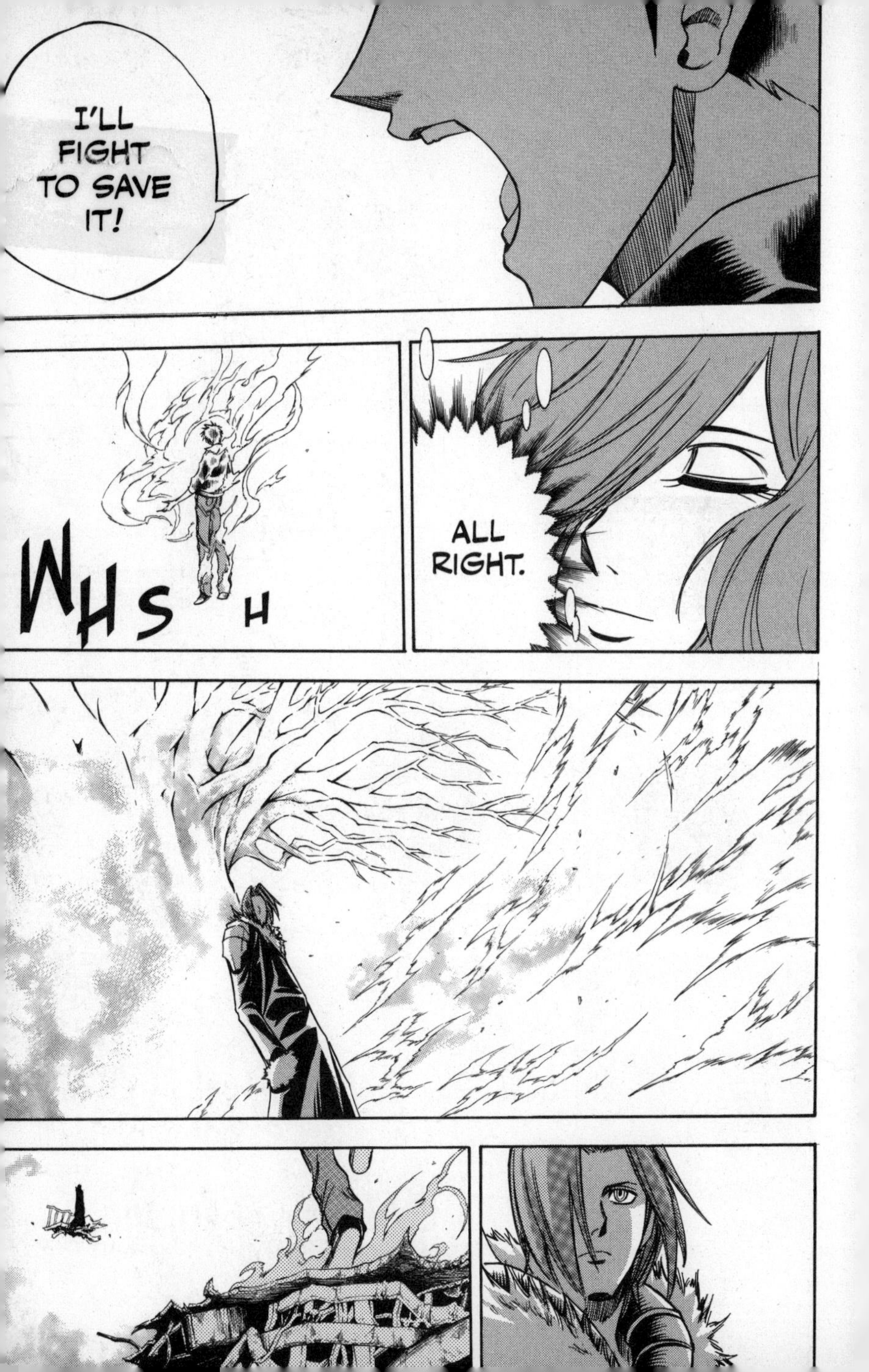
I'LL FIGHT TO SAVE IT!
ALL RIGHT.
WHSH

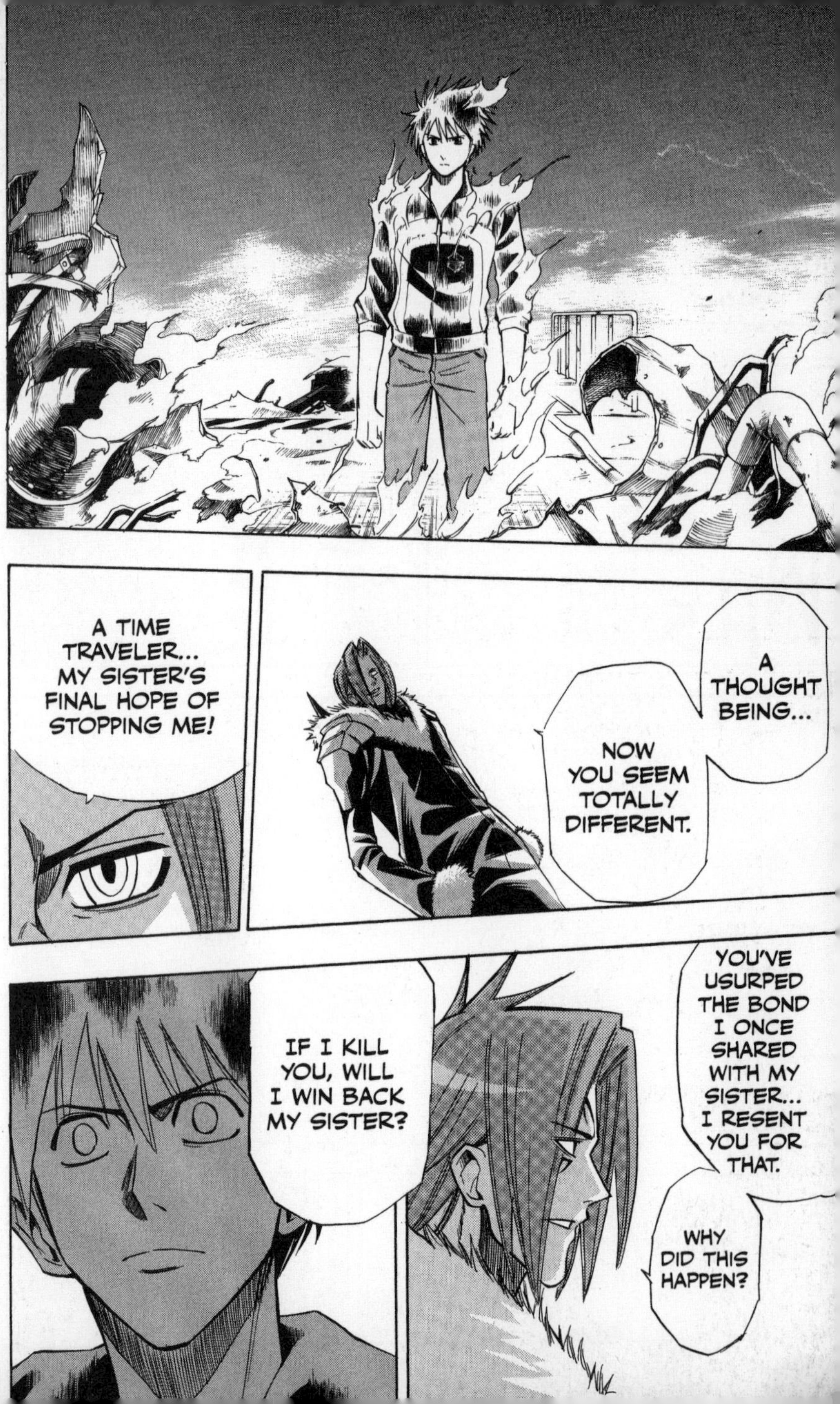
A THOUGHT BEING...
NOW YOU SEEM TOTALLY DIFFERENT.
A TIME TRAVELER... MY SISTER'S FINAL HOPE OF STOPPING ME!
YOU'VE USURPED THE BOND I ONCE SHARED WITH MY SISTER... I RESENT YOU FOR THAT.
WHY DID THIS HAPPEN?
IF I KILL YOU, WILL I WIN BACK MY SISTER?

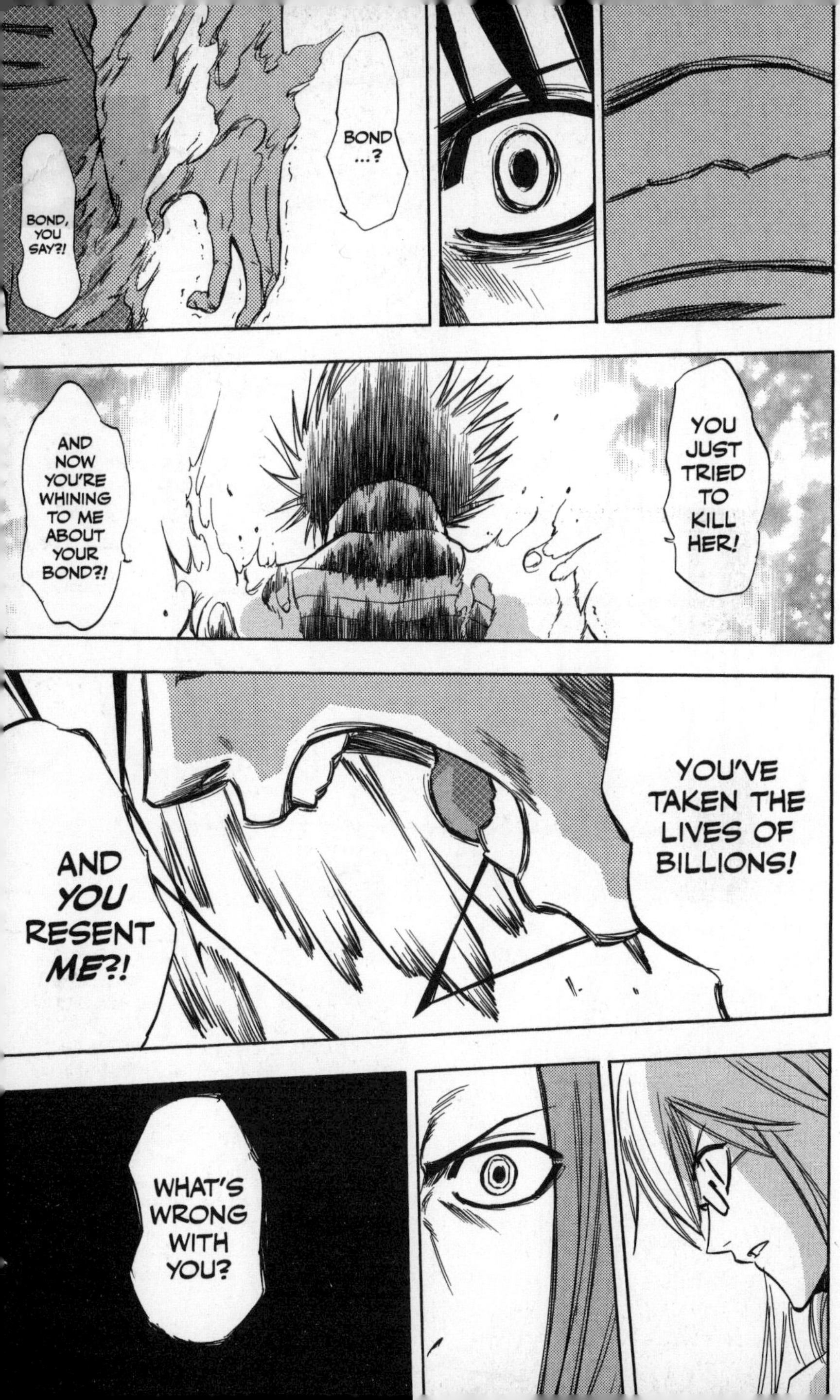
BOND ...?
BOND, YOU SAY?!
YOU JUST TRIED TO KILL HER!
AND NOW YOU'RE WHINING TO ME ABOUT YOUR BOND?!
YOU'VE TAKEN THE LIVES OF BILLIONS!
AND *YOU* RESENT *ME*?!
WHAT'S WRONG WITH YOU?

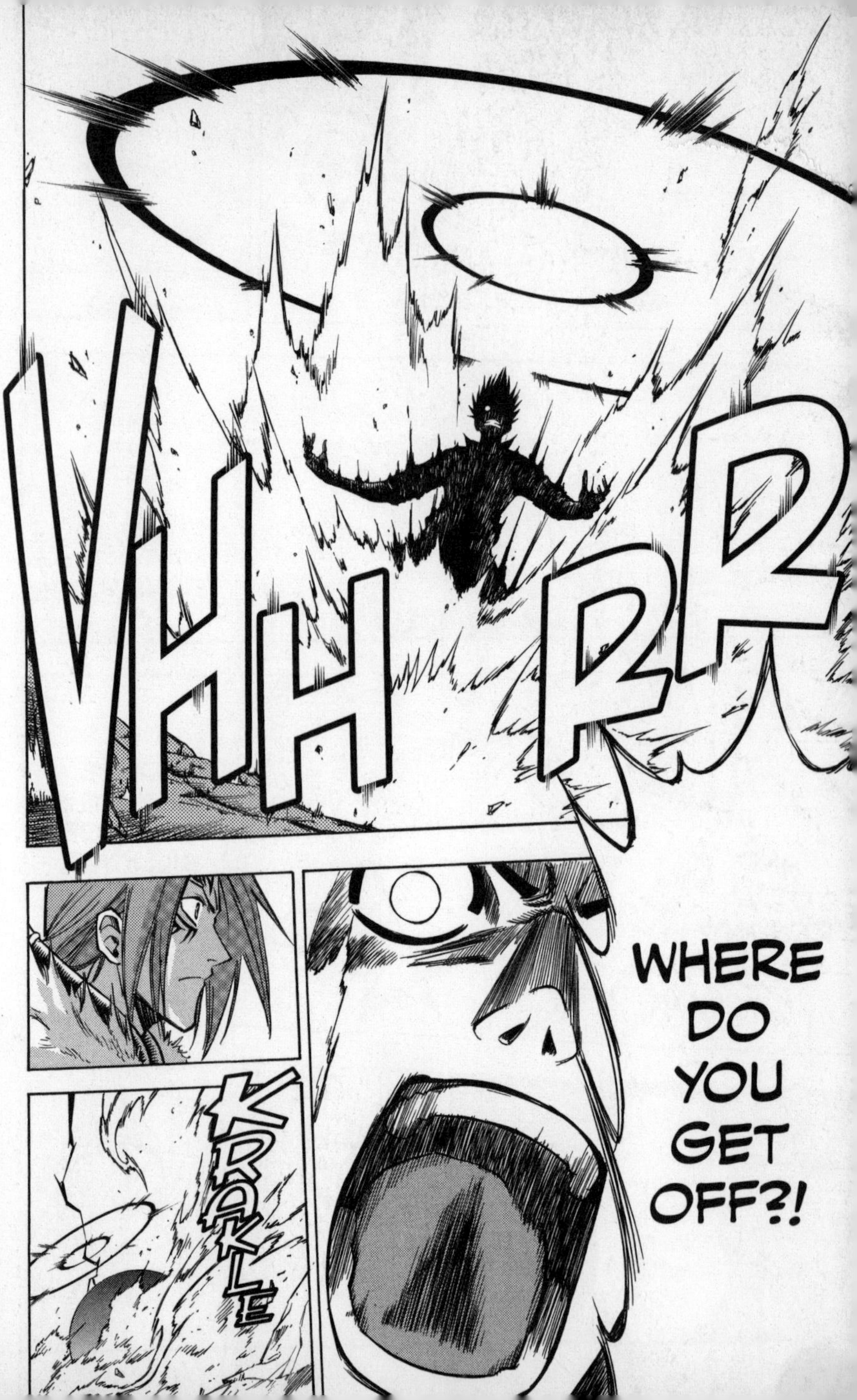
VHHRR
WHERE DO YOU GET OFF?!
KRAKLE

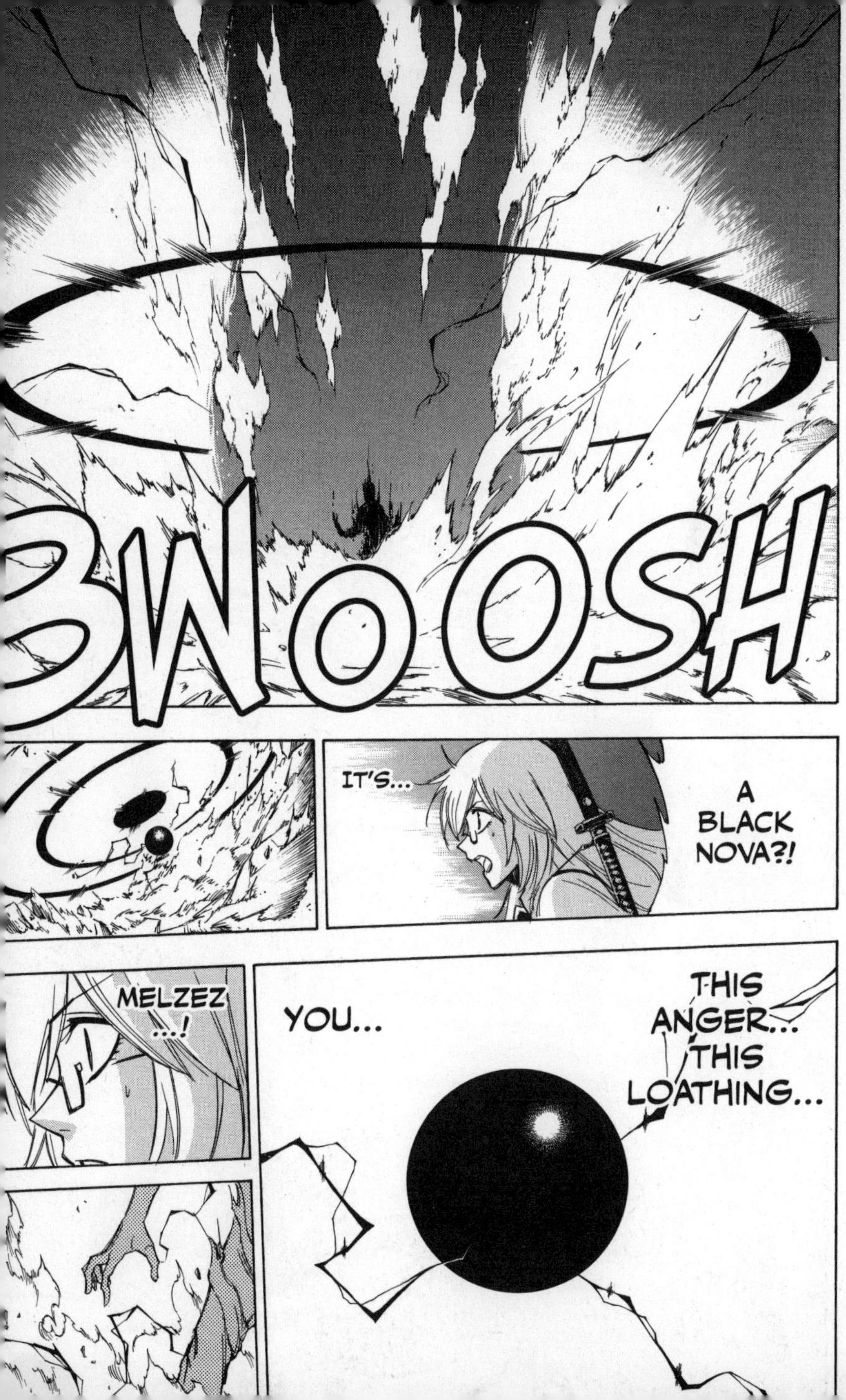
BWOOSH
IT'S...
A BLACK NOVA?!
THIS ANGER... THIS LOATHING...
YOU...
MELZEZ ...!

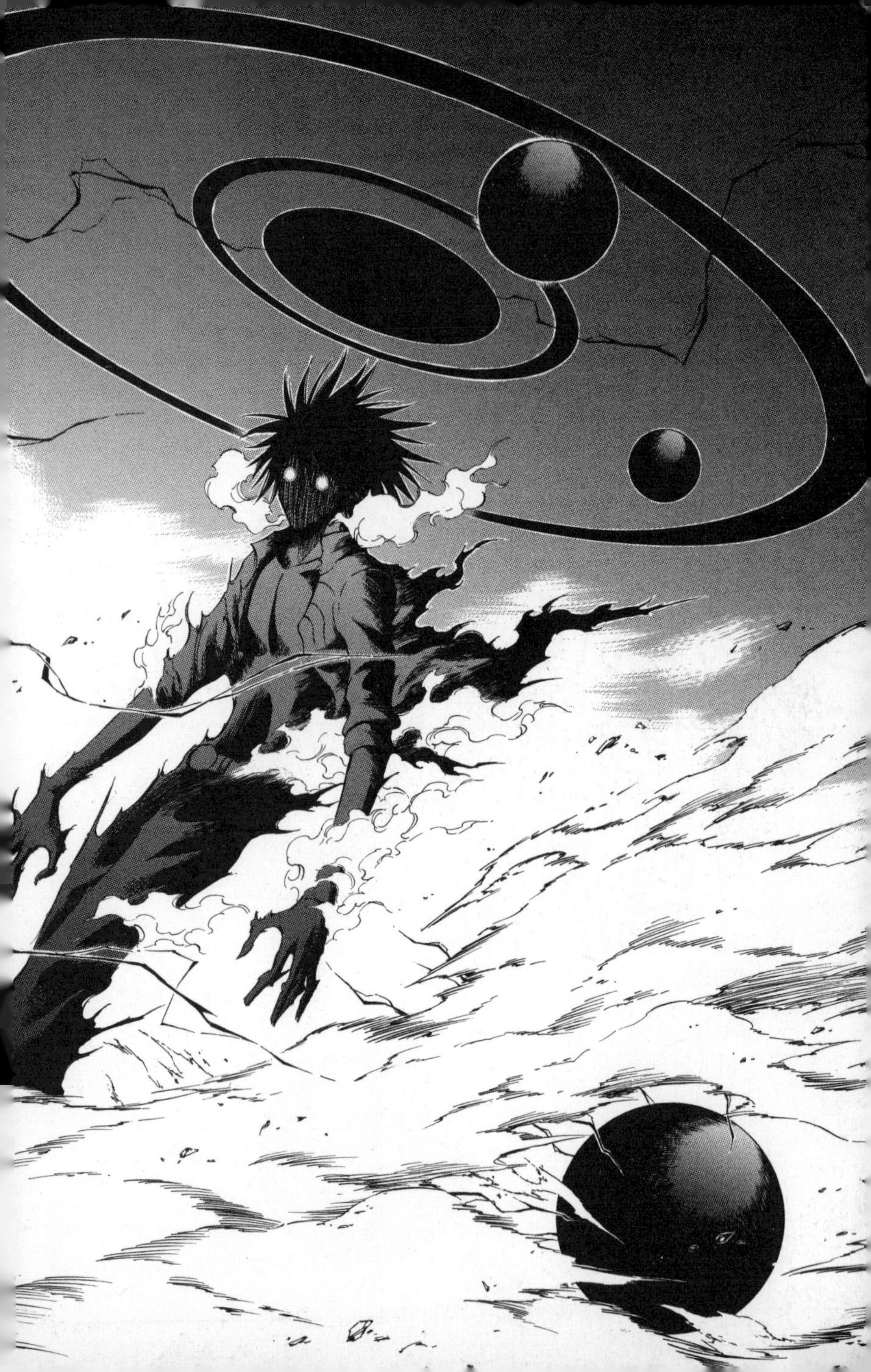

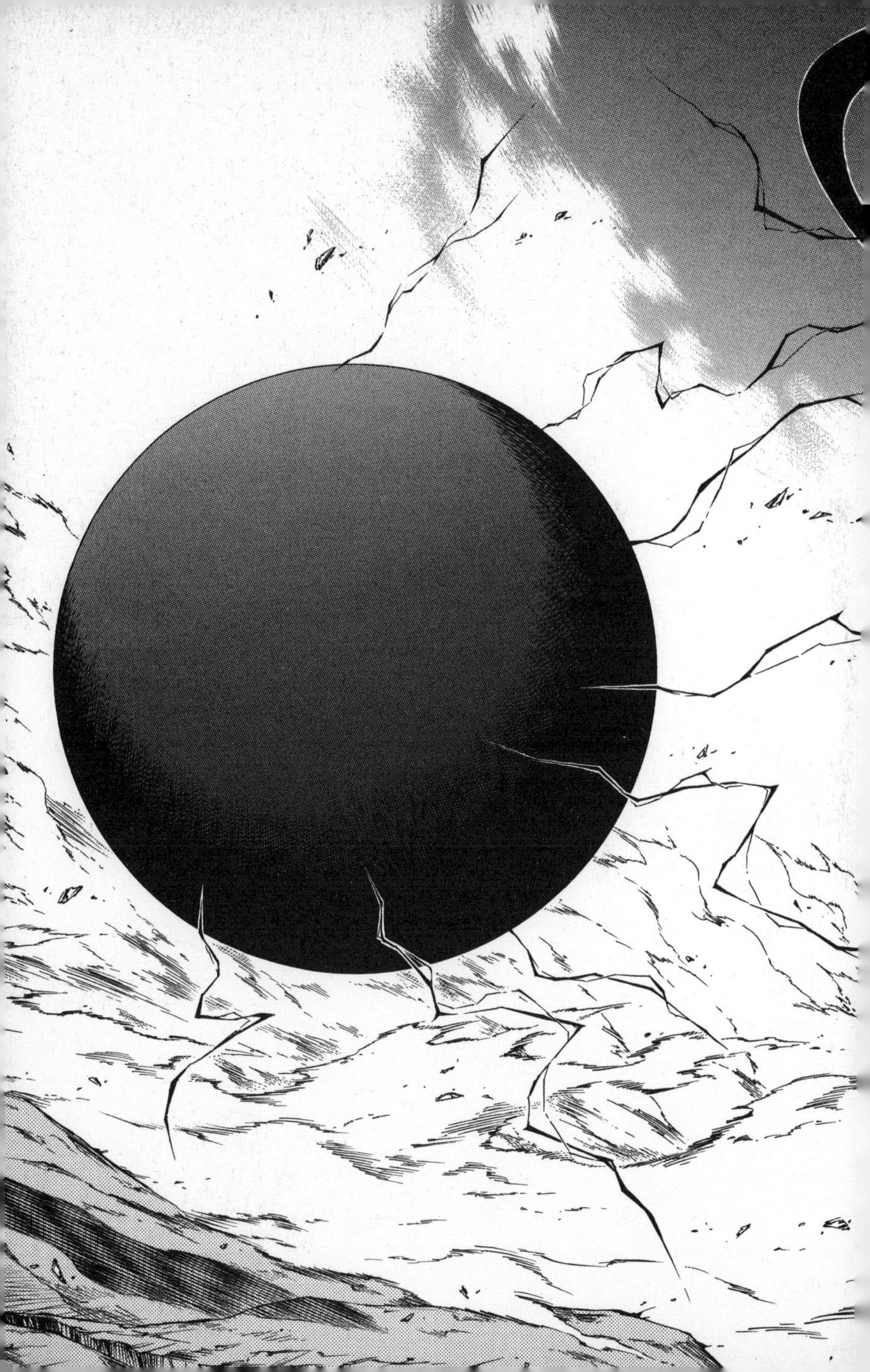

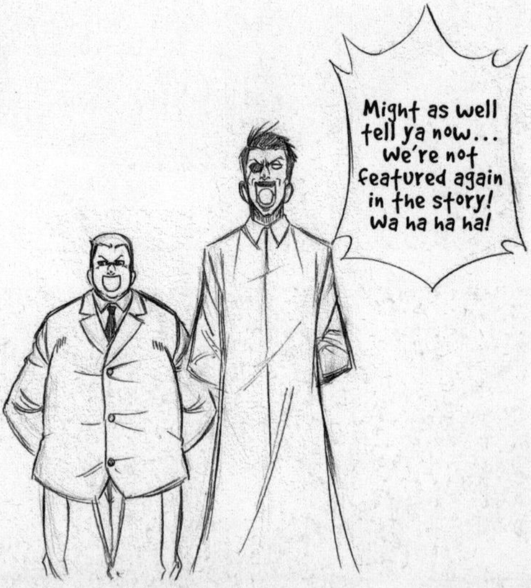
Might as well tell ya now... We're not featured again in the story! Wa ha ha ha!

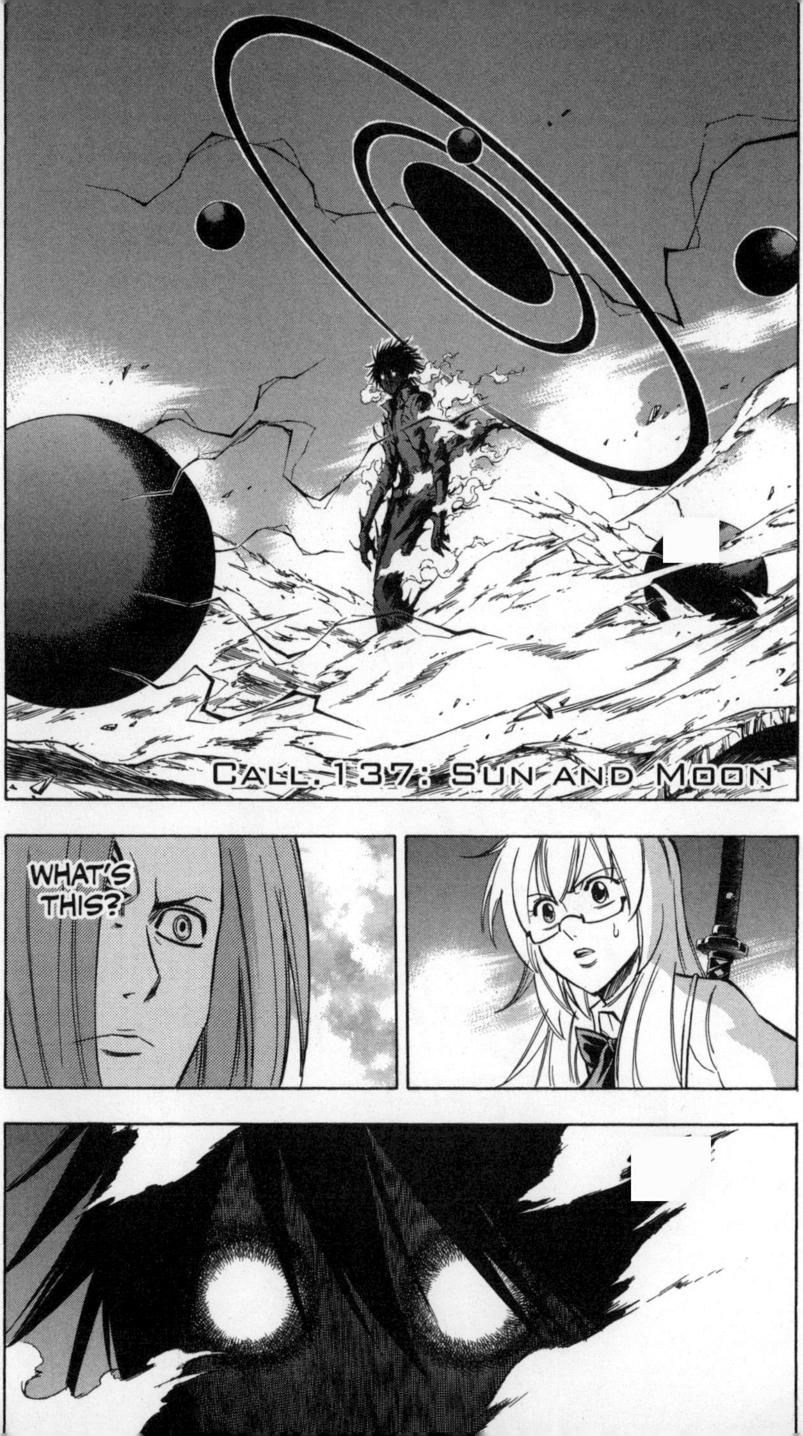
CALL. 137: SUN AND MOON
WHAT'S THIS?

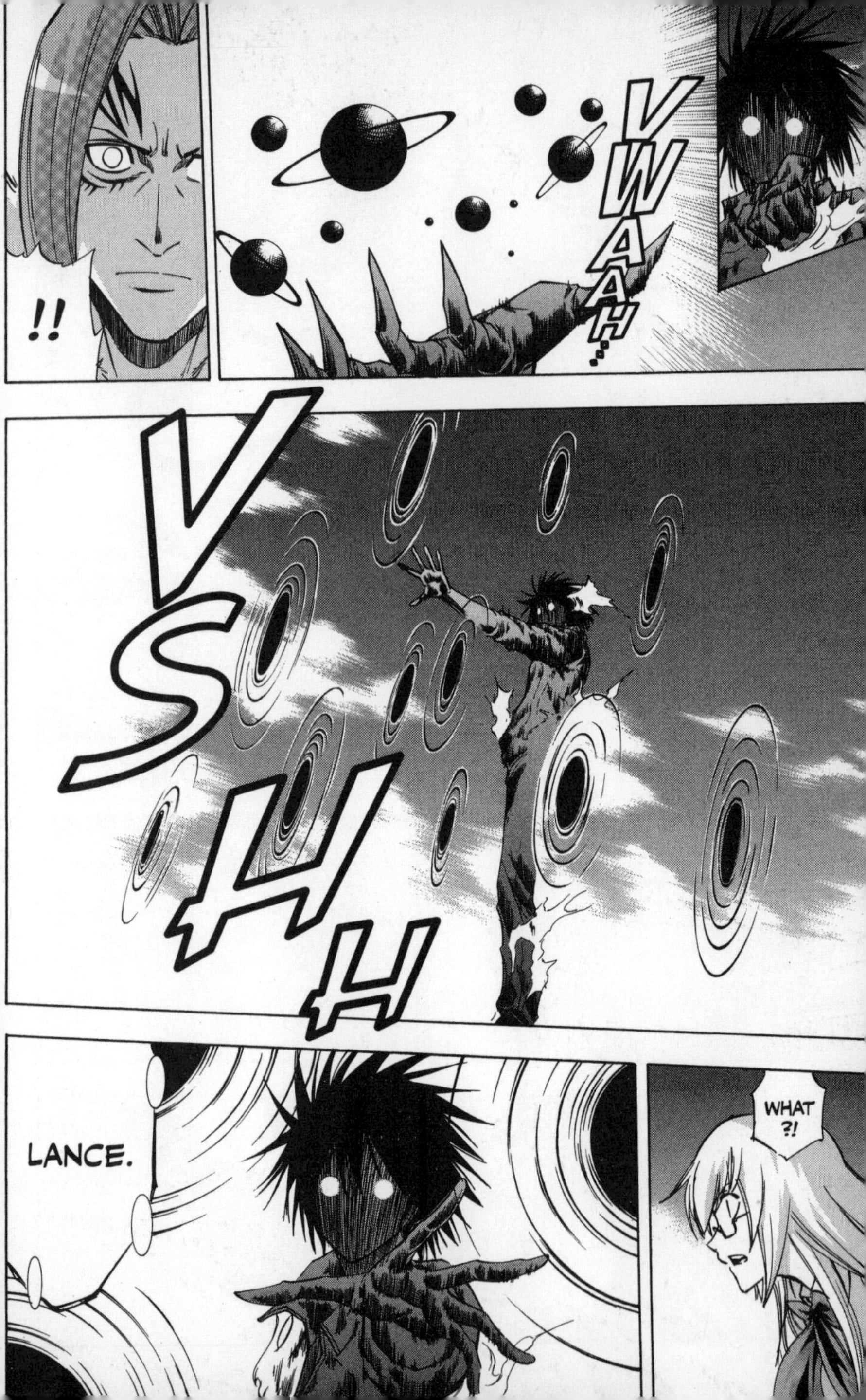
VWAAAH...
!!
VSHH
WHAT?!
LANCE.

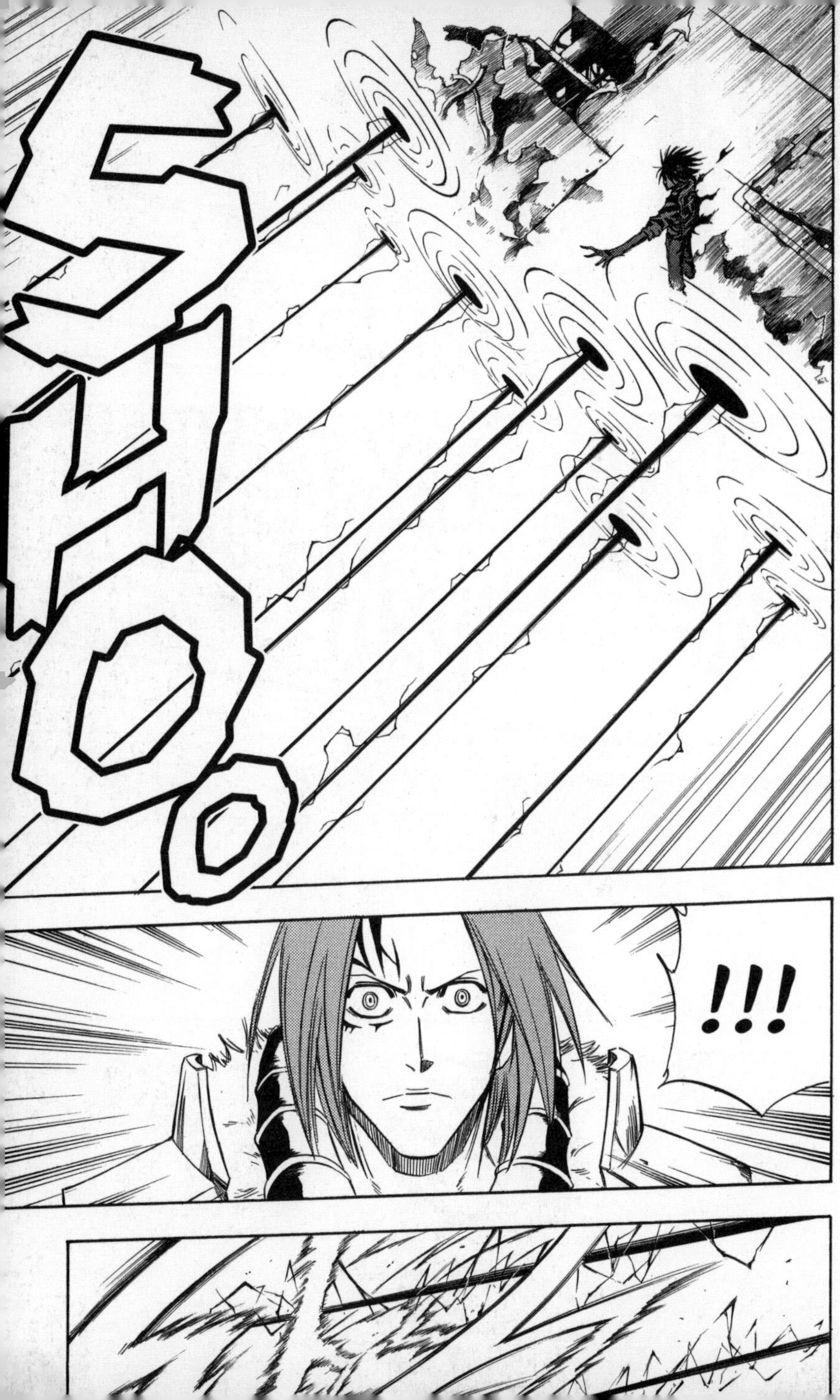
!!!

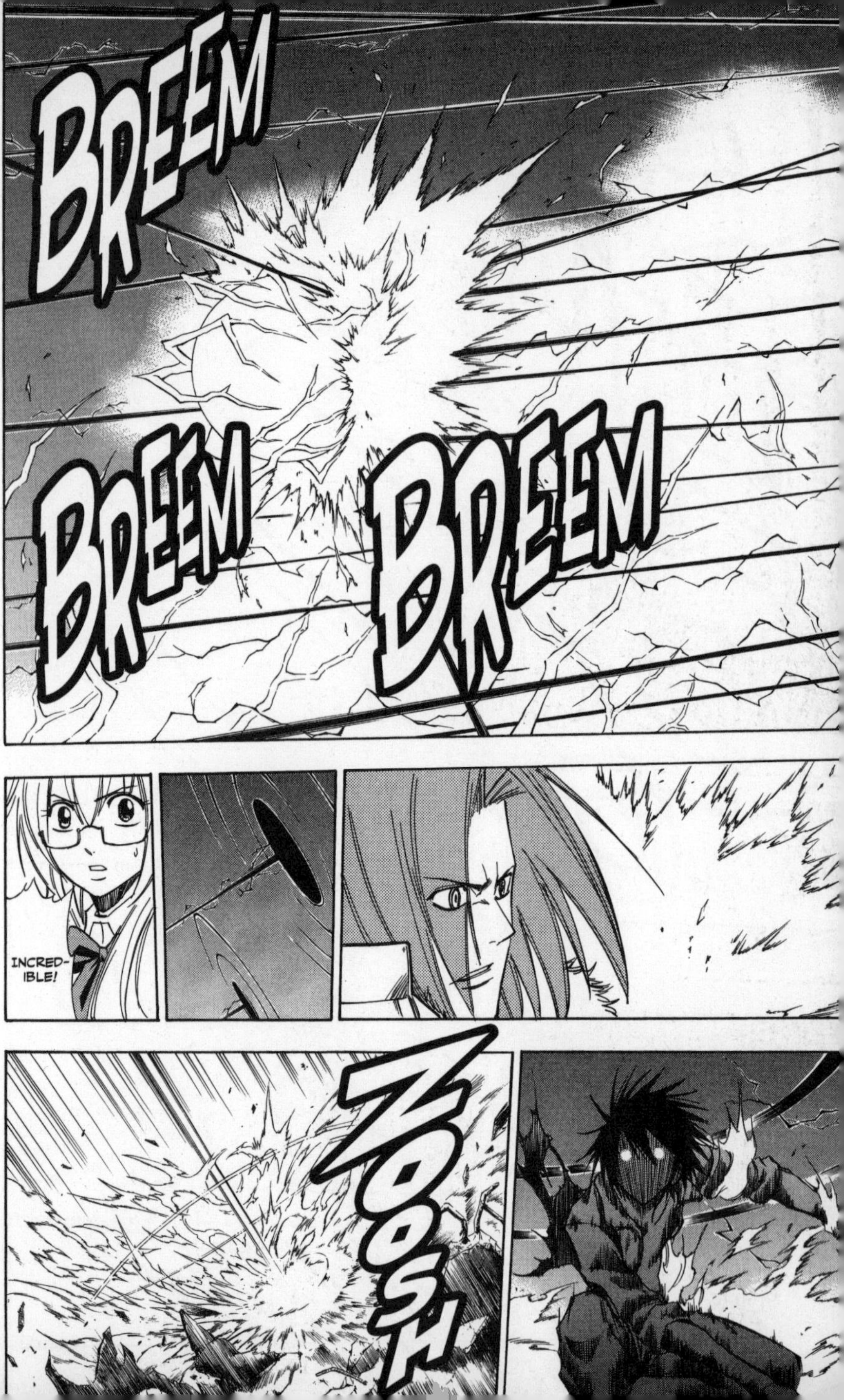
BREEM
BREEM
BREEM
INCRED-IBLE!
ZOOSH

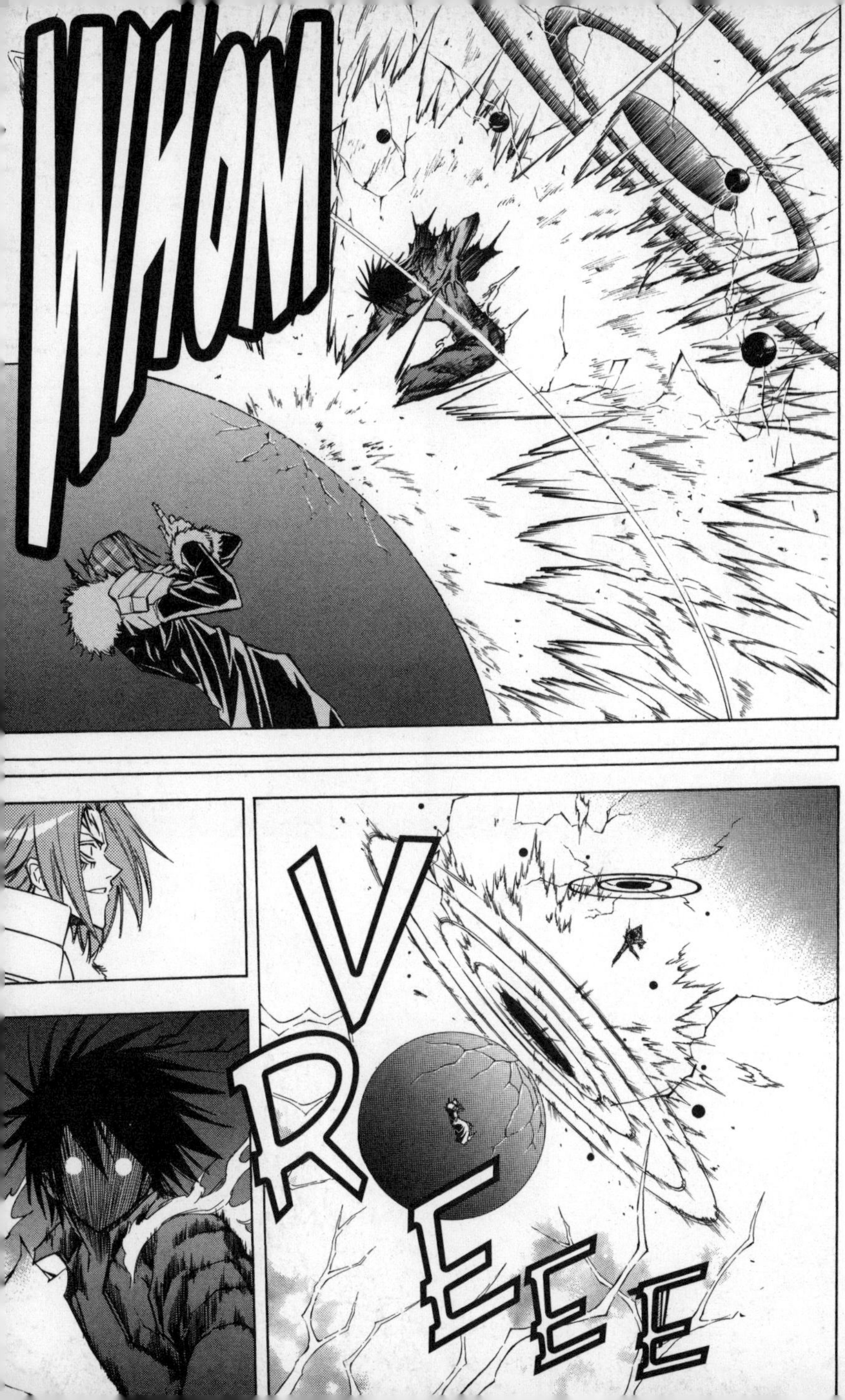
WHOM
VROEEE

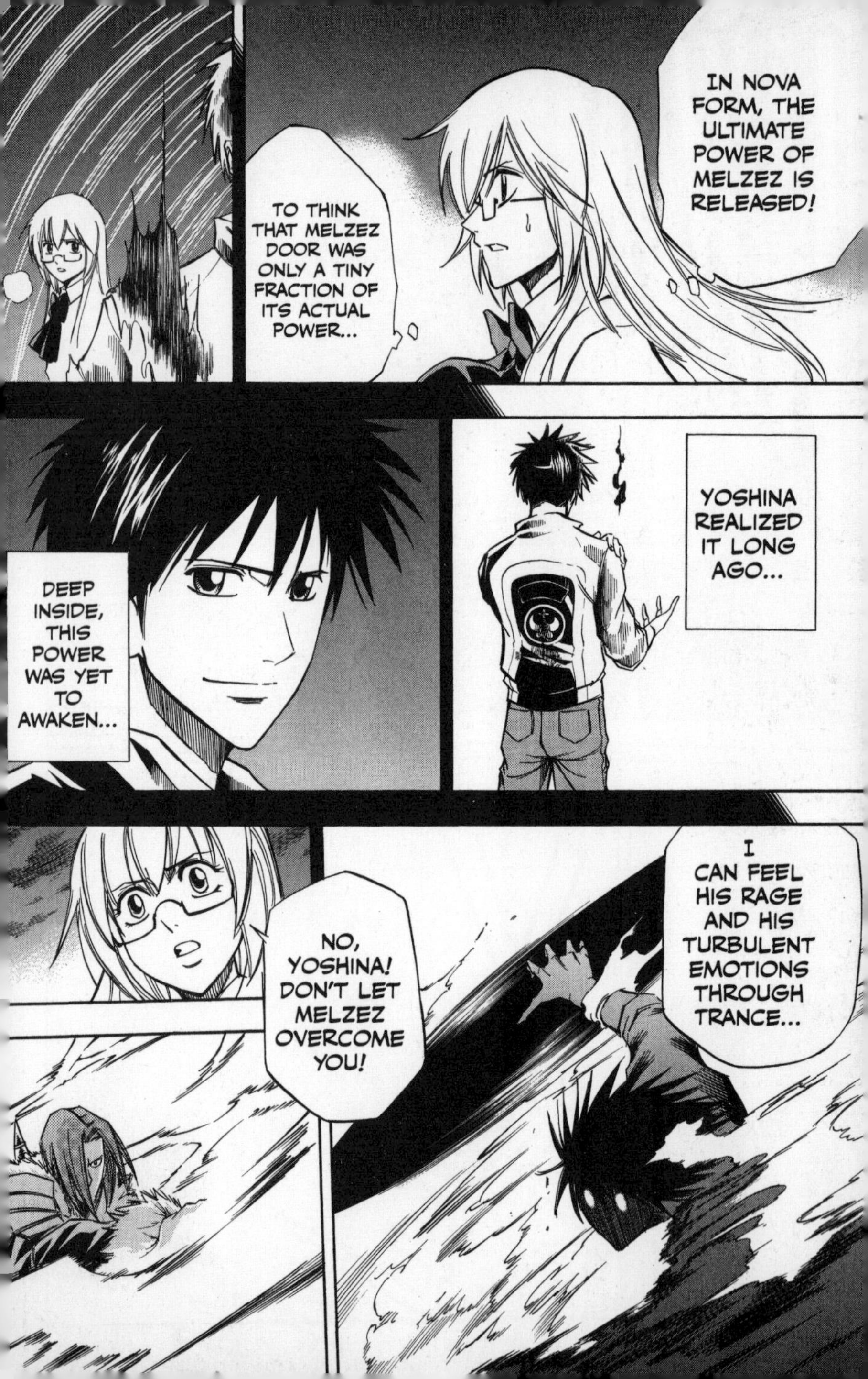
IN NOVA FORM, THE ULTIMATE POWER OF MELZEZ IS RELEASED!
TO THINK THAT MELZEZ DOOR WAS ONLY A TINY FRACTION OF ITS ACTUAL POWER...
YOSHINA REALIZED IT LONG AGO...
DEEP INSIDE, THIS POWER WAS YET TO AWAKEN...
I CAN FEEL HIS RAGE AND HIS TURBULENT EMOTIONS THROUGH TRANCE...
NO, YOSHINA! DON'T LET MELZEZ OVERCOME YOU!

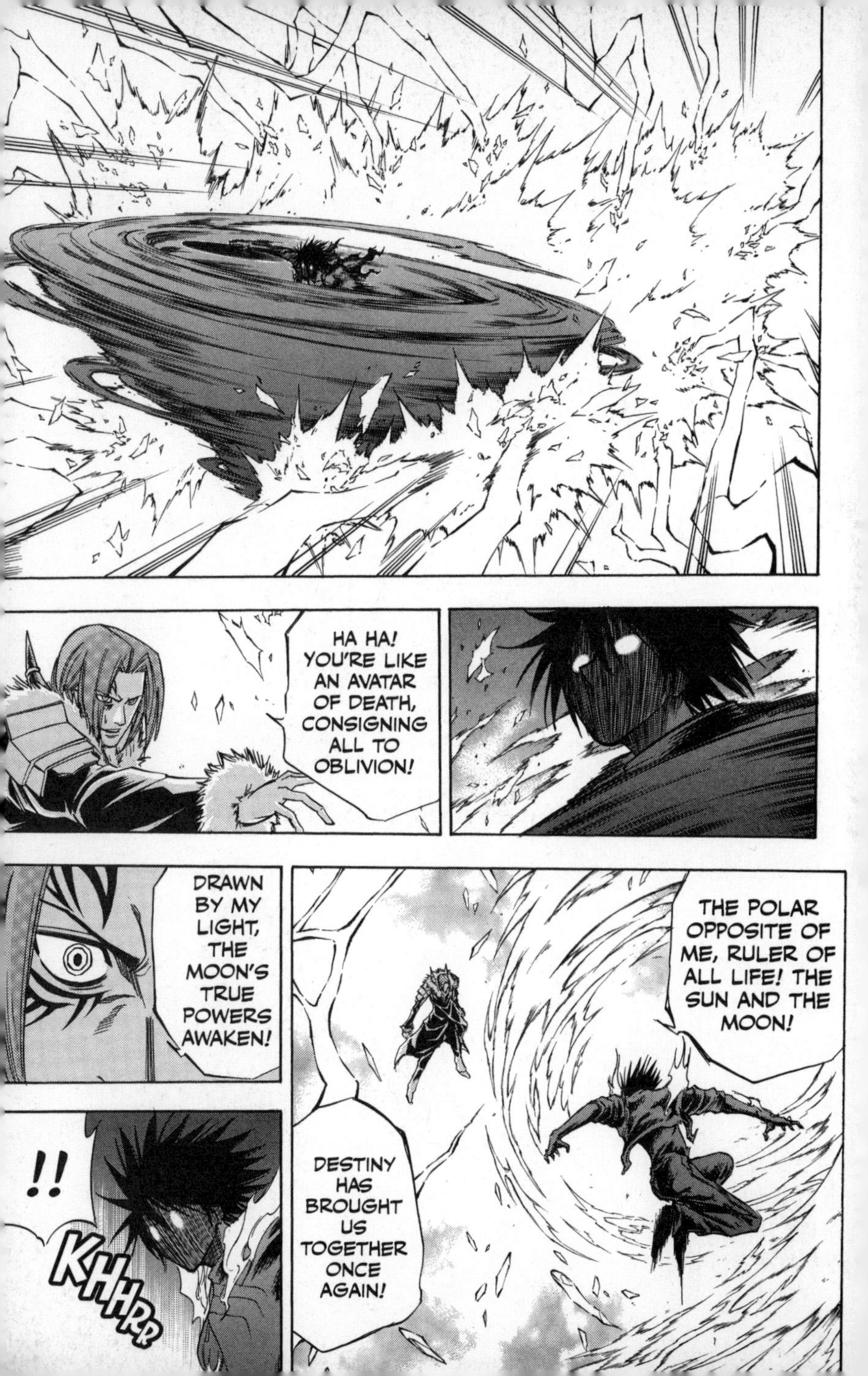
HA HA! YOU'RE LIKE AN AVATAR OF DEATH, CONSIGNING ALL TO OBLIVION!
THE POLAR OPPOSITE OF ME, RULER OF ALL LIFE! THE SUN AND THE MOON!
DESTINY HAS BROUGHT US TOGETHER ONCE AGAIN!
DRAWN BY MY LIGHT, THE MOON'S TRUE POWERS AWAKEN!
!!
KHHRR

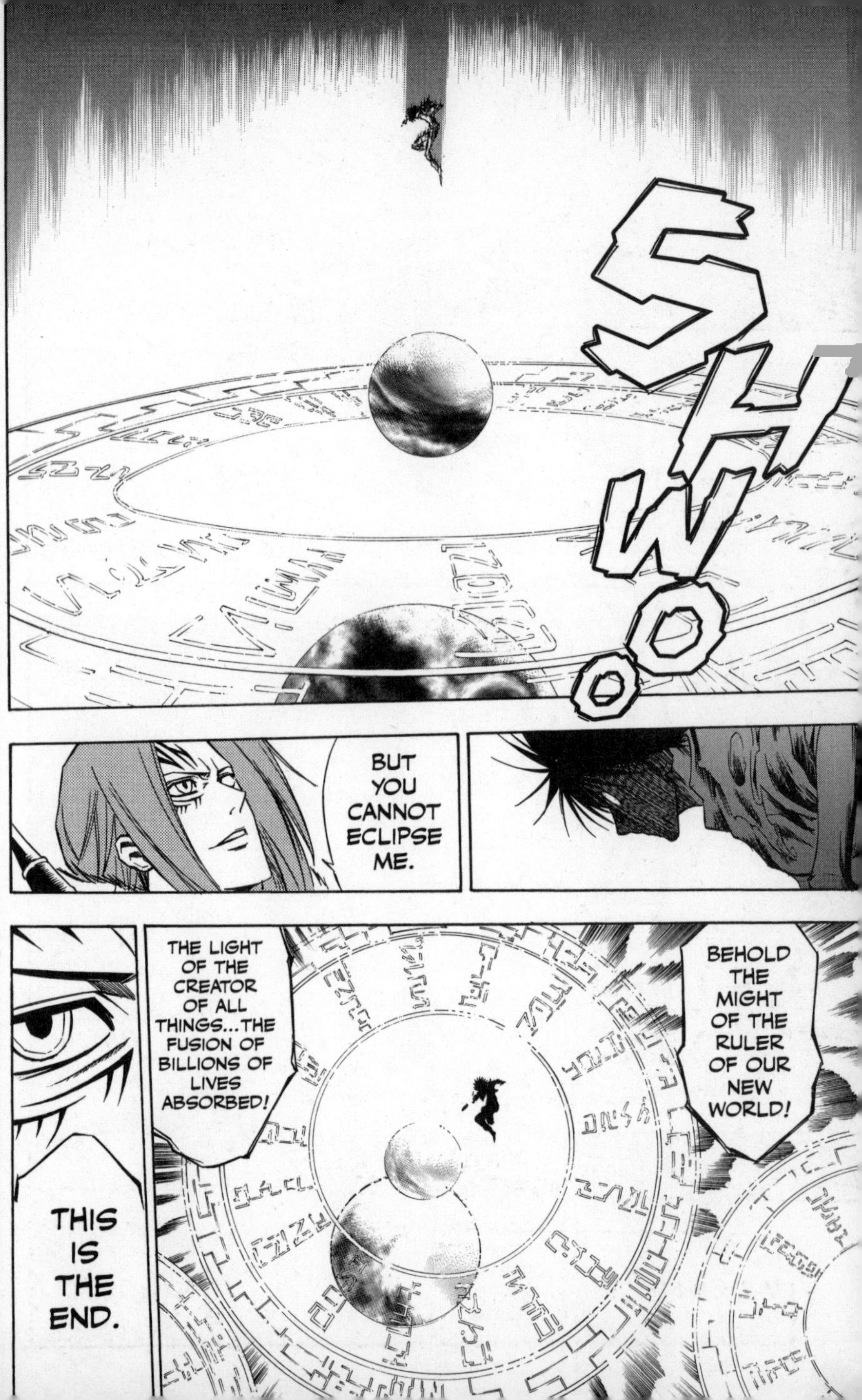
SHWOOO
BUT YOU CANNOT ECLIPSE ME.
BEHOLD THE MIGHT OF THE RULER OF OUR NEW WORLD!
THE LIGHT OF THE CREATOR OF ALL THINGS...THE FUSION OF BILLIONS OF LIVES ABSORBED!
THIS IS THE END.

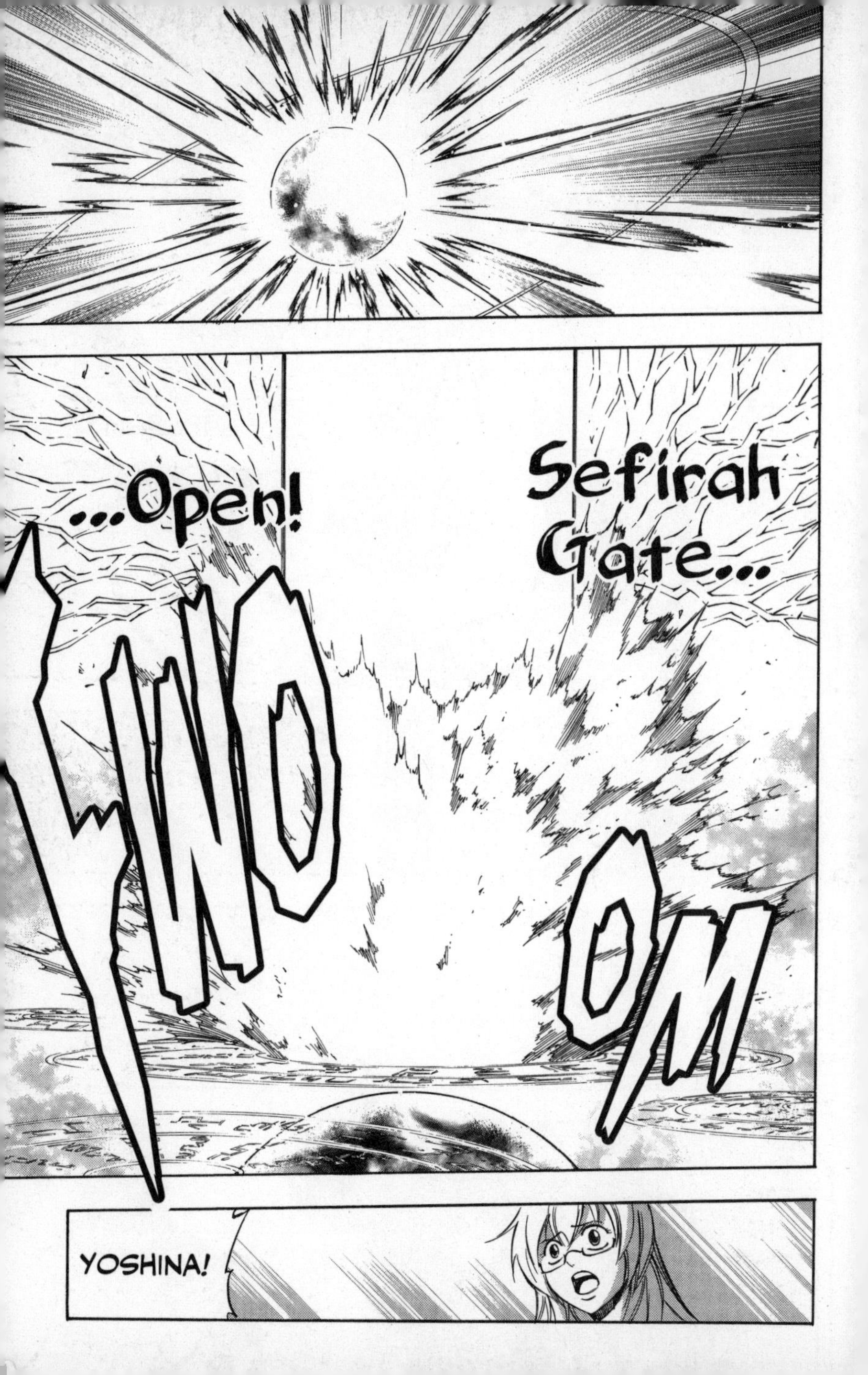
Sefirah Gate...
...Open!
WHOOM
YOSHINA!

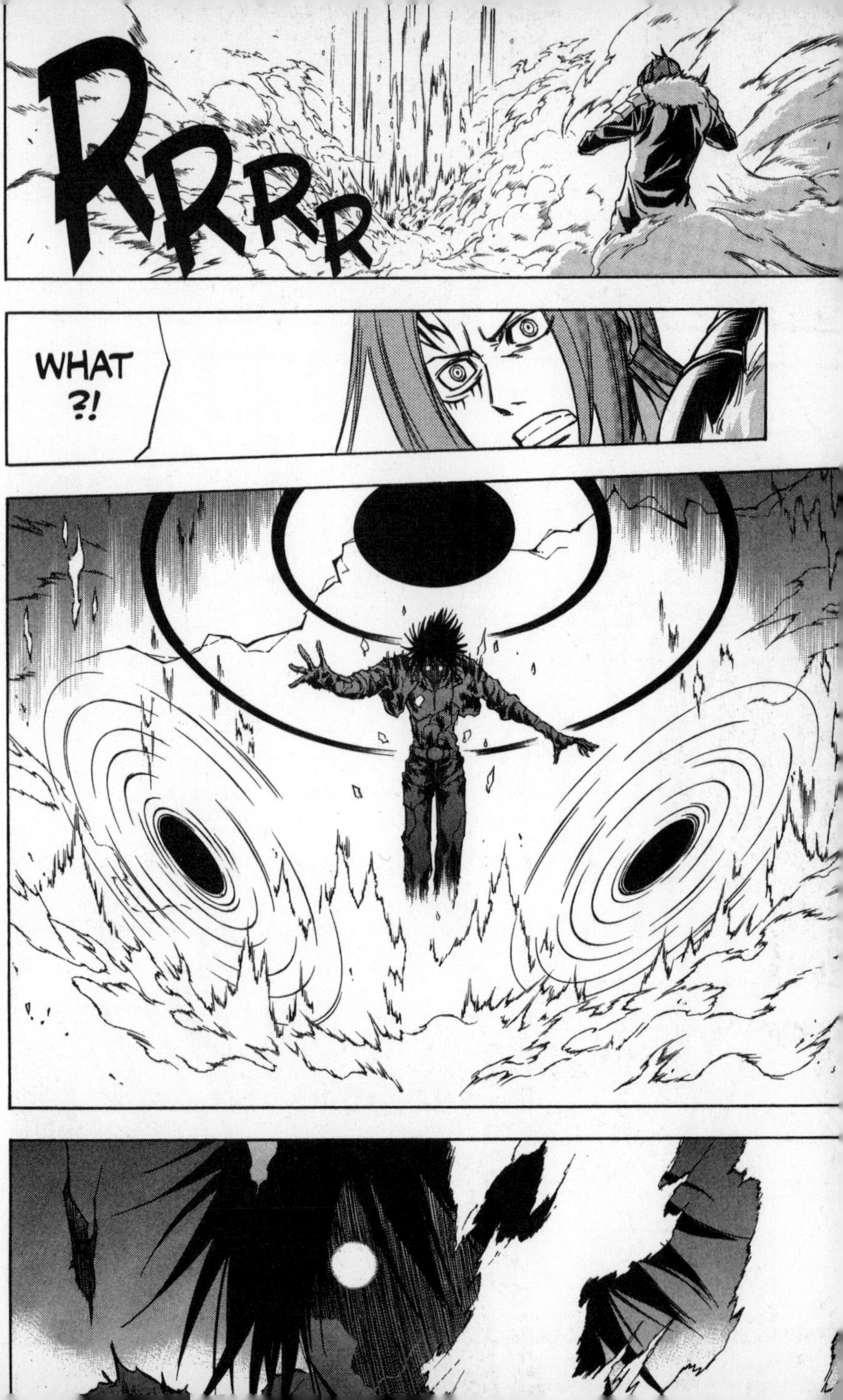
RRRRR
WHAT ?!

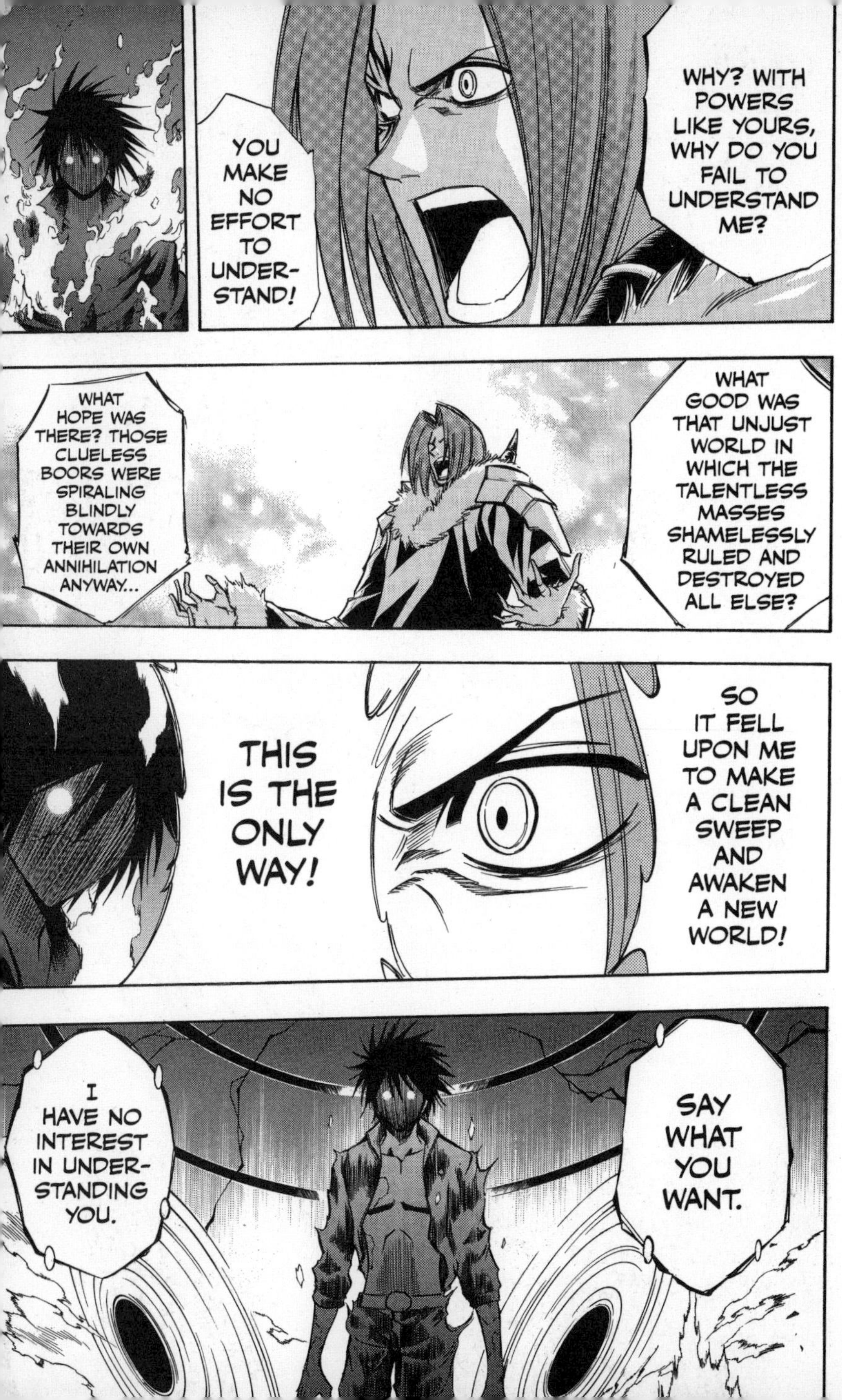
WHY? WITH POWERS LIKE YOURS, WHY DO YOU FAIL TO UNDERSTAND ME?
YOU MAKE NO EFFORT TO UNDER-STAND!
WHAT GOOD WAS THAT UNJUST WORLD IN WHICH THE TALENTLESS MASSES SHAMELESSLY RULED AND DESTROYED ALL ELSE?
WHAT HOPE WAS THERE? THOSE CLUELESS BOORS WERE SPIRALING BLINDLY TOWARDS THEIR OWN ANNIHILATION ANYWAY...
SO IT FELL UPON ME TO MAKE A CLEAN SWEEP AND AWAKEN A NEW WORLD!
THIS IS THE ONLY WAY!
SAY WHAT YOU WANT.
I HAVE NO INTEREST IN UNDER-STANDING YOU.

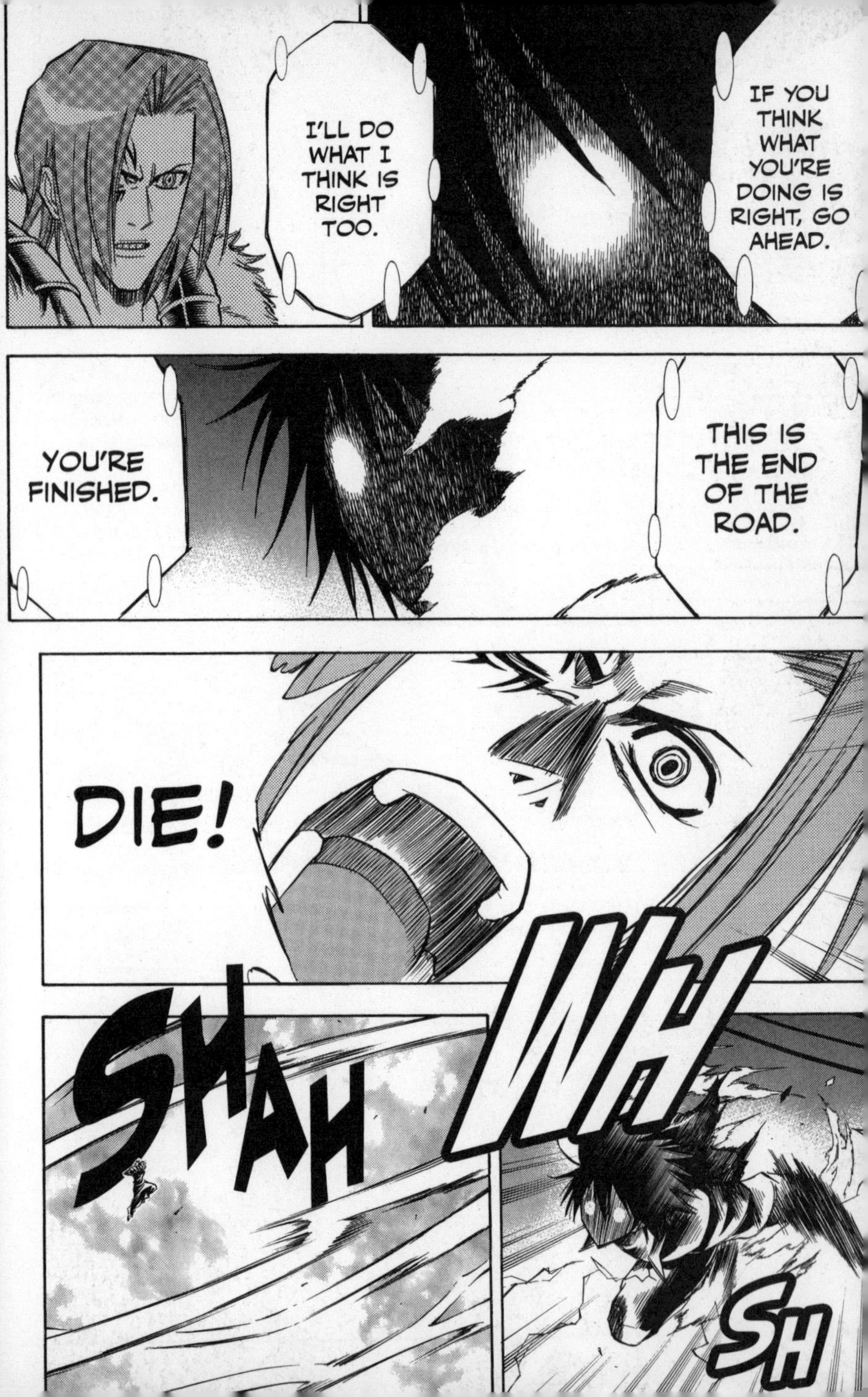
IF YOU THINK WHAT YOU'RE DOING IS RIGHT, GO AHEAD.
I'LL DO WHAT I THINK IS RIGHT TOO.
THIS IS THE END OF THE ROAD.
YOU'RE FINISHED.
DIE!
WH
SH
SHAH

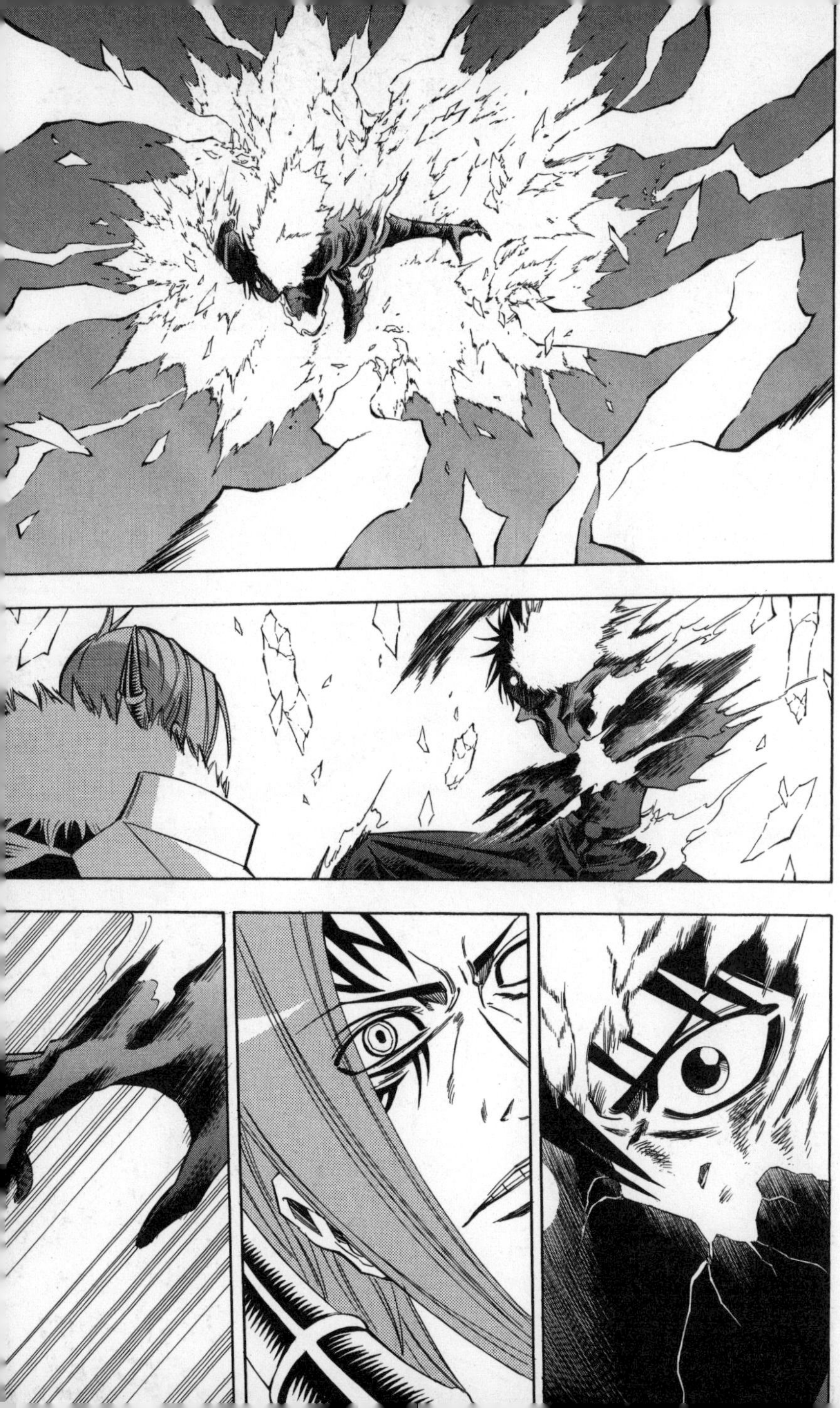

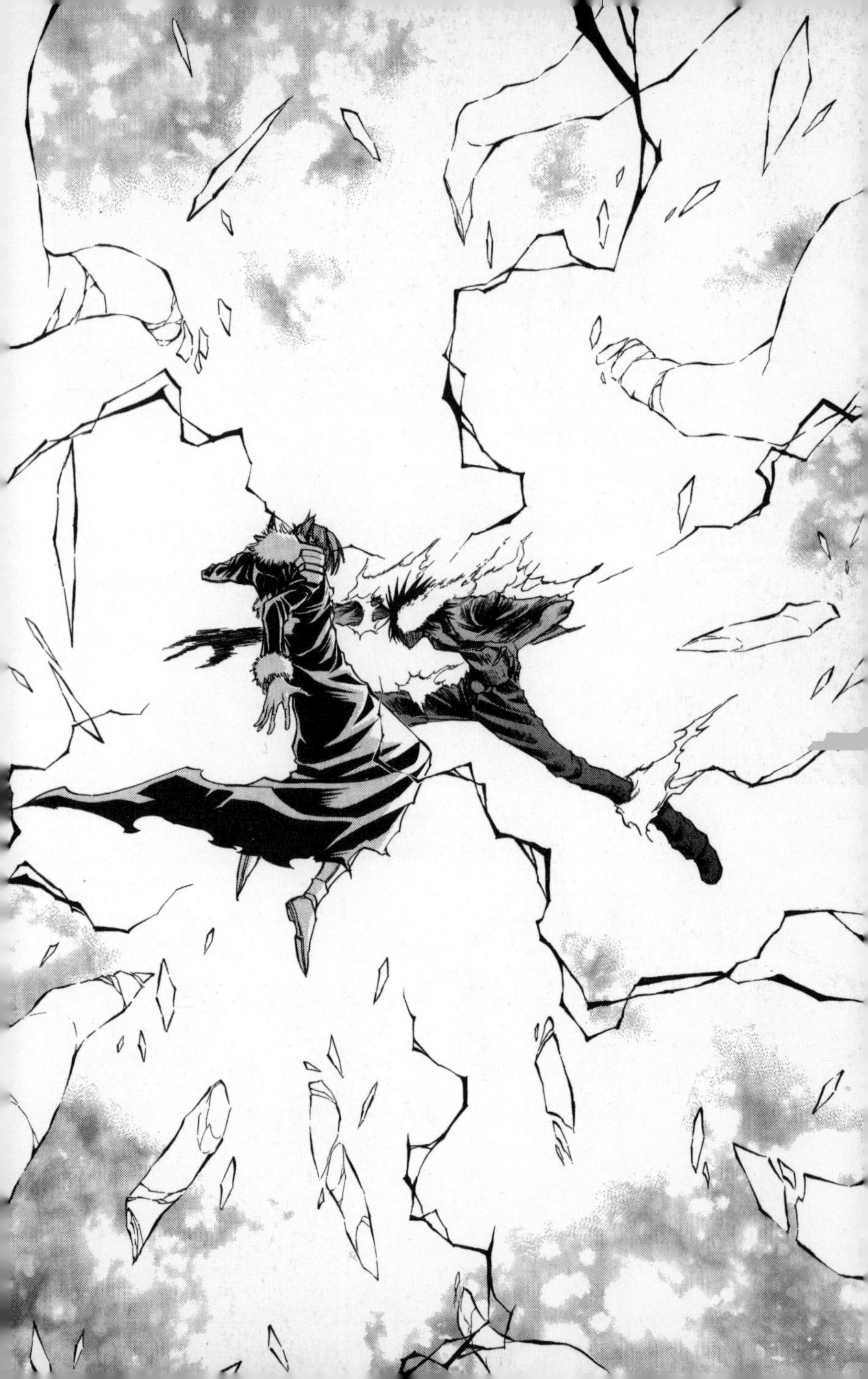

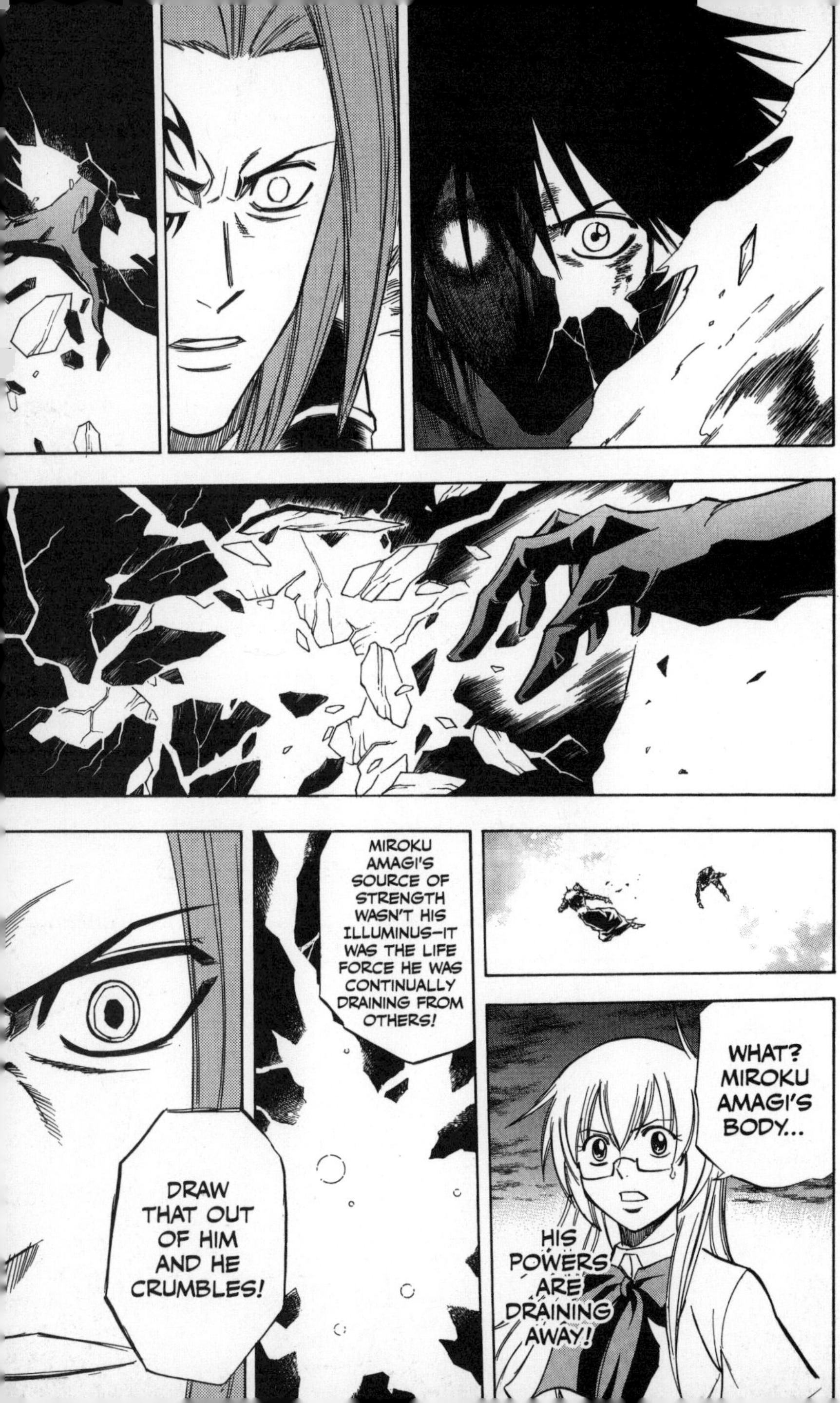
WHAT? MIROKU AMAGI'S BODY...
HIS POWERS ARE DRAINING AWAY!
MIROKU AMAGI'S SOURCE OF STRENGTH WASN'T HIS ILLUMINUS—IT WAS THE LIFE FORCE HE WAS CONTINUALLY DRAINING FROM OTHERS!
DRAW THAT OUT OF HIM AND HE CRUMBLES!

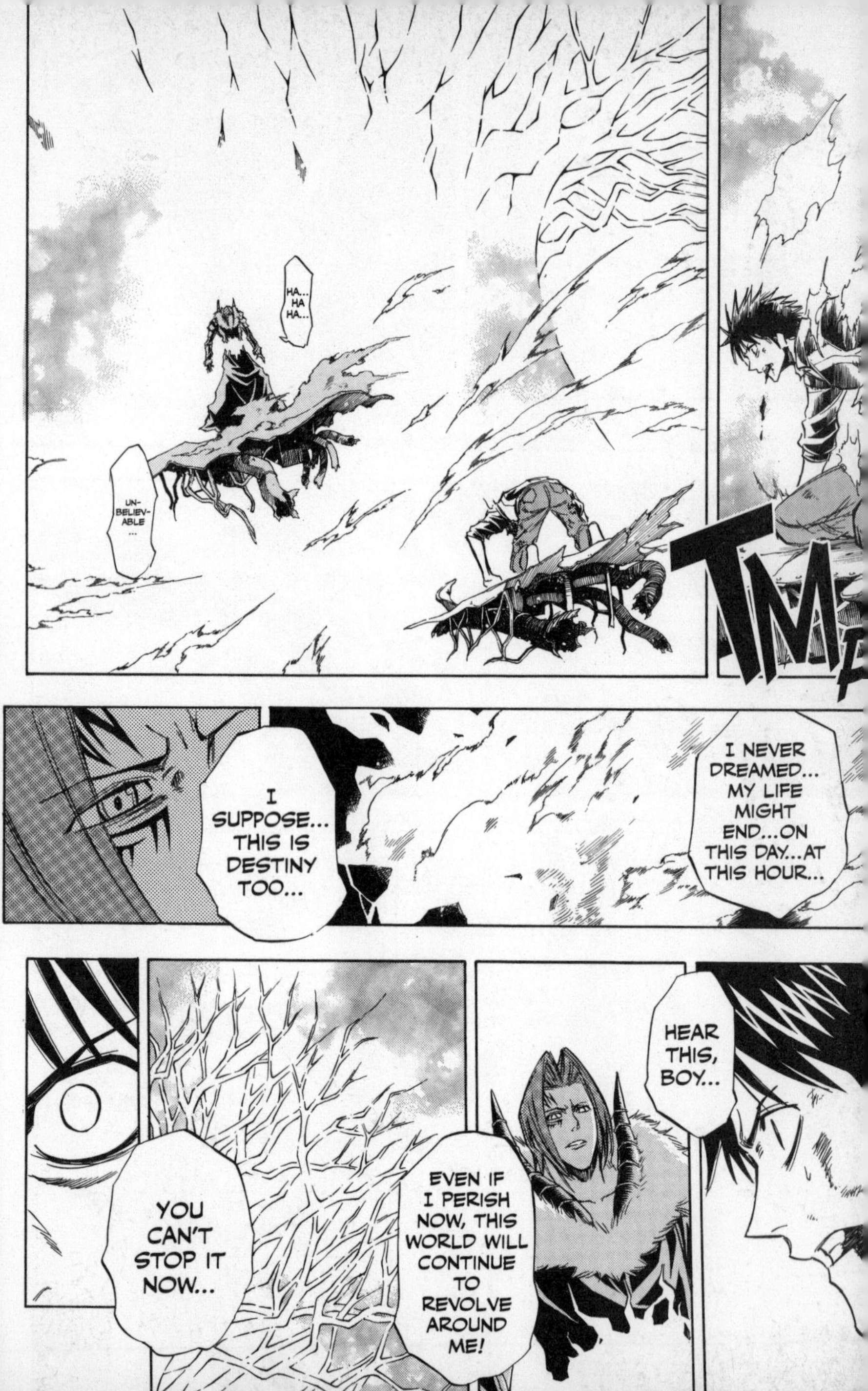
HA... HA HA...
UN-BELIEV-ABLE...
I NEVER DREAMED... MY LIFE MIGHT END...ON THIS DAY...AT THIS HOUR...
I SUPPOSE... THIS IS DESTINY TOO...
HEAR THIS, BOY...
EVEN IF I PERISH NOW, THIS WORLD WILL CONTINUE TO REVOLVE AROUND ME!
YOU CAN'T STOP IT NOW...

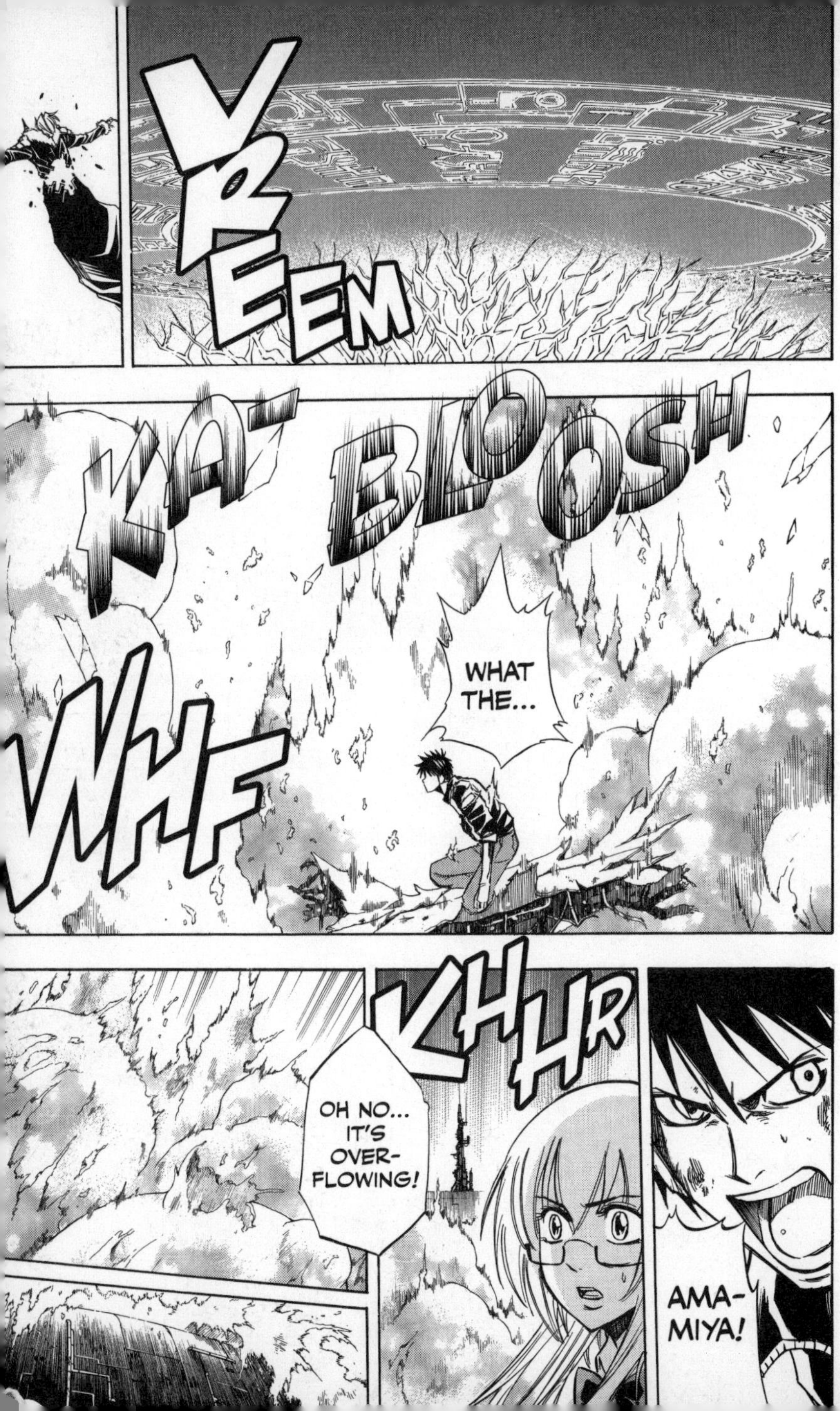
VREEM
KA-BLOOSH
WHAT THE...
WHF
AMA-MIYA!
KHR
OH NO... IT'S OVER-FLOWING!

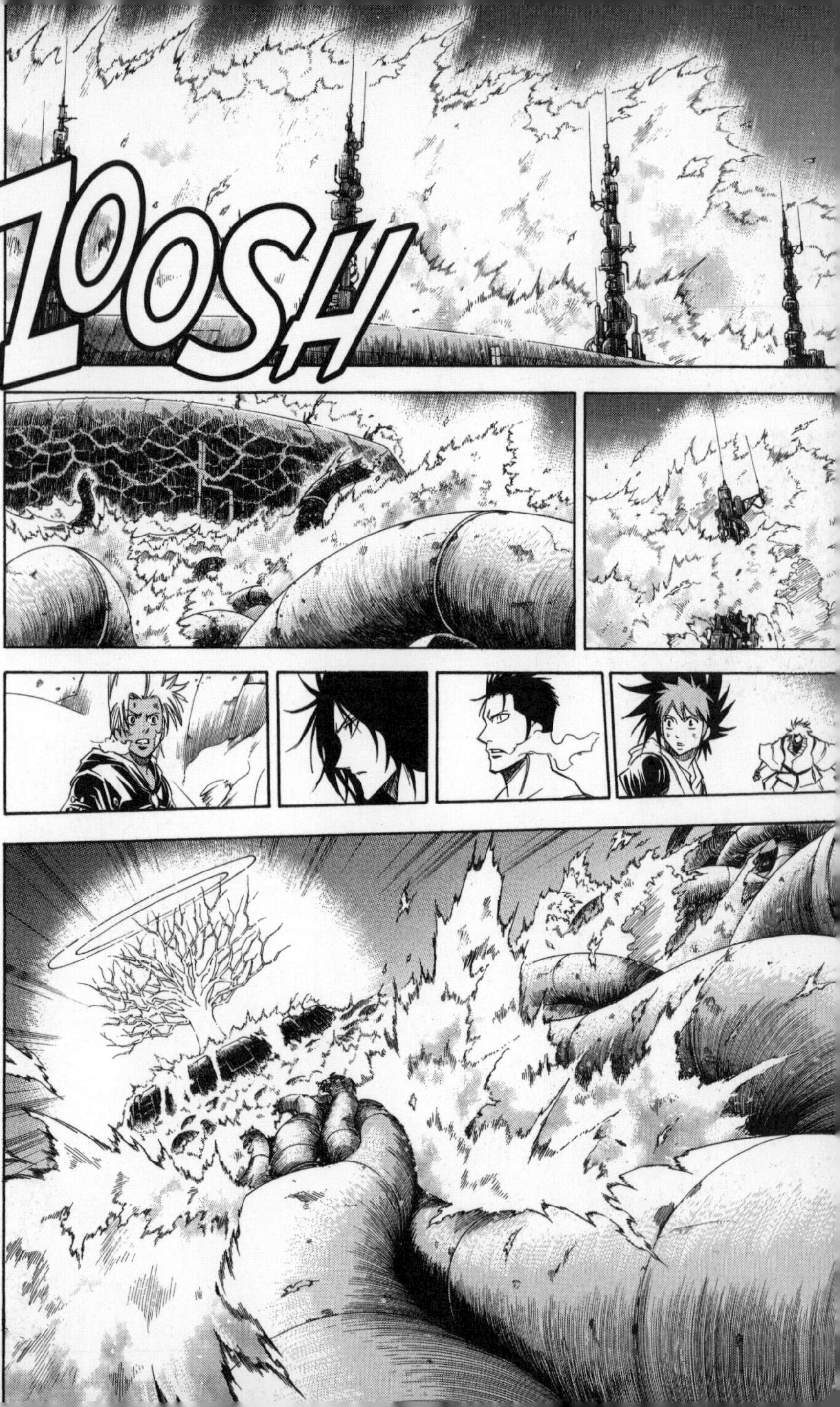
ZOOSH

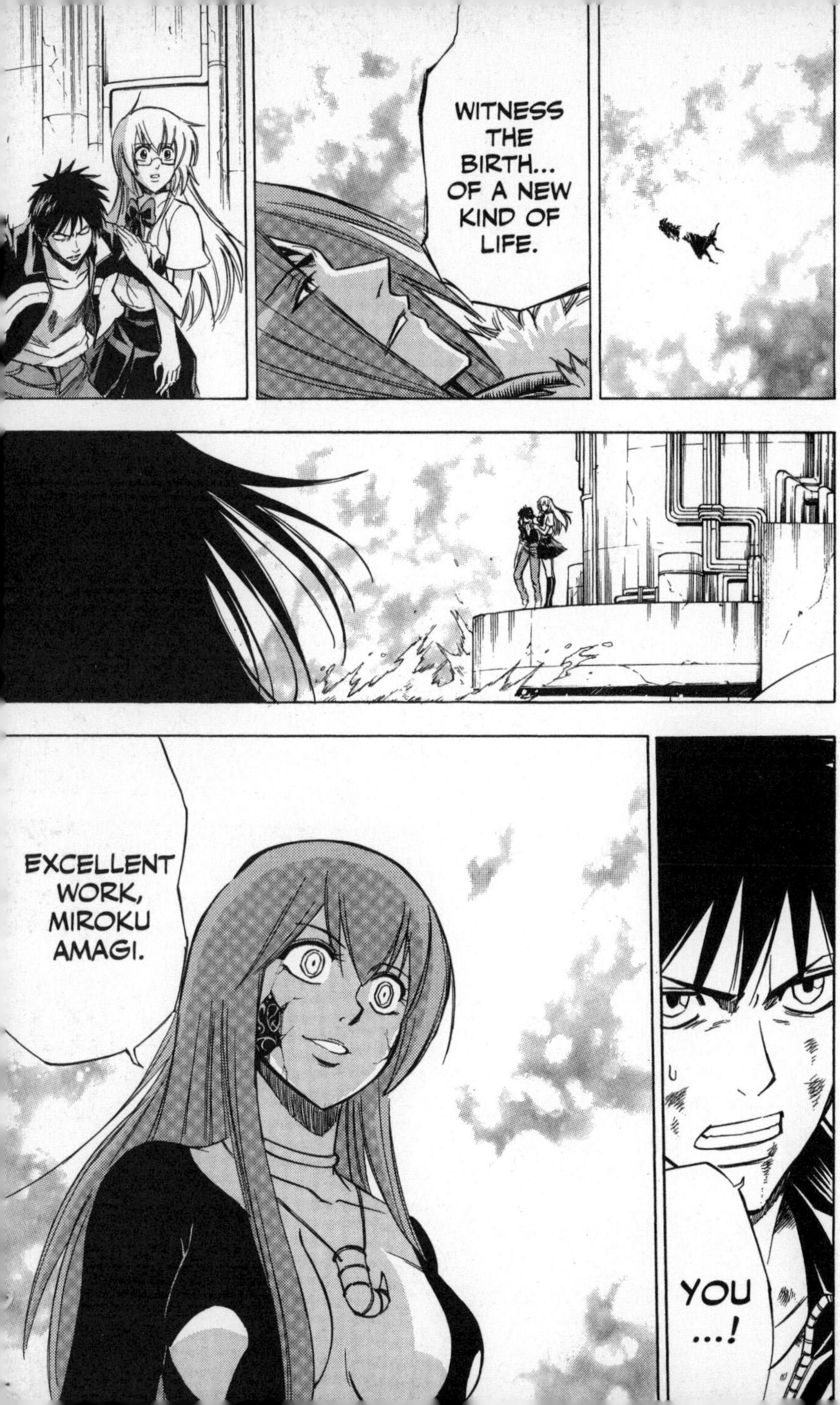
WITNESS THE BIRTH... OF A NEW KIND OF LIFE.
YOU ...!
EXCELLENT WORK, MIROKU AMAGI.

Mutters and mumblings...

GRANAR

GRANAR'S CHARACTER CHANGED QUITE A BIT OVER THE
COURSE OF THE STORY, ESPECIALLY IN TERMS OF HIS
PHYSICAL APPEARANCE.
I INITIALLY DREW GRANAR AS A MUCH MORE GENTLE,
GOOFY GUY. GRANAR'S BASIC INCLINATION TO IMITATE
HUMAN EMOTION HASN'T CHANGED. BUT EARLY ON IN
THE STORY I IMAGINED A MORE FAMILIAL RELATIONSHIP
BETWEEN THE STAR COMMANDERS, AND I THINK THAT
INFLUENCED HOW I IMAGINED GRANAR'S CHARACTER.
(TO BE CONTINUED...)

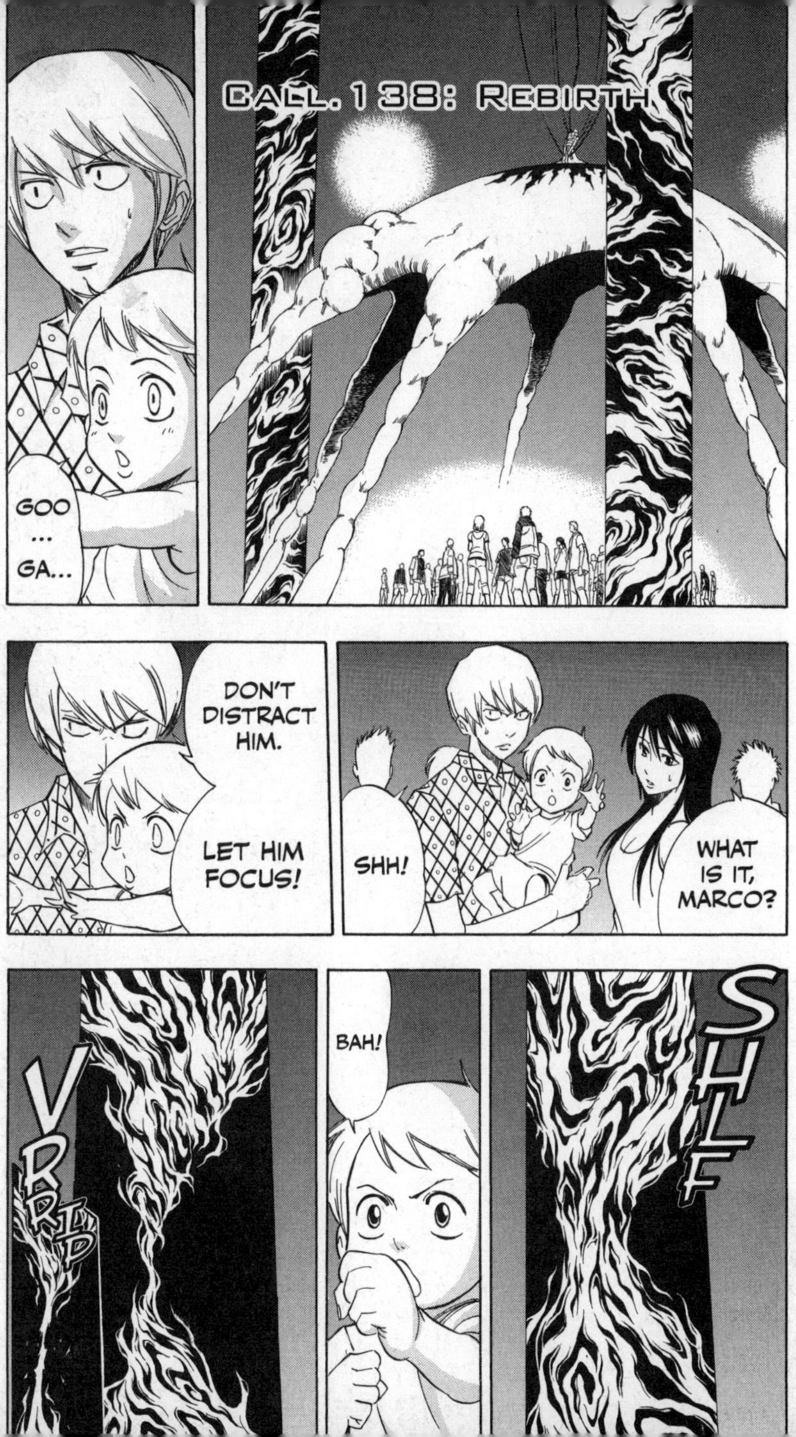
CALL. 138: REBIRTH
GOO ... GA...
WHAT IS IT, MARCO?
SHH!
DON'T DISTRACT HIM.
LET HIM FOCUS!
SHLF
BAH!
VRRIP

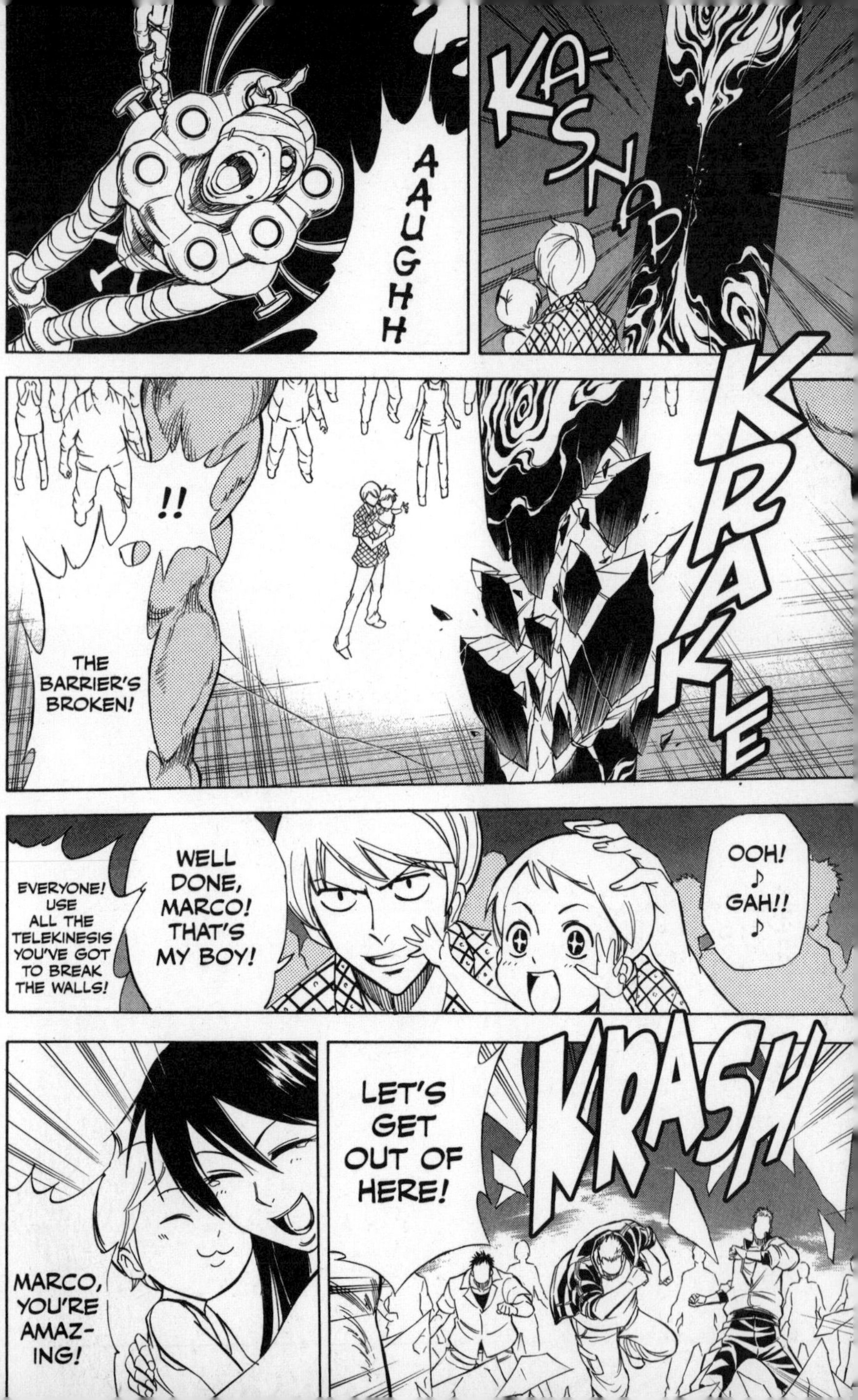
KA-SHAP
AAAUGHH
KRAKLE
!!
THE BARRIER'S BROKEN!
OOH! ♪ GAH!! ♪
WELL DONE, MARCO! THAT'S MY BOY!
EVERYONE! USE ALL THE TELEKINESIS YOU'VE GOT TO BREAK THE WALLS!
KRASH
LET'S GET OUT OF HERE!
MARCO, YOU'RE AMAZ-ING!

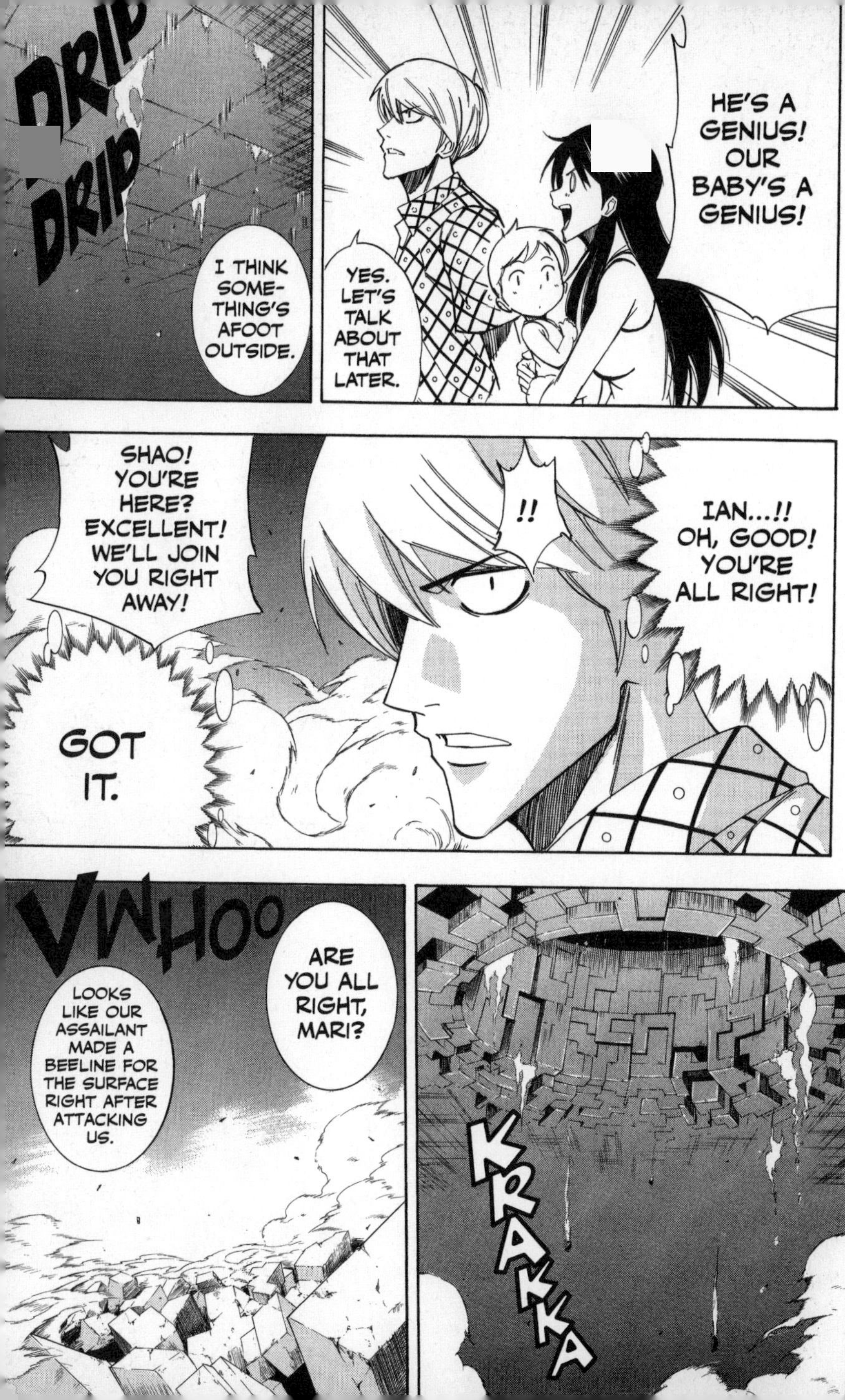
HE'S A GENIUS! OUR BABY'S A GENIUS!
YES. LET'S TALK ABOUT THAT LATER.
DRIP DRIP
I THINK SOMETHING'S AFOOT OUTSIDE.
IAN...!! OH, GOOD! YOU'RE ALL RIGHT!
!!
SHAO! YOU'RE HERE? EXCELLENT! WE'LL JOIN YOU RIGHT AWAY!
GOT IT.
KRAKKA
VWHOO
ARE YOU ALL RIGHT, MARI?
LOOKS LIKE OUR ASSAILANT MADE A BEELINE FOR THE SURFACE RIGHT AFTER ATTACKING US.

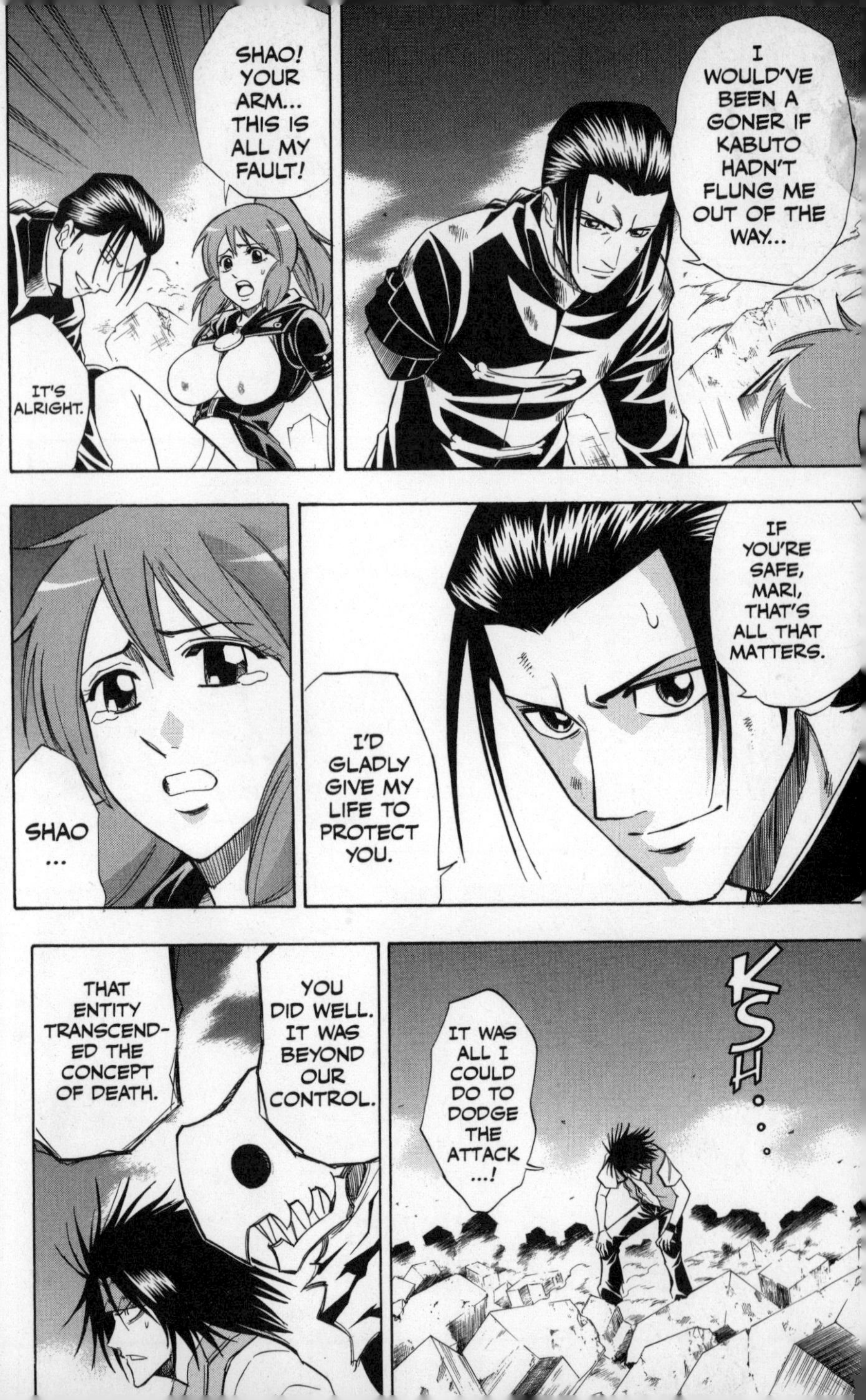
I WOULD'VE BEEN A GONER IF KABUTO HADN'T FLUNG ME OUT OF THE WAY...
SHAO! YOUR ARM... THIS IS ALL MY FAULT!
IT'S ALRIGHT.
IF YOU'RE SAFE, MARI, THAT'S ALL THAT MATTERS.
I'D GLADLY GIVE MY LIFE TO PROTECT YOU.
SHAO ...
KSH...
IT WAS ALL I COULD DO TO DODGE THE ATTACK ...!
YOU DID WELL. IT WAS BEYOND OUR CONTROL.
THAT ENTITY TRANSCEND-ED THE CONCEPT OF DEATH.

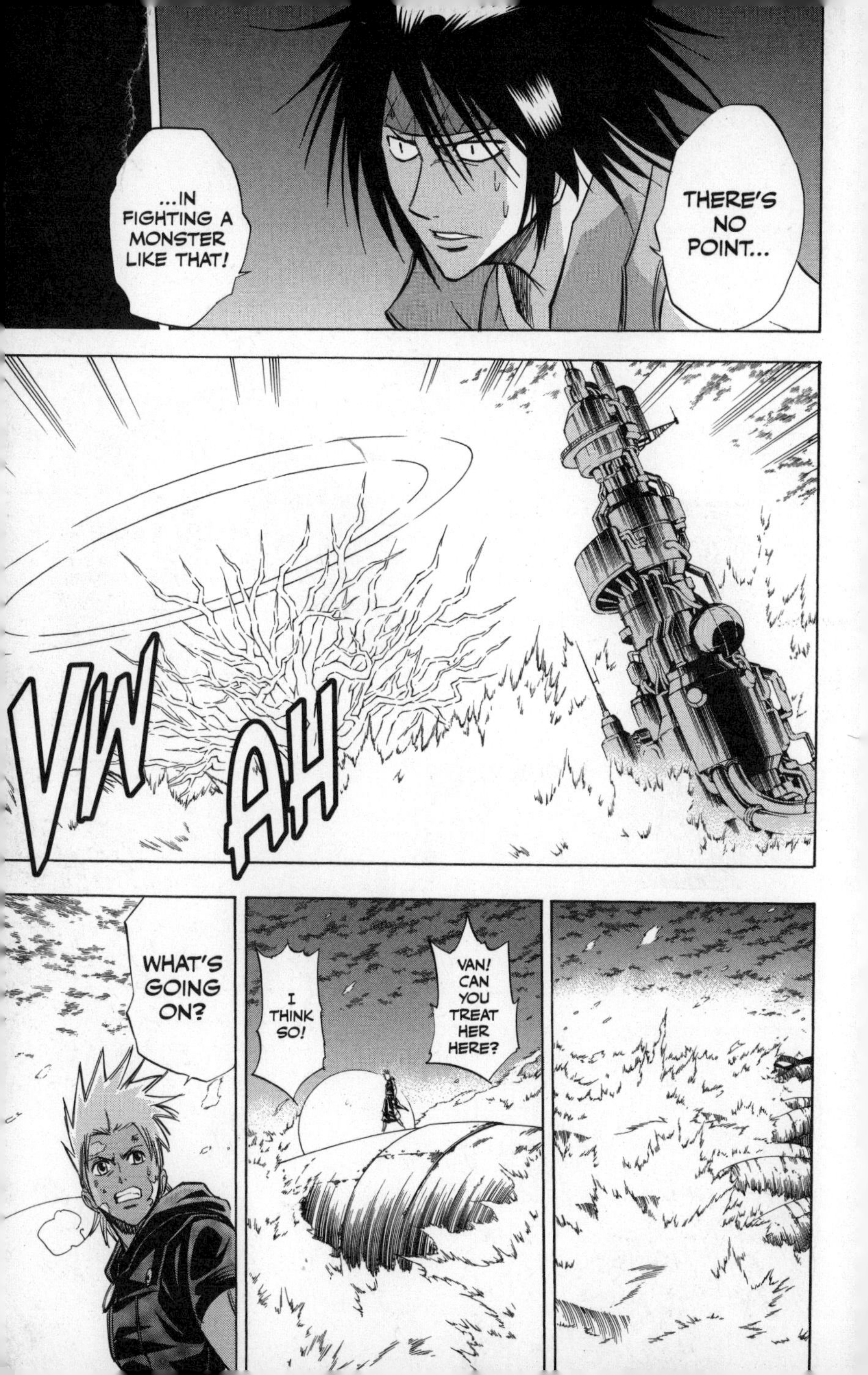
THERE'S NO POINT...
...IN FIGHTING A MONSTER LIKE THAT!
VWAH
VAN! CAN YOU TREAT HER HERE?
I THINK SO!
WHAT'S GOING ON?

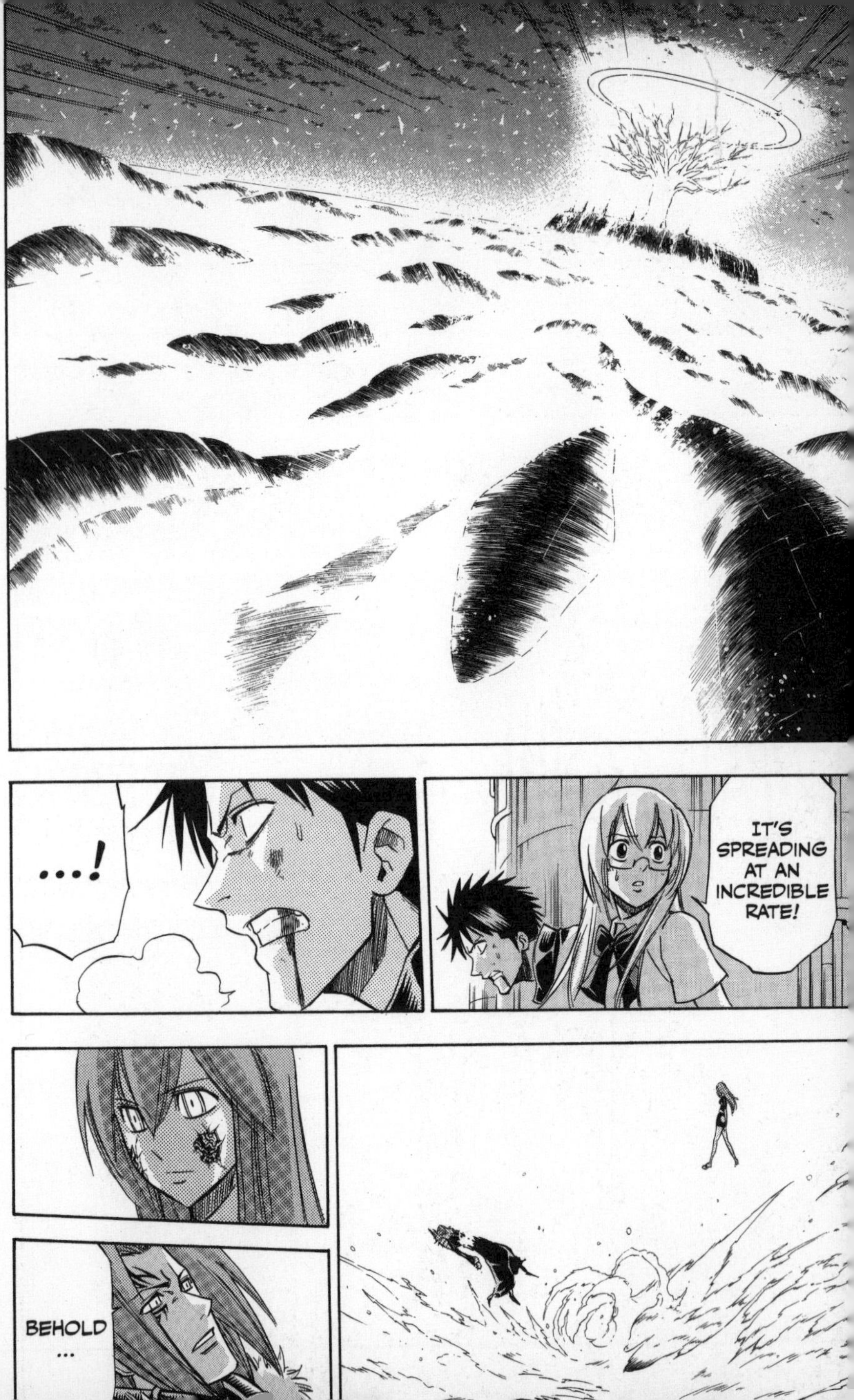
IT'S SPREADING AT AN INCREDIBLE RATE!
...!
BEHOLD ...

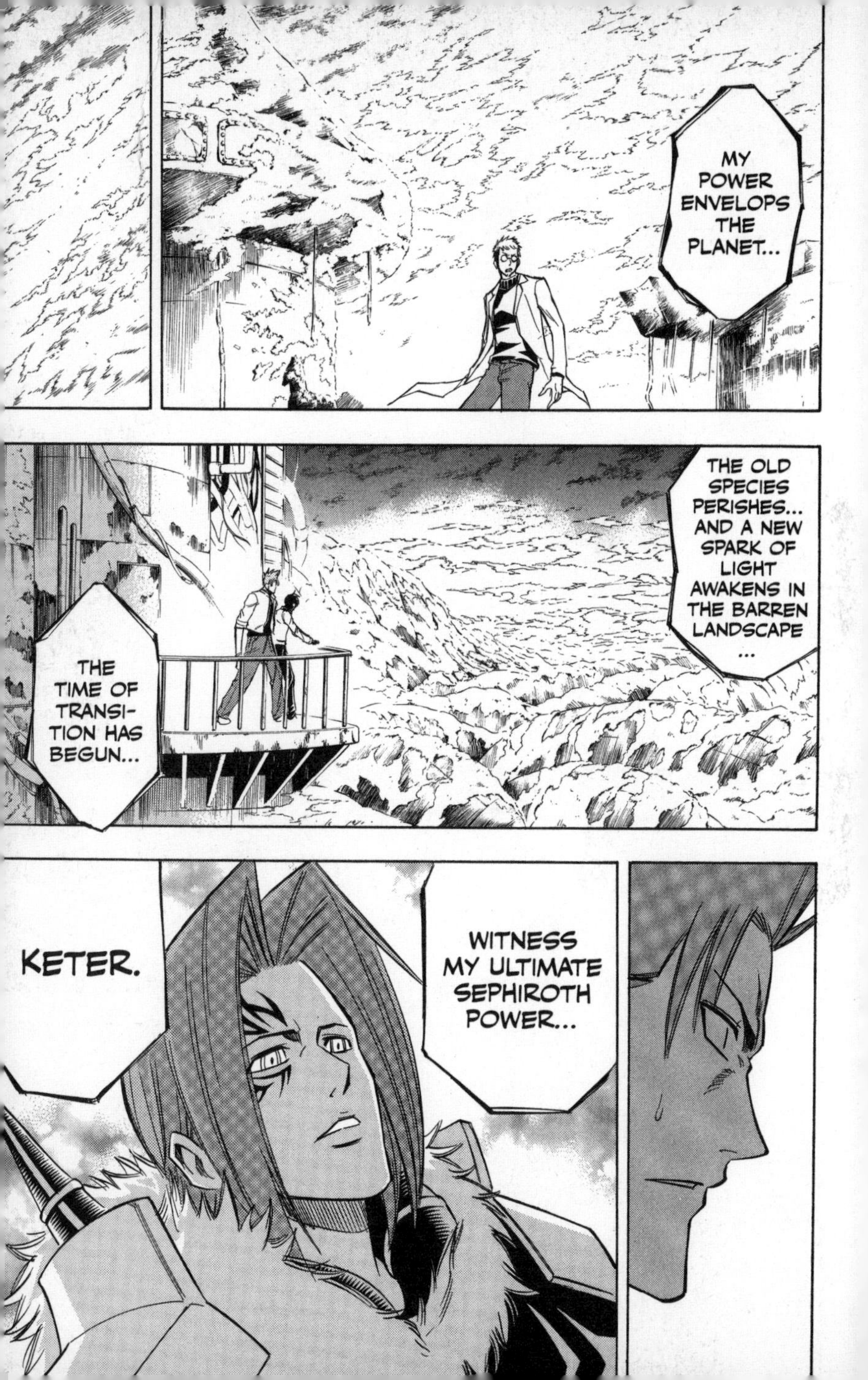
MY POWER ENVELOPS THE PLANET...
THE OLD SPECIES PERISHES... AND A NEW SPARK OF LIGHT AWAKENS IN THE BARREN LANDSCAPE ...
THE TIME OF TRANSITION HAS BEGUN...
WITNESS MY ULTIMATE SEPHIROTH POWER...
KETER.

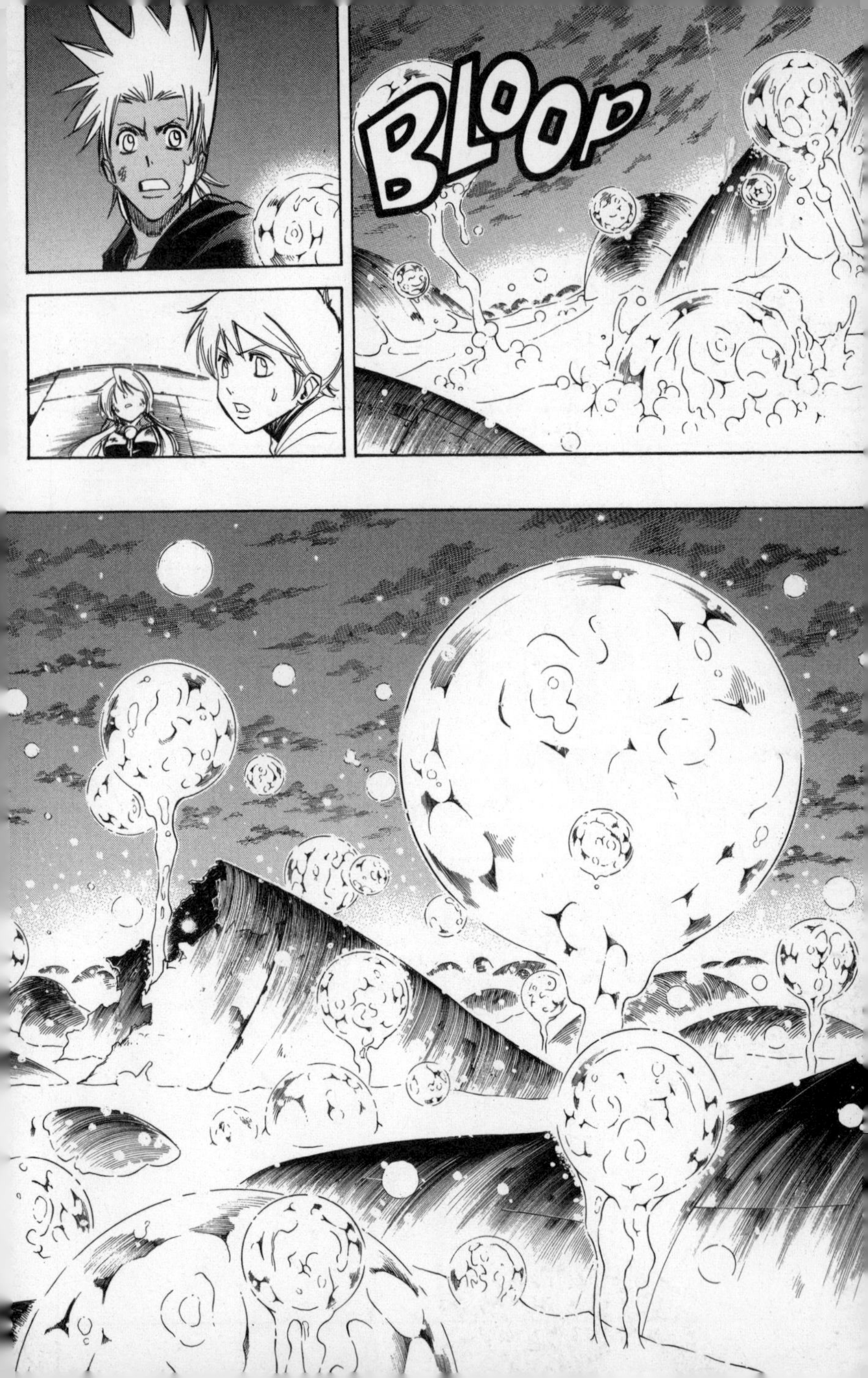
BLOOP

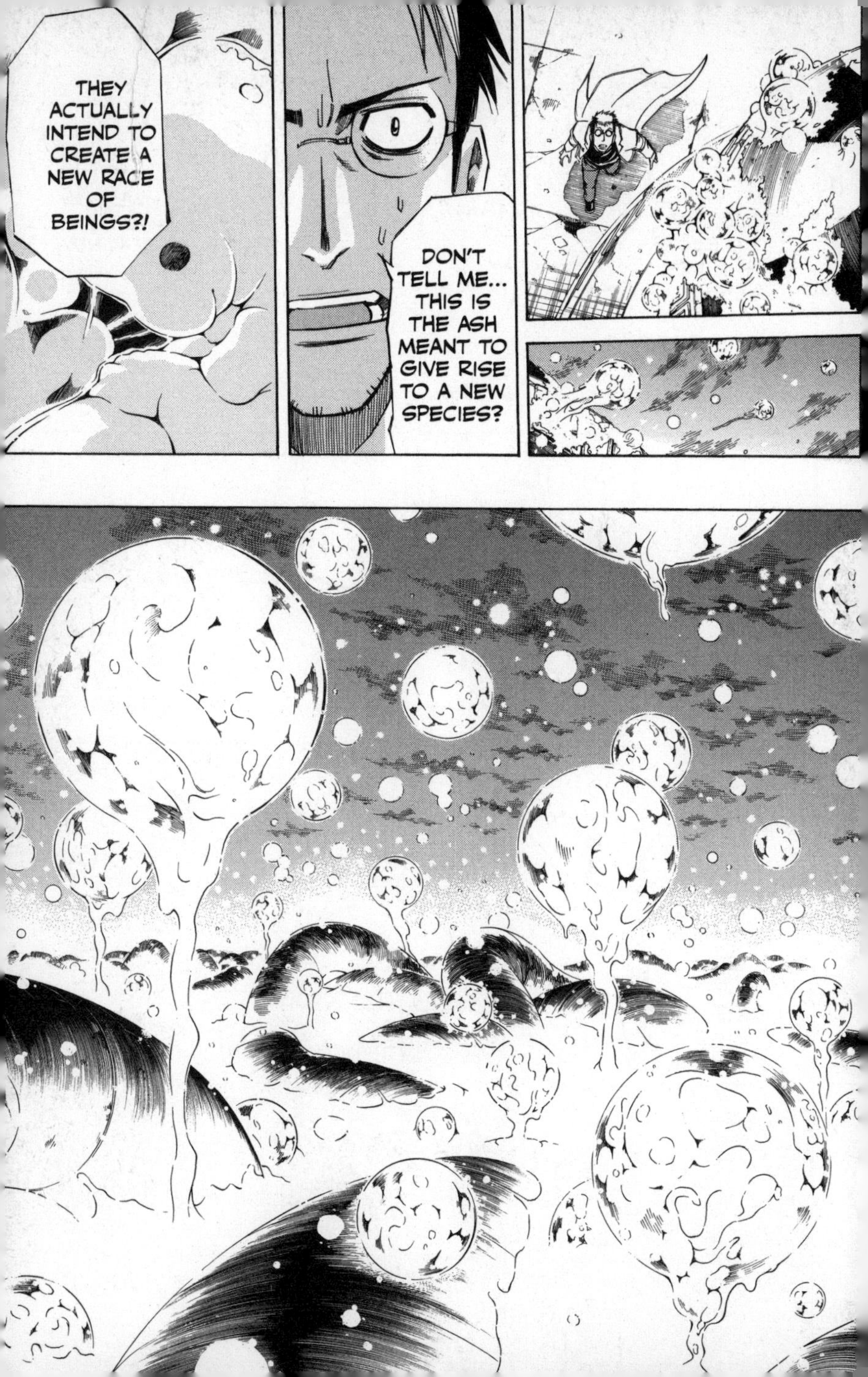
DON'T TELL ME... THIS IS THE ASH MEANT TO GIVE RISE TO A NEW SPECIES?
THEY ACTUALLY INTEND TO CREATE A NEW RACE OF BEINGS?!

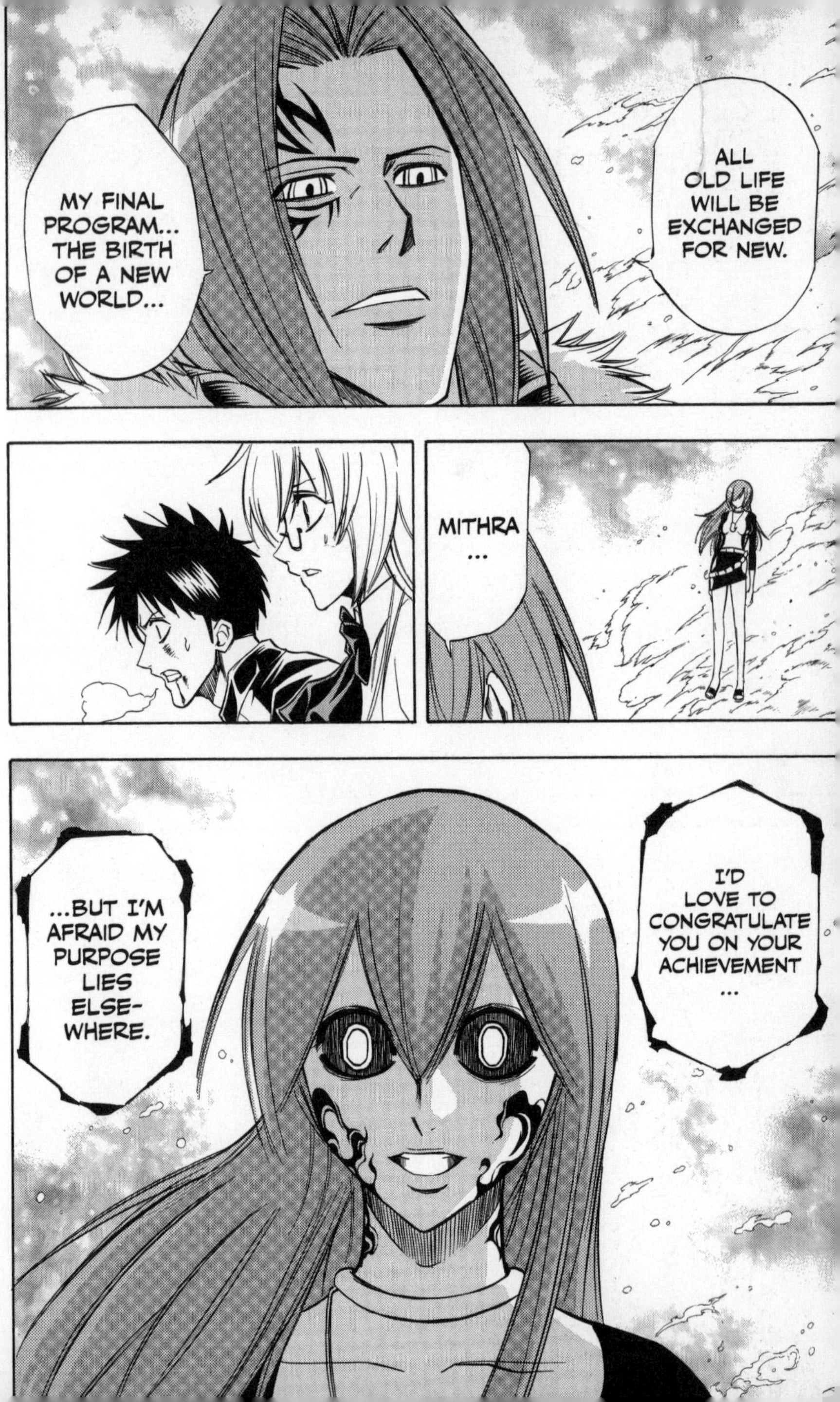
ALL OLD LIFE WILL BE EXCHANGED FOR NEW.
MY FINAL PROGRAM... THE BIRTH OF A NEW WORLD...
MITHRA ...
I'D LOVE TO CONGRATULATE YOU ON YOUR ACHIEVEMENT ...
...BUT I'M AFRAID MY PURPOSE LIES ELSE-WHERE.

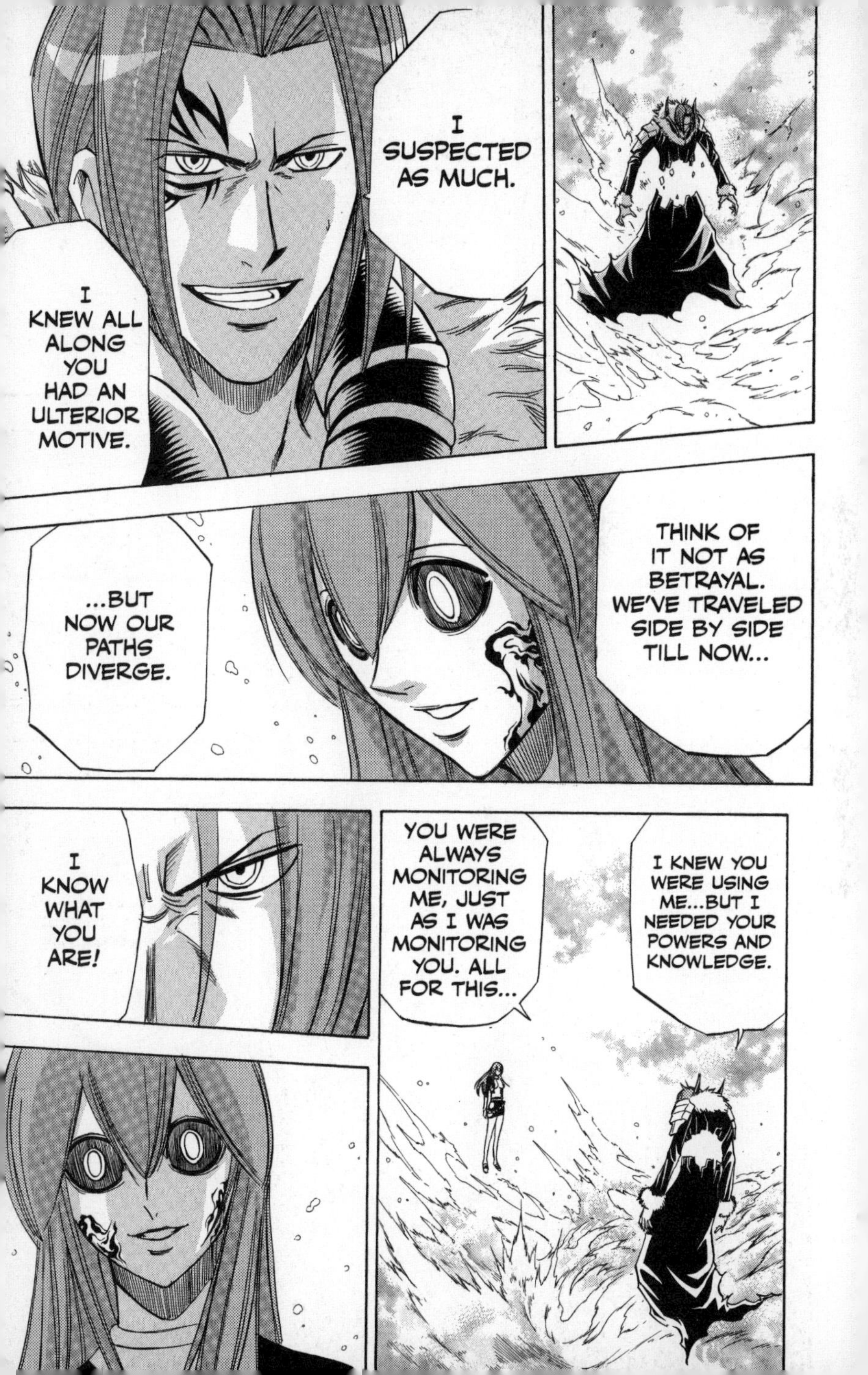
I SUSPECTED AS MUCH.
I KNEW ALL ALONG YOU HAD AN ULTERIOR MOTIVE.
THINK OF IT NOT AS BETRAYAL. WE'VE TRAVELED SIDE BY SIDE TILL NOW...
...BUT NOW OUR PATHS DIVERGE.
I KNEW YOU WERE USING ME...BUT I NEEDED YOUR POWERS AND KNOWLEDGE.
YOU WERE ALWAYS MONITORING ME, JUST AS I WAS MONITORING YOU. ALL FOR THIS...
I KNOW WHAT YOU ARE!

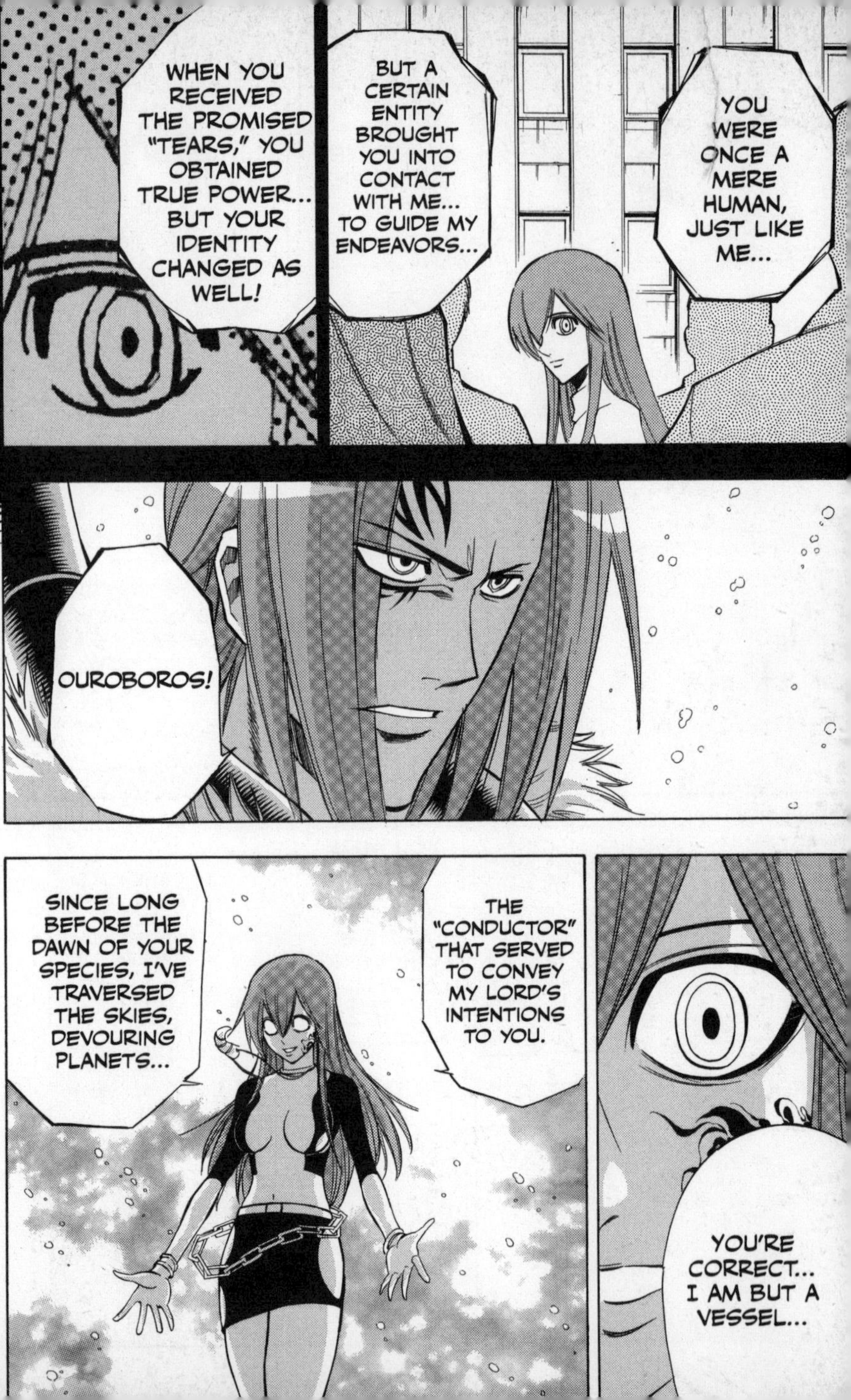
YOU WERE ONCE A MERE HUMAN, JUST LIKE ME...
BUT A CERTAIN ENTITY BROUGHT YOU INTO CONTACT WITH ME... TO GUIDE MY ENDEAVORS...
WHEN YOU RECEIVED THE PROMISED "TEARS," YOU OBTAINED TRUE POWER... BUT YOUR IDENTITY CHANGED AS WELL!
OUROBOROS!
YOU'RE CORRECT... I AM BUT A VESSEL...
THE "CONDUCTOR" THAT SERVED TO CONVEY MY LORD'S INTENTIONS TO YOU.
SINCE LONG BEFORE THE DAWN OF YOUR SPECIES, I'VE TRAVERSED THE SKIES, DEVOURING PLANETS...

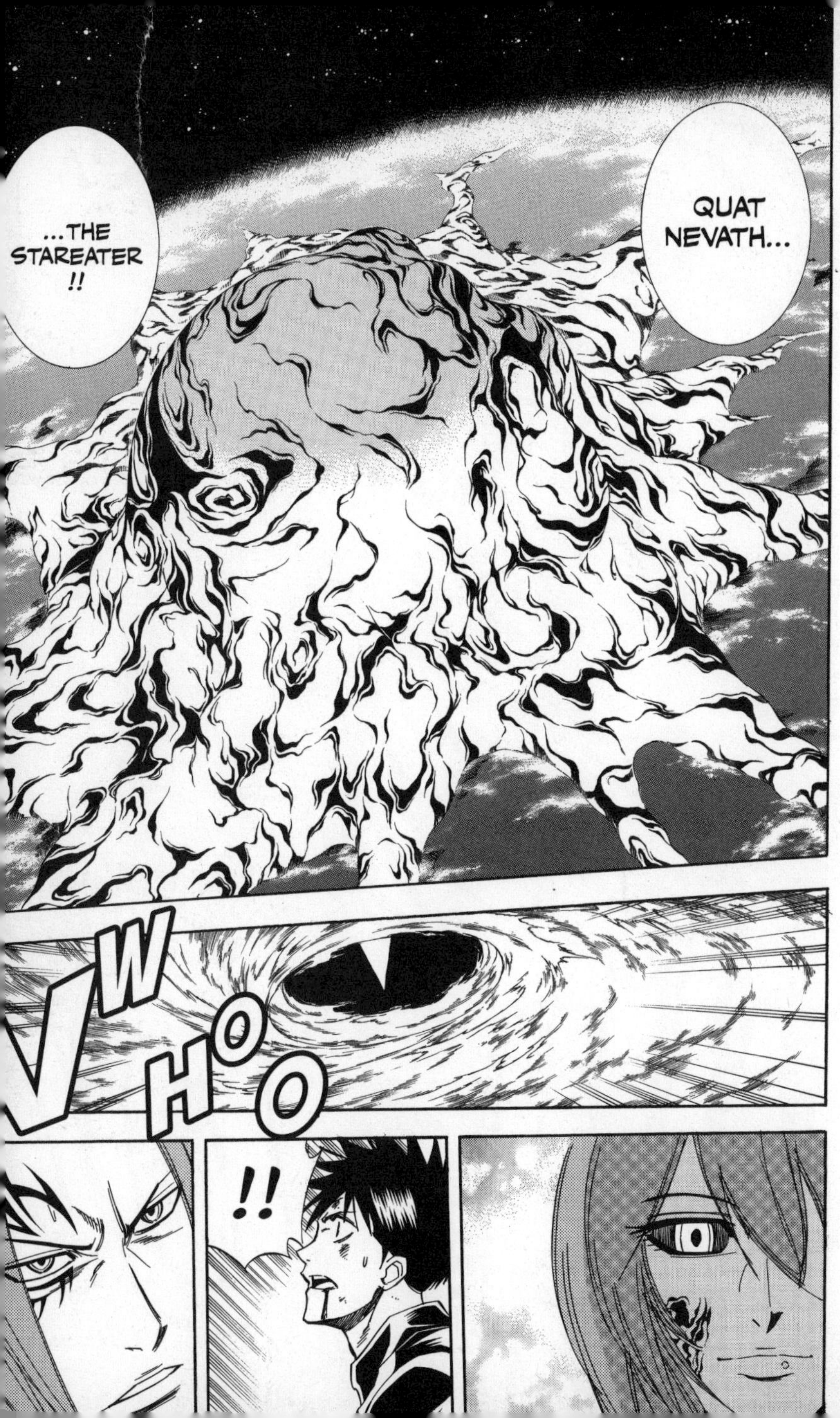
QUAT NEVATH...
...THE STAREATER !!
VWHOOO
!!

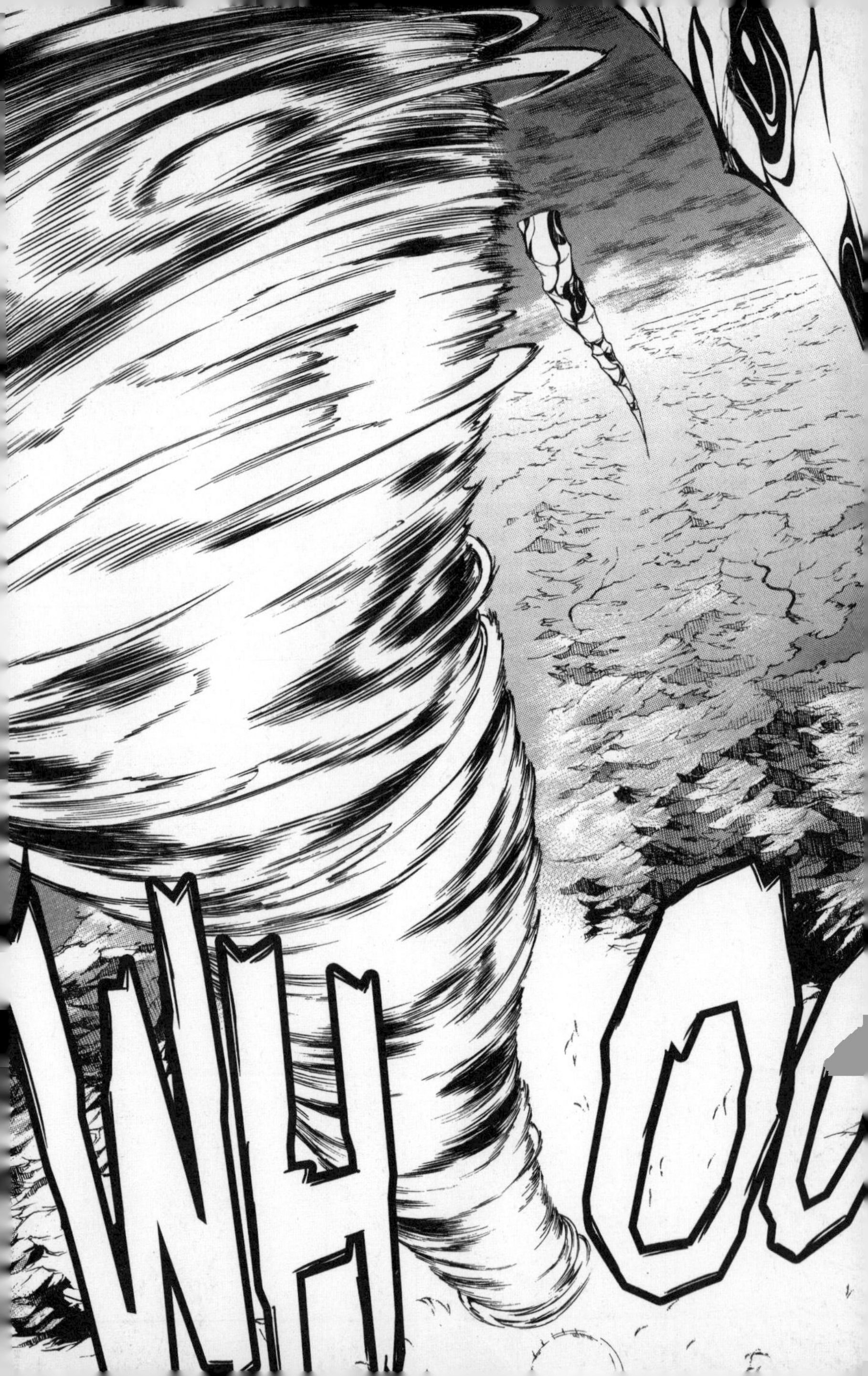
WHOO

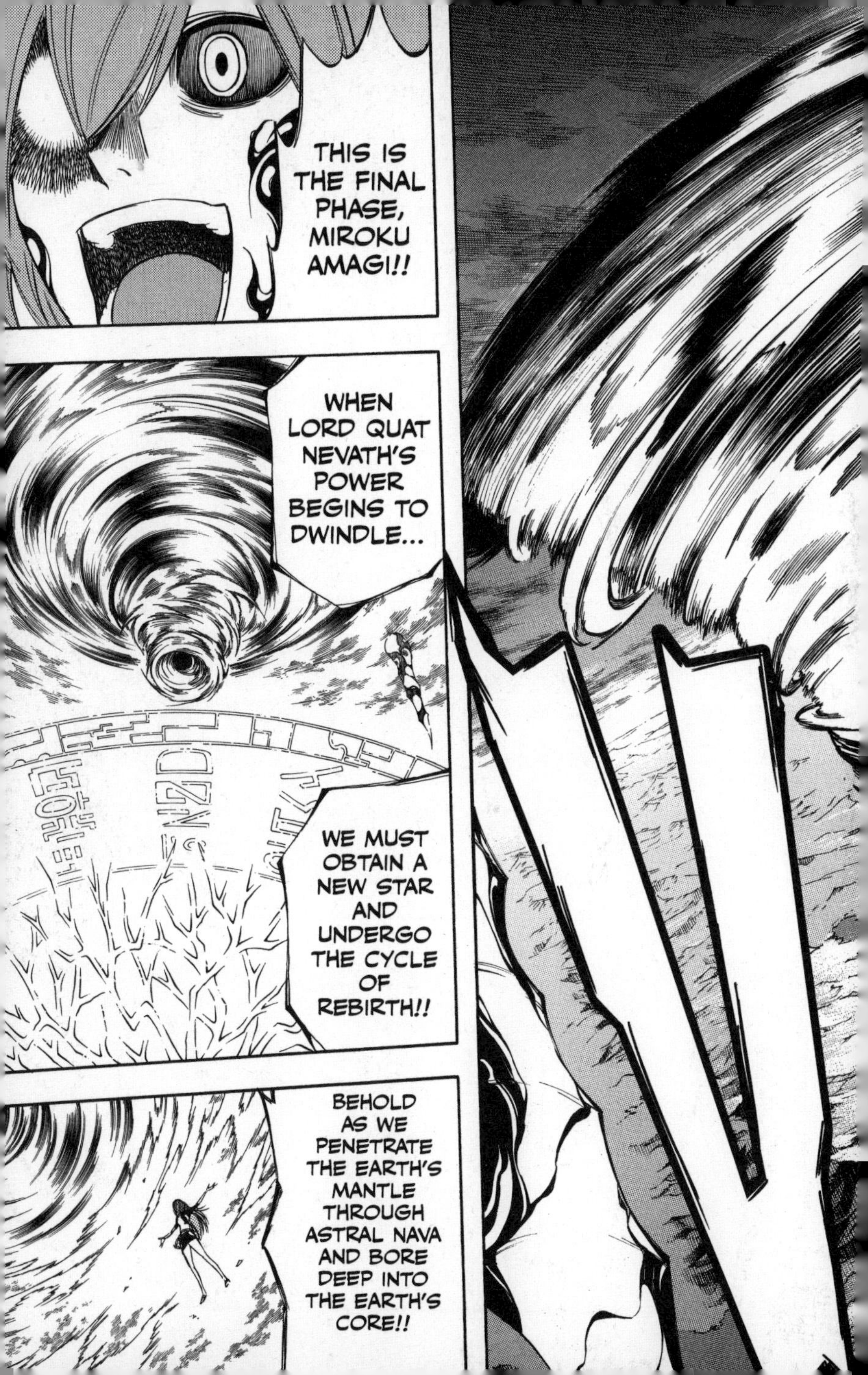
THIS IS THE FINAL PHASE, MIROKU AMAGI!!
WHEN LORD QUAT NEVATH'S POWER BEGINS TO DWINDLE...
WE MUST OBTAIN A NEW STAR AND UNDERGO THE CYCLE OF REBIRTH!!
BEHOLD AS WE PENETRATE THE EARTH'S MANTLE THROUGH ASTRAL NAVA AND BORE DEEP INTO THE EARTH'S CORE!!

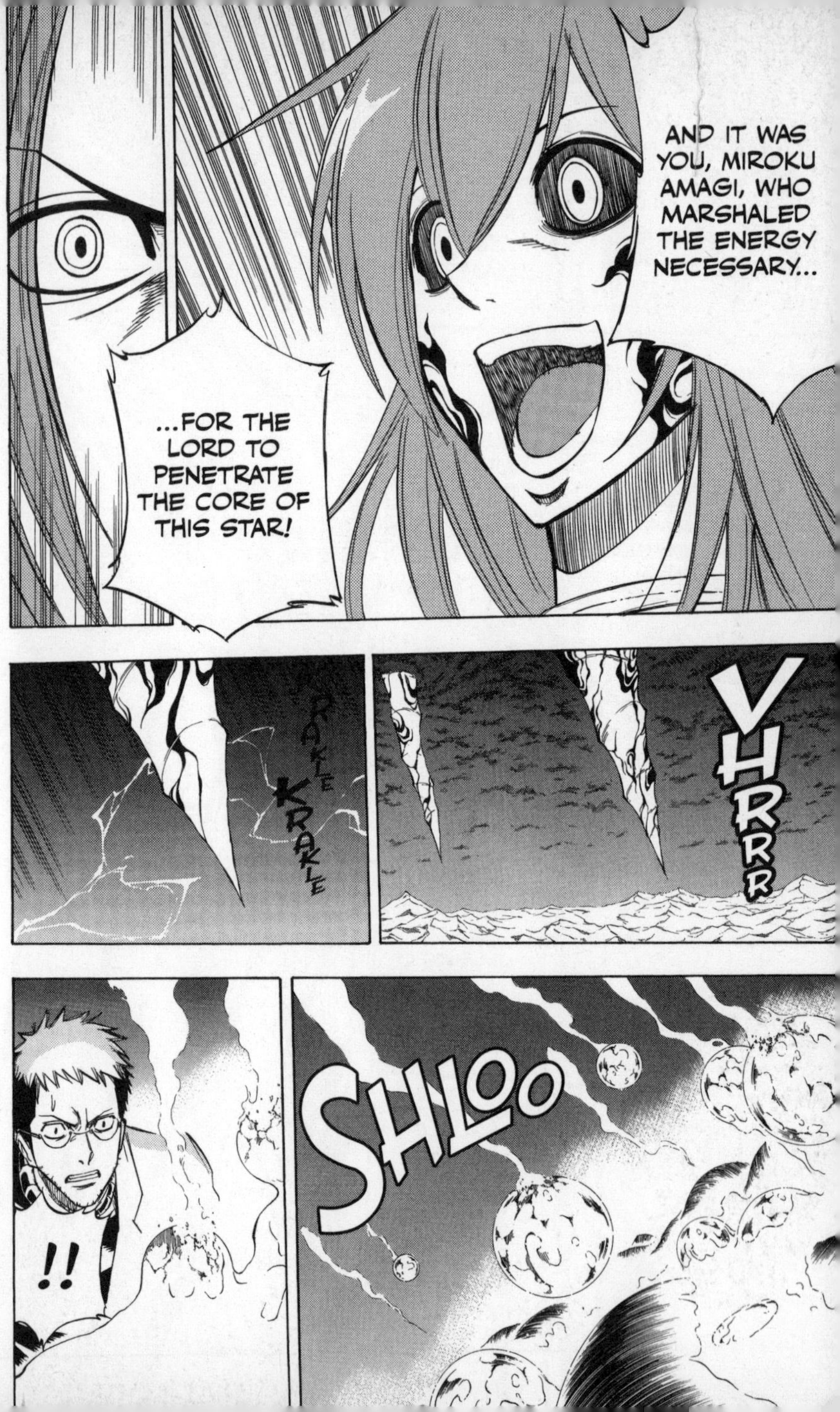
AND IT WAS YOU, MIROKU AMAGI, WHO MARSHALED THE ENERGY NECESSARY...
...FOR THE LORD TO PENETRATE THE CORE OF THIS STAR!
VHRRR
KRAKLE KRAKLE
SHLOO
!!

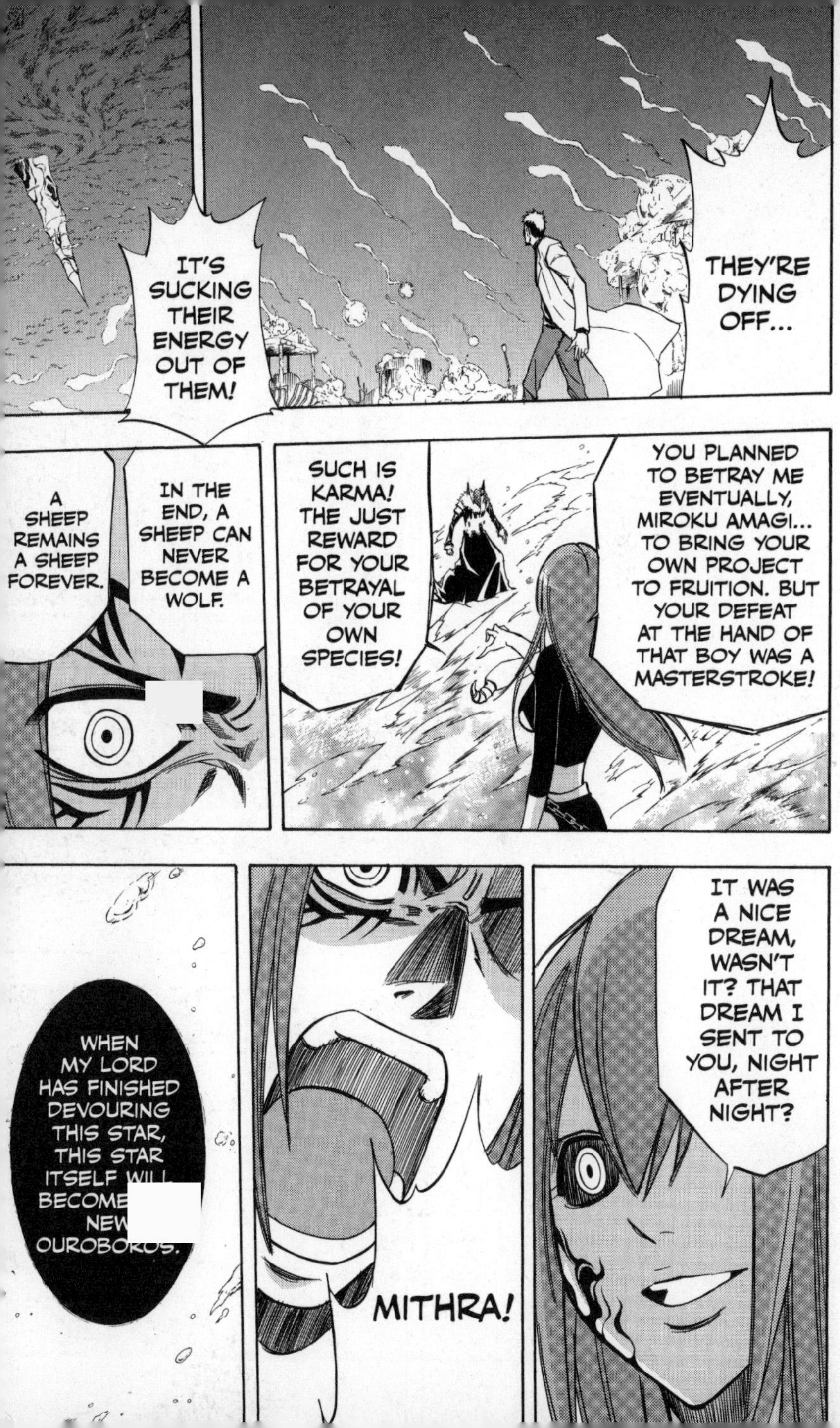
THEY'RE DYING OFF...
IT'S SUCKING THEIR ENERGY OUT OF THEM!
YOU PLANNED TO BETRAY ME EVENTUALLY, MIROKU AMAGI... TO BRING YOUR OWN PROJECT TO FRUITION. BUT YOUR DEFEAT AT THE HAND OF THAT BOY WAS A MASTERSTROKE!
SUCH IS KARMA! THE JUST REWARD FOR YOUR BETRAYAL OF YOUR OWN SPECIES!
IN THE END, A SHEEP CAN NEVER BECOME A WOLF.
A SHEEP REMAINS A SHEEP FOREVER.
IT WAS A NICE DREAM, WASN'T IT? THAT DREAM I SENT TO YOU, NIGHT AFTER NIGHT?
MITHRA!
WHEN MY LORD HAS FINISHED DEVOURING THIS STAR, THIS STAR ITSELF WILL BECOME NEW OUROBOROS.

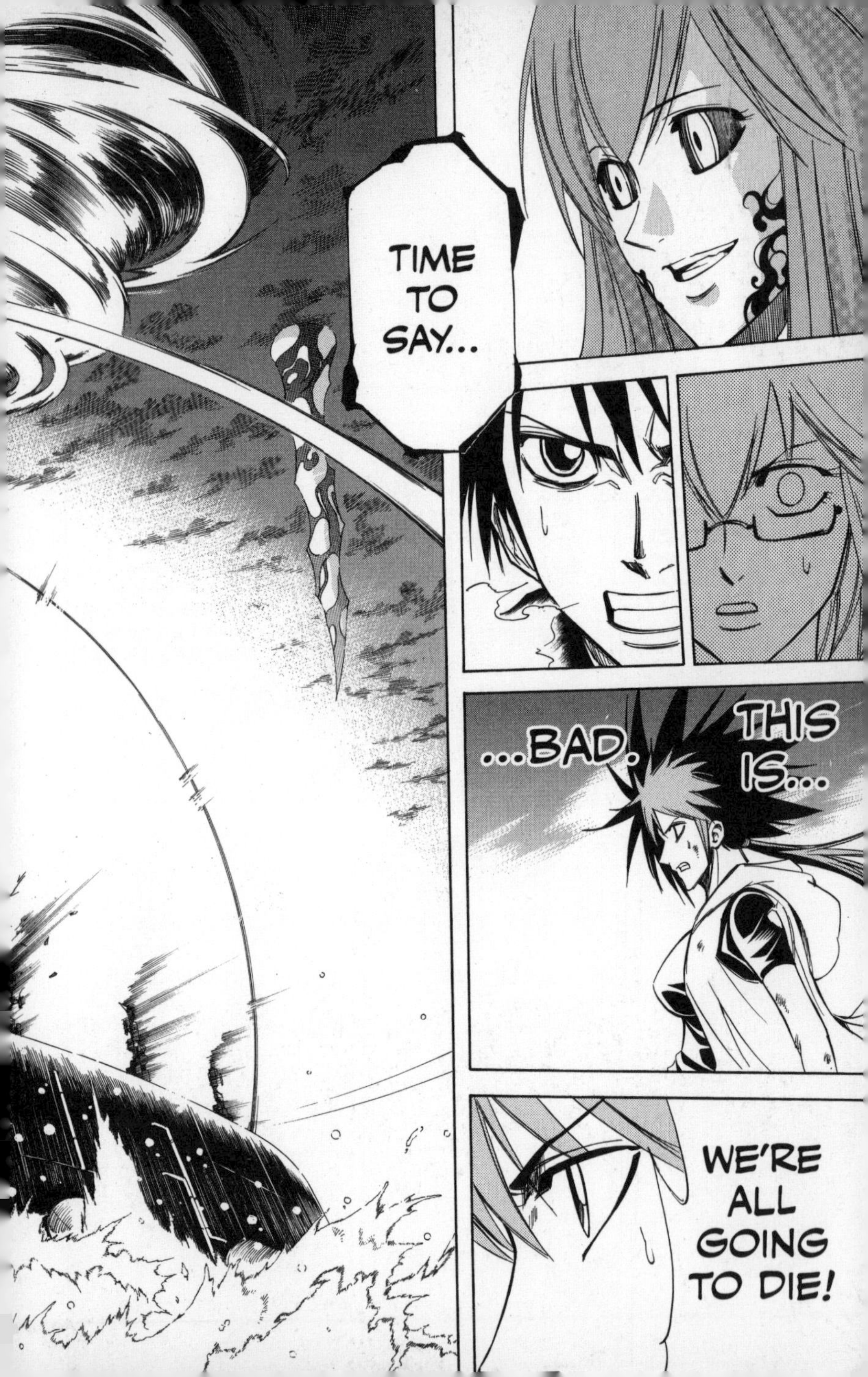
TIME TO SAY...
THIS IS...
...BAD.
WE'RE ALL GOING TO DIE!

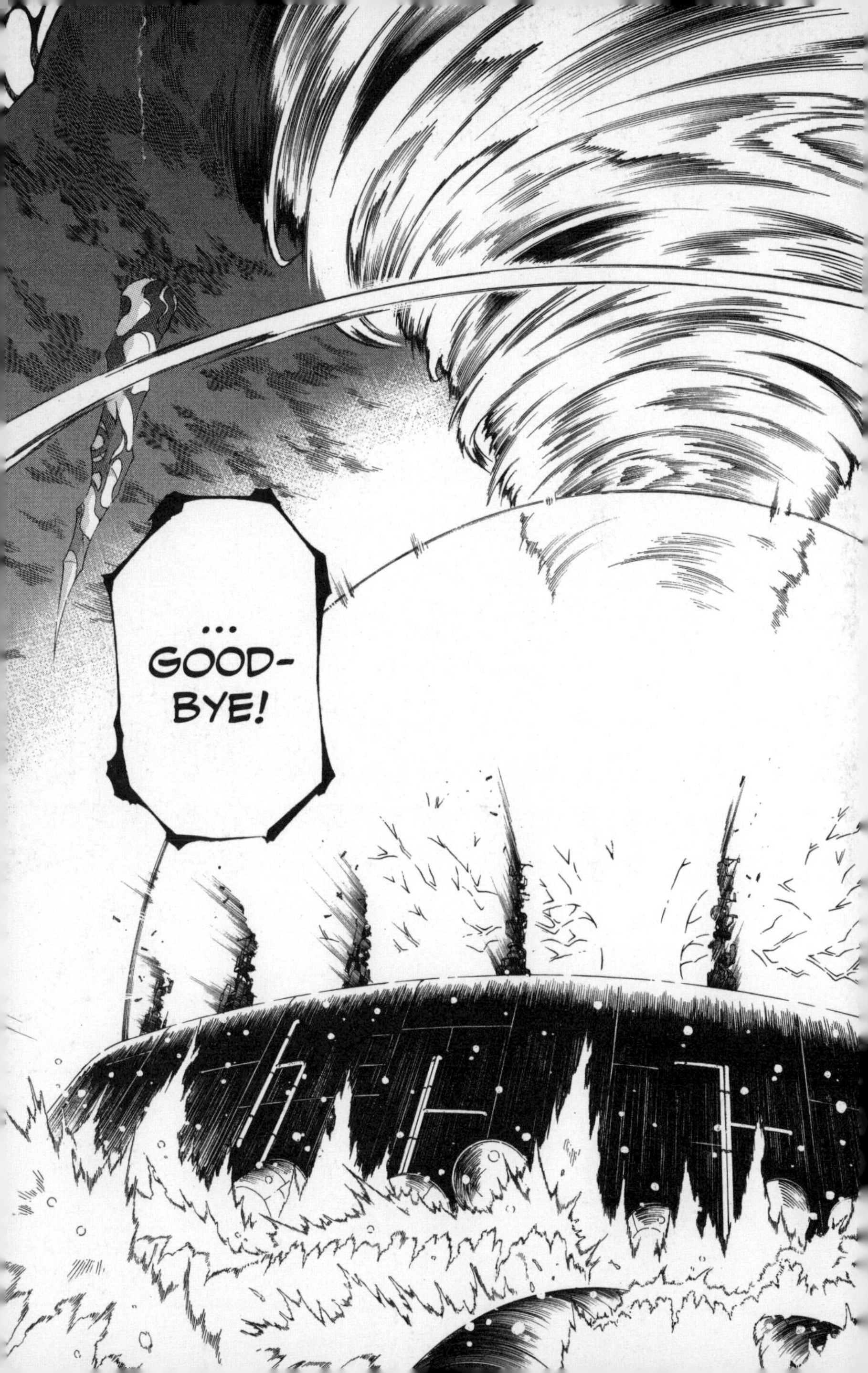
... GOOD-BYE!

Mutters and mumblings

(CONTINUED)

BUT AS THE STORY DEVELOPED, THERE WERE ISSUES WITH
DEPICTING W.I.S.E AS A LOVEY-DOVEY FAMILY AS THEY
CONSPIRED TO DESTROY THE WORLD AND EXTINGUISH THE
HUMAN RACE, INCLUDING THE CHALLENGE OF PORTRAYING
THE INDIVIDUAL MEMBERS OF W.I.S.E'S FEELINGS AND IDEAS
ABOUT THEIR EVIL DEEDS. SO I BACKED OFF A STEP FROM
GRANAR'S AMICABILITY AND HE BECAME A CHARACTER WHO
WITNESSES AND OBSERVES MIROKU'S ACTIONS. I ALSO
WANTED HIM TO COME ACROSS AS SUPER BUFF, SO I
MODIFIED HIS CLOTHING TOO.

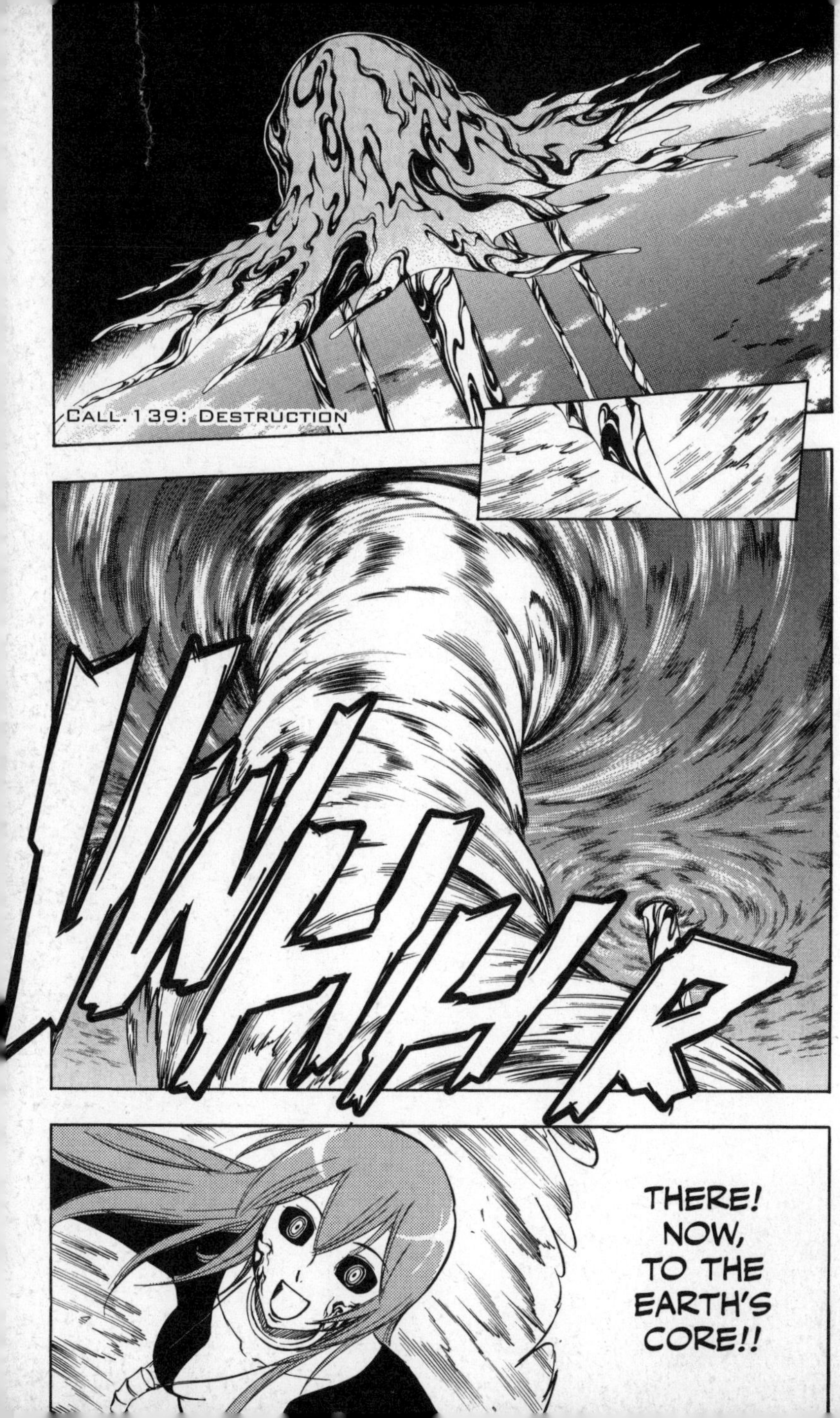
Call. 139: Destruction
WHHR
THERE! NOW, TO THE EARTH'S CORE!!

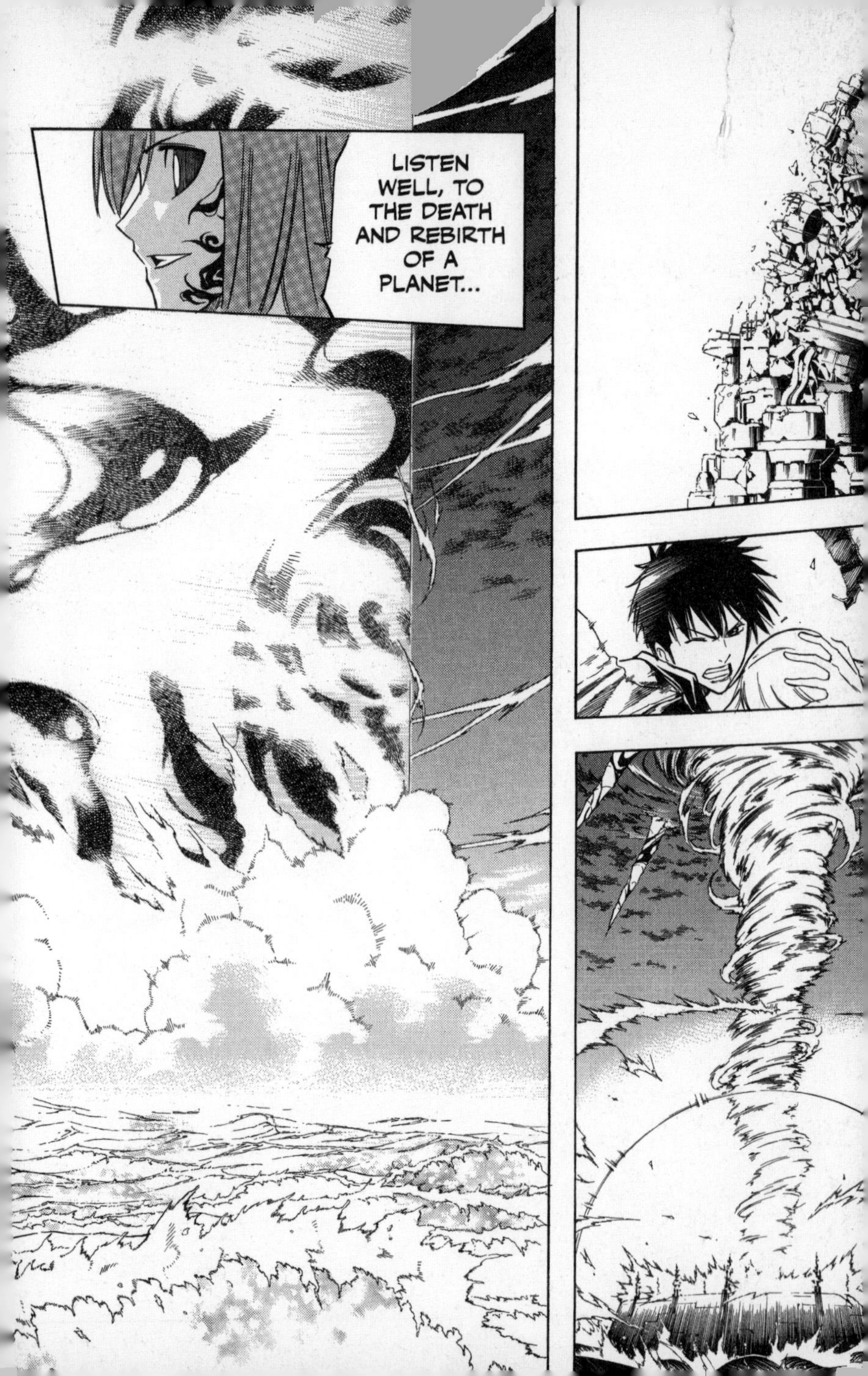
LISTEN WELL, TO THE DEATH AND REBIRTH OF A PLANET...

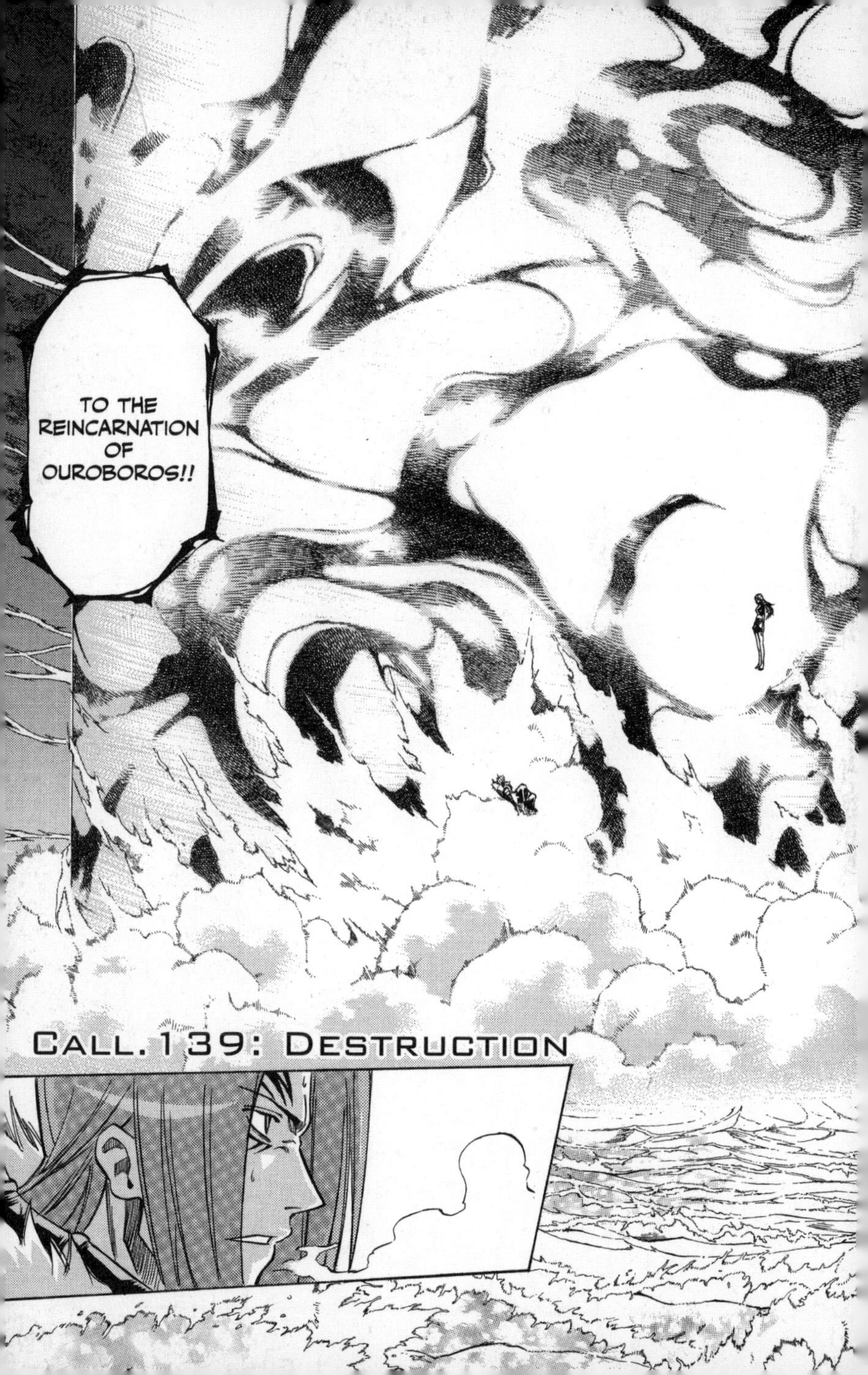
TO THE REINCARNATION OF OUROBOROS!!
CALL. 139: DESTRUCTION

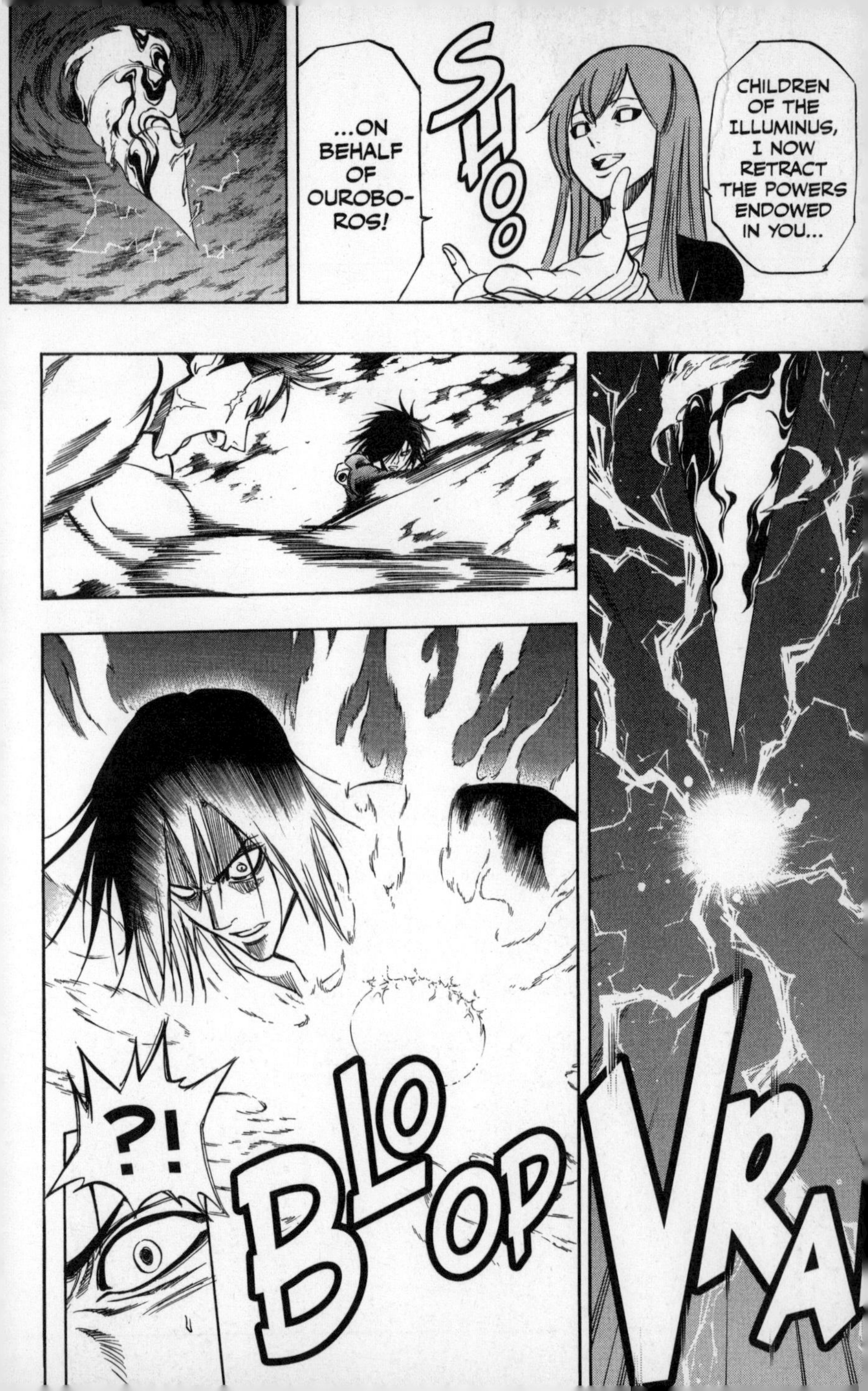
CHILDREN OF THE ILLUMINUS, I NOW RETRACT THE POWERS ENDOWED IN YOU...
SHOO
...ON BEHALF OF OUROBO-ROS!
VRA
BLOOP
?!

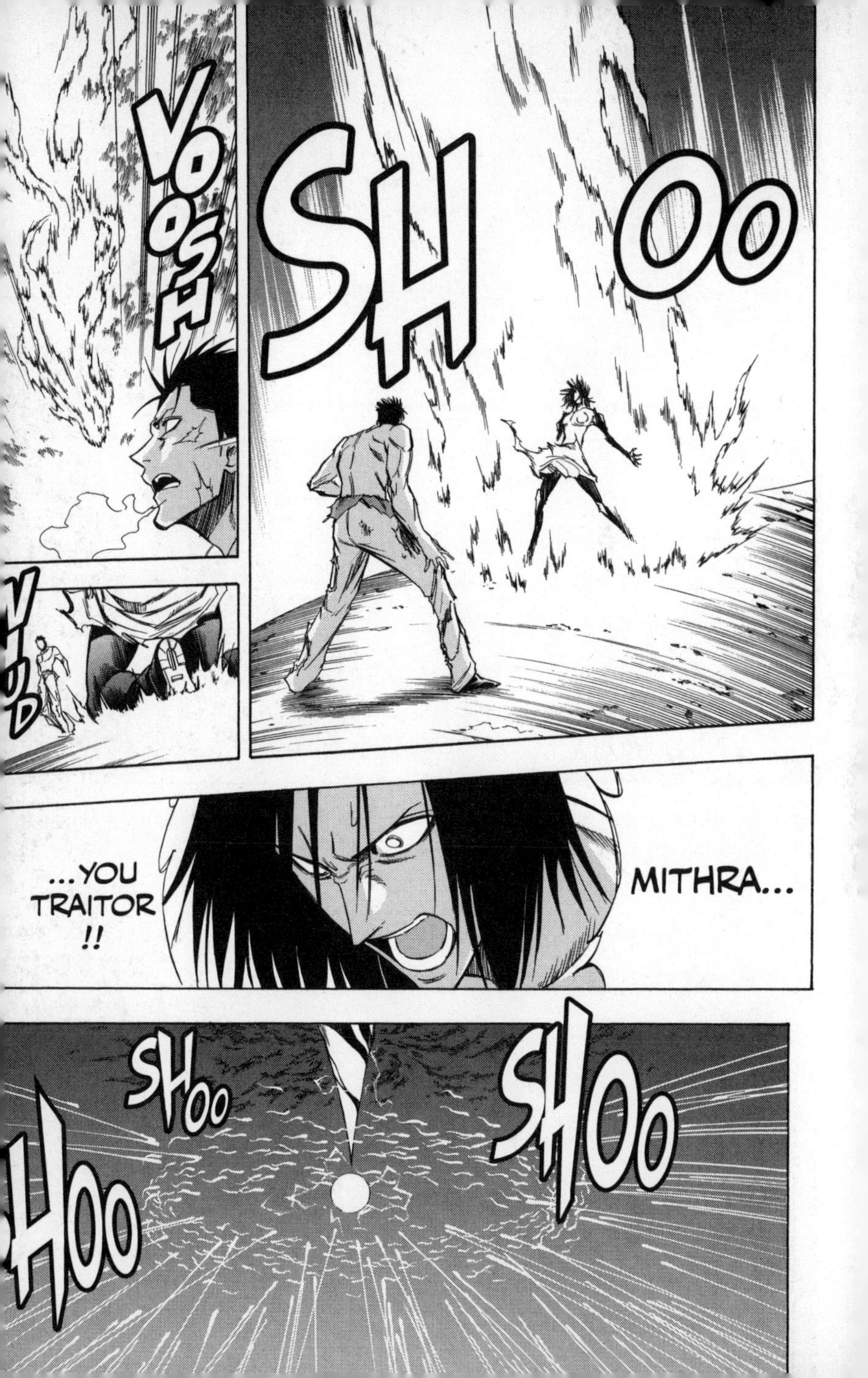
SHOO
VOOSH
VUD
MITHRA...
...YOU TRAITOR!!
SHOO
SHOO
HOO

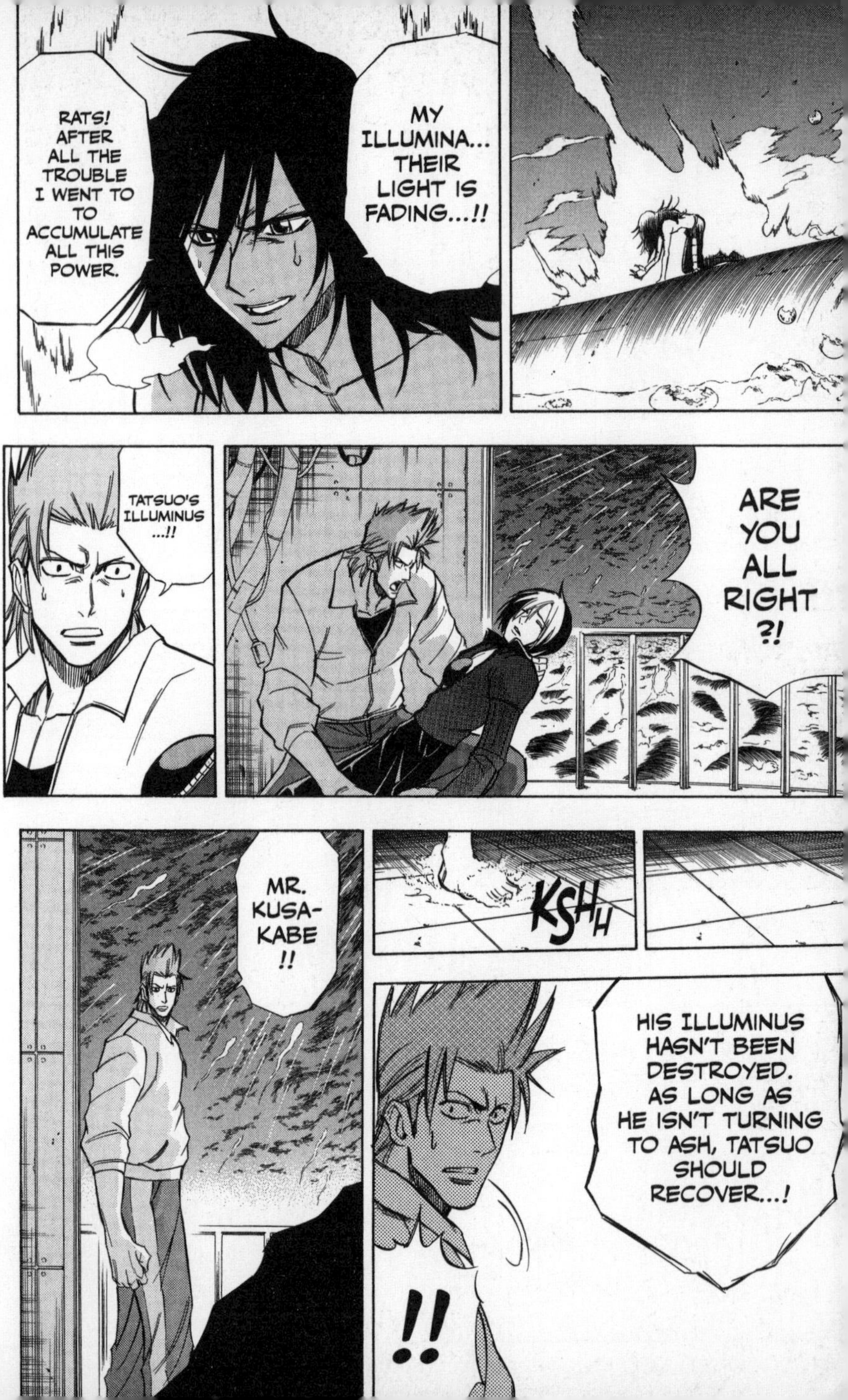
MY ILLUMINA... THEIR LIGHT IS FADING...!!
RATS! AFTER ALL THE TROUBLE I WENT TO TO ACCUMULATE ALL THIS POWER.
ARE YOU ALL RIGHT?!
TATSUO'S ILLUMINUS ...!!
KSHH
HIS ILLUMINUS HASN'T BEEN DESTROYED. AS LONG AS HE ISN'T TURNING TO ASH, TATSUO SHOULD RECOVER...!
!!
MR. KUSA-KABE!!

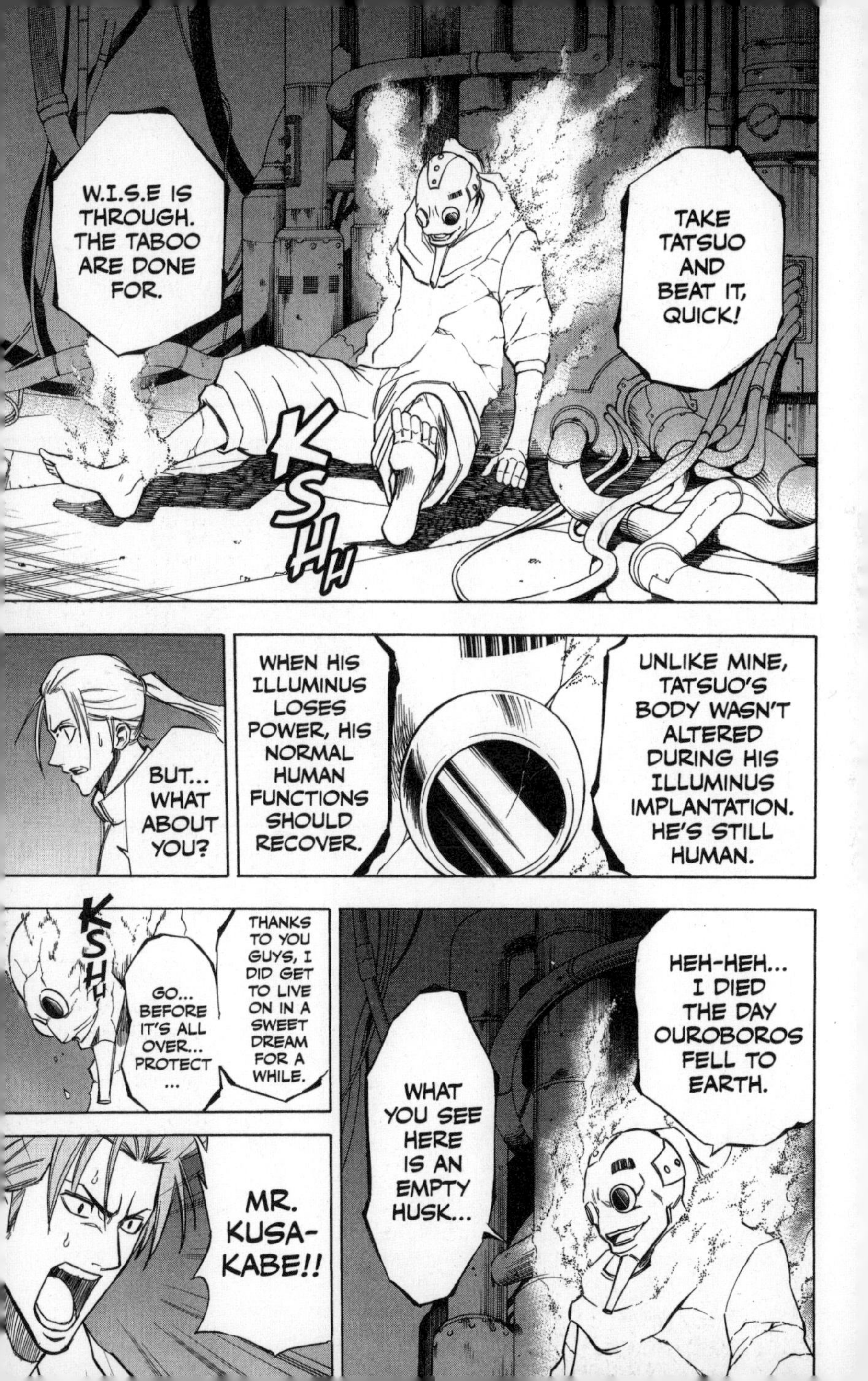
TAKE TATSUO AND BEAT IT, QUICK!
W.I.S.E IS THROUGH. THE TABOO ARE DONE FOR.
KSHH
UNLIKE MINE, TATSUO'S BODY WASN'T ALTERED DURING HIS ILLUMINUS IMPLANTATION. HE'S STILL HUMAN.
WHEN HIS ILLUMINUS LOSES POWER, HIS NORMAL HUMAN FUNCTIONS SHOULD RECOVER.
BUT... WHAT ABOUT YOU?
HEH-HEH... I DIED THE DAY OUROBOROS FELL TO EARTH.
WHAT YOU SEE HERE IS AN EMPTY HUSK...
THANKS TO YOU GUYS, I DID GET TO LIVE ON IN A SWEET DREAM FOR A WHILE.
GO... BEFORE IT'S ALL OVER... PROTECT ...
KSHH
MR. KUSA-KABE!!

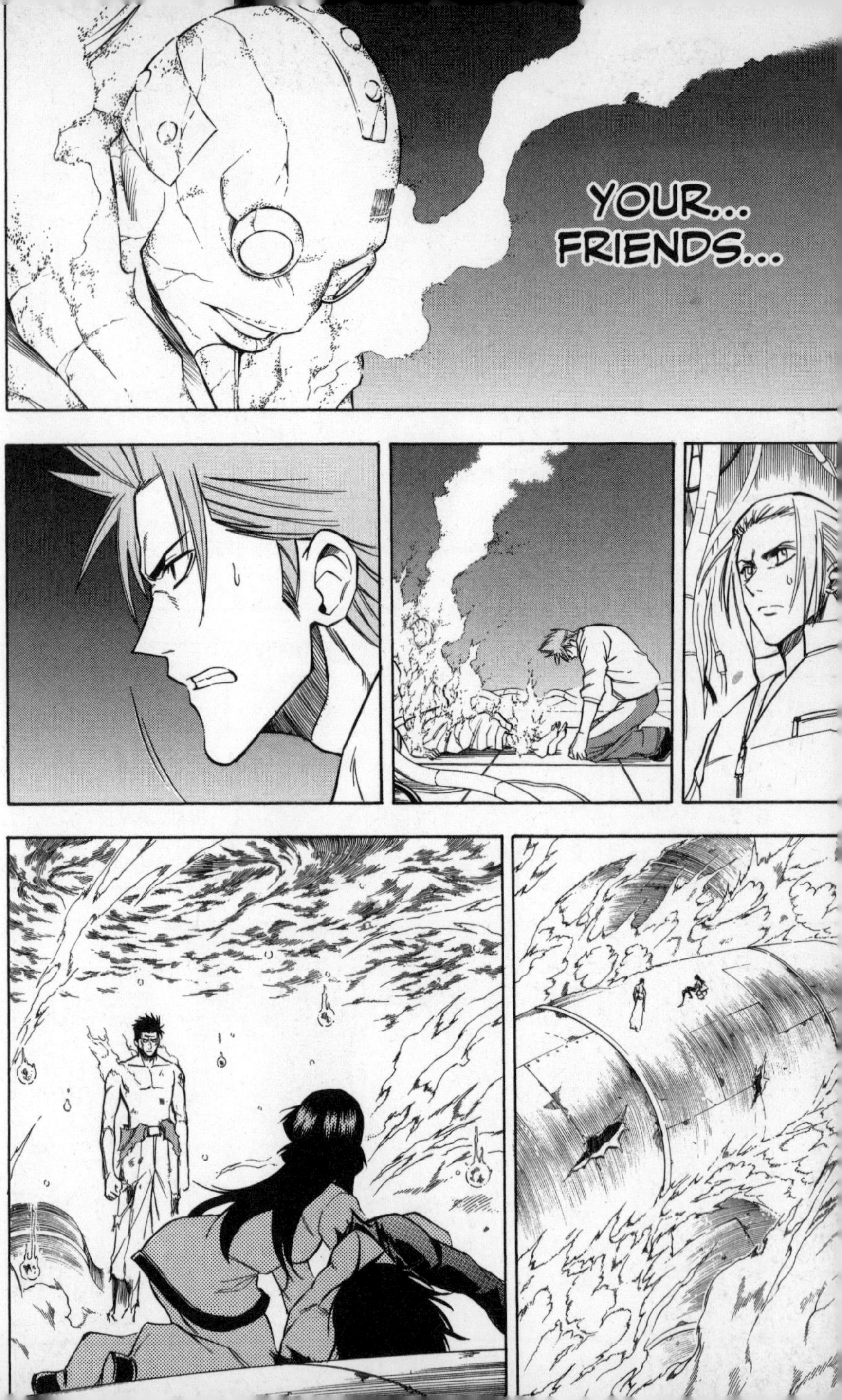
YOUR... FRIENDS...

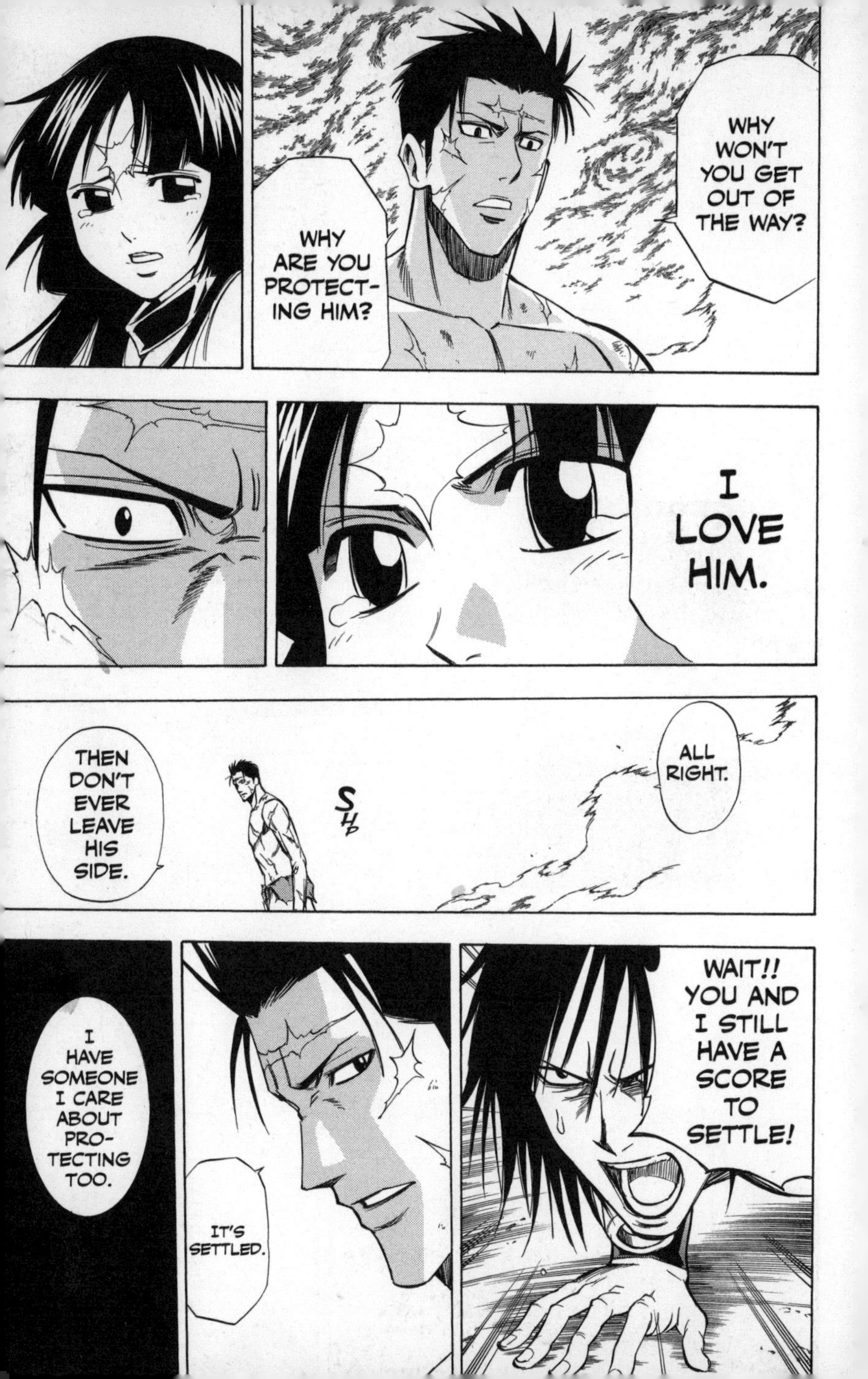
WHY WON'T YOU GET OUT OF THE WAY?
WHY ARE YOU PROTECT-ING HIM?
I LOVE HIM.
ALL RIGHT.
THEN DON'T EVER LEAVE HIS SIDE.
WAIT!! YOU AND I STILL HAVE A SCORE TO SETTLE!
IT'S SETTLED.
I HAVE SOMEONE I CARE ABOUT PRO-TECTING TOO.

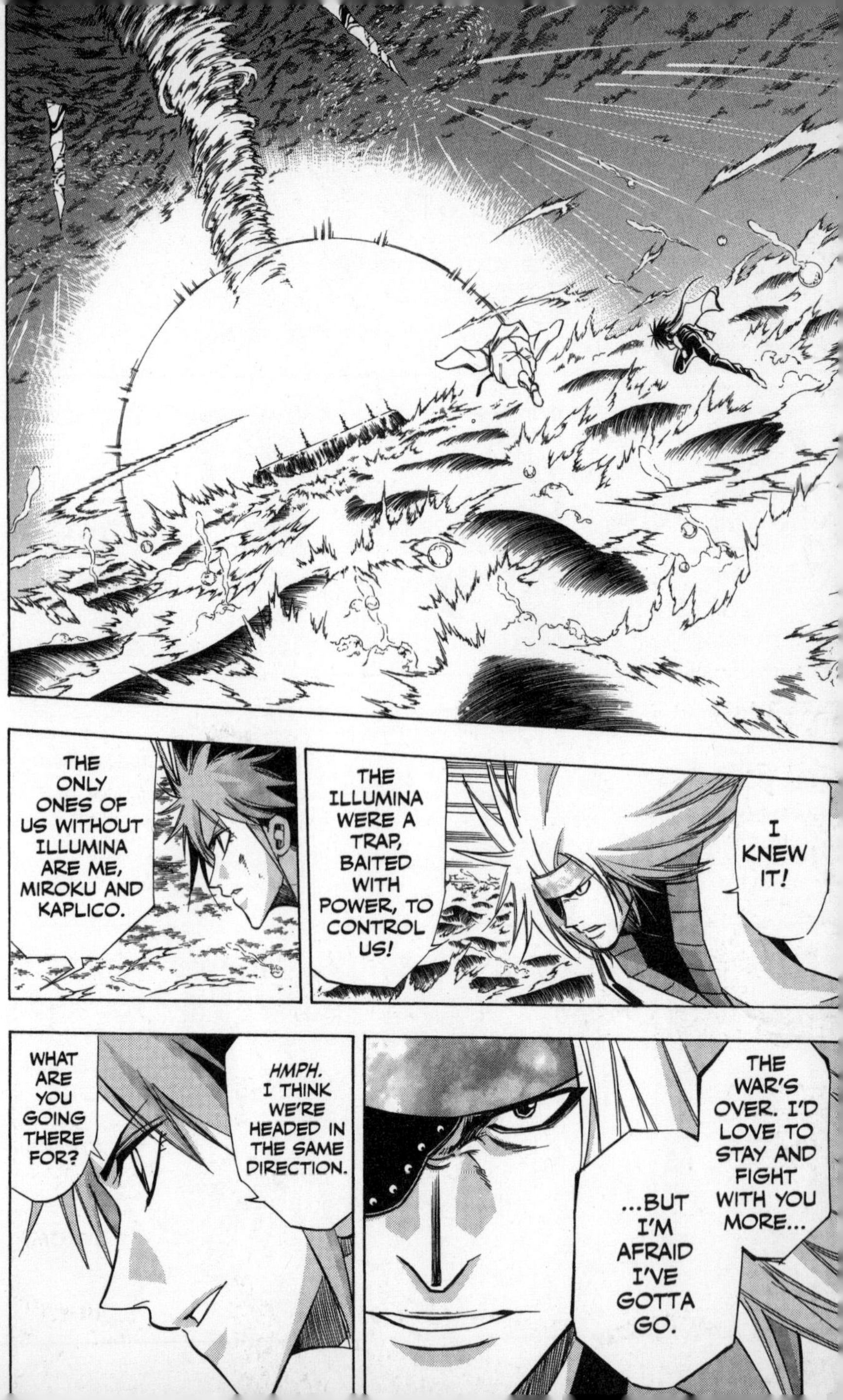
I KNEW IT!
THE ILLUMINA WERE A TRAP, BAITED WITH POWER, TO CONTROL US!
THE ONLY ONES OF US WITHOUT ILLUMINA ARE ME, MIROKU AND KAPLICO.
THE WAR'S OVER. I'D LOVE TO STAY AND FIGHT WITH YOU MORE...
...BUT I'M AFRAID I'VE GOTTA GO.
HMPH. I THINK WE'RE HEADED IN THE SAME DIRECTION.
WHAT ARE YOU GOING THERE FOR?

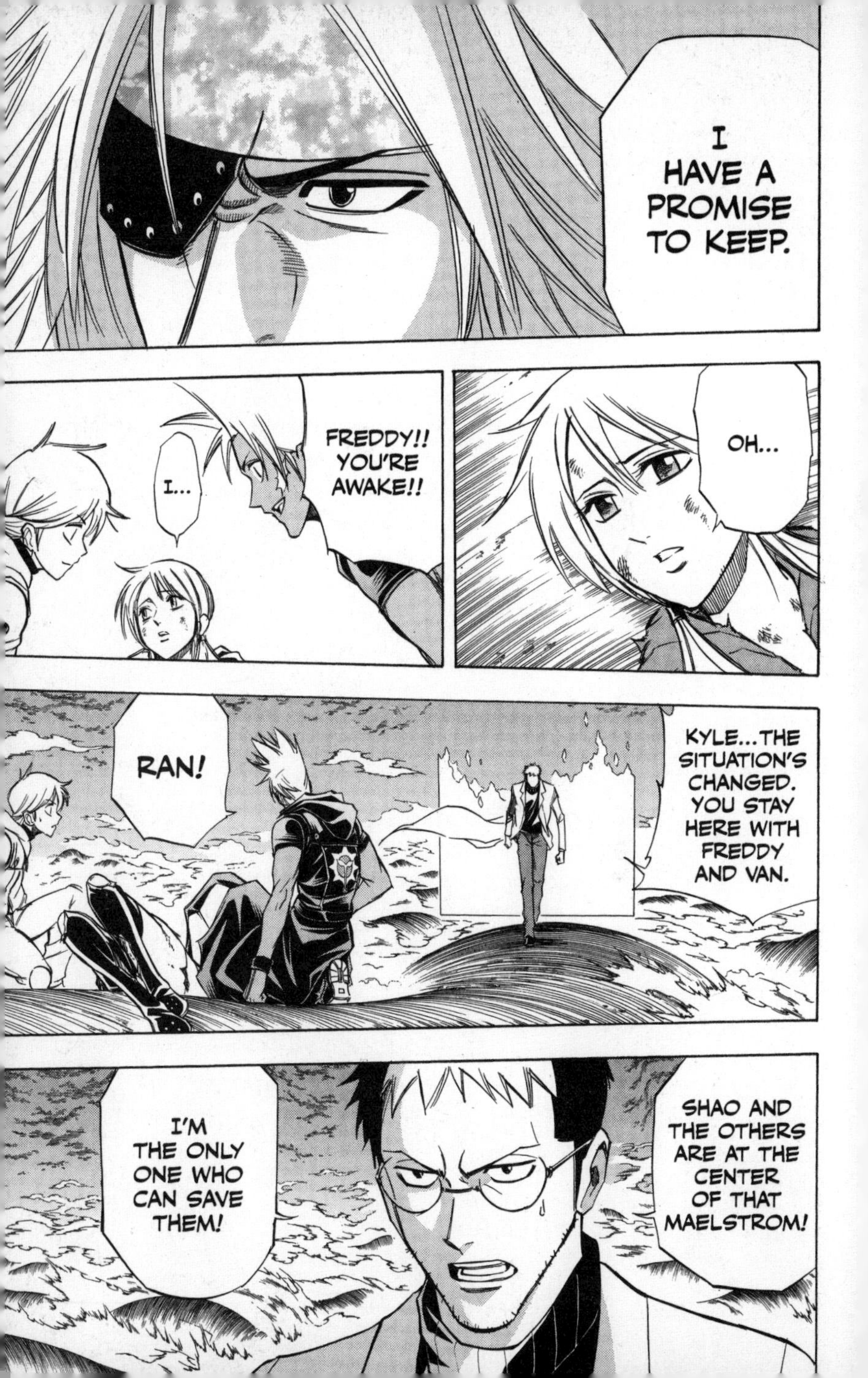
I HAVE A PROMISE TO KEEP.
OH...
FREDDY!! YOU'RE AWAKE!!
I...
KYLE...THE SITUATION'S CHANGED. YOU STAY HERE WITH FREDDY AND VAN.
RAN!
SHAO AND THE OTHERS ARE AT THE CENTER OF THAT MAELSTROM!
I'M THE ONLY ONE WHO CAN SAVE THEM!

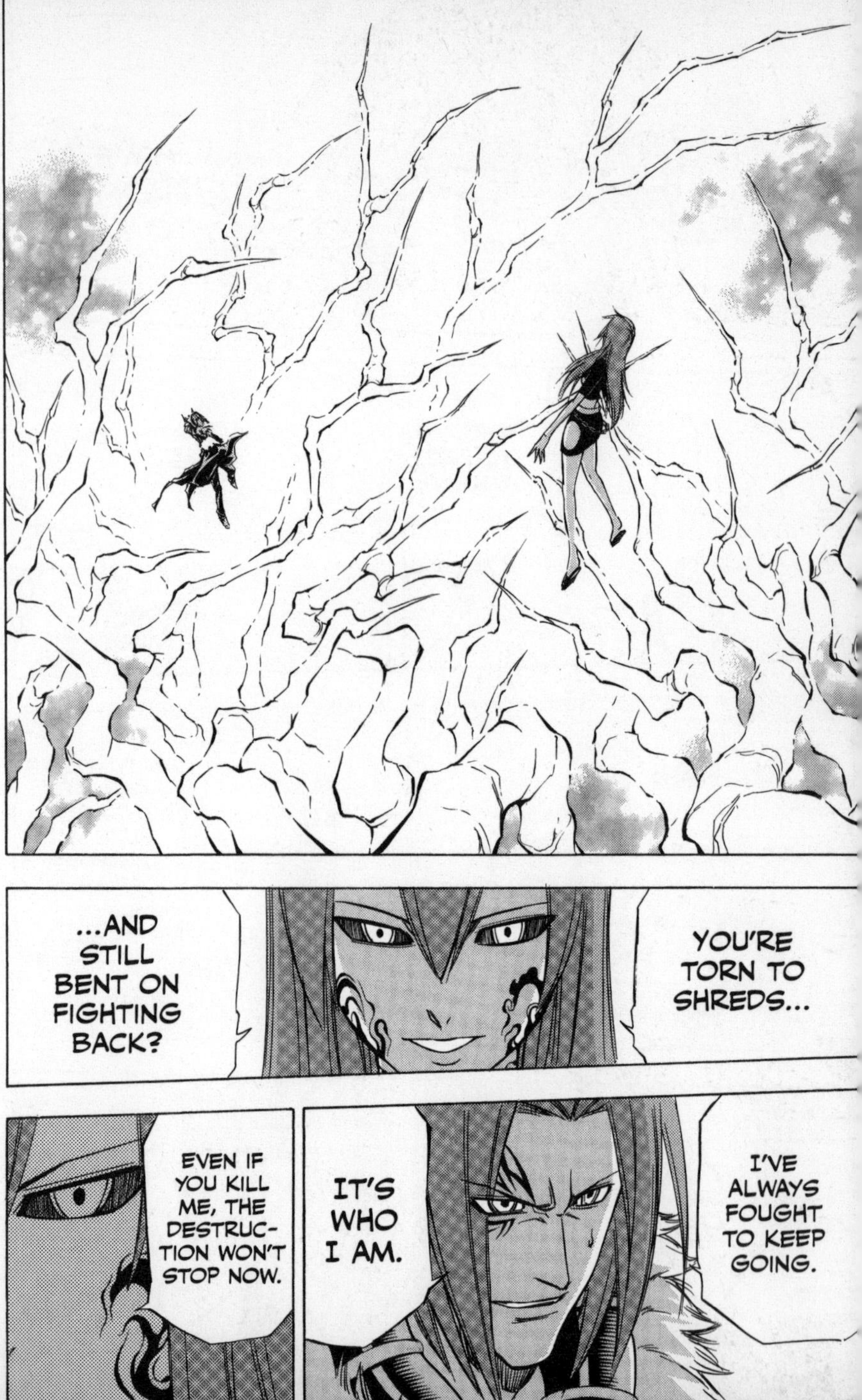
YOU'RE TORN TO SHREDS...
...AND STILL BENT ON FIGHTING BACK?
I'VE ALWAYS FOUGHT TO KEEP GOING.
IT'S WHO I AM.
EVEN IF YOU KILL ME, THE DESTRUCTION WON'T STOP NOW.

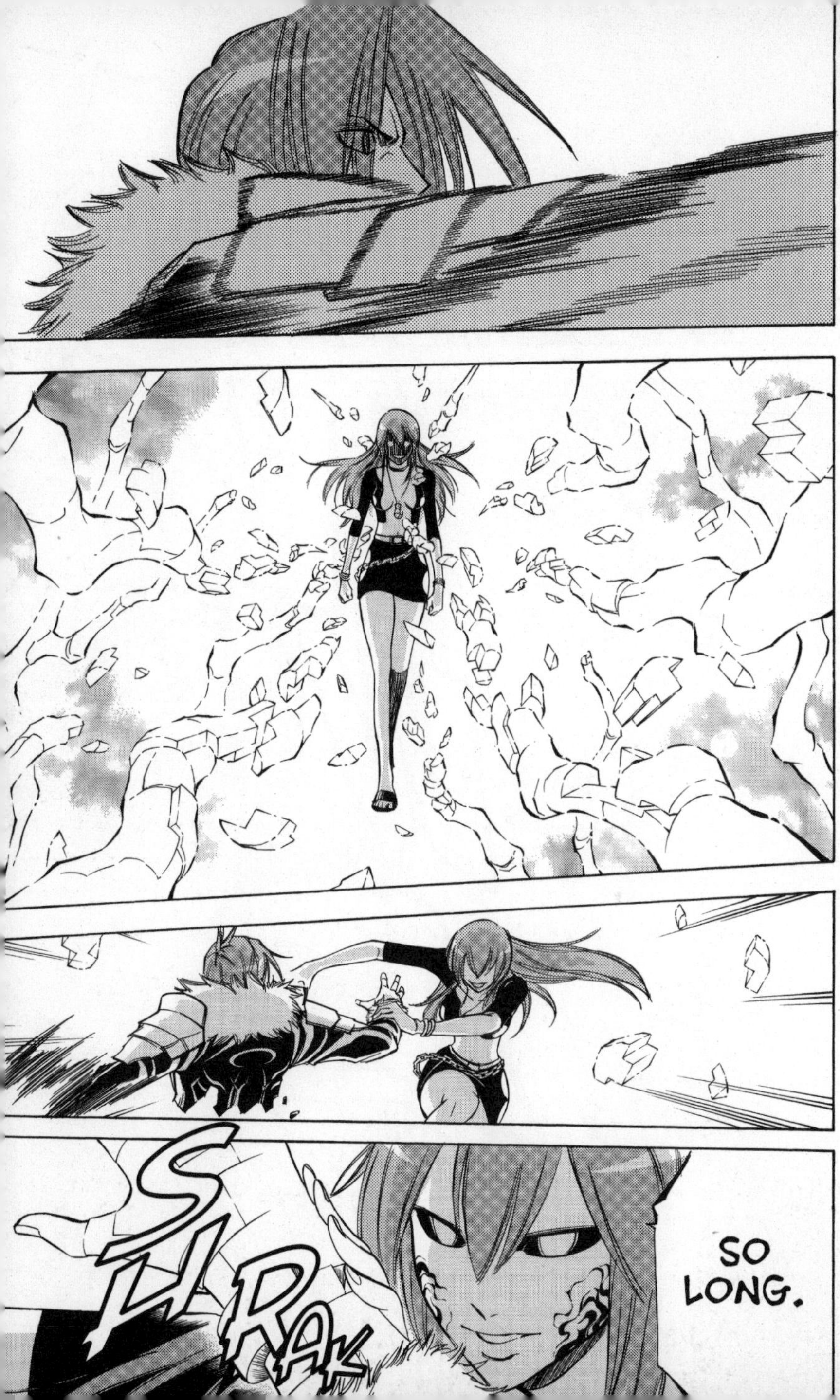
SO LONG.
SHRAK

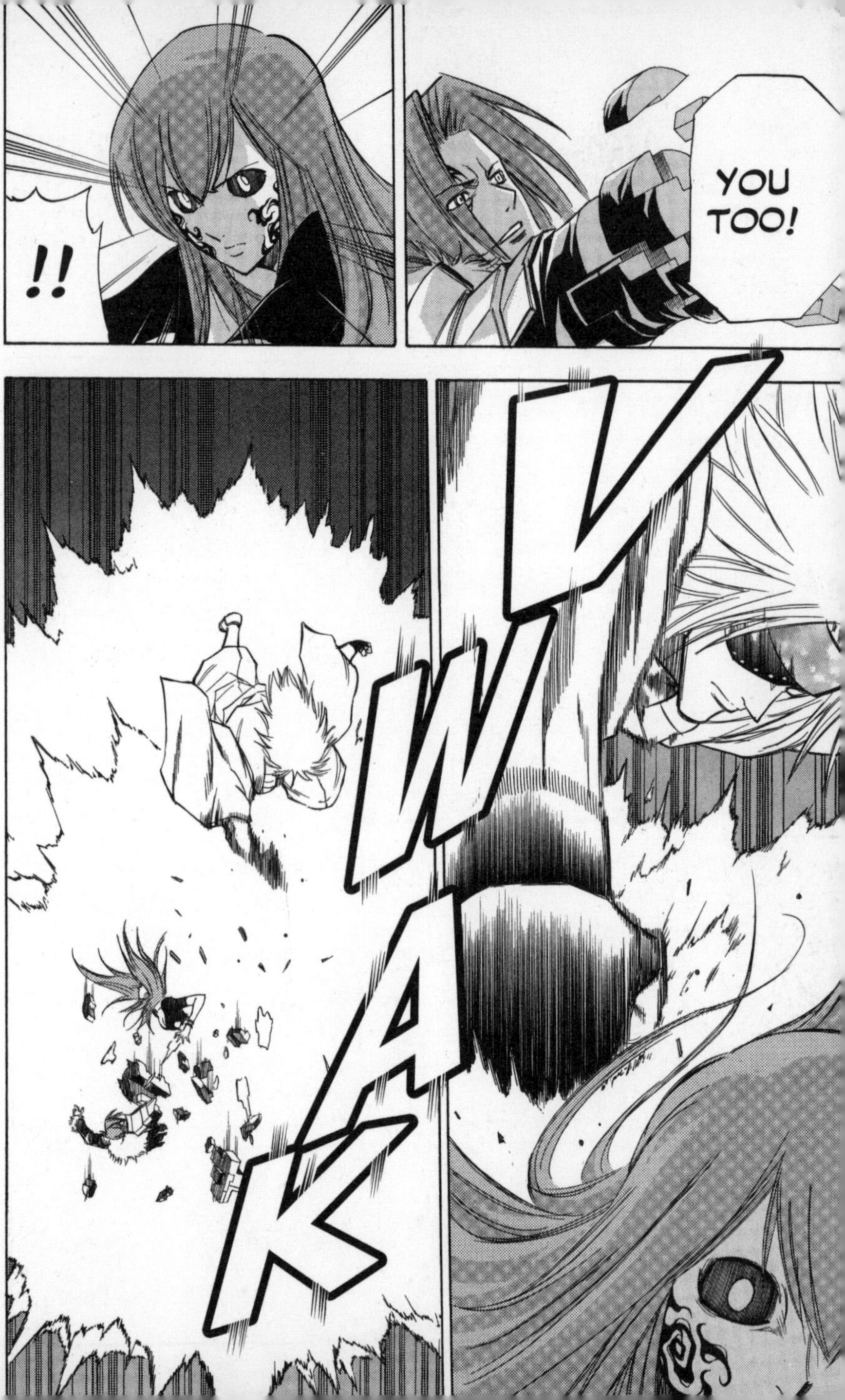
YOU TOO!
!!
WHAK

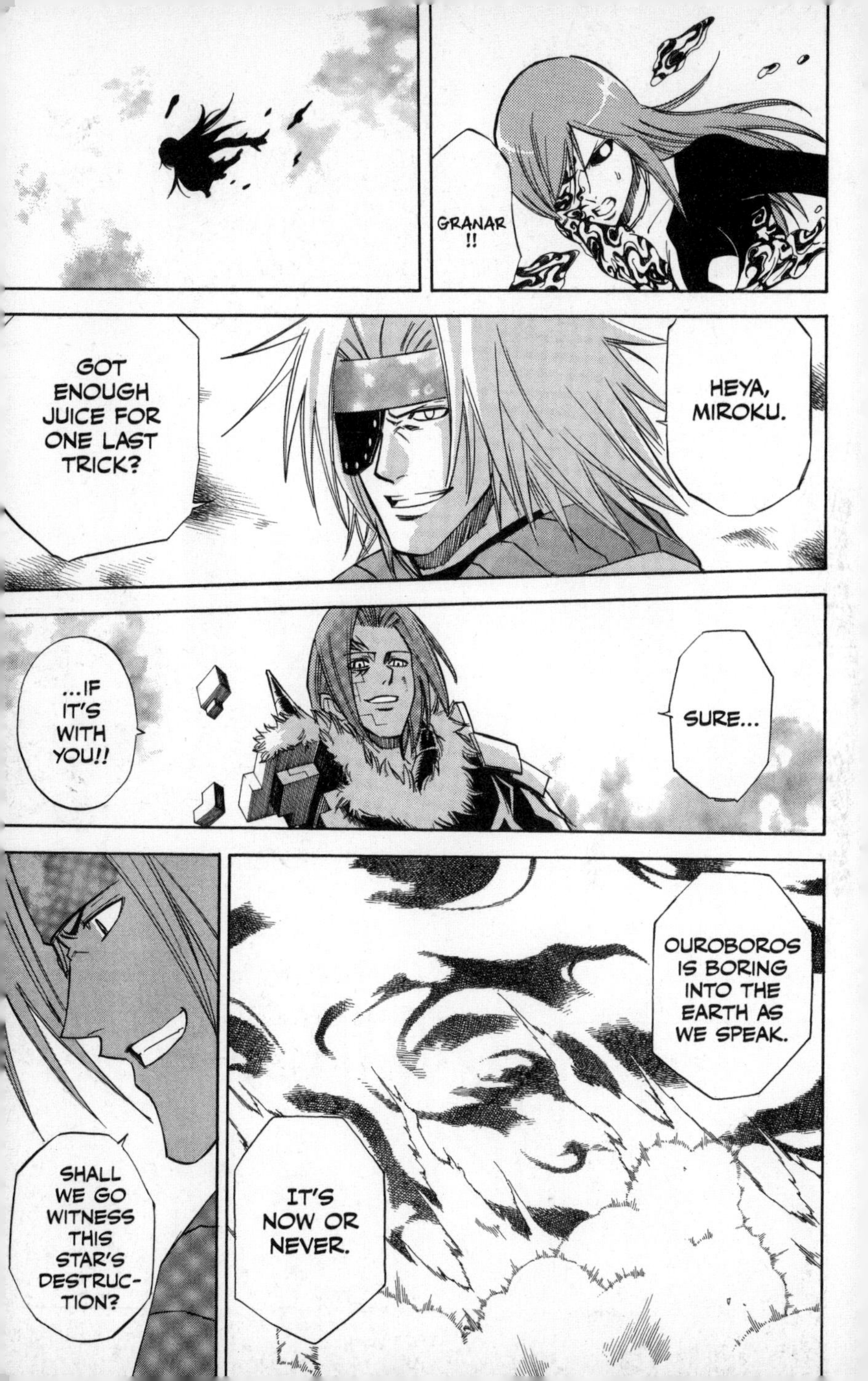
GRANAR !!
HEYA, MIROKU.
GOT ENOUGH JUICE FOR ONE LAST TRICK?
SURE...
...IF IT'S WITH YOU!!
OUROBOROS IS BORING INTO THE EARTH AS WE SPEAK.
IT'S NOW OR NEVER.
SHALL WE GO WITNESS THIS STAR'S DESTRUC-TION?

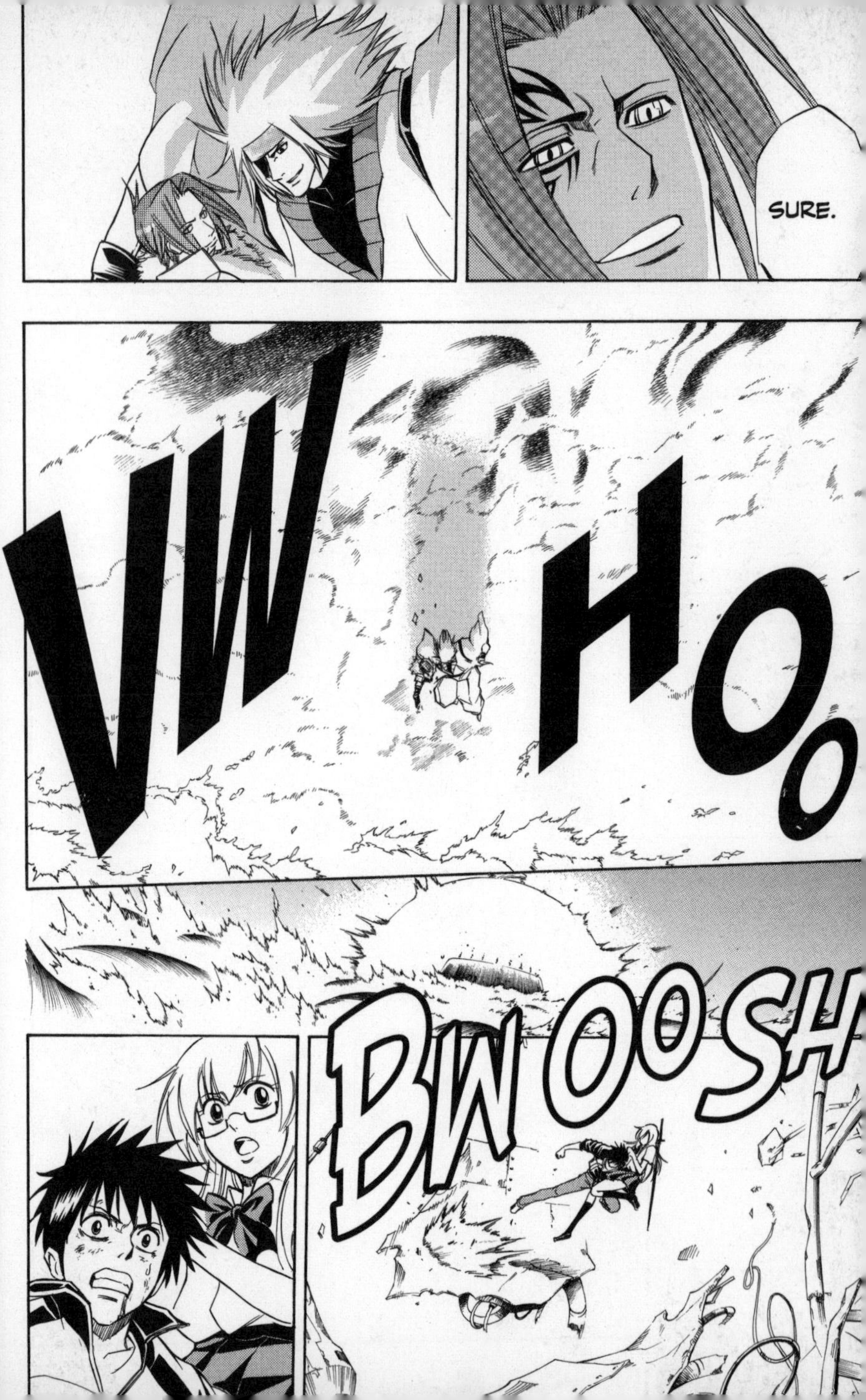
SURE.
VW HOO
BWOOSH

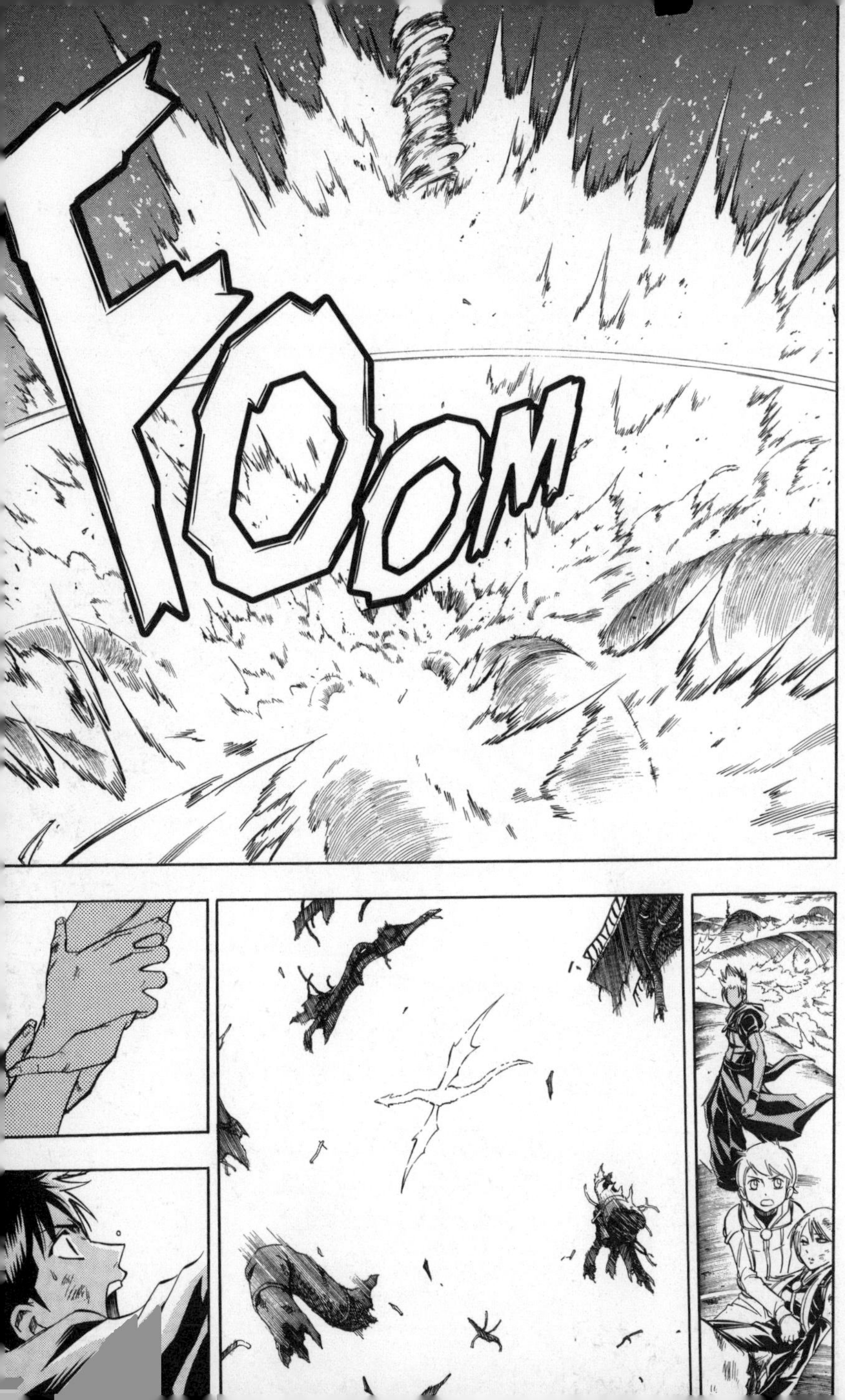
FOOOM

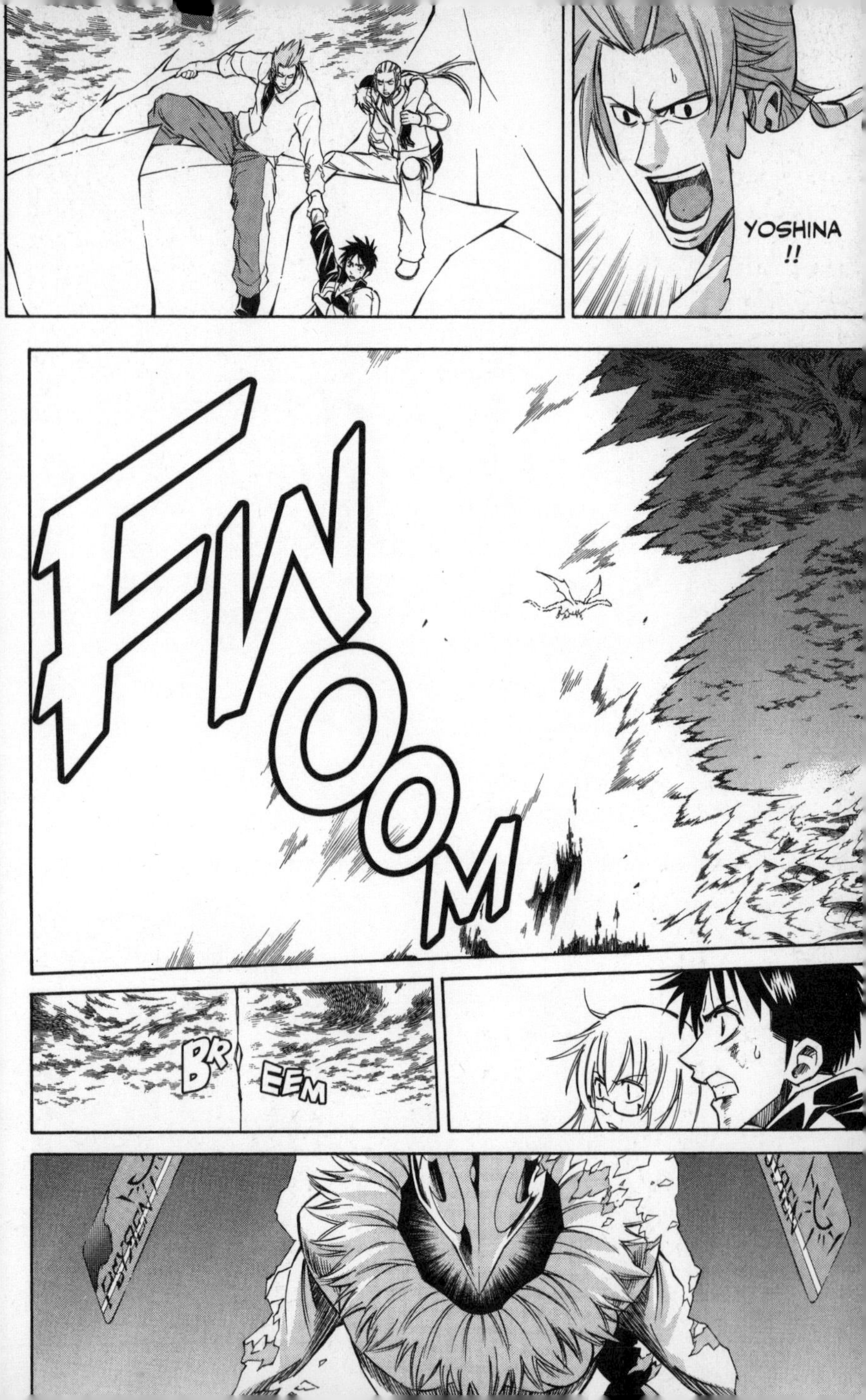
YOSHINA !!
FWOOOM
BR EEM

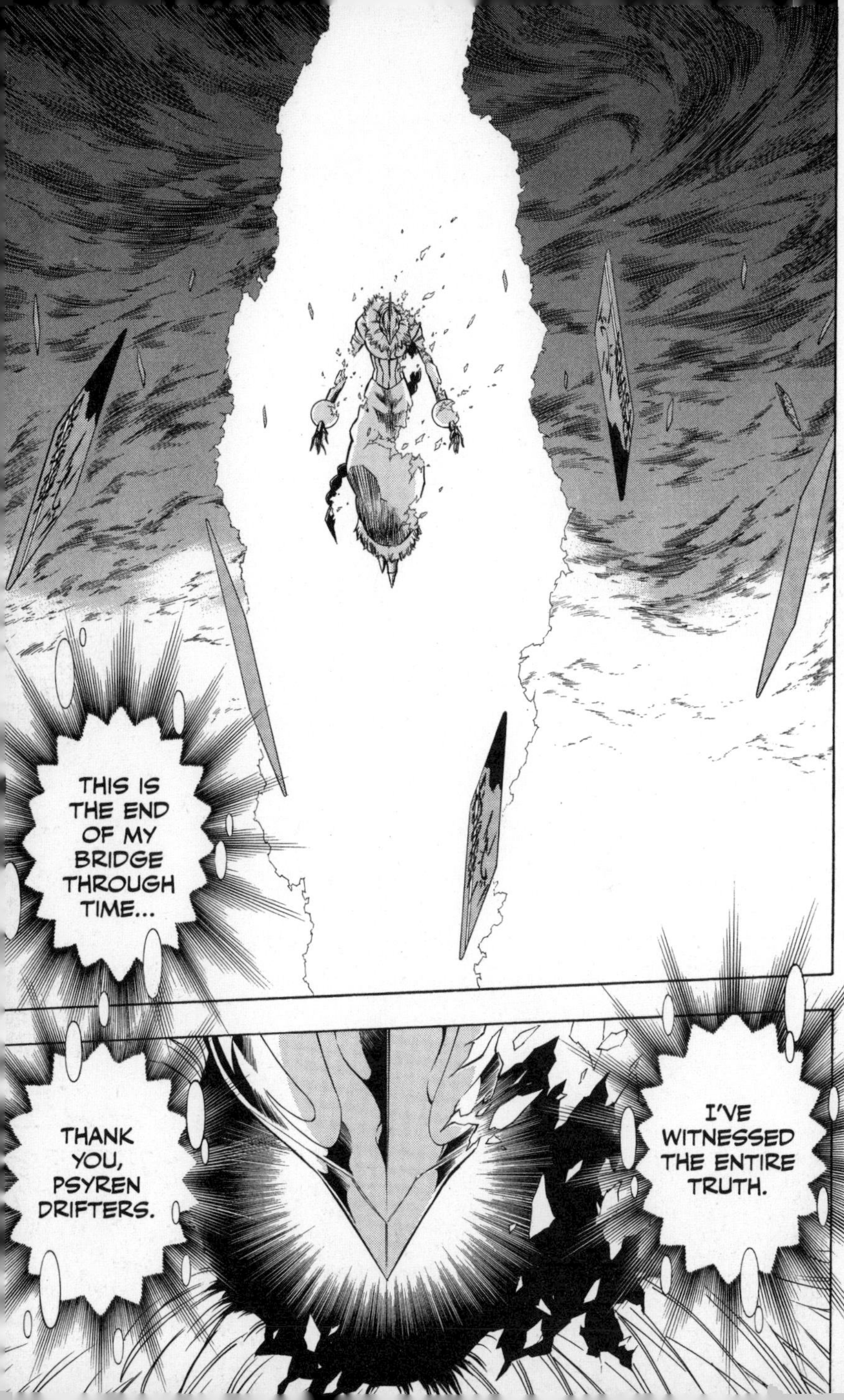
THIS IS THE END OF MY BRIDGE THROUGH TIME...
I'VE WITNESSED THE ENTIRE TRUTH.
THANK YOU, PSYREN DRIFTERS.

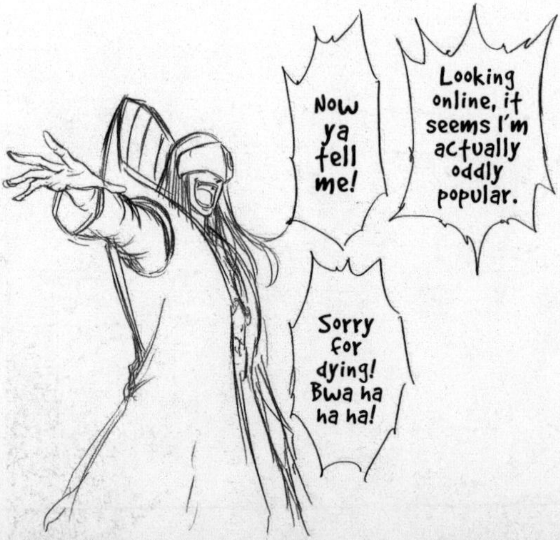
Looking online, it seems I'm actually oddly popular.
Now ya tell me!
Sorry for dying! Bwa ha ha ha!

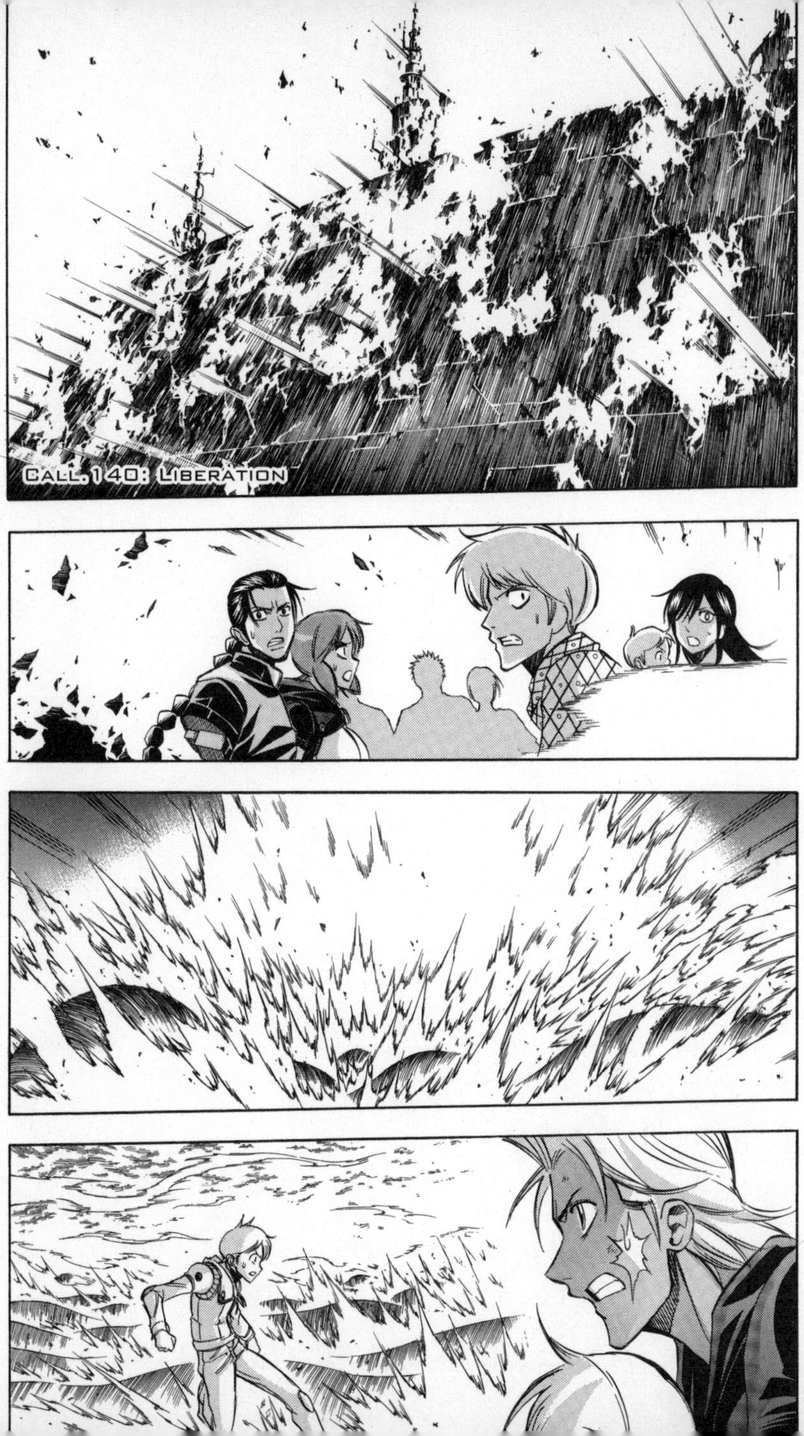
Call. 140: Liberation

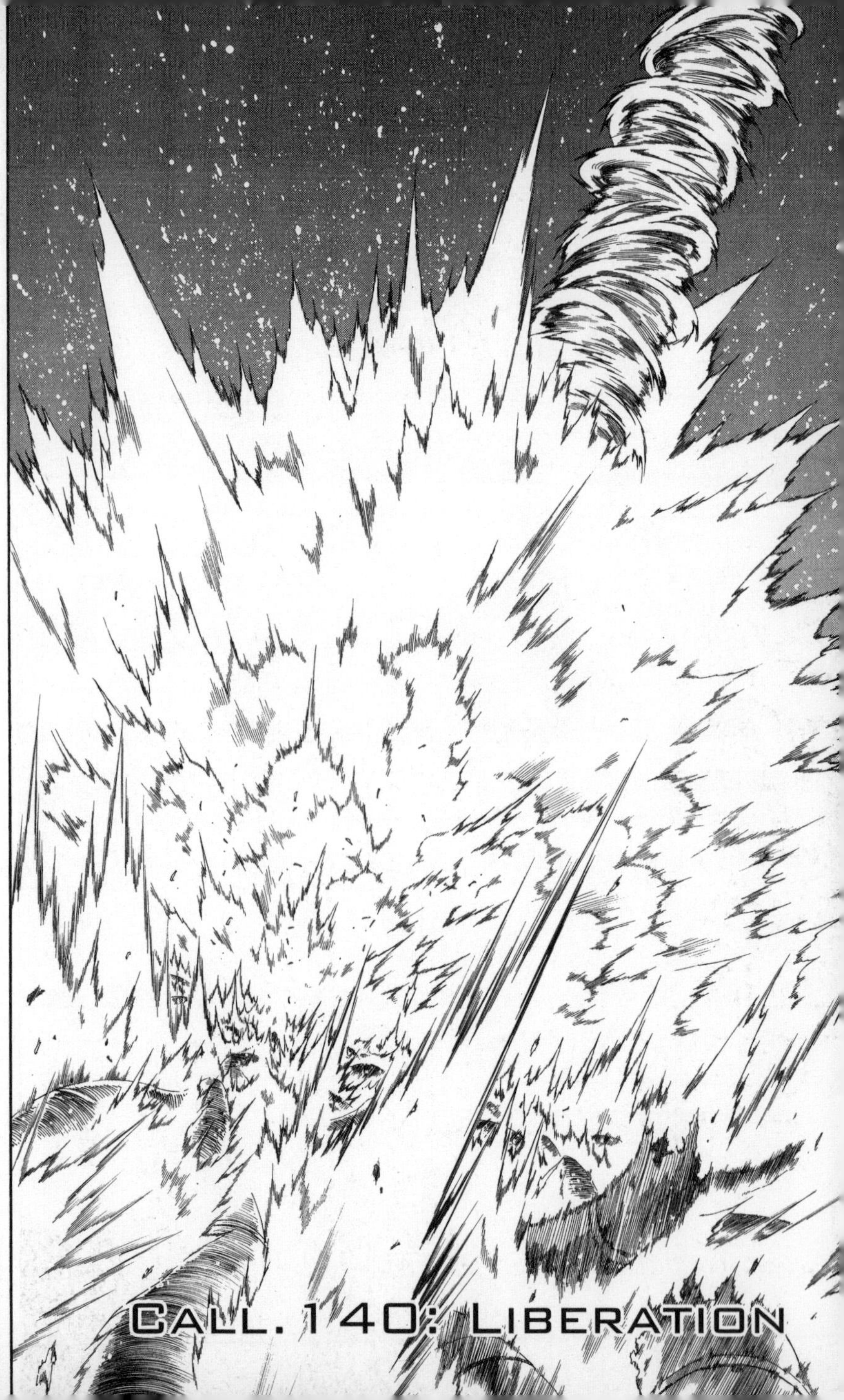
CALL. 140: LIBERATION

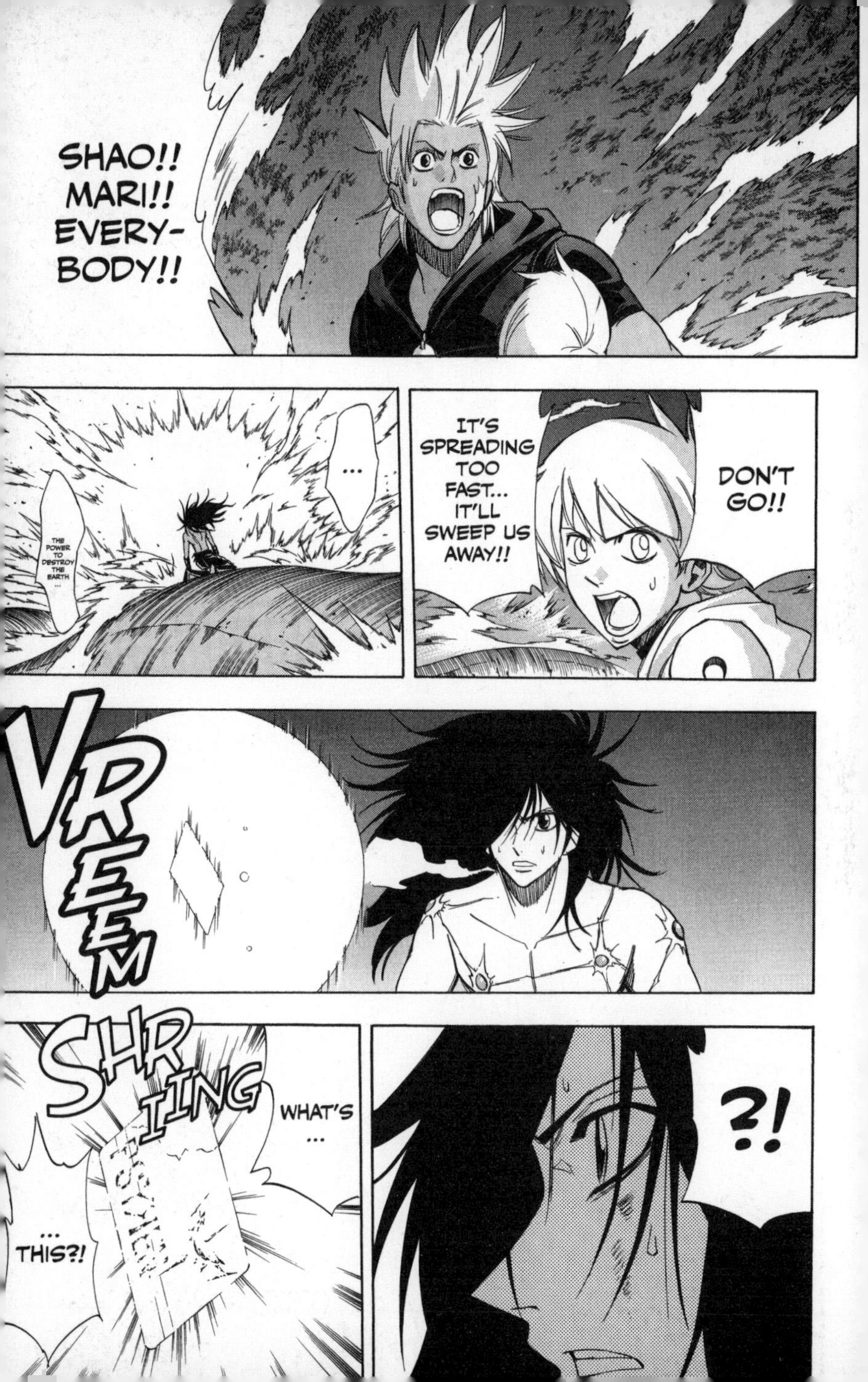
SHAO!! MARI!! EVERY-BODY!!
DON'T GO!!
IT'S SPREADING TOO FAST... IT'LL SWEEP US AWAY!!
...
THE POWER TO DESTROY THE EARTH ...
VREEEM
?!
SHRIING
WHAT'S ...
... THIS?!

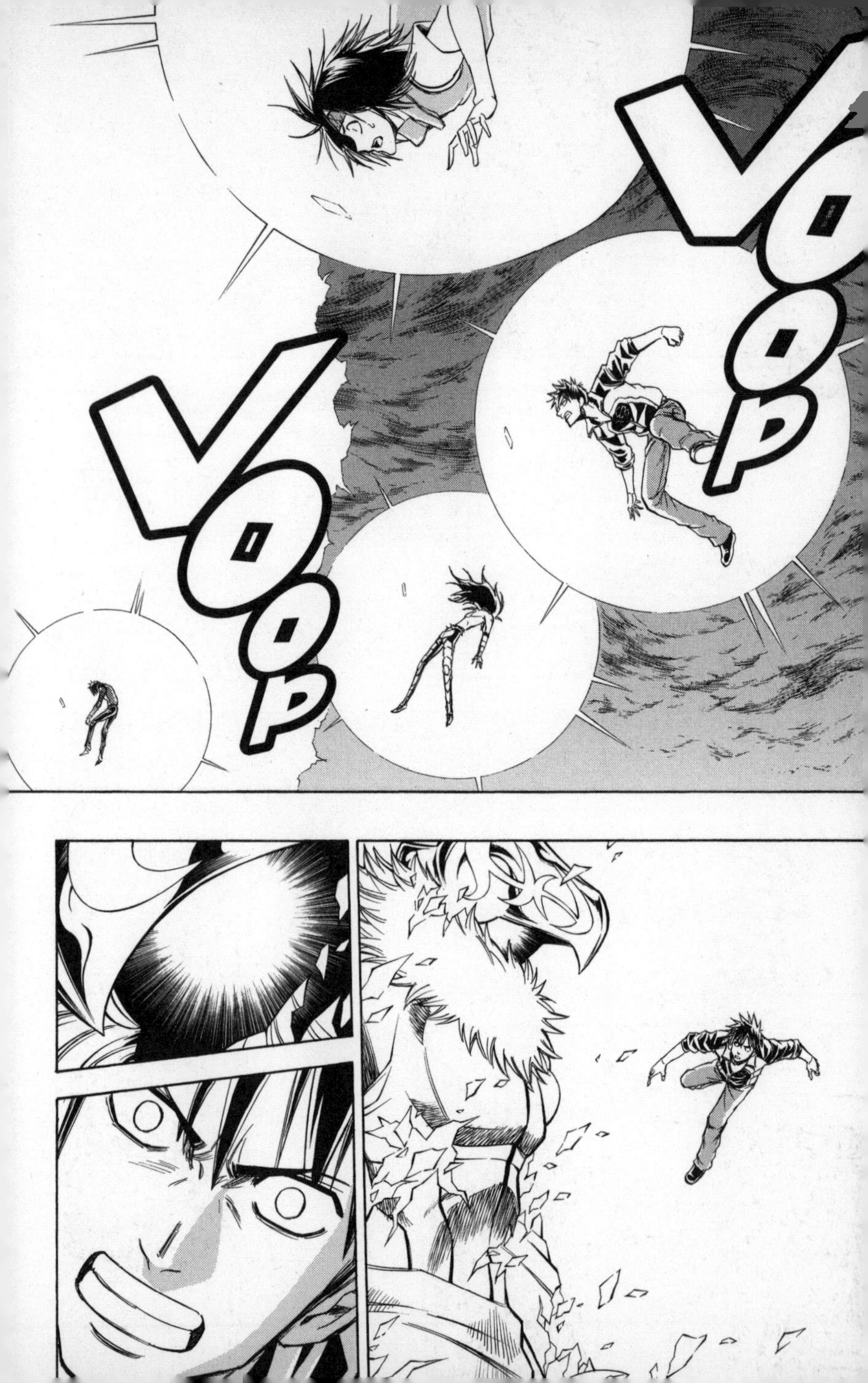
VOOP
VOOP

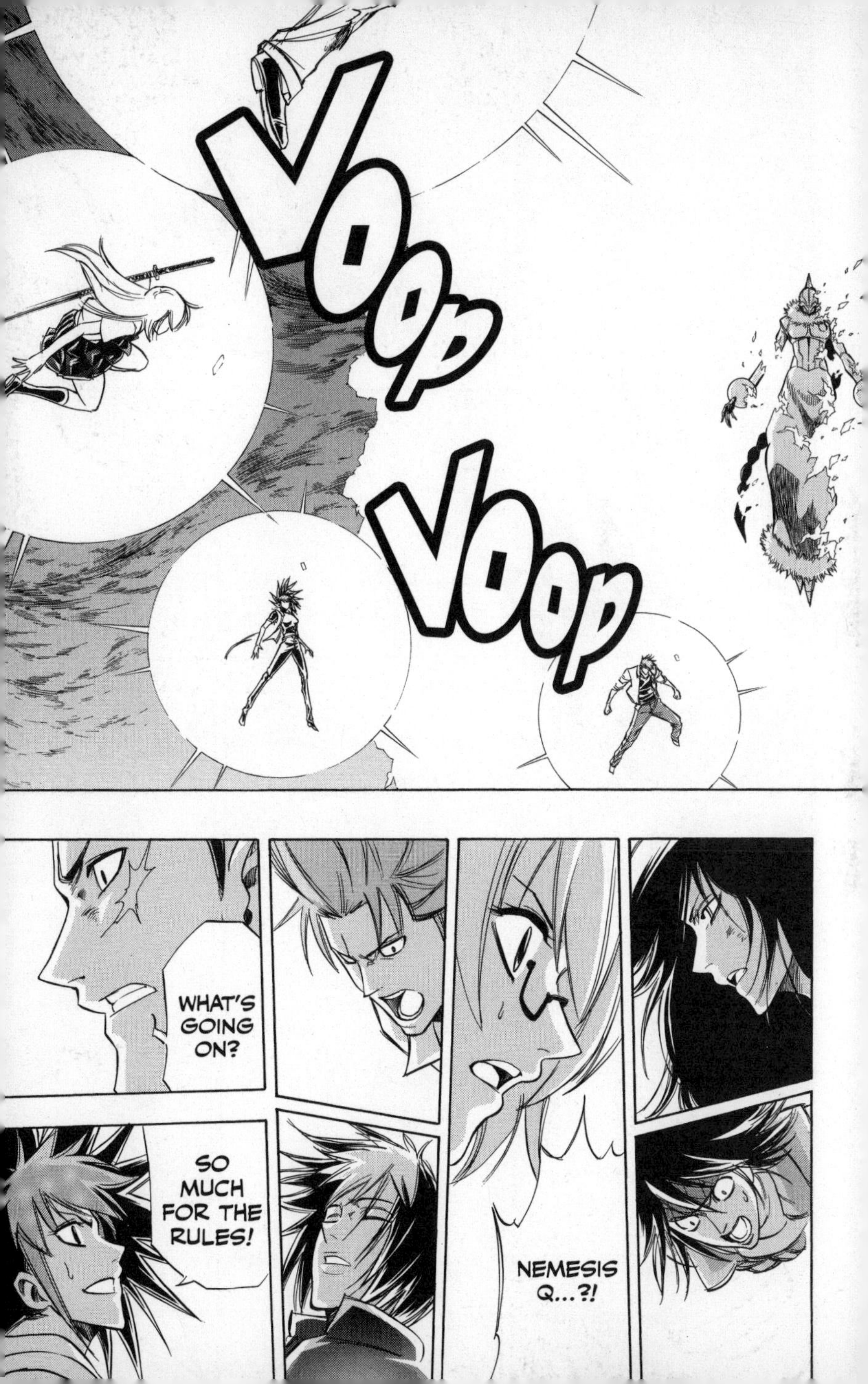
VOOP
VOOP
NEMESIS Q...?!
WHAT'S GOING ON?
SO MUCH FOR THE RULES!

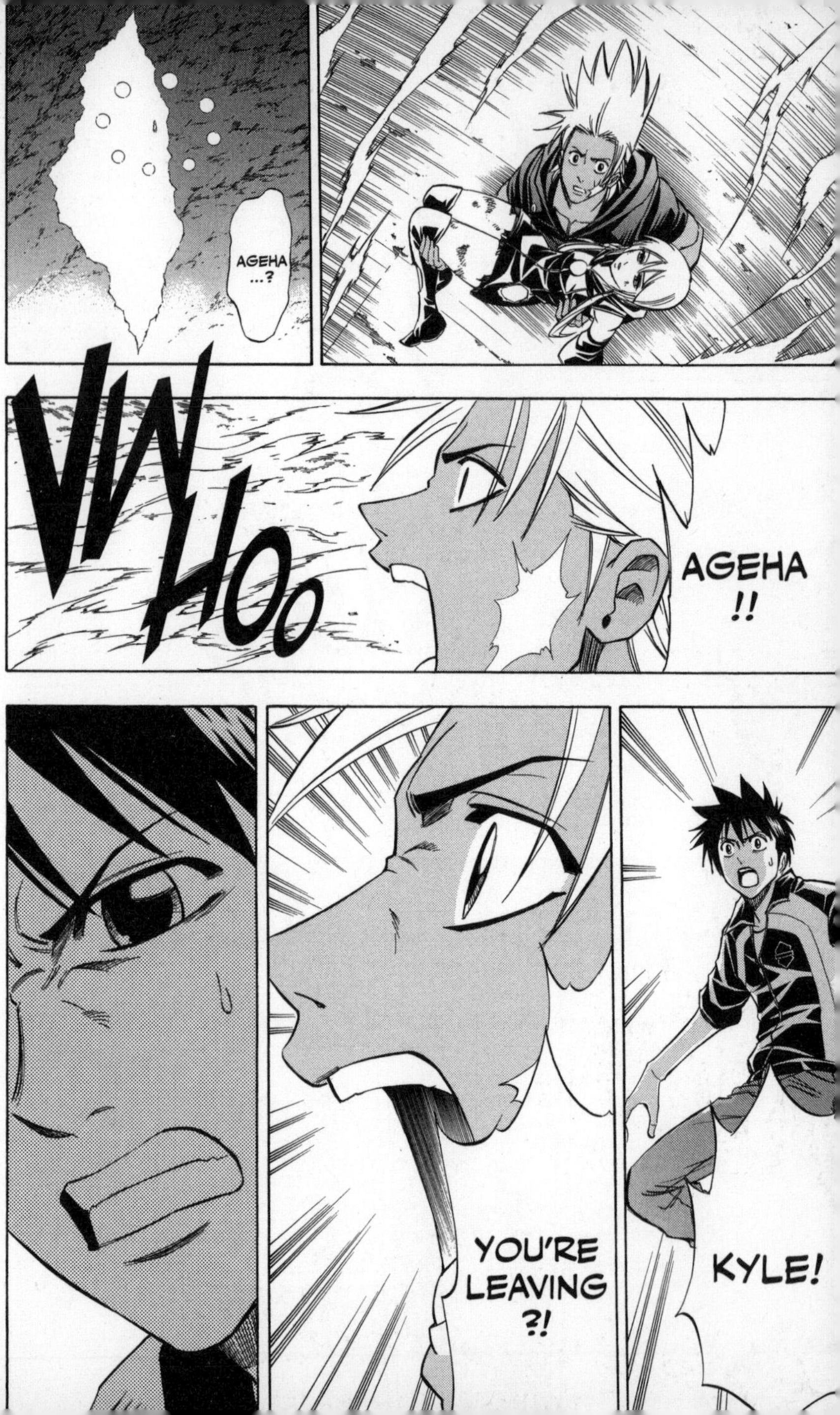
AGEHA ...?
AGEHA !!
VWHOO
KYLE!
YOU'RE LEAVING ?!

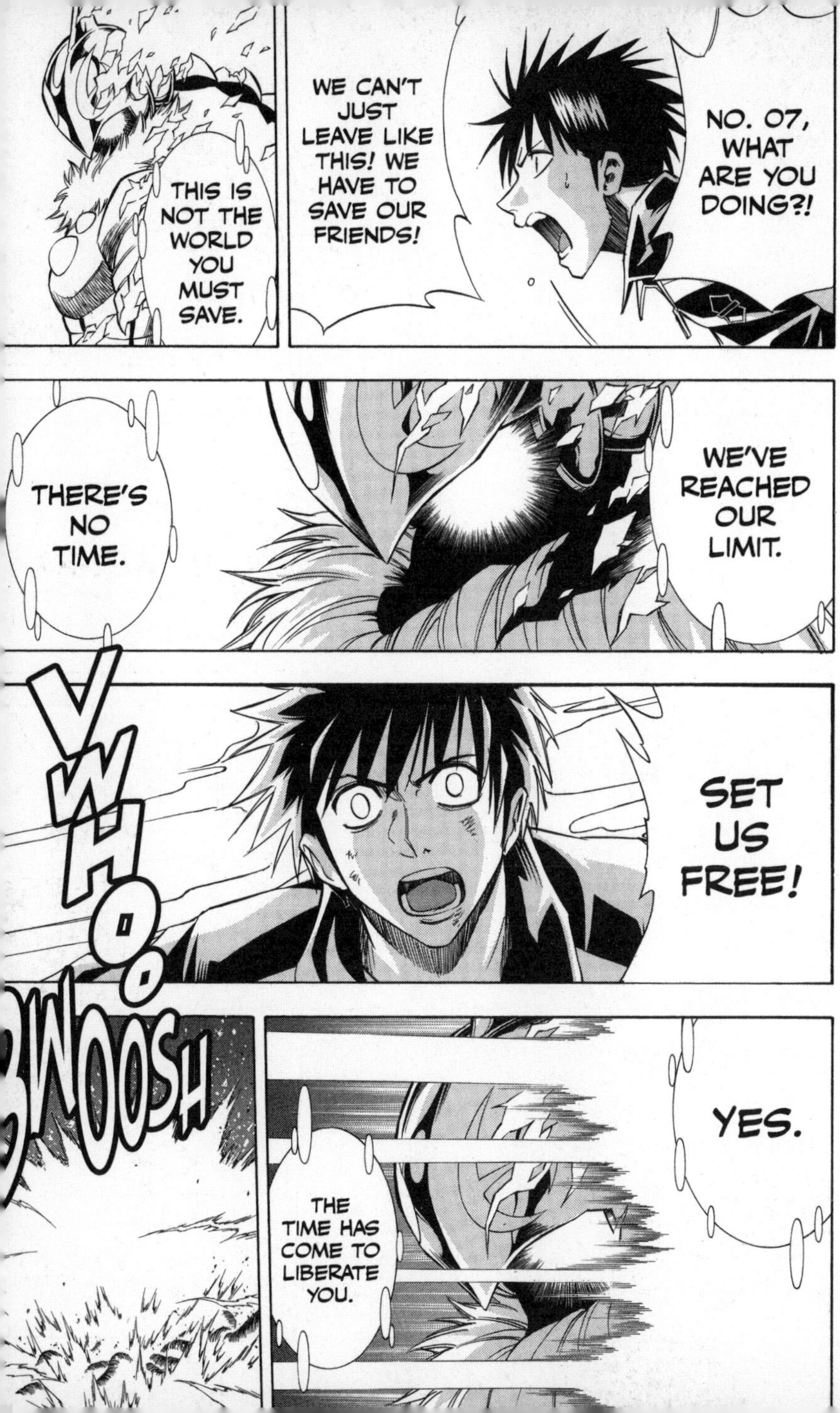
NO. 07, WHAT ARE YOU DOING?!
WE CAN'T JUST LEAVE LIKE THIS! WE HAVE TO SAVE OUR FRIENDS!
THIS IS NOT THE WORLD YOU MUST SAVE.
WE'VE REACHED OUR LIMIT.
THERE'S NO TIME.
SET US FREE!
VWHO..
YES.
THE TIME HAS COME TO LIBERATE YOU.
BWOOSH

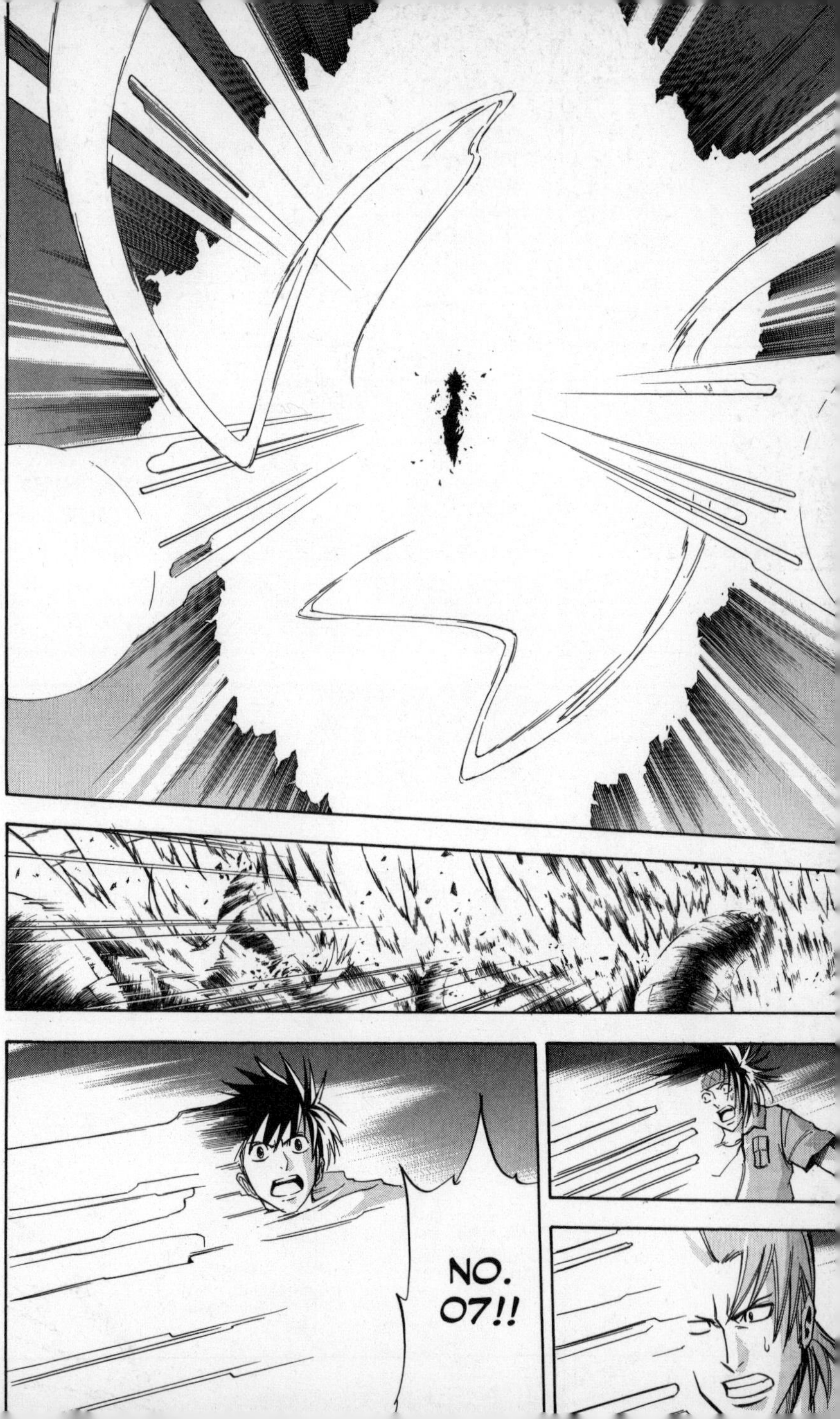
NO. 07!!

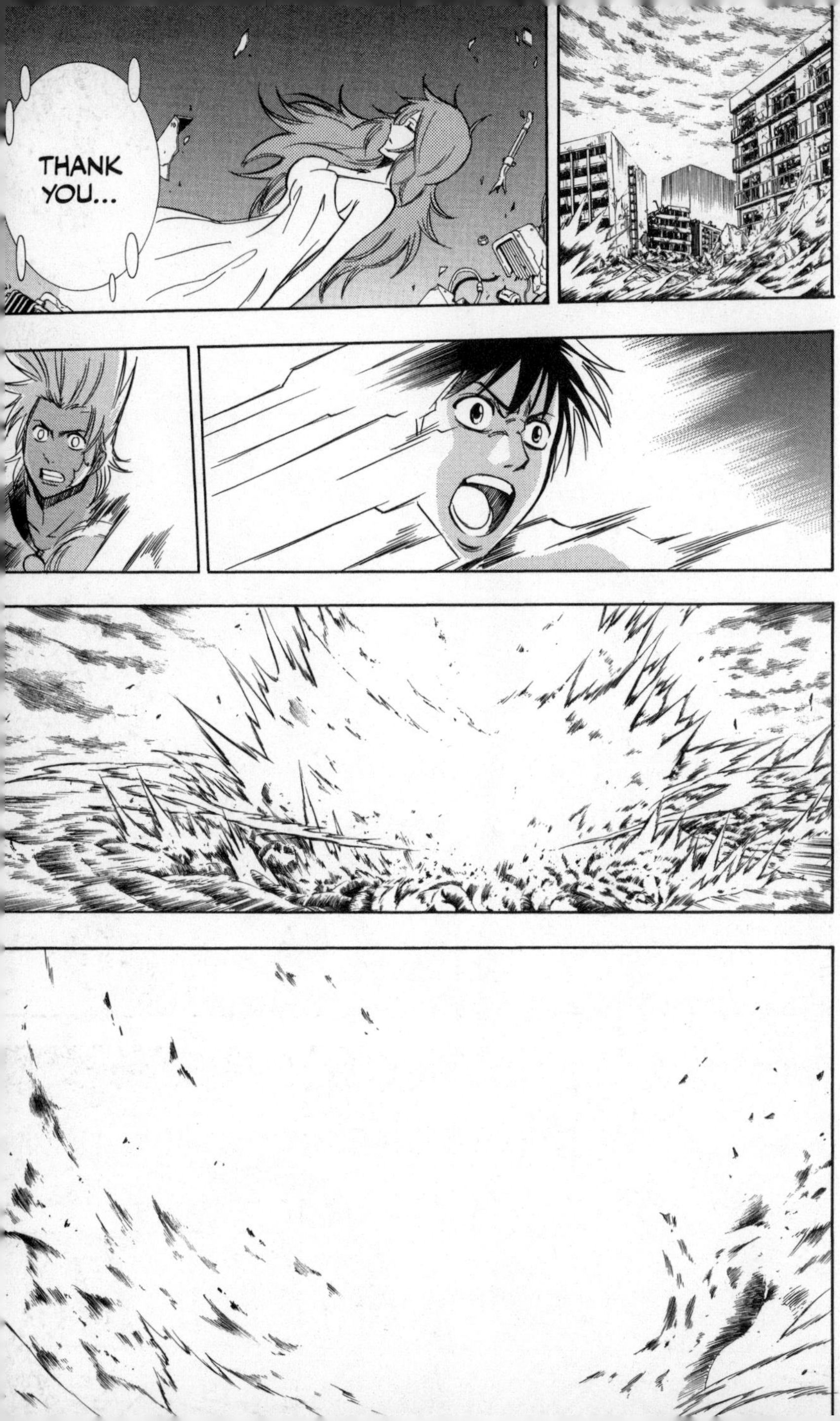
THANK YOU...

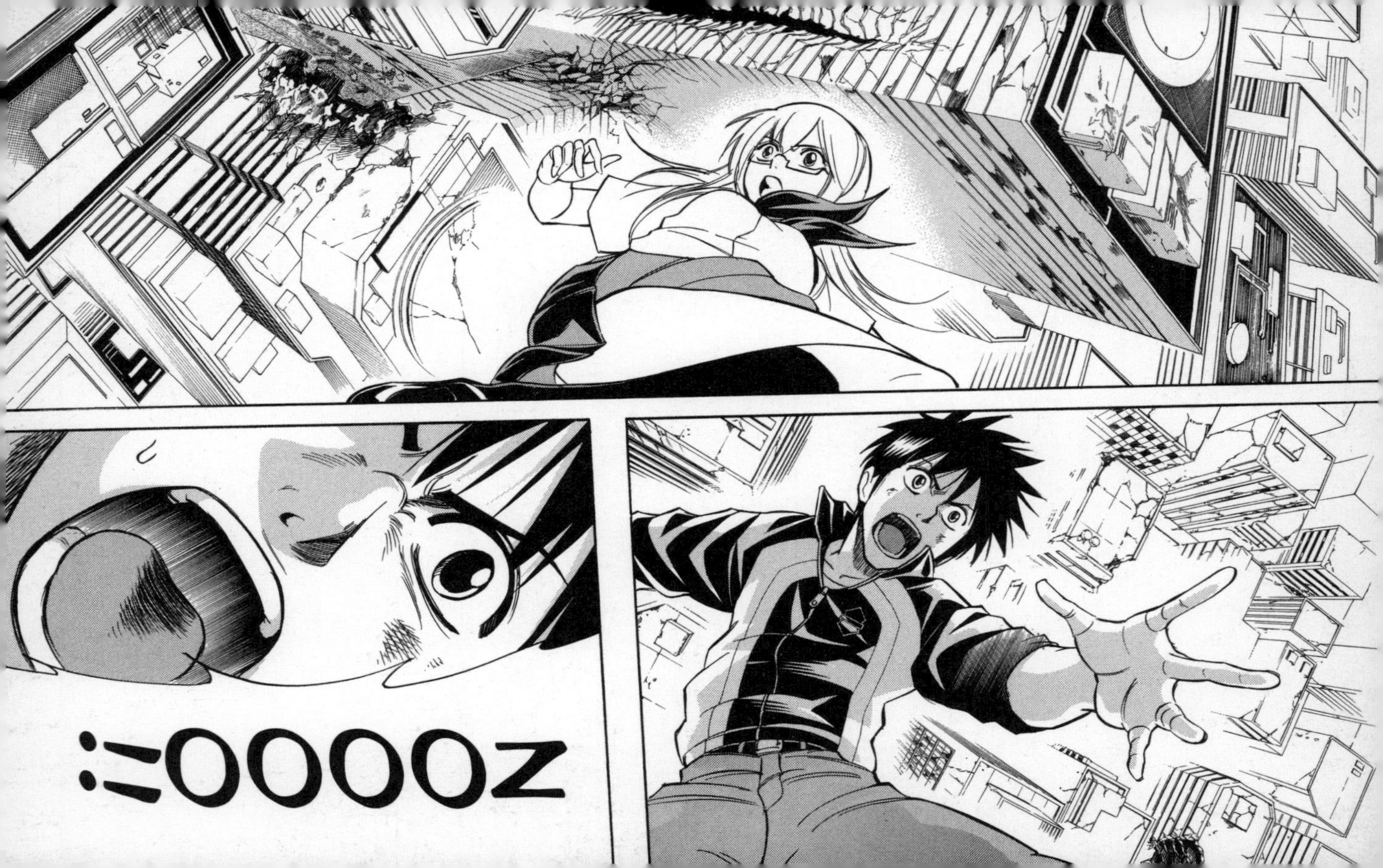
NOOOO!!

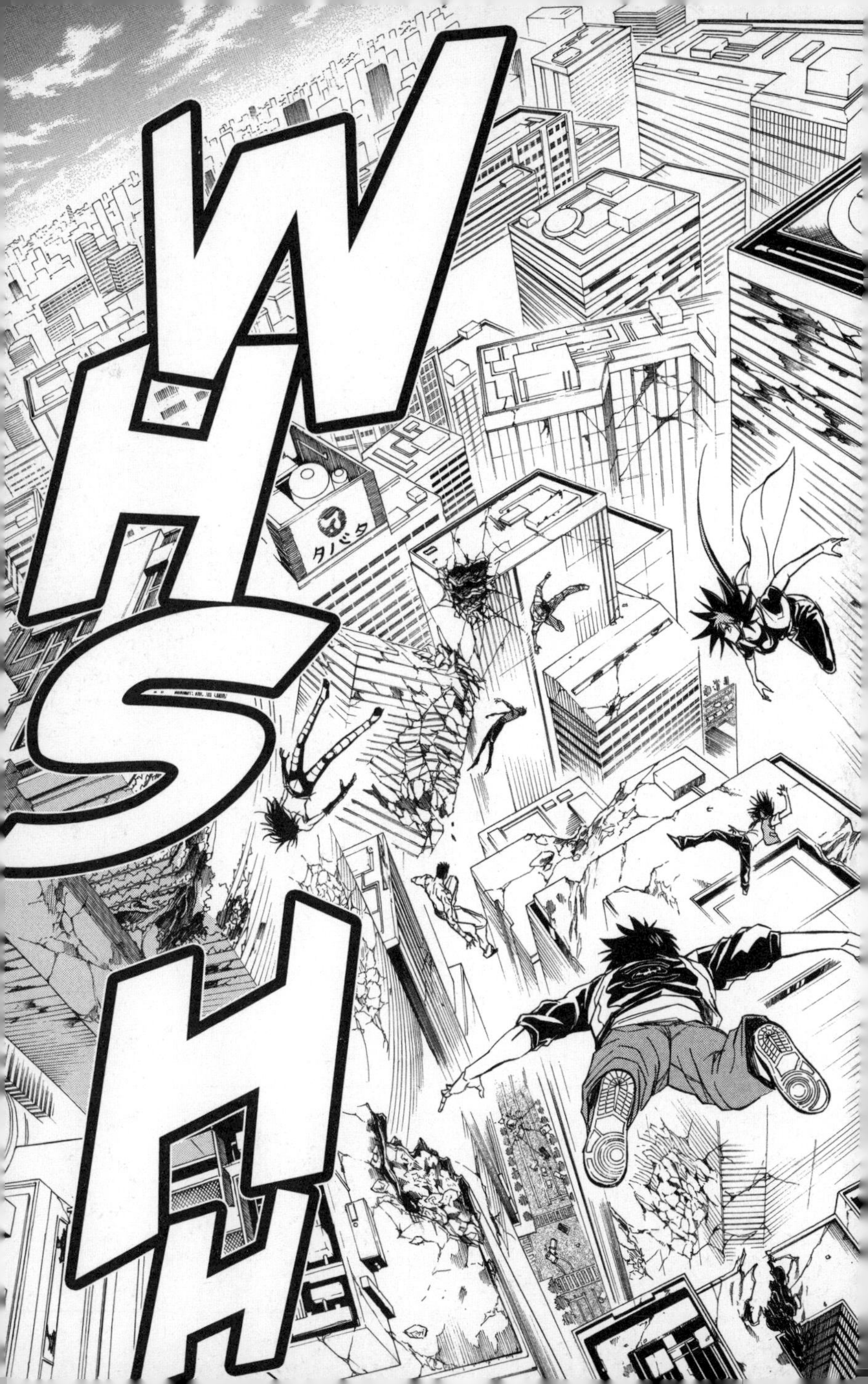
WHSHH

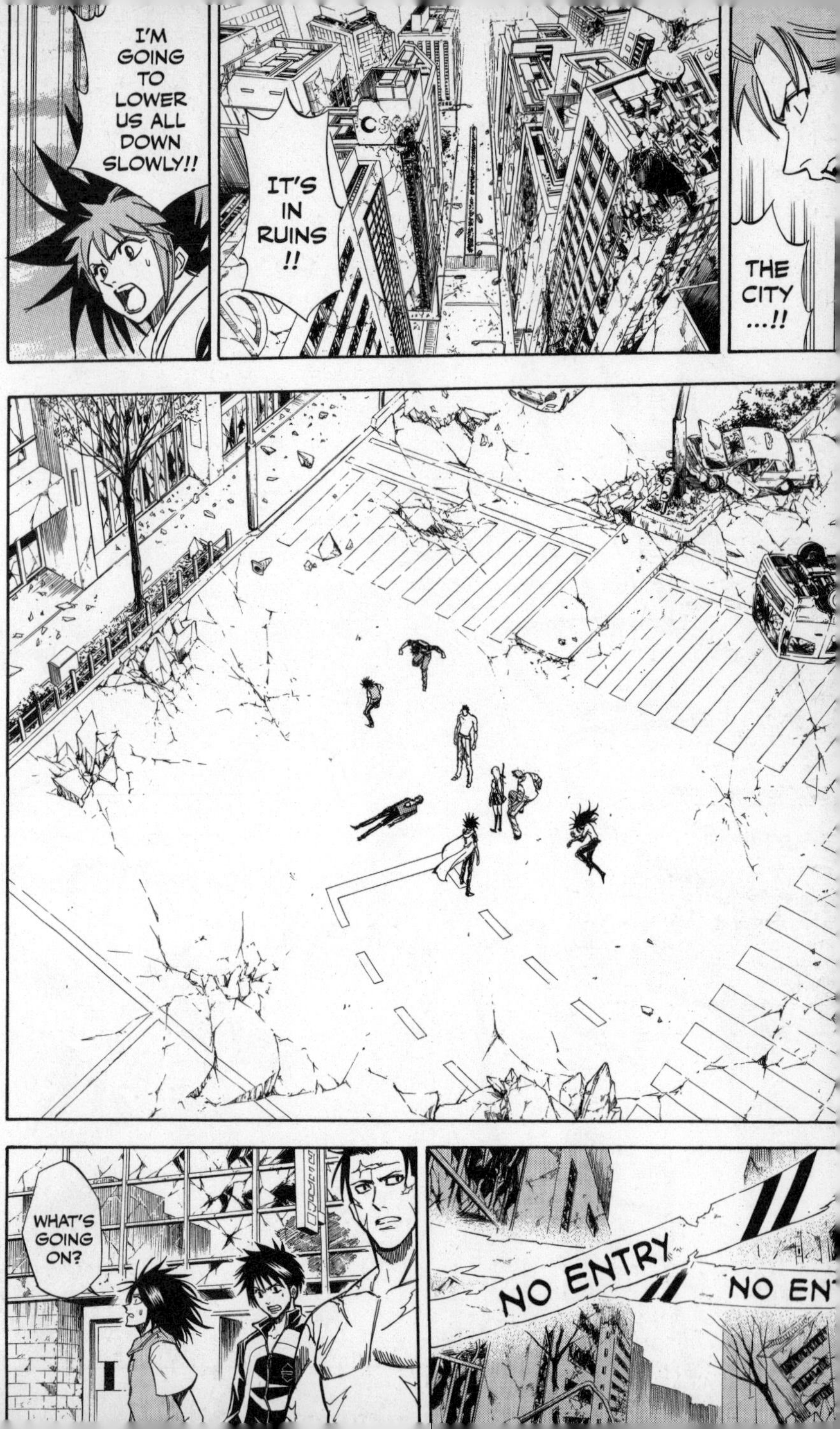
THE CITY ...!!
IT'S IN RUINS!!
I'M GOING TO LOWER US ALL DOWN SLOWLY!!
NO ENTRY
NO EN
WHAT'S GOING ON?

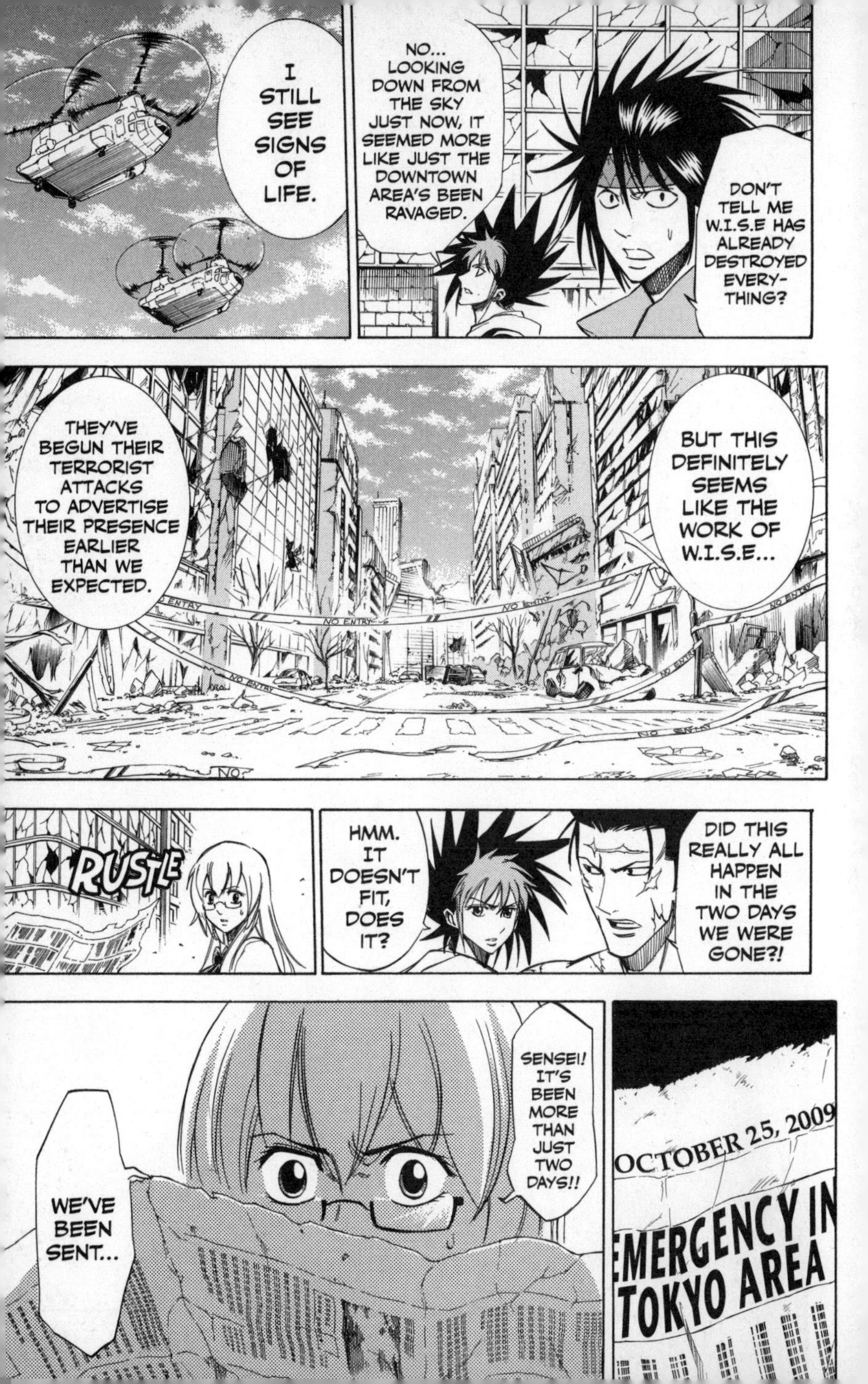
DON'T TELL ME W.I.S.E HAS ALREADY DESTROYED EVERY-THING?
NO... LOOKING DOWN FROM THE SKY JUST NOW, IT SEEMED MORE LIKE JUST THE DOWNTOWN AREA'S BEEN RAVAGED.
I STILL SEE SIGNS OF LIFE.
BUT THIS DEFINITELY SEEMS LIKE THE WORK OF W.I.S.E...
THEY'VE BEGUN THEIR TERRORIST ATTACKS TO ADVERTISE THEIR PRESENCE EARLIER THAN WE EXPECTED.
NO ENTRY
DID THIS REALLY ALL HAPPEN IN THE TWO DAYS WE WERE GONE?!
HMM. IT DOESN'T FIT, DOES IT?
RUSTLE
OCTOBER 25, 2009
EMERGENCY IN TOKYO AREA
SENSEI! IT'S BEEN MORE THAN JUST TWO DAYS!!
WE'VE BEEN SENT...

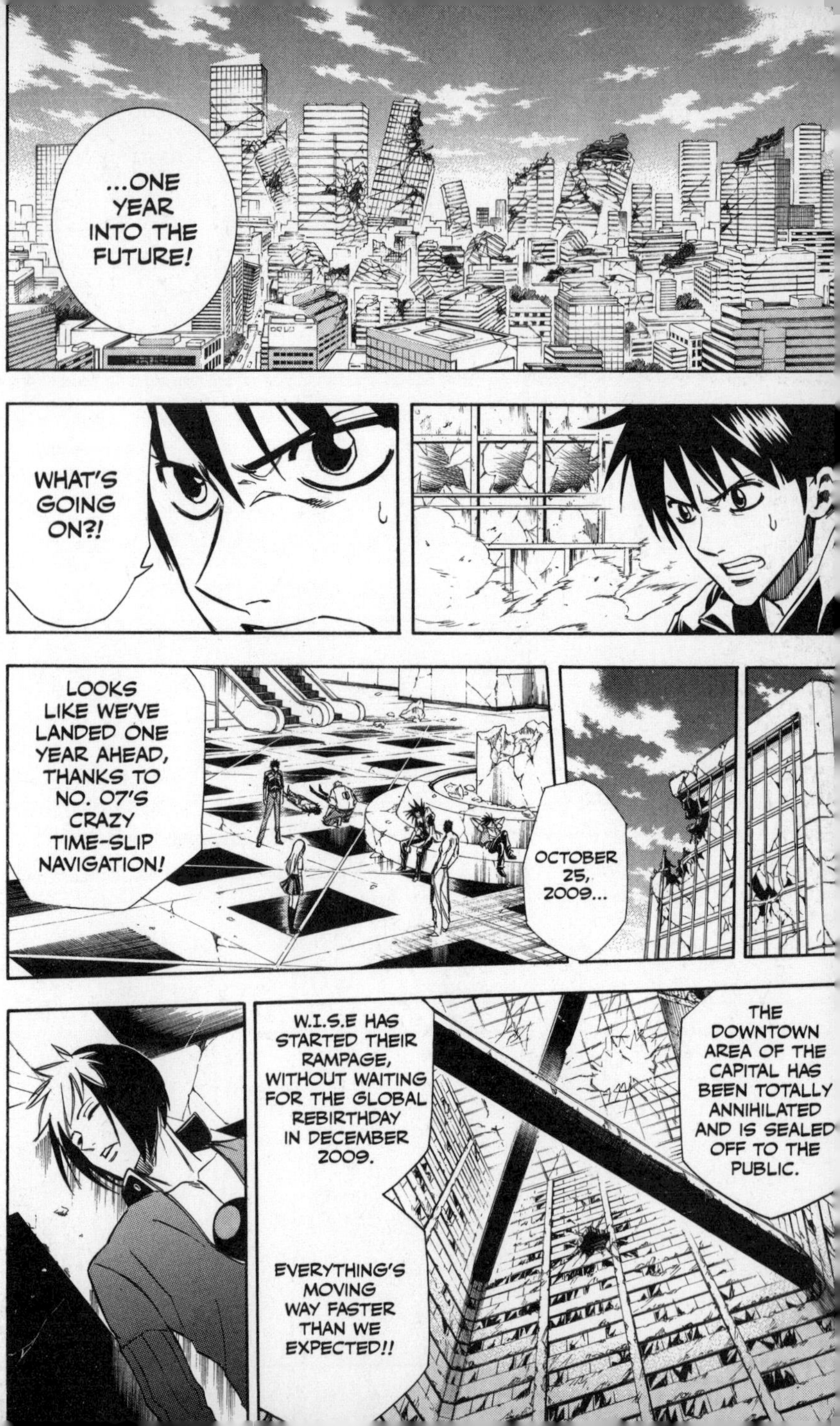
...ONE YEAR INTO THE FUTURE!
WHAT'S GOING ON?!
OCTOBER 25, 2009...
LOOKS LIKE WE'VE LANDED ONE YEAR AHEAD, THANKS TO NO. 07'S CRAZY TIME-SLIP NAVIGATION!
THE DOWNTOWN AREA OF THE CAPITAL HAS BEEN TOTALLY ANNIHILATED AND IS SEALED OFF TO THE PUBLIC.
W.I.S.E HAS STARTED THEIR RAMPAGE, WITHOUT WAITING FOR THE GLOBAL REBIRTHDAY IN DECEMBER 2009.
EVERYTHING'S MOVING WAY FASTER THAN WE EXPECTED!!

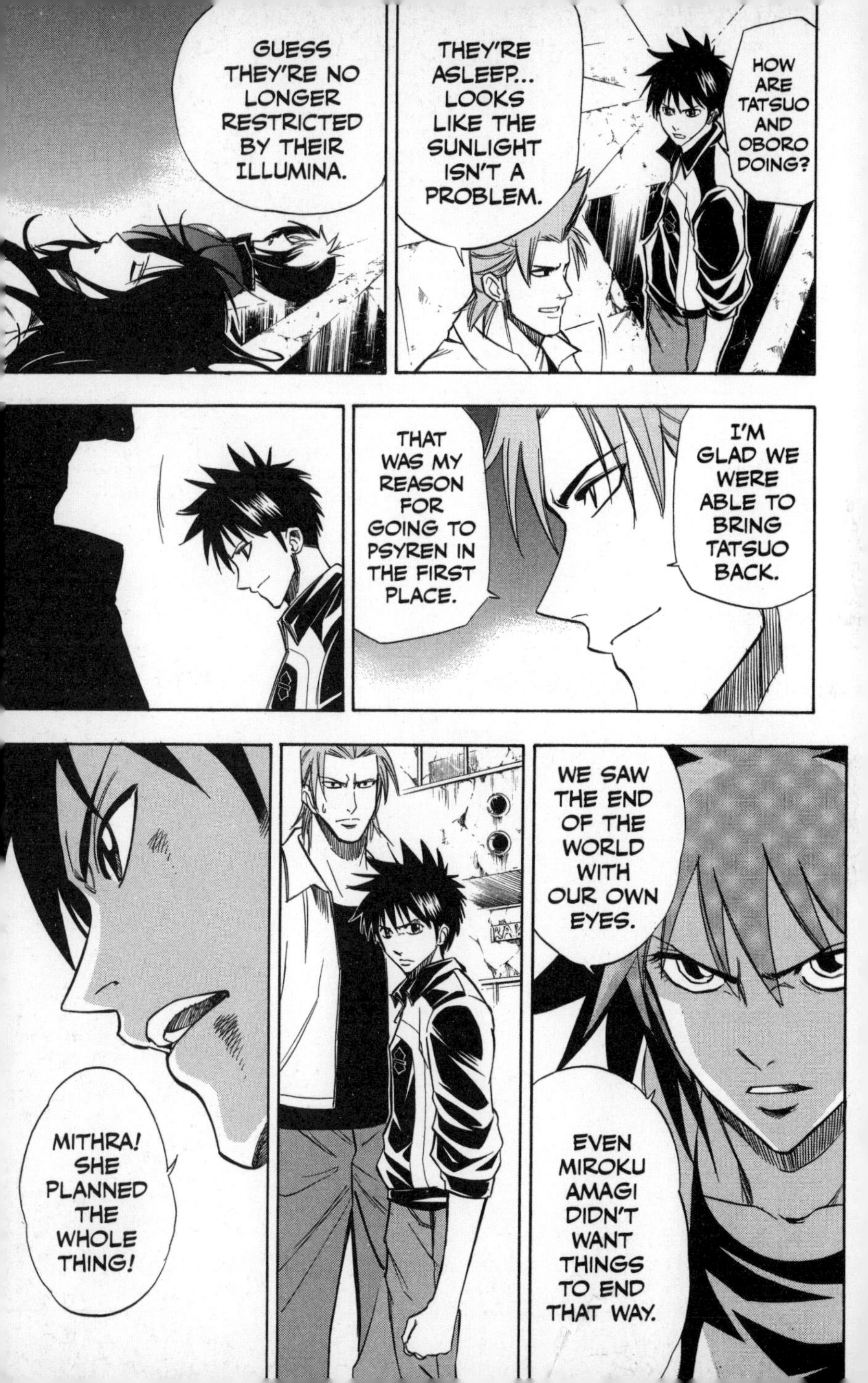
HOW ARE TATSUO AND OBORO DOING?
THEY'RE ASLEEP... LOOKS LIKE THE SUNLIGHT ISN'T A PROBLEM.
GUESS THEY'RE NO LONGER RESTRICTED BY THEIR ILLUMINA.
I'M GLAD WE WERE ABLE TO BRING TATSUO BACK.
THAT WAS MY REASON FOR GOING TO PSYREN IN THE FIRST PLACE.
WE SAW THE END OF THE WORLD WITH OUR OWN EYES.
EVEN MIROKU AMAGI DIDN'T WANT THINGS TO END THAT WAY.
MITHRA! SHE PLANNED THE WHOLE THING!

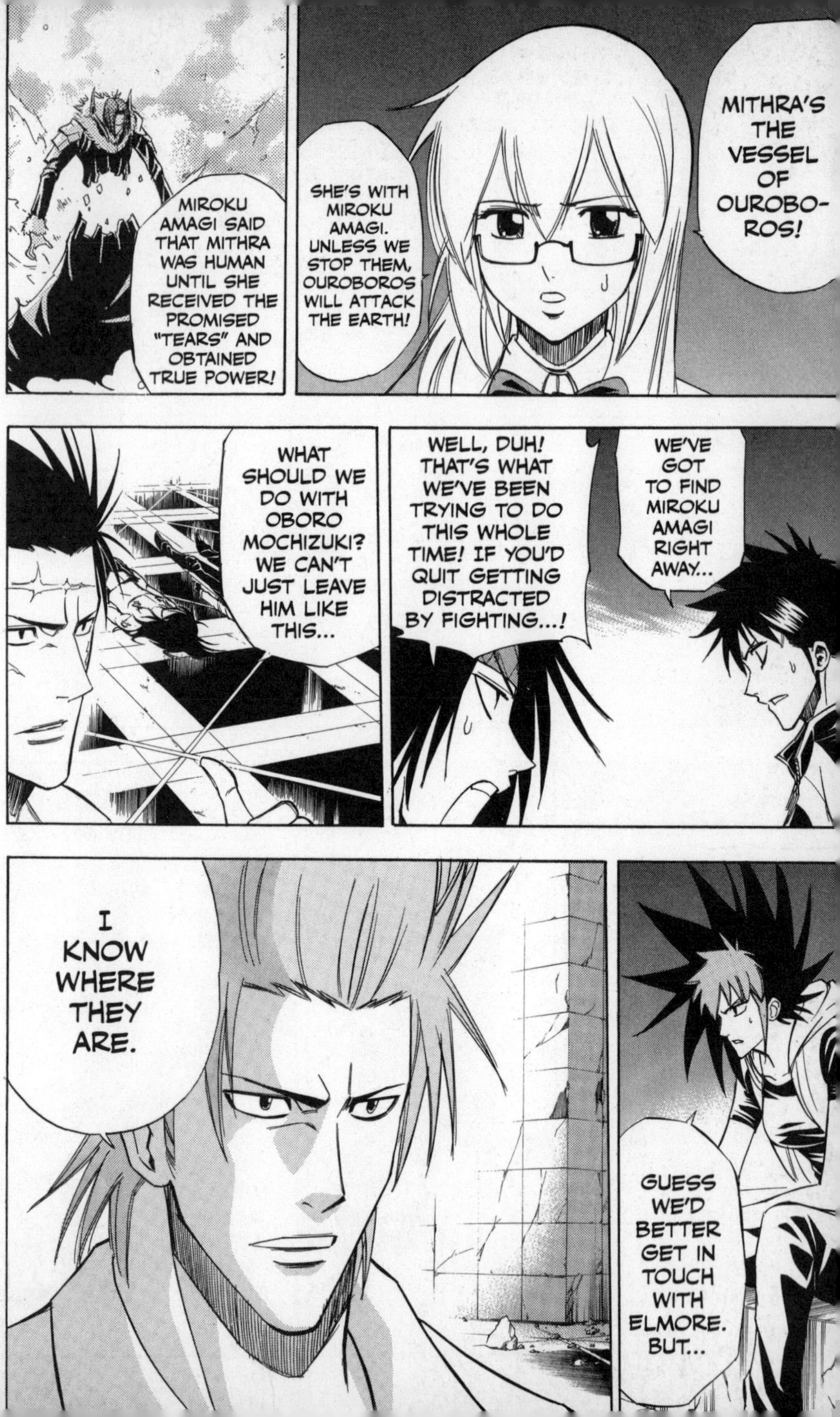
MITHRA'S THE VESSEL OF OUROBO-ROS!
SHE'S WITH MIROKU AMAGI. UNLESS WE STOP THEM, OUROBOROS WILL ATTACK THE EARTH!
MIROKU AMAGI SAID THAT MITHRA WAS HUMAN UNTIL SHE RECEIVED THE PROMISED "TEARS" AND OBTAINED TRUE POWER!
WE'VE GOT TO FIND MIROKU AMAGI RIGHT AWAY...
WELL, DUH! THAT'S WHAT WE'VE BEEN TRYING TO DO THIS WHOLE TIME! IF YOU'D QUIT GETTING DISTRACTED BY FIGHTING...!
WHAT SHOULD WE DO WITH OBORO MOCHIZUKI? WE CAN'T JUST LEAVE HIM LIKE THIS...
GUESS WE'D BETTER GET IN TOUCH WITH ELMORE. BUT...
I KNOW WHERE THEY ARE.

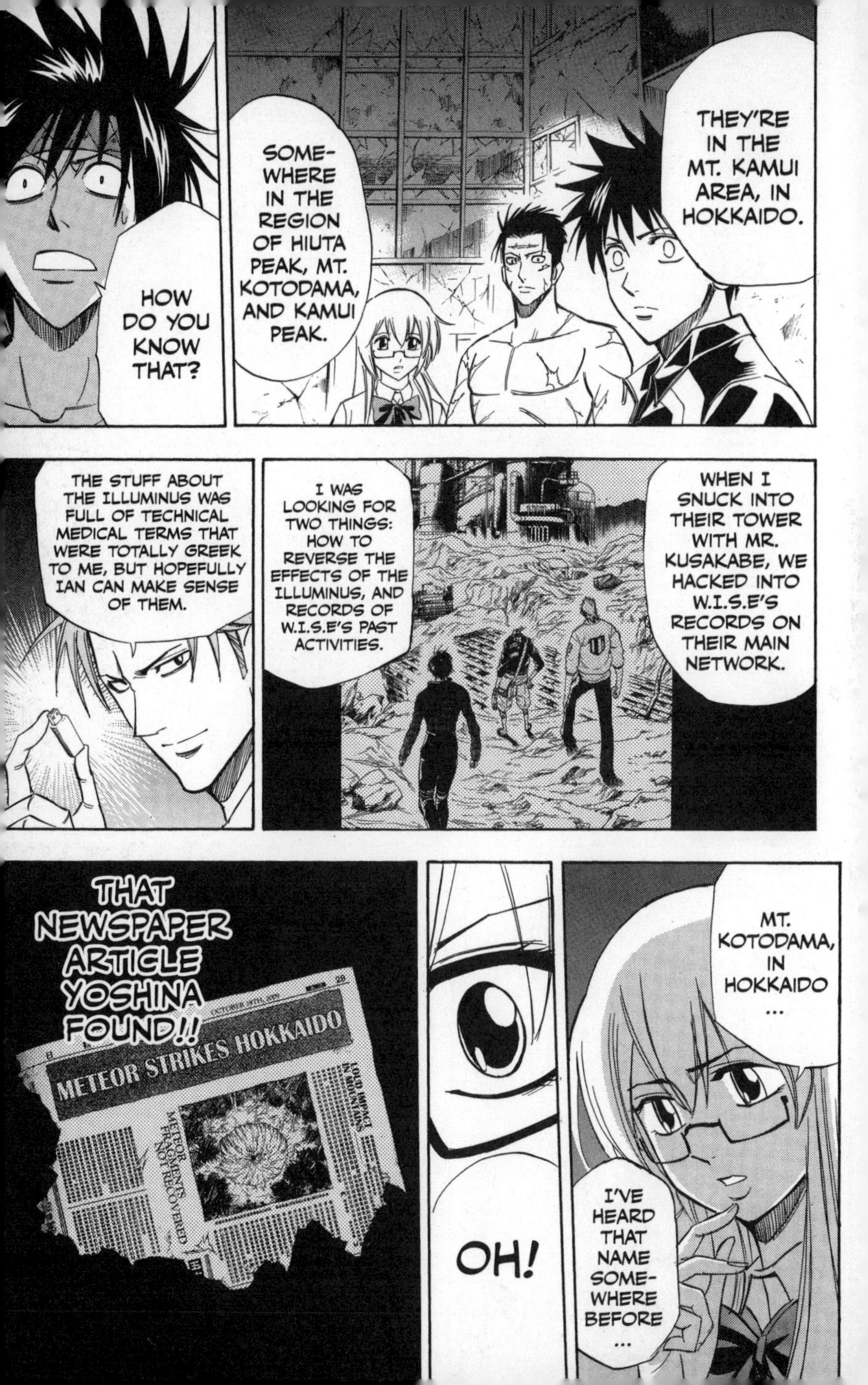
THEY'RE IN THE MT. KAMUI AREA, IN HOKKAIDO.
SOME-WHERE IN THE REGION OF HIUTA PEAK, MT. KOTODAMA, AND KAMUI PEAK.
HOW DO YOU KNOW THAT?
WHEN I SNUCK INTO THEIR TOWER WITH MR. KUSAKABE, WE HACKED INTO W.I.S.E'S RECORDS ON THEIR MAIN NETWORK.
I WAS LOOKING FOR TWO THINGS: HOW TO REVERSE THE EFFECTS OF THE ILLUMINUS, AND RECORDS OF W.I.S.E'S PAST ACTIVITIES.
THE STUFF ABOUT THE ILLUMINUS WAS FULL OF TECHNICAL MEDICAL TERMS THAT WERE TOTALLY GREEK TO ME, BUT HOPEFULLY IAN CAN MAKE SENSE OF THEM.
MT. KOTODAMA, IN HOKKAIDO ...
I'VE HEARD THAT NAME SOME-WHERE BEFORE ...
OH!
THAT NEWSPAPER ARTICLE YOSHINA FOUND!!
METEOR STRIKES HOKKAIDO
LOUD IMPACT IN MOUNTAINS
METEOR FRAGMENTS NOT RECOVERED

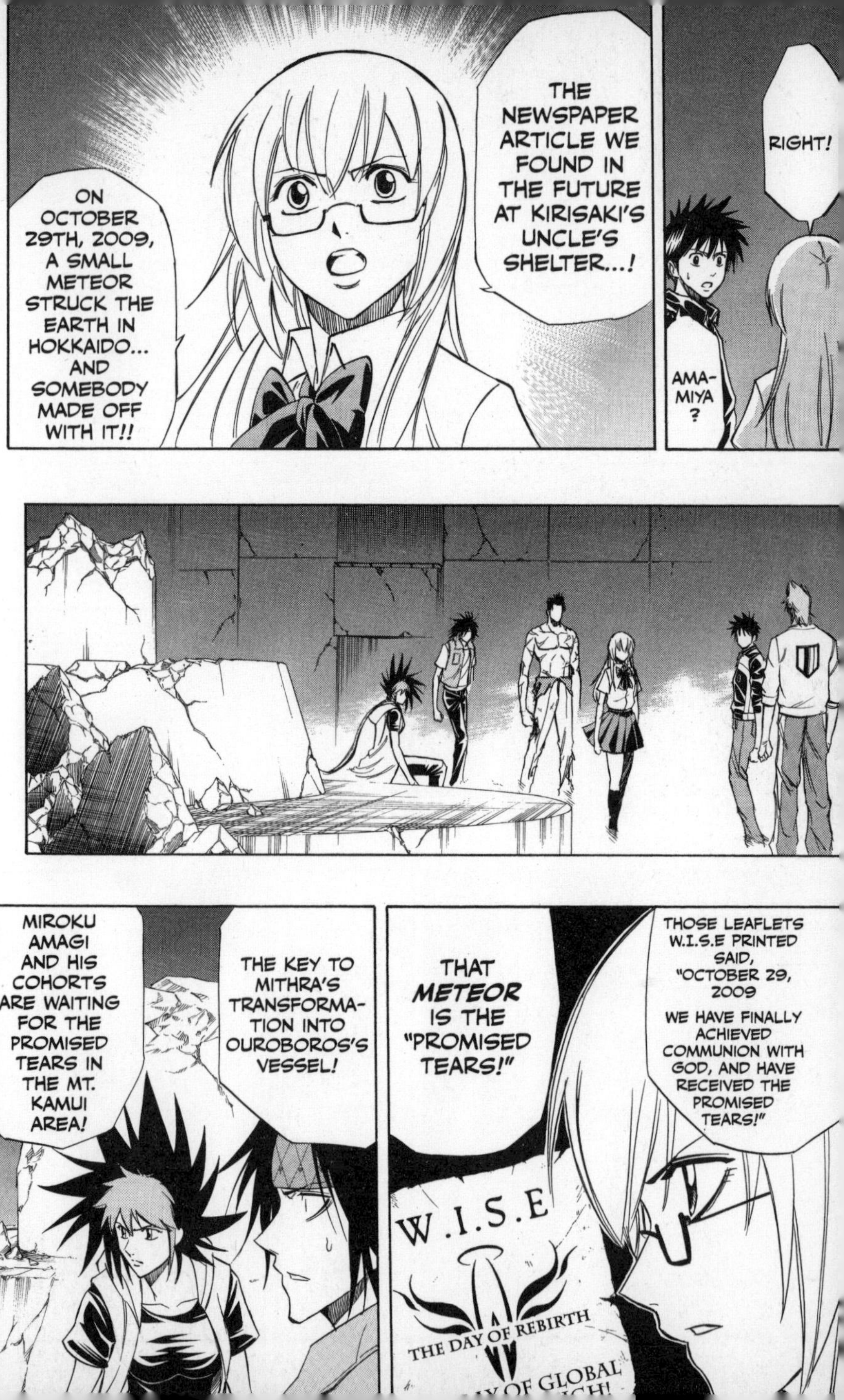
RIGHT!
AMA-MIYA?
THE NEWSPAPER ARTICLE WE FOUND IN THE FUTURE AT KIRISAKI'S UNCLE'S SHELTER...!
ON OCTOBER 29TH, 2009, A SMALL METEOR STRUCK THE EARTH IN HOKKAIDO... AND SOMEBODY MADE OFF WITH IT!!
THOSE LEAFLETS W.I.S.E PRINTED SAID, "OCTOBER 29, 2009
WE HAVE FINALLY ACHIEVED COMMUNION WITH GOD, AND HAVE RECEIVED THE PROMISED TEARS!"
THAT *METEOR* IS THE "PROMISED TEARS!"
W.I.S.E
THE DAY OF REBIRTH
THE KEY TO MITHRA'S TRANSFORMATION INTO OUROBOROS'S VESSEL!
MIROKU AMAGI AND HIS COHORTS ARE WAITING FOR THE PROMISED TEARS IN THE MT. KAMUI AREA!

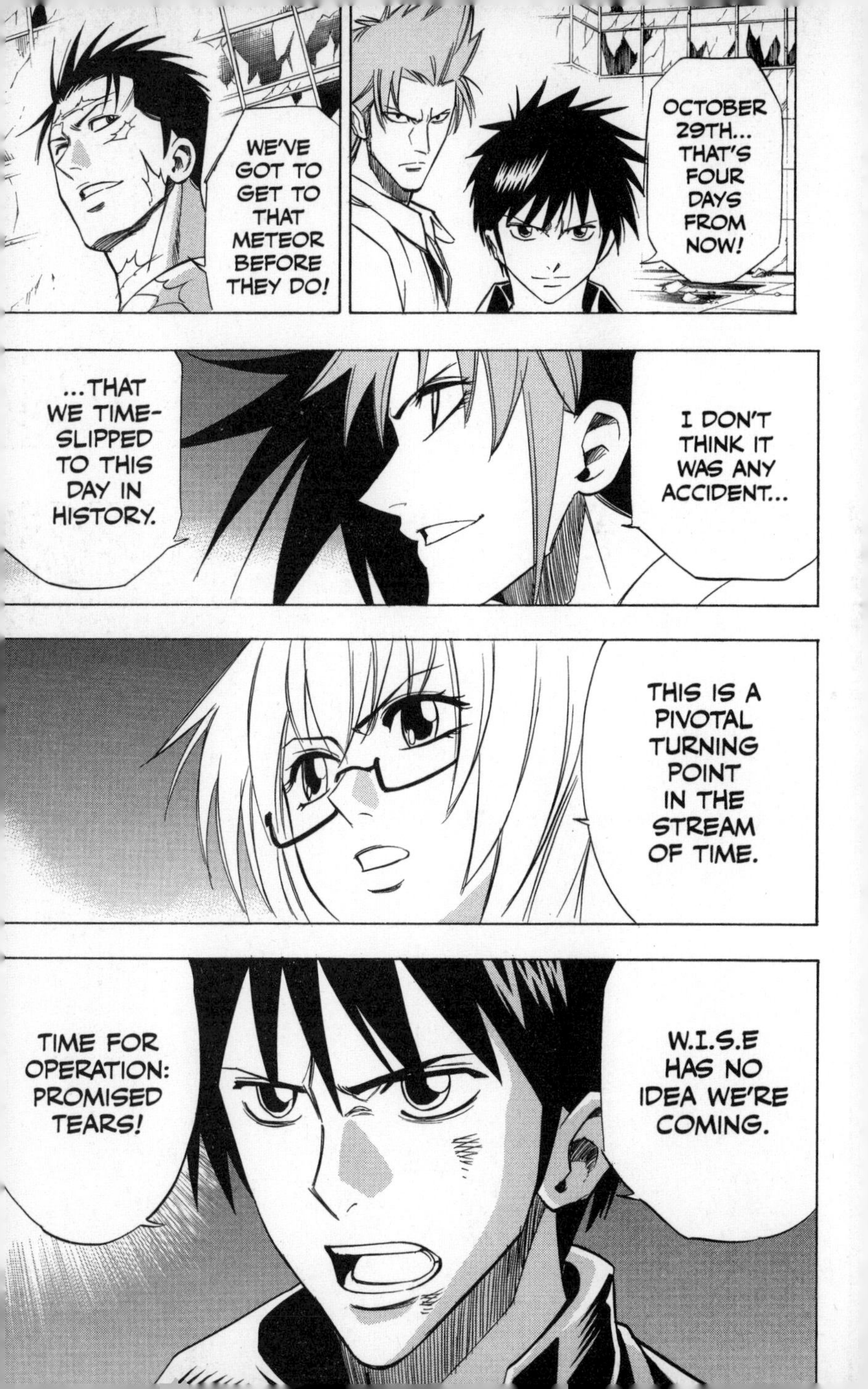
OCTOBER 29TH... THAT'S FOUR DAYS FROM NOW!
WE'VE GOT TO GET TO THAT METEOR BEFORE THEY DO!
I DON'T THINK IT WAS ANY ACCIDENT...
...THAT WE TIME-SLIPPED TO THIS DAY IN HISTORY.
THIS IS A PIVOTAL TURNING POINT IN THE STREAM OF TIME.
W.I.S.E HAS NO IDEA WE'RE COMING.
TIME FOR OPERATION: PROMISED TEARS!

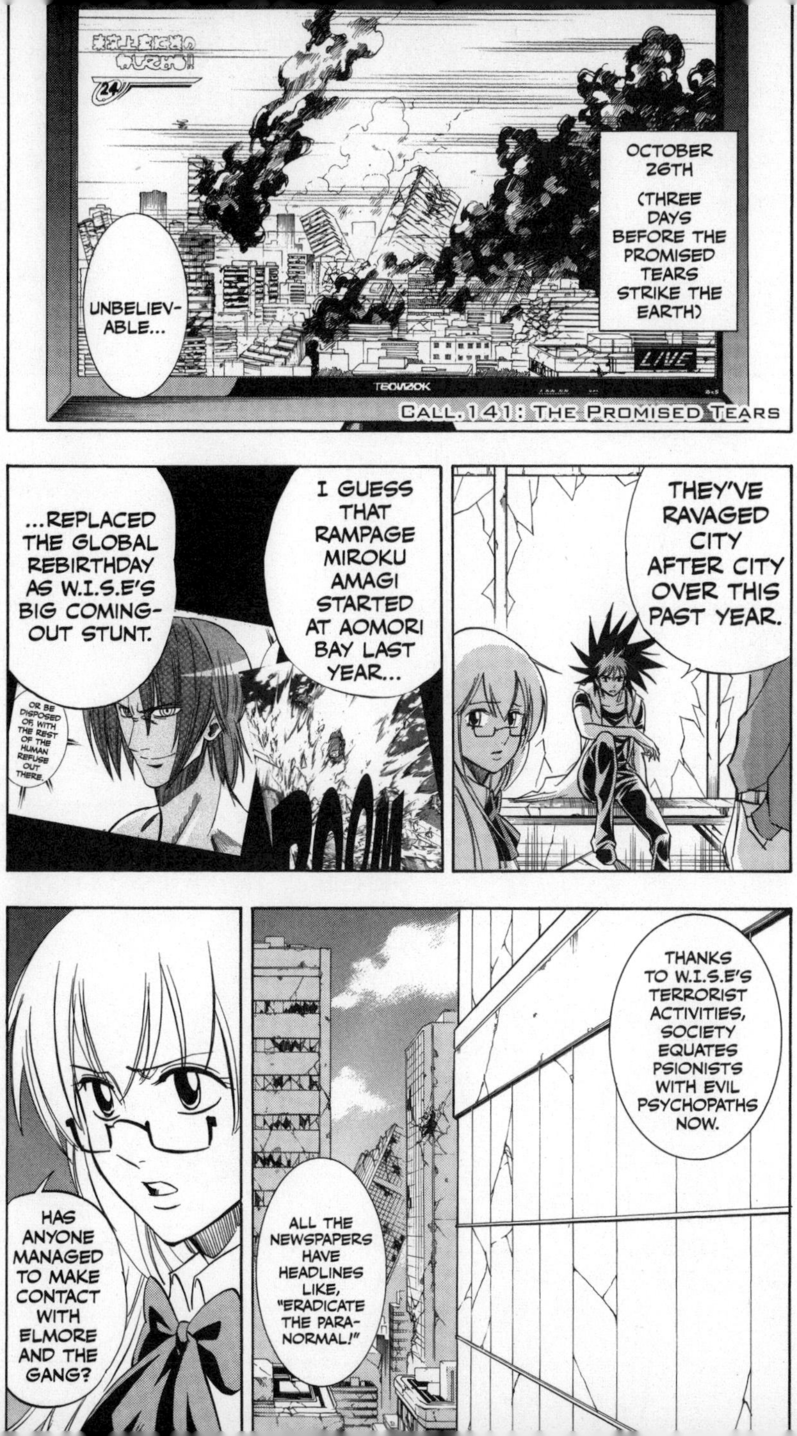
OCTOBER 26TH (THREE DAYS BEFORE THE PROMISED TEARS STRIKE THE EARTH)
LIVE
UNBELIEVABLE...
CALL. 141: THE PROMISED TEARS
THEY'VE RAVAGED CITY AFTER CITY OVER THIS PAST YEAR.
I GUESS THAT RAMPAGE MIROKU AMAGI STARTED AT AOMORI BAY LAST YEAR...
...REPLACED THE GLOBAL REBIRTHDAY AS W.I.S.E'S BIG COMING-OUT STUNT.
OR BE DISPOSED OF WITH THE REST OF THE HUMAN REFUSE OUT THERE.
THANKS TO W.I.S.E'S TERRORIST ACTIVITIES, SOCIETY EQUATES PSIONISTS WITH EVIL PSYCHOPATHS NOW.
ALL THE NEWSPAPERS HAVE HEADLINES LIKE, "ERADICATE THE PARA-NORMAL!"
HAS ANYONE MANAGED TO MAKE CONTACT WITH ELMORE AND THE GANG?

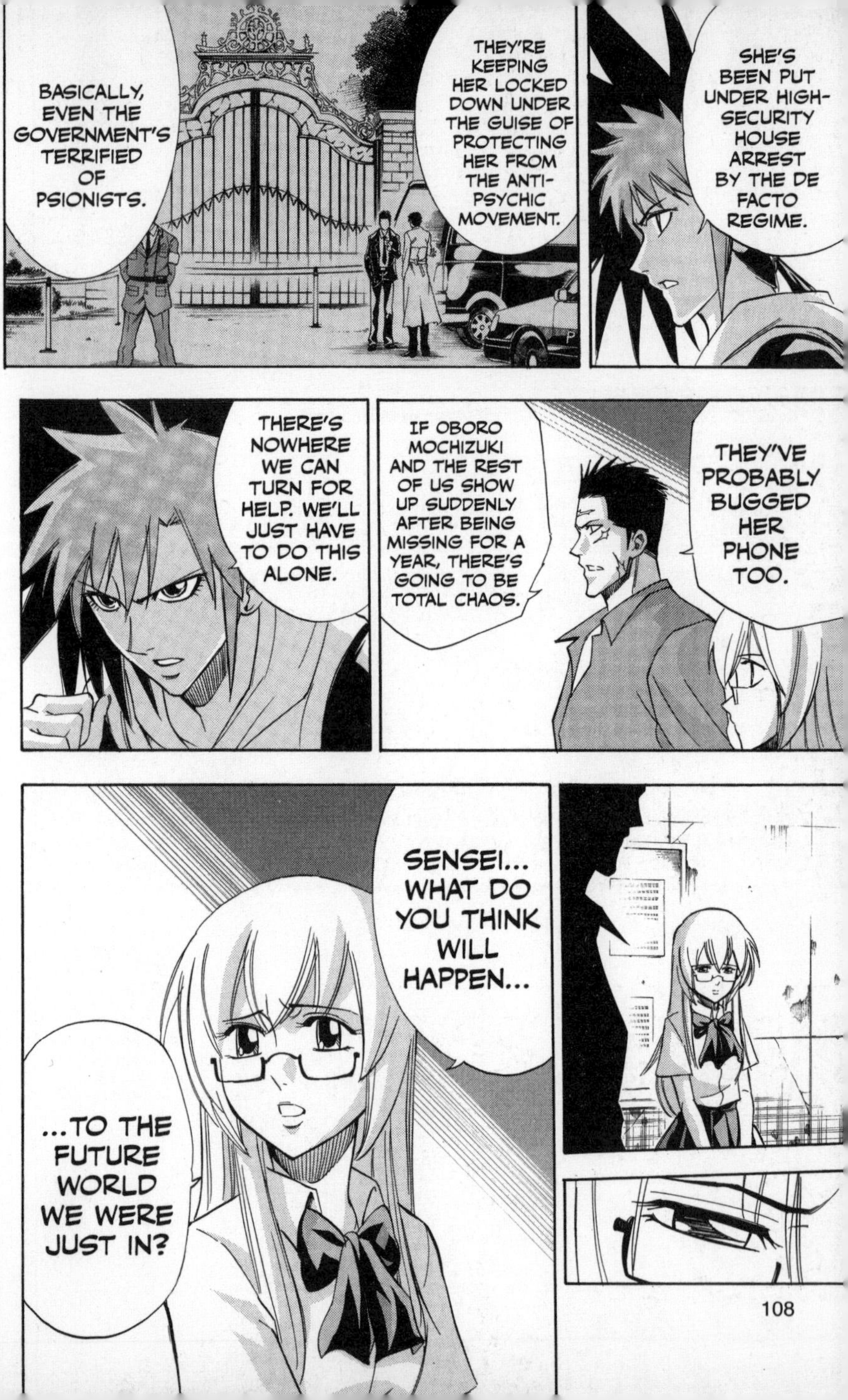
SHE'S BEEN PUT UNDER HIGH-SECURITY HOUSE ARREST BY THE DE FACTO REGIME.
THEY'RE KEEPING HER LOCKED DOWN UNDER THE GUISE OF PROTECTING HER FROM THE ANTI-PSYCHIC MOVEMENT.
BASICALLY, EVEN THE GOVERNMENT'S TERRIFIED OF PSIONISTS.
THEY'VE PROBABLY BUGGED HER PHONE TOO.
IF OBORO MOCHIZUKI AND THE REST OF US SHOW UP SUDDENLY AFTER BEING MISSING FOR A YEAR, THERE'S GOING TO BE TOTAL CHAOS.
THERE'S NOWHERE WE CAN TURN FOR HELP. WE'LL JUST HAVE TO DO THIS ALONE.
SENSEI... WHAT DO YOU THINK WILL HAPPEN...
...TO THE FUTURE WORLD WE WERE JUST IN?

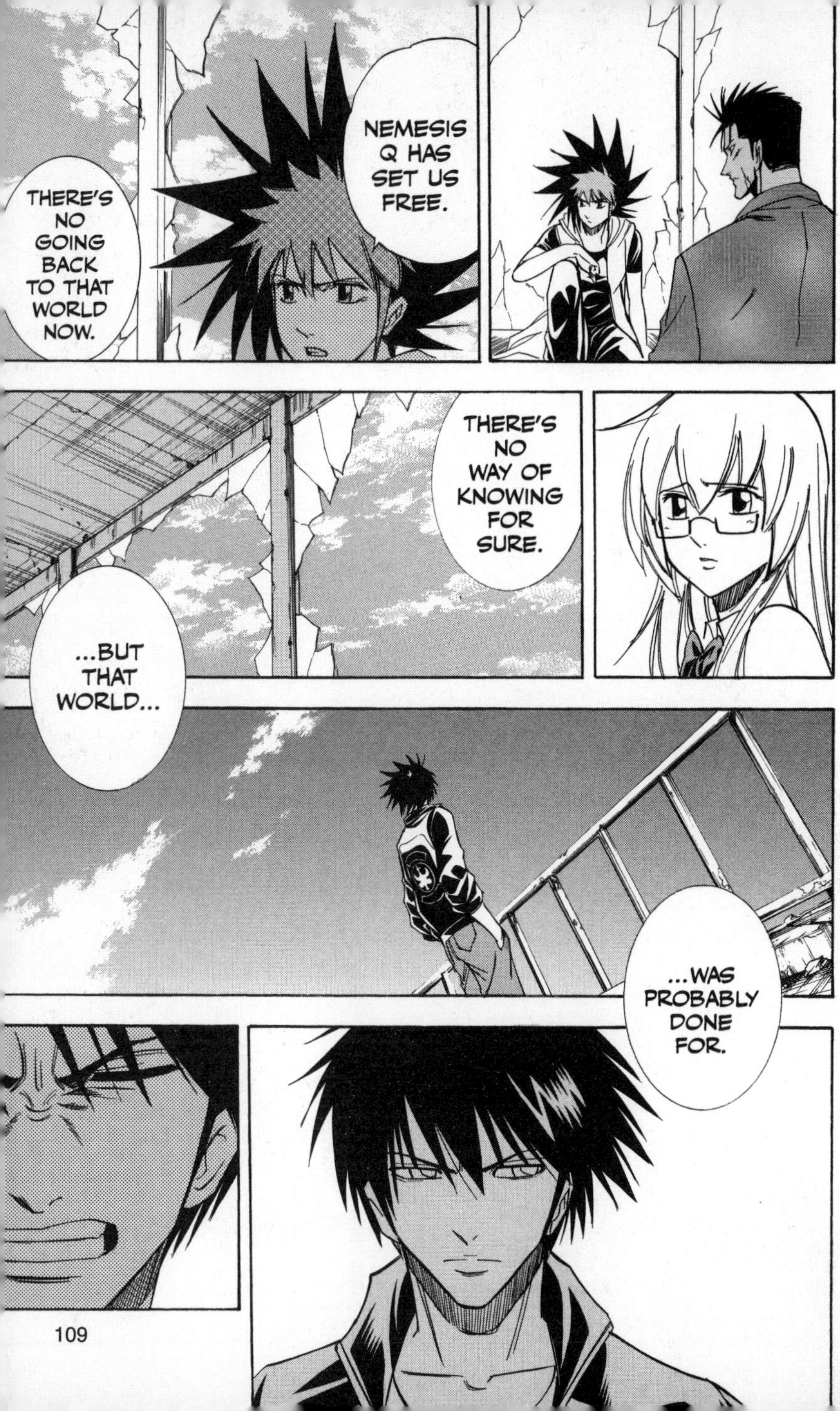
NEMESIS Q HAS SET US FREE.
THERE'S NO GOING BACK TO THAT WORLD NOW.
THERE'S NO WAY OF KNOWING FOR SURE.
...BUT THAT WORLD...
...WAS PROBABLY DONE FOR.

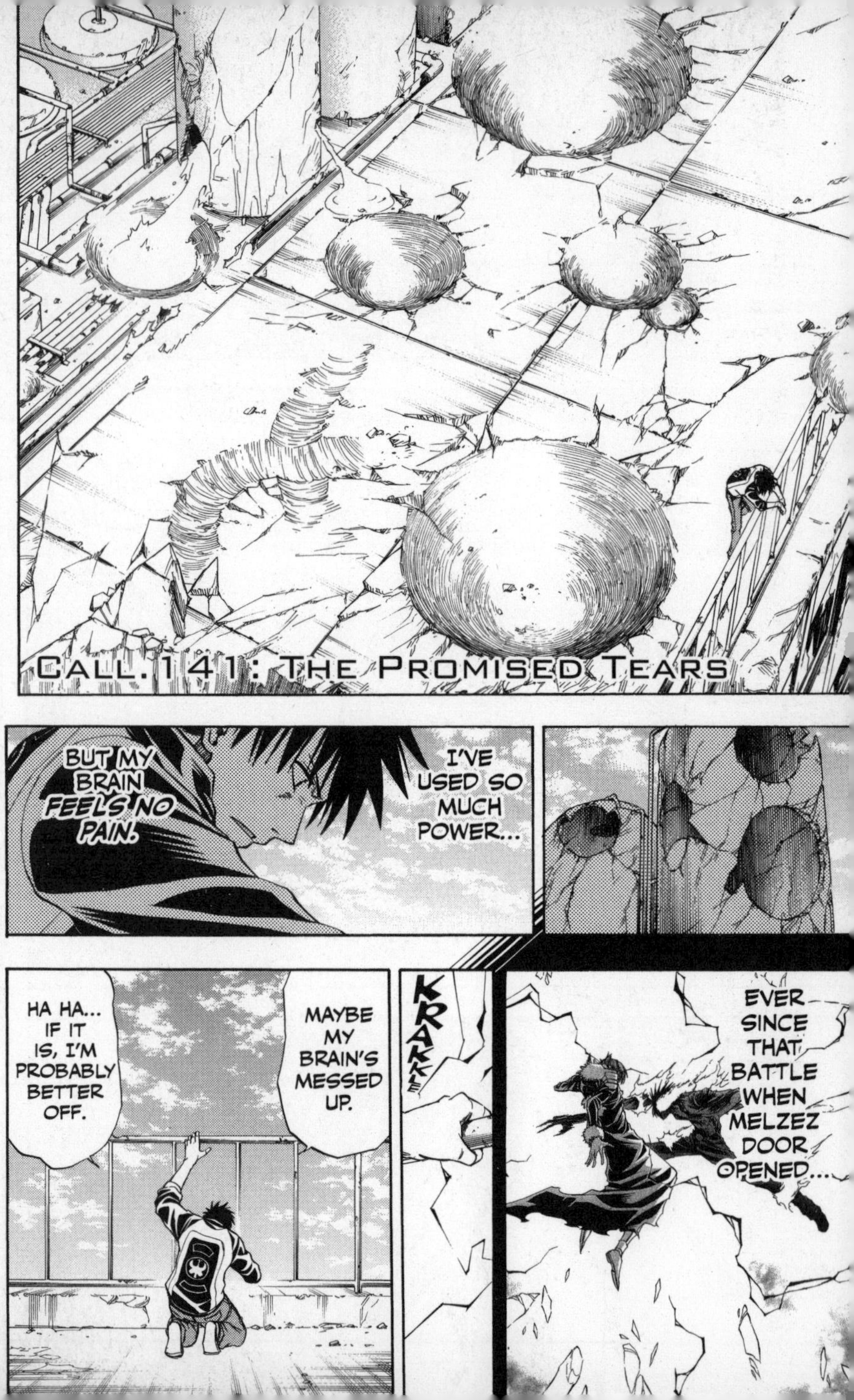
CALL. 141: THE PROMISED TEARS
I'VE USED SO MUCH POWER...
BUT MY BRAIN FEELS NO PAIN.
EVER SINCE THAT BATTLE WHEN MELZEZ DOOR OPENED...
KRAKKLE
MAYBE MY BRAIN'S MESSED UP.
HA HA... IF IT IS, I'M PROBABLY BETTER OFF.

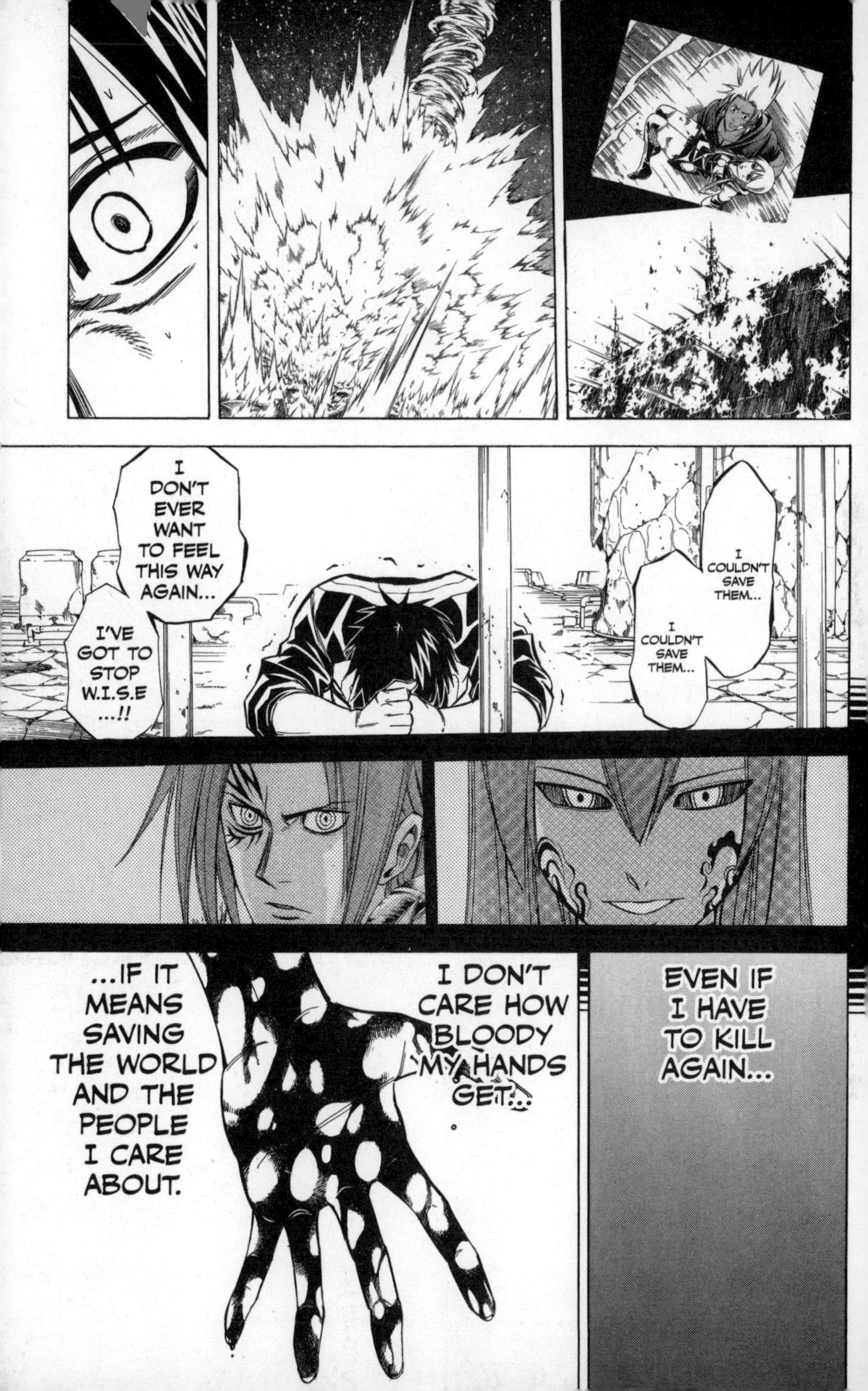
I COULDN'T SAVE THEM...
I COULDN'T SAVE THEM...
I DON'T EVER WANT TO FEEL THIS WAY AGAIN...
I'VE GOT TO STOP W.I.S.E ...!!
EVEN IF I HAVE TO KILL AGAIN...
I DON'T CARE HOW BLOODY MY HANDS GET...
...IF IT MEANS SAVING THE WORLD AND THE PEOPLE I CARE ABOUT.

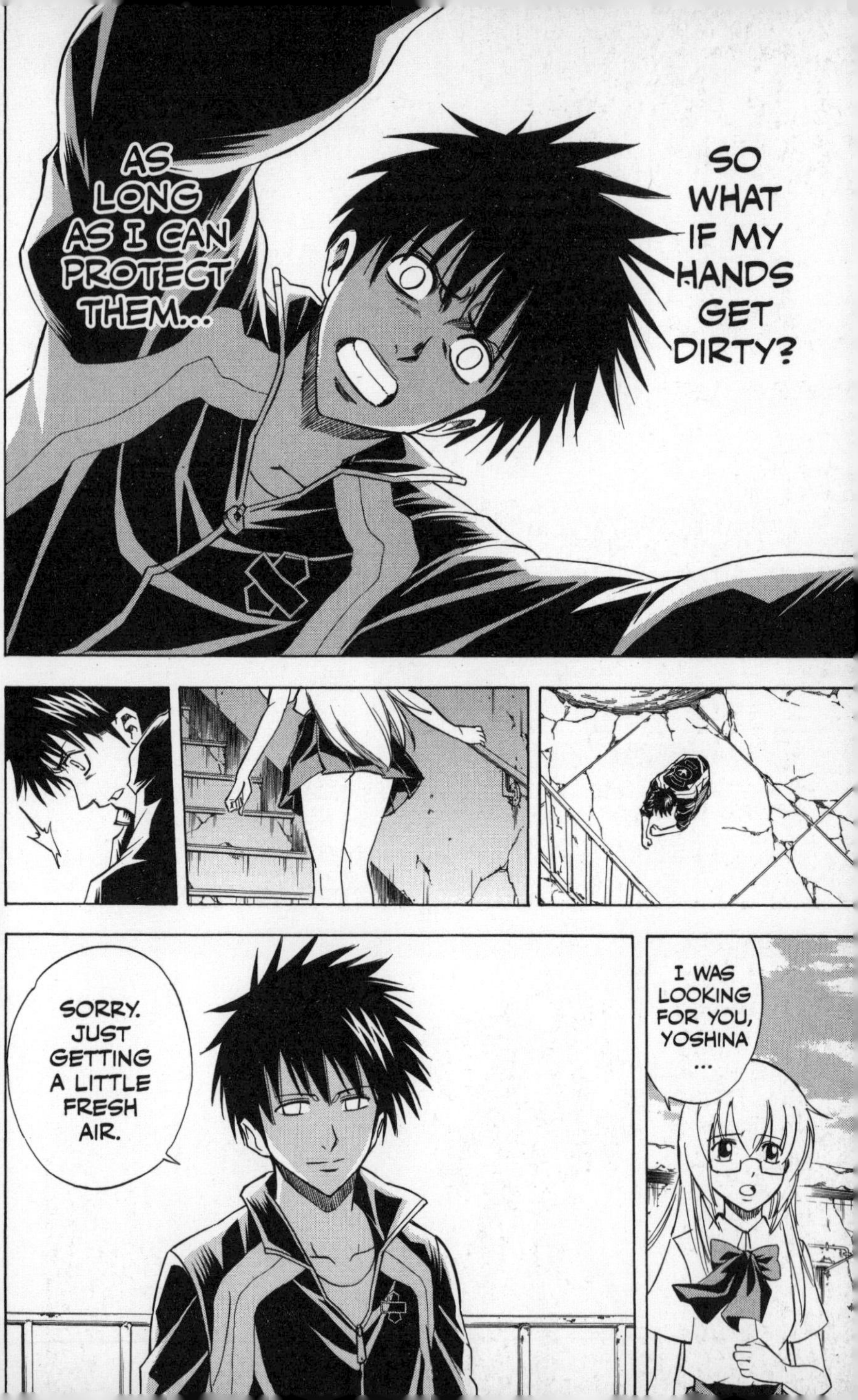
SO WHAT IF MY HANDS GET DIRTY?
AS LONG AS I CAN PROTECT THEM...
I WAS LOOKING FOR YOU, YOSHINA...
SORRY. JUST GETTING A LITTLE FRESH AIR.

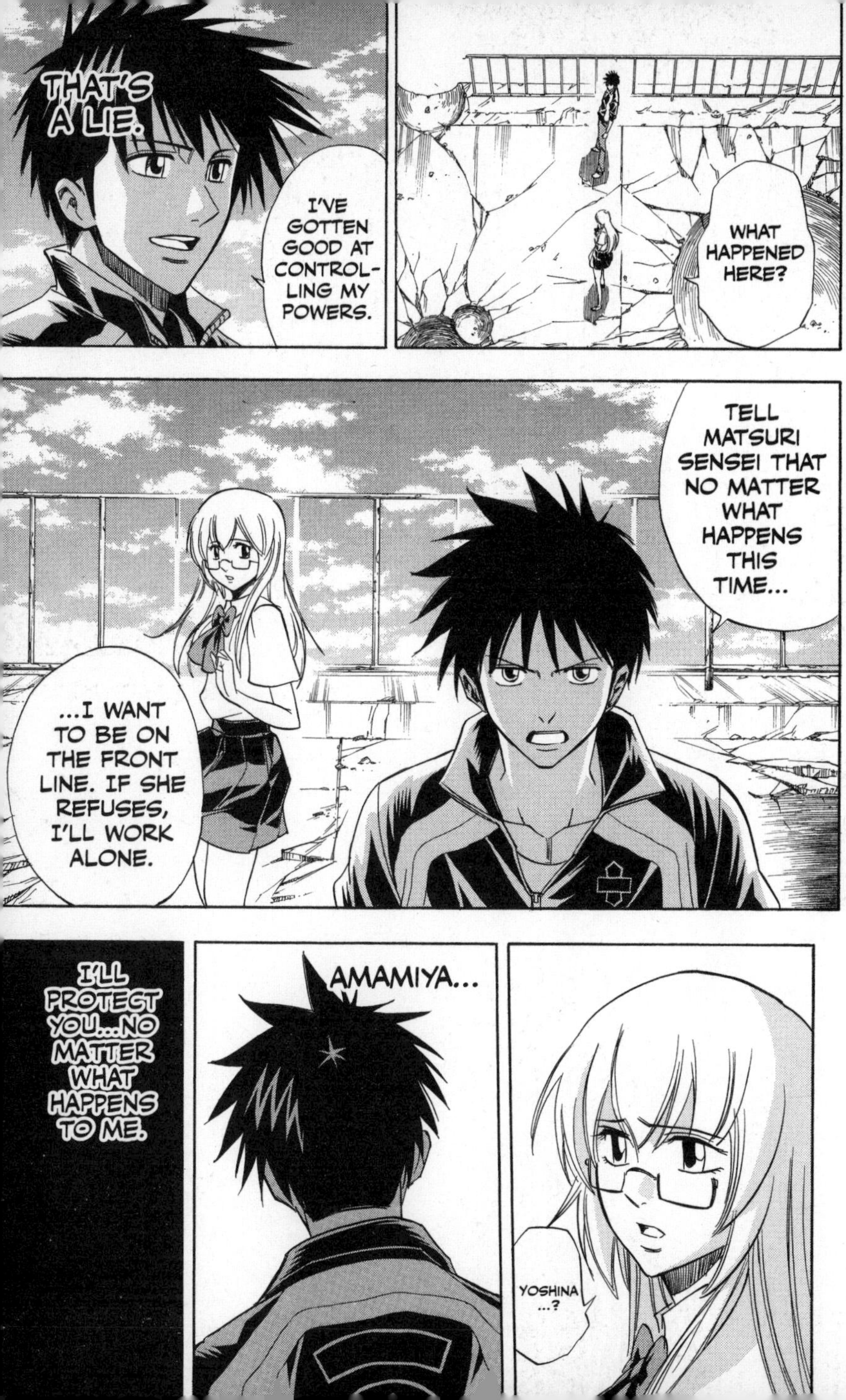
WHAT HAPPENED HERE?
I'VE GOTTEN GOOD AT CONTROL-LING MY POWERS.
THAT'S A LIE.
TELL MATSURI SENSEI THAT NO MATTER WHAT HAPPENS THIS TIME...
...I WANT TO BE ON THE FRONT LINE. IF SHE REFUSES, I'LL WORK ALONE.
YOSHINA ...?
AMAMIYA...
I'LL PROTECT YOU...NO MATTER WHAT HAPPENS TO ME.

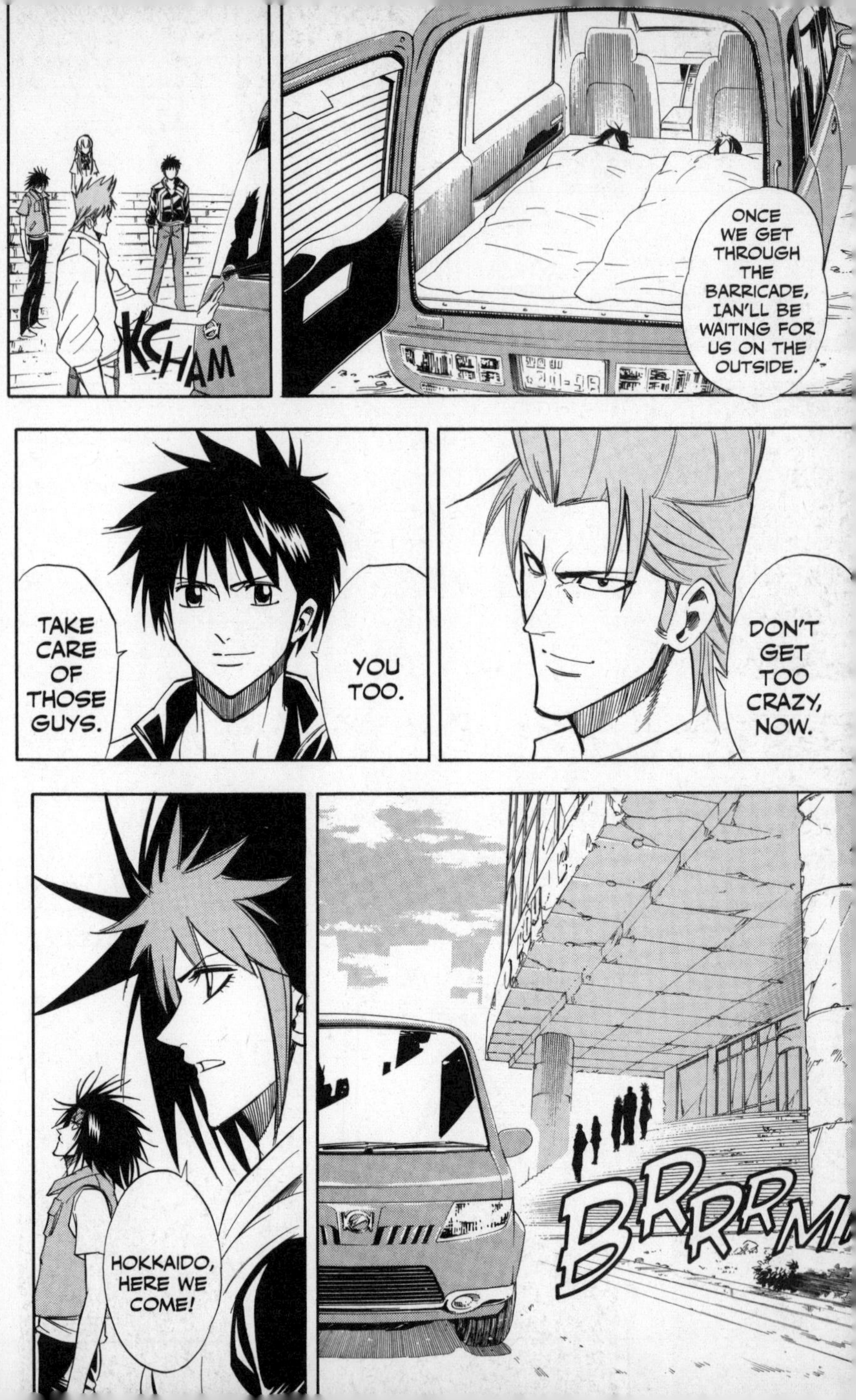
ONCE WE GET THROUGH THE BARRICADE, IAN'LL BE WAITING FOR US ON THE OUTSIDE.
KCHAM
DON'T GET TOO CRAZY, NOW.
YOU TOO.
TAKE CARE OF THOSE GUYS.
BRRRM
HOKKAIDO, HERE WE COME!

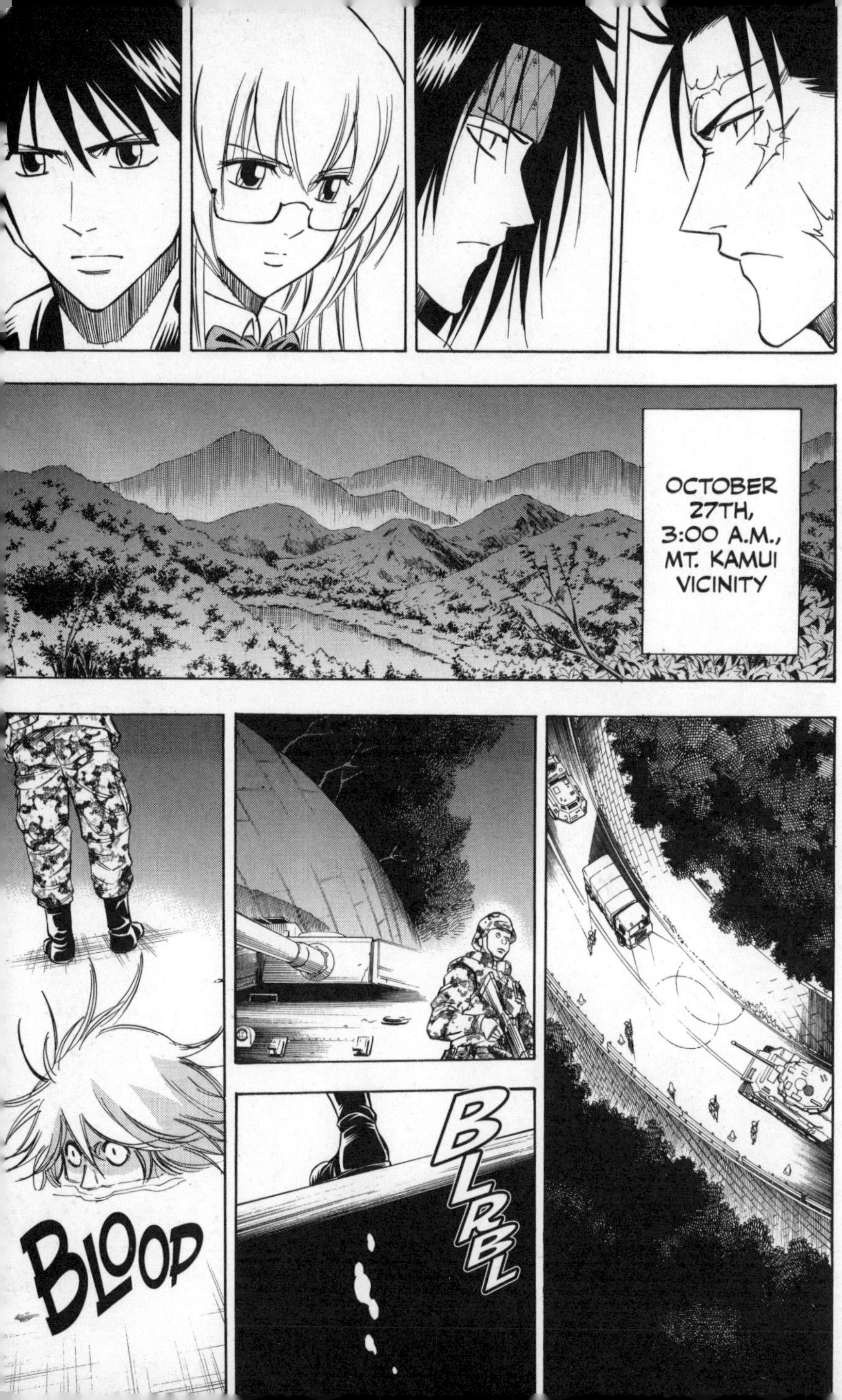
OCTOBER 27TH, 3:00 A.M., MT. KAMUI VICINITY
BLRBL
BLOOP

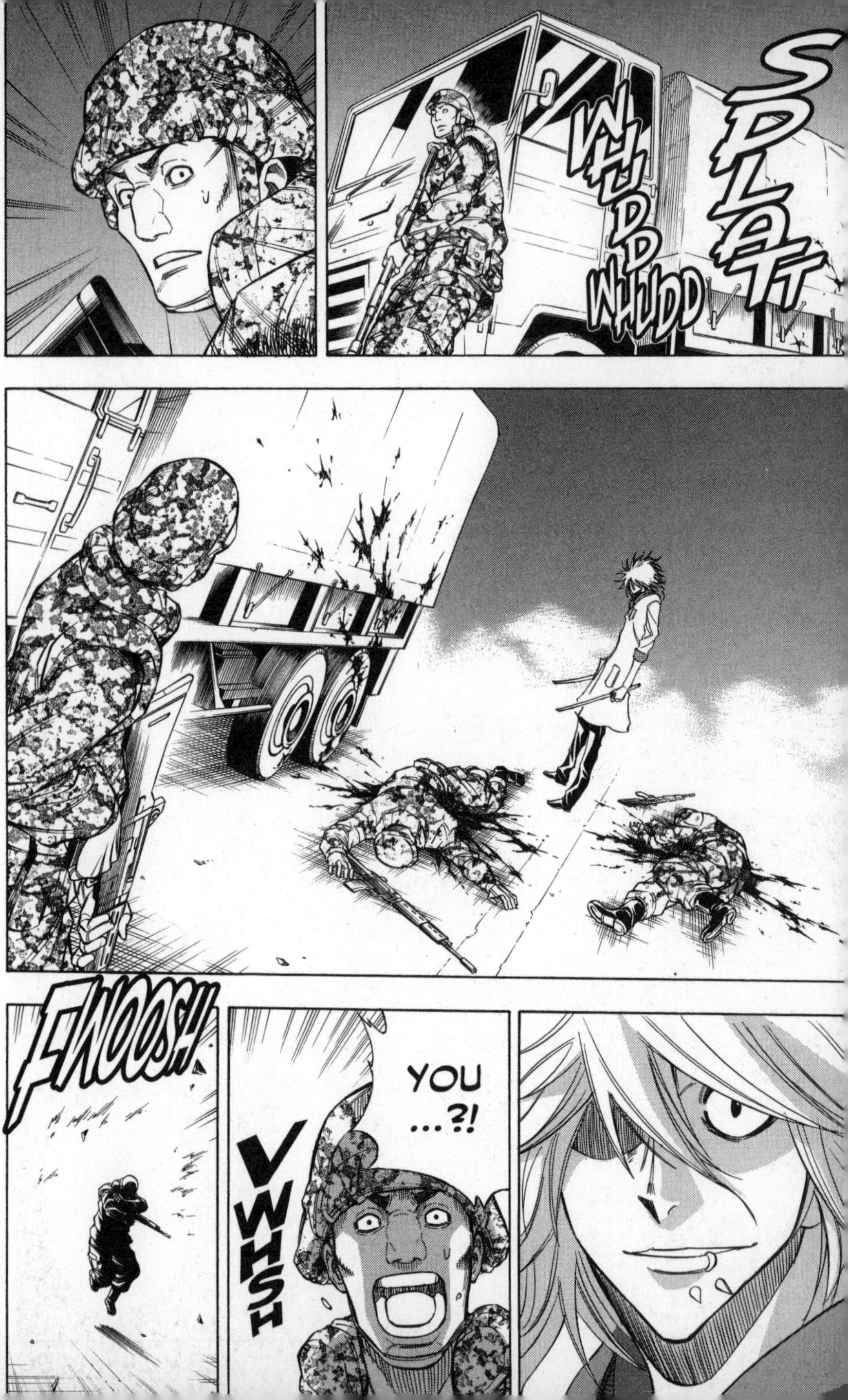
SPLATT
WHUDD WHUDD
YOU ...?!
VWHSH
FWOOSH

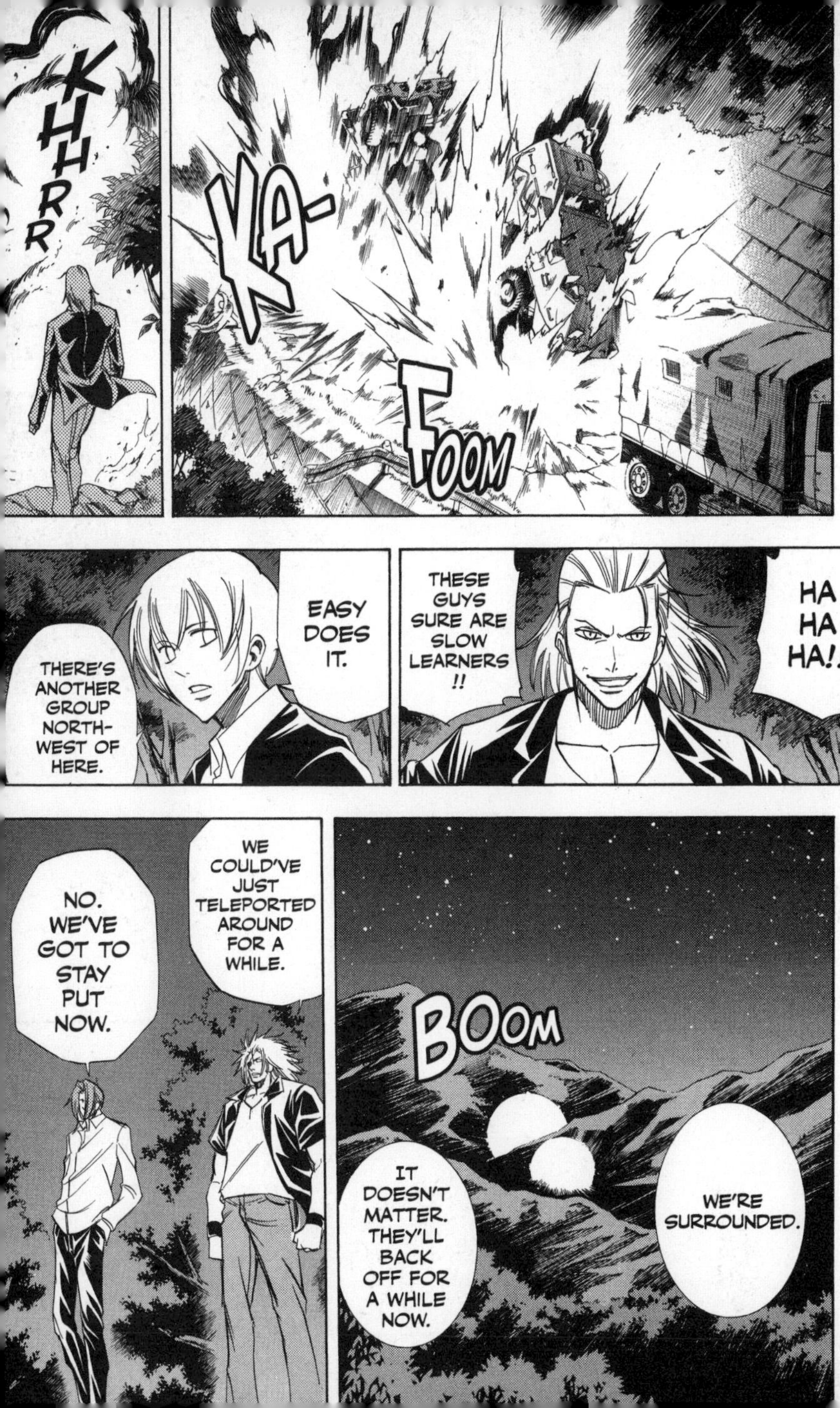
KA-
FOOM
KHHRR
HA HA HA!!
THESE GUYS SURE ARE SLOW LEARNERS!!
EASY DOES IT.
THERE'S ANOTHER GROUP NORTH-WEST OF HERE.
BOOM
WE'RE SURROUNDED.
IT DOESN'T MATTER. THEY'LL BACK OFF FOR A WHILE NOW.
WE COULD'VE JUST TELEPORTED AROUND FOR A WHILE.
NO. WE'VE GOT TO STAY PUT NOW.

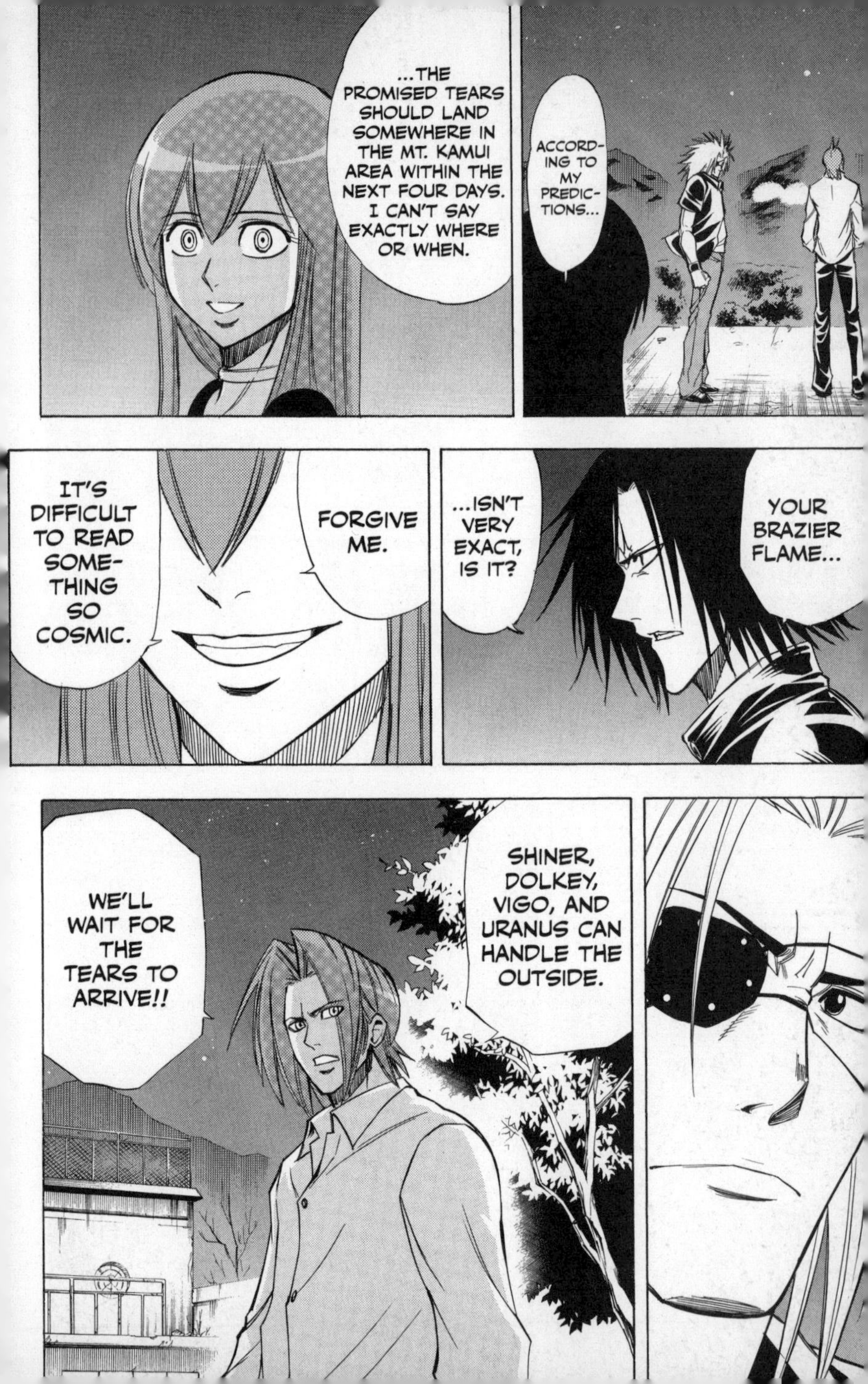
ACCORDING TO MY PREDICTIONS...
...THE PROMISED TEARS SHOULD LAND SOMEWHERE IN THE MT. KAMUI AREA WITHIN THE NEXT FOUR DAYS. I CAN'T SAY EXACTLY WHERE OR WHEN.
YOUR BRAZIER FLAME...
...ISN'T VERY EXACT, IS IT?
FORGIVE ME.
IT'S DIFFICULT TO READ SOMETHING SO COSMIC.
SHINER, DOLKEY, VIGO, AND URANUS CAN HANDLE THE OUTSIDE.
WE'LL WAIT FOR THE TEARS TO ARRIVE!!

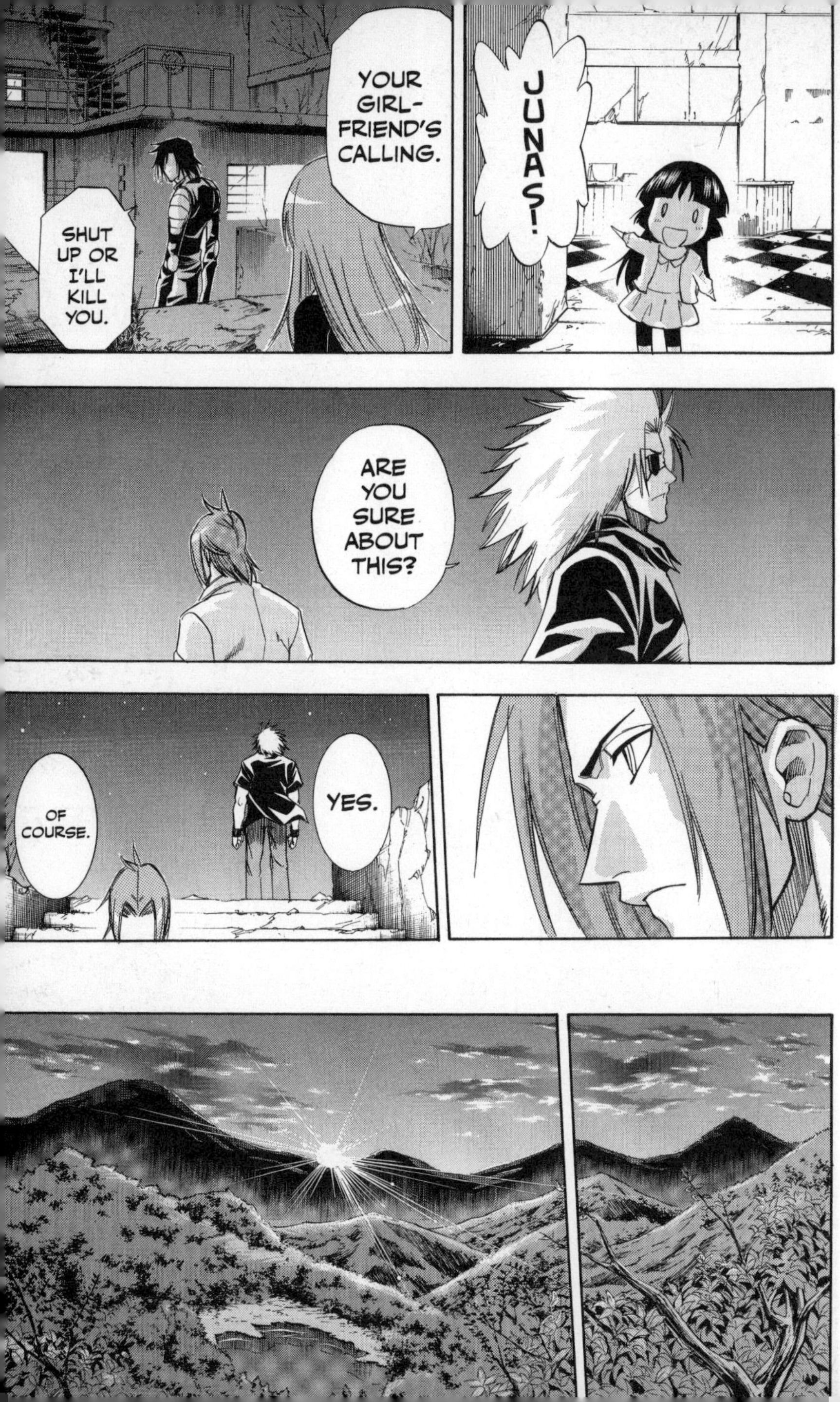
JUNAS!
YOUR GIRL-FRIEND'S CALLING.
SHUT UP OR I'LL KILL YOU.
ARE YOU SURE ABOUT THIS?
YES.
OF COURSE.

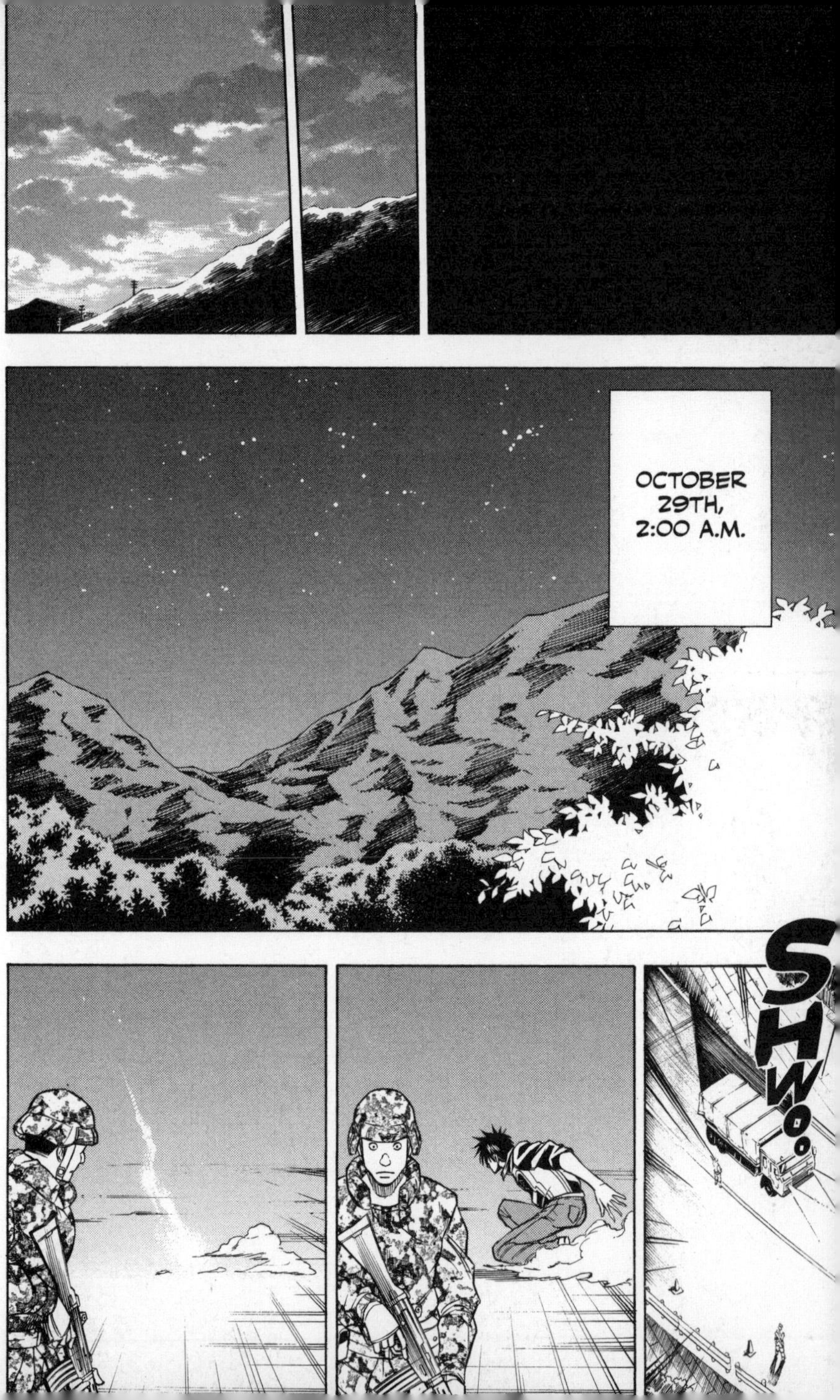
OCTOBER 29TH, 2:00 A.M.
SHWOO

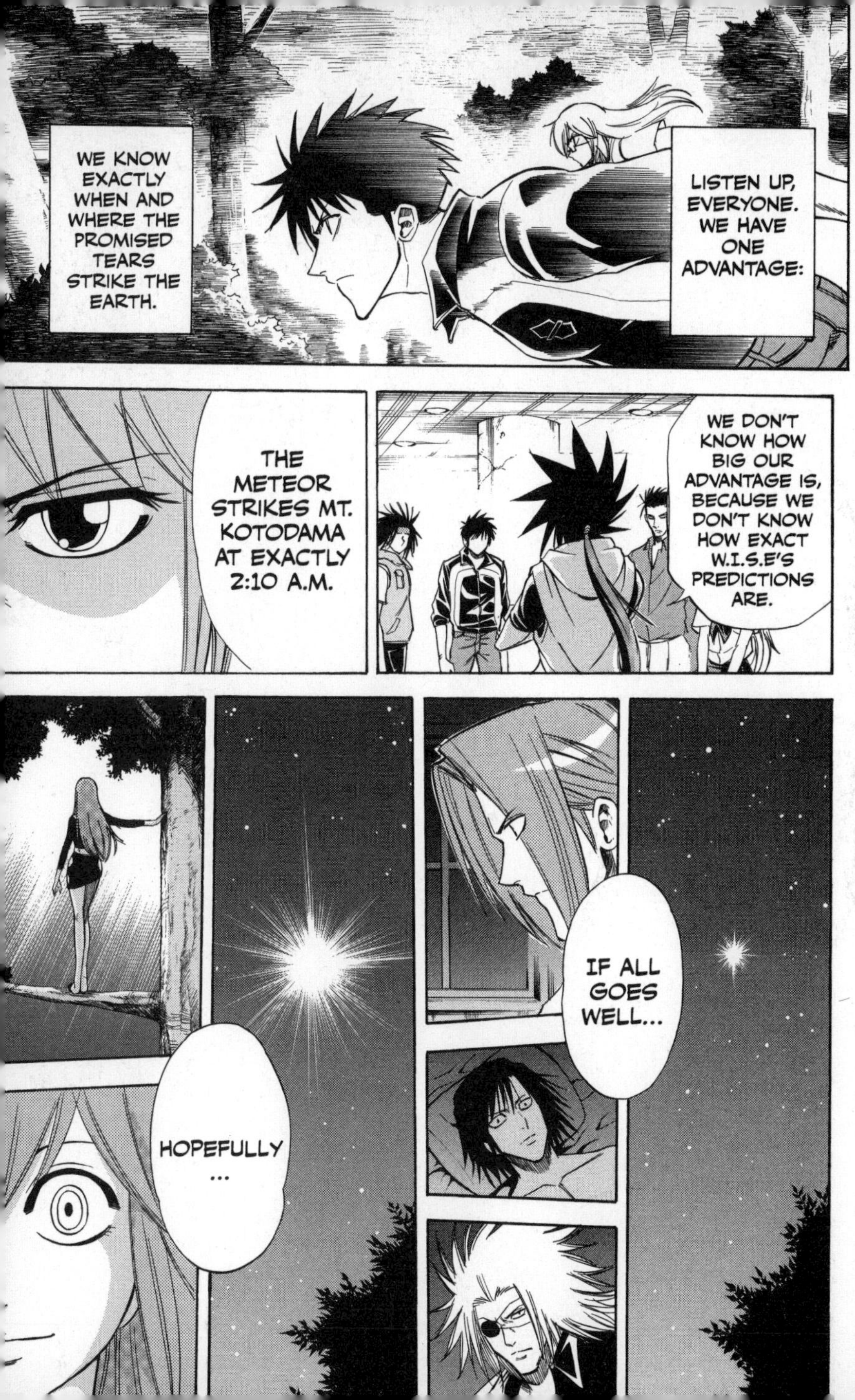
LISTEN UP, EVERYONE. WE HAVE ONE ADVANTAGE:
WE KNOW EXACTLY WHEN AND WHERE THE PROMISED TEARS STRIKE THE EARTH.
WE DON'T KNOW HOW BIG OUR ADVANTAGE IS, BECAUSE WE DON'T KNOW HOW EXACT W.I.S.E'S PREDICTIONS ARE.
THE METEOR STRIKES MT. KOTODAMA AT EXACTLY 2:10 A.M.
IF ALL GOES WELL...
HOPEFULLY ...

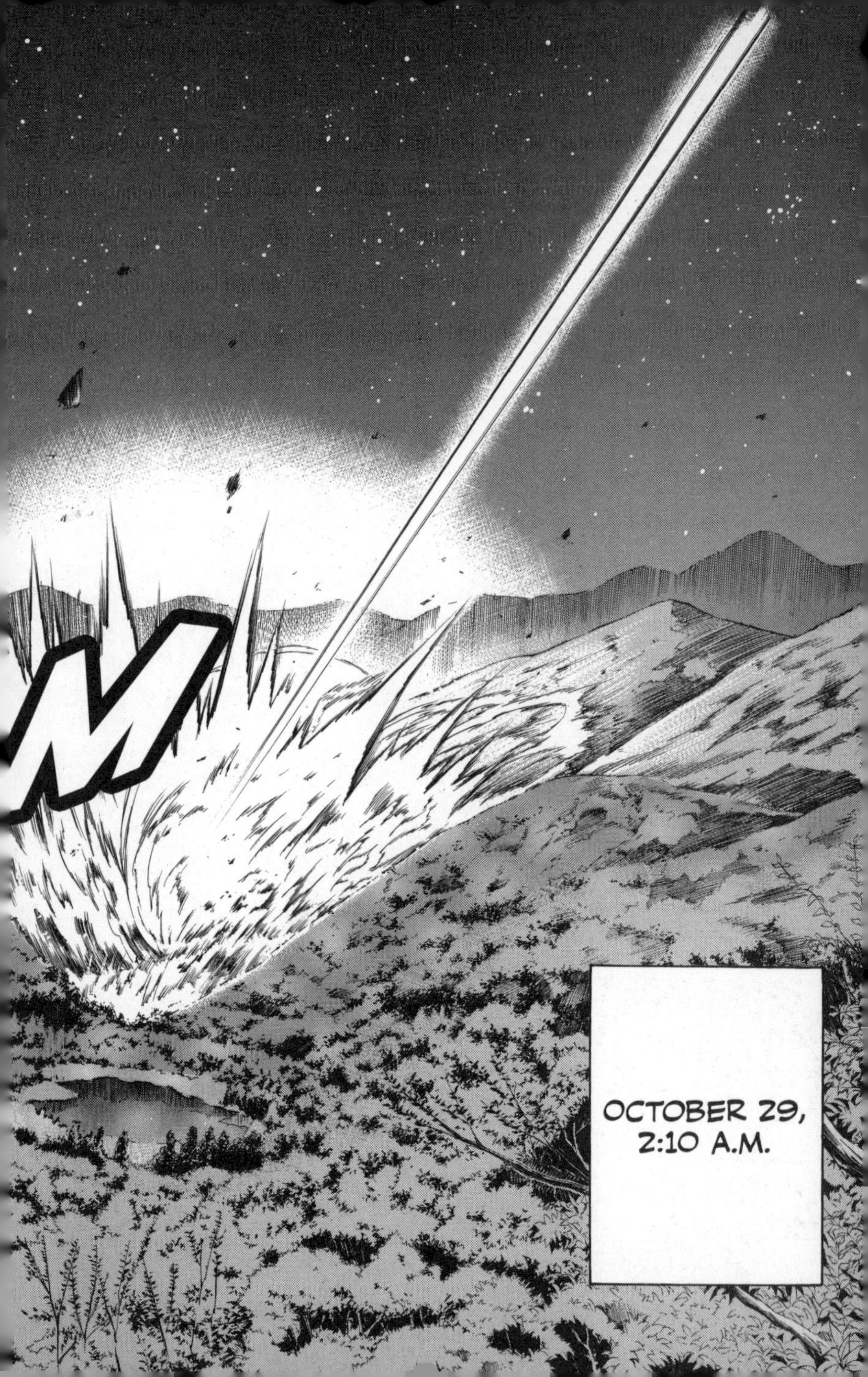
OCTOBER 29,
2:10 A.M.
M

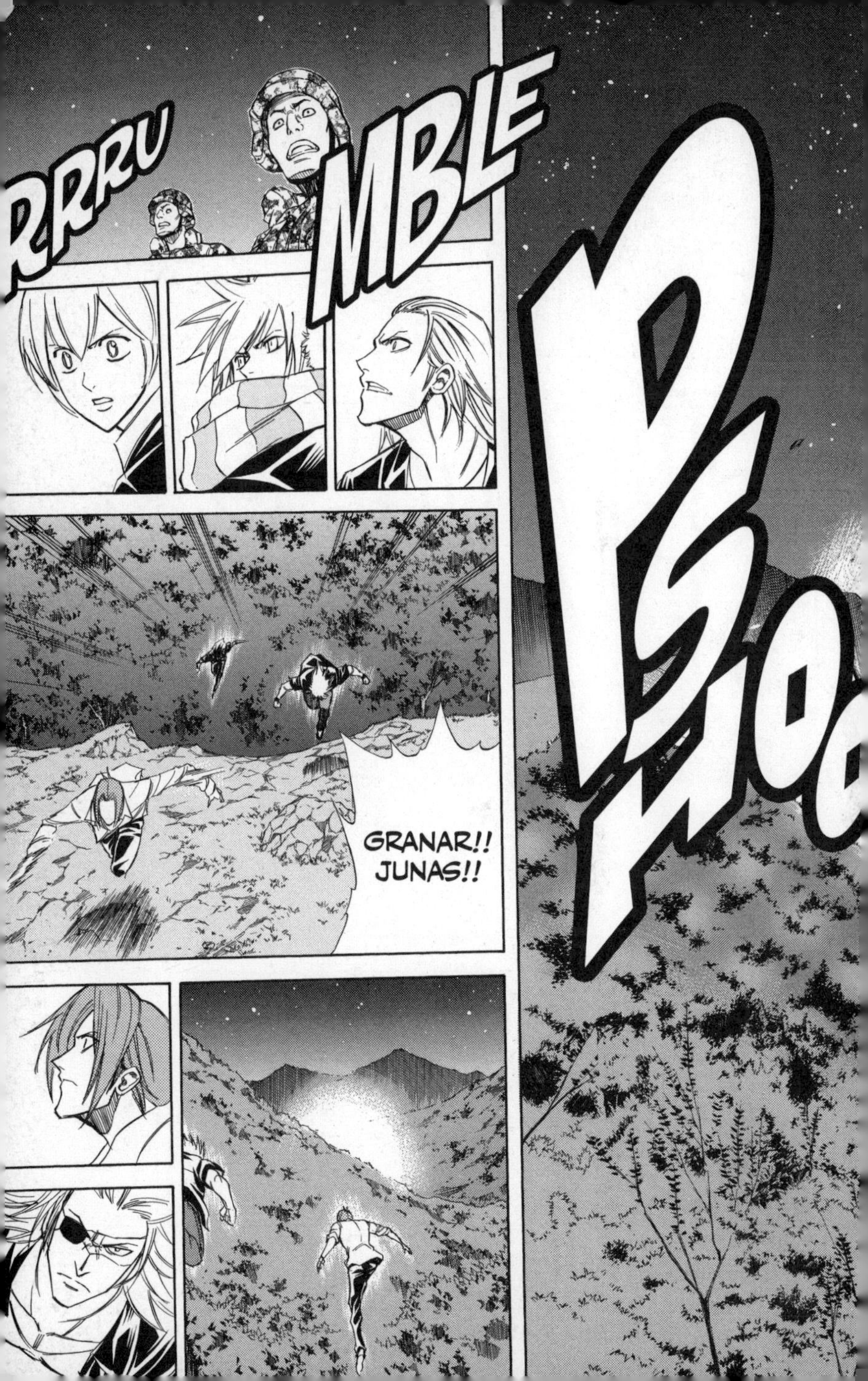
RRRU MBLE
GRANAR!! JUNAS!!

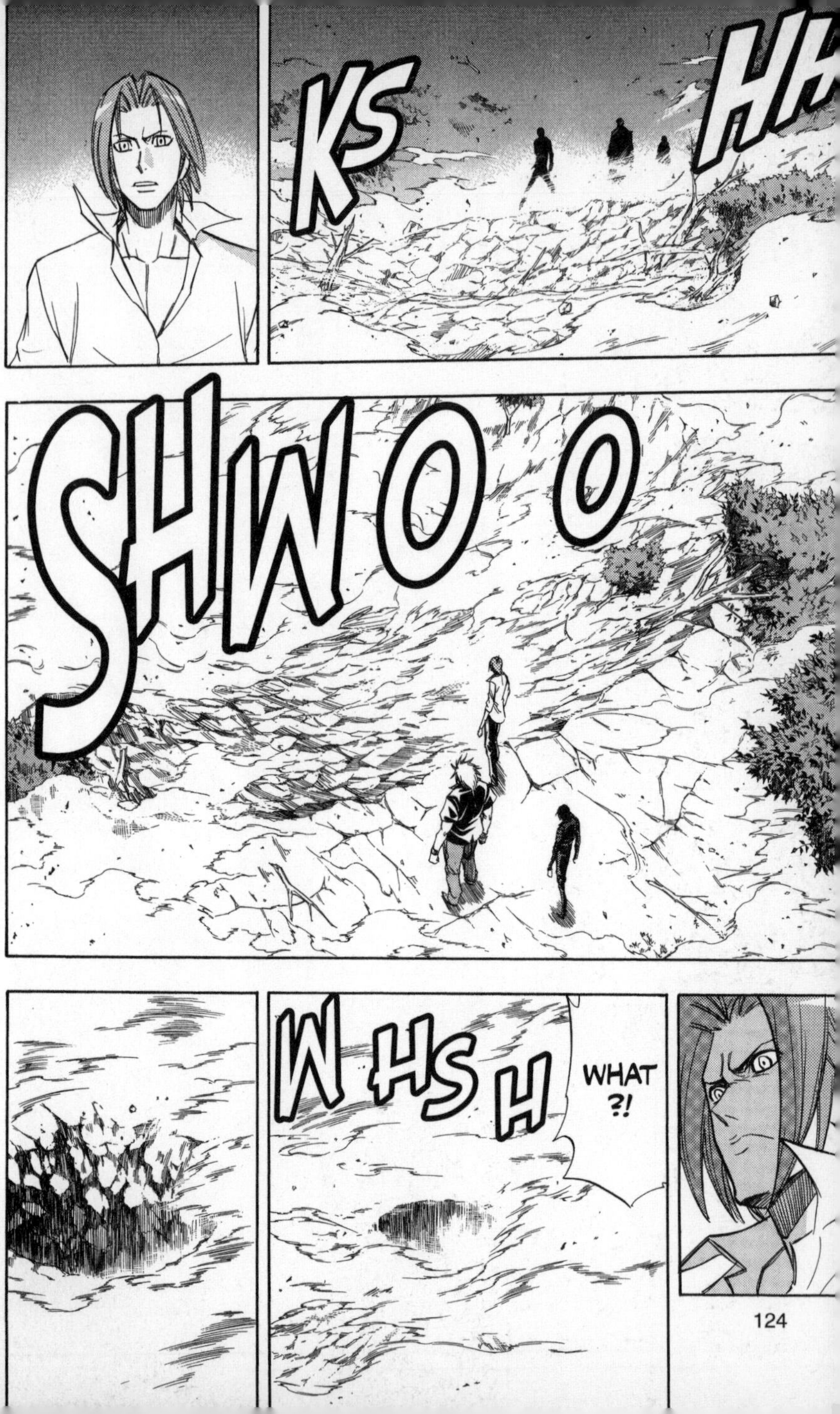
KS
SHWO O
WHSH
WHAT?!

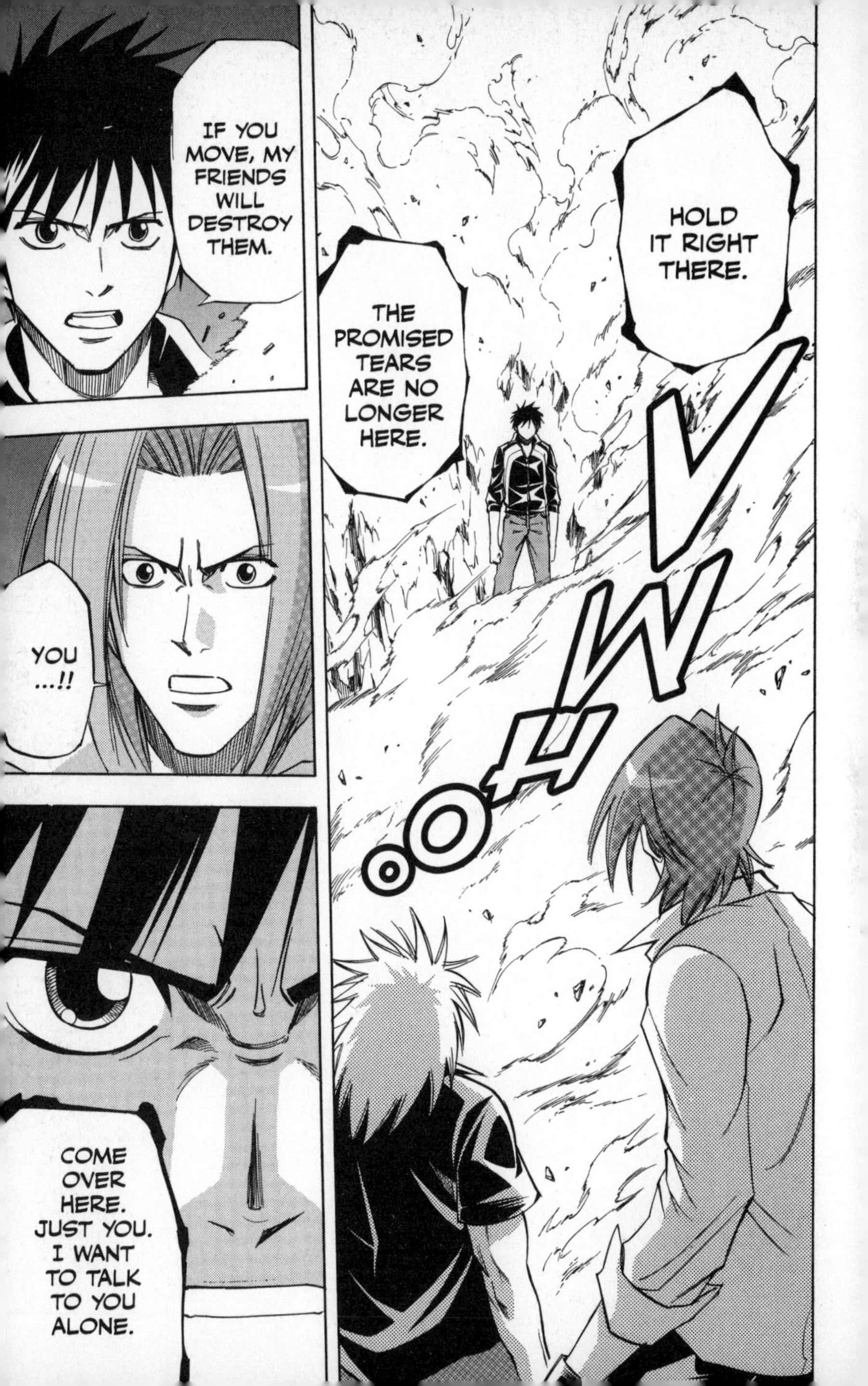
HOLD IT RIGHT THERE.
THE PROMISED TEARS ARE NO LONGER HERE.
VWHOO
IF YOU MOVE, MY FRIENDS WILL DESTROY THEM.
YOU ...!!
COME OVER HERE. JUST YOU. I WANT TO TALK TO YOU ALONE.

Mutters and mumblings...

I HAD ACTUALLY INTENDED FOR KABUTO TO DIE IN VOLUME
7 OR 8.
I SERIOUSLY INTENDED TO KILL HIM OFF, TO INFLUENCE
THE DEVELOPMENT OF AGEHA'S CHARACTER, BUT I HAD
SECOND THOUGHTS WHEN I WAS FINISHING THE LAST
CHAPTER OF VOLUME 7 AND DECIDED NOT TO.
SINCE THEN, HE'S DEVELOPED INTO A REALLY GREAT CHAR-
ACTER.
I'M SO GLAD I DIDN'T KILL HIM OFF.
KIRISAKI KABUTO HAS AN AMAZING ABILITY TO EVADE THE
GRIM REAPER.
HE EVEN MANAGED TO MANIPULATE THE INTENTIONS OF HIS
CREATOR. NOW THAT'S SCARY.

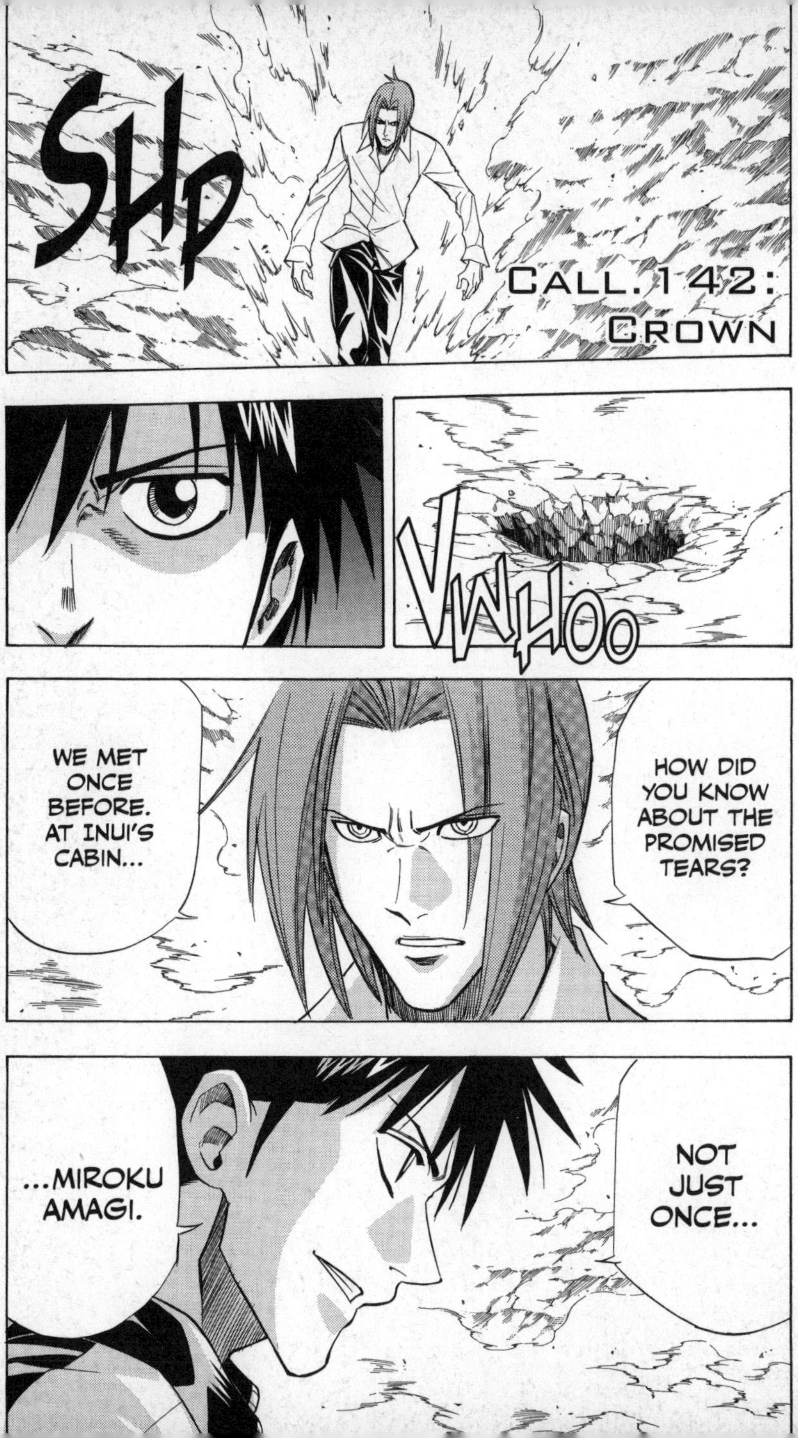
SHP
CALL. 142: CROWN
VWHOO
HOW DID YOU KNOW ABOUT THE PROMISED TEARS?
WE MET ONCE BEFORE. AT INUI'S CABIN...
NOT JUST ONCE...
...MIROKU AMAGI.

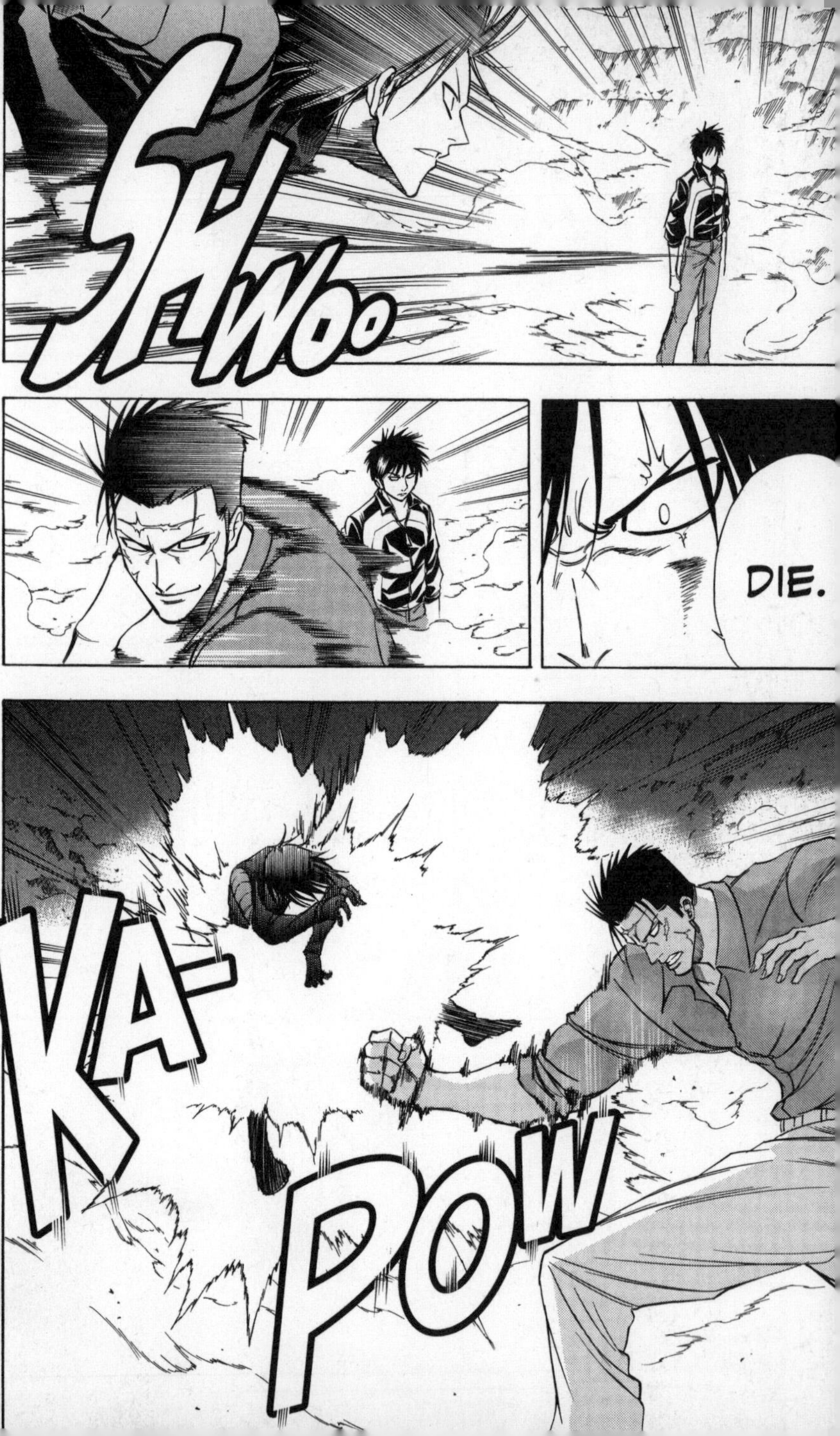
SHWOO
DIE.
KA-POW

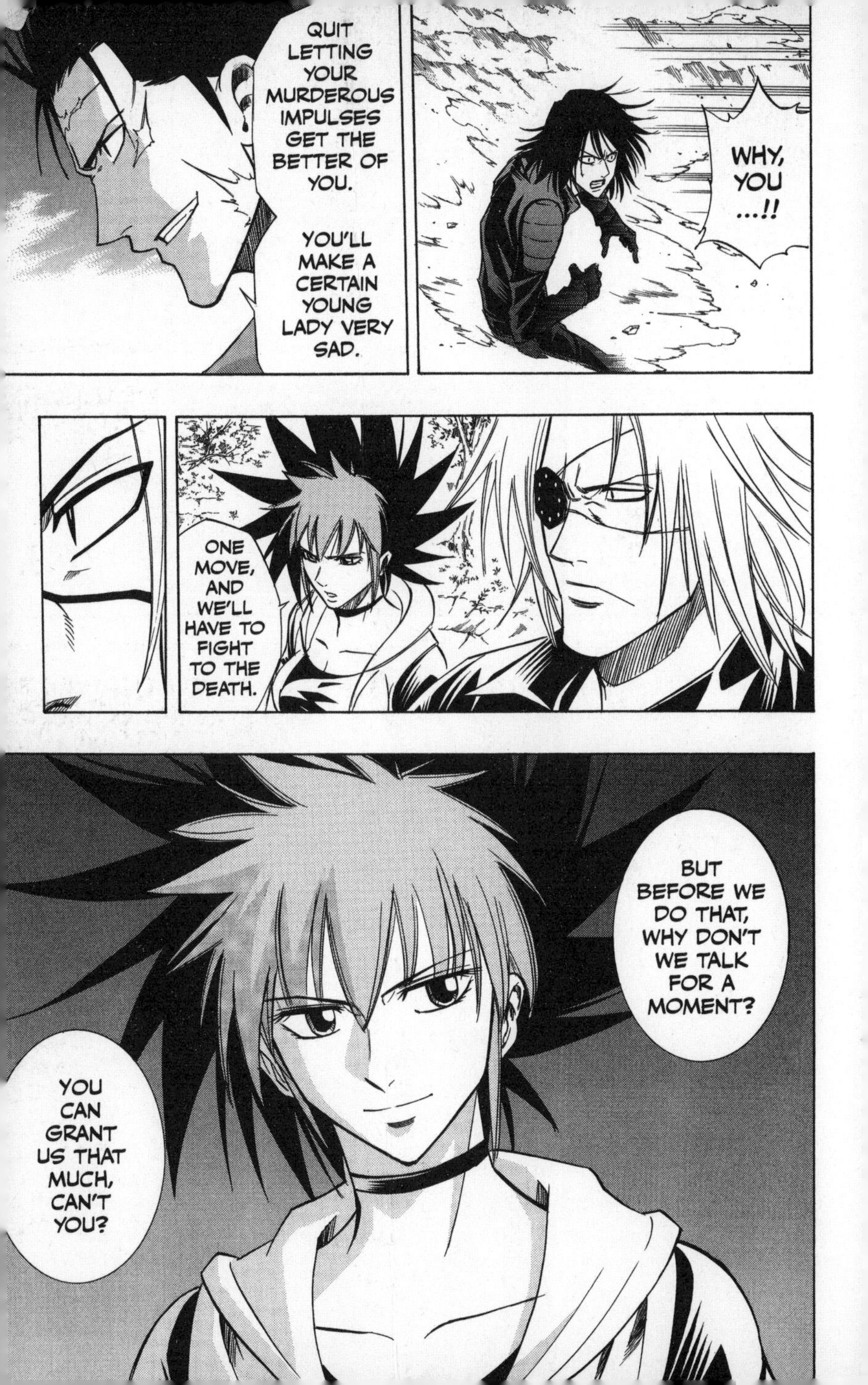
WHY, YOU ...!!
QUIT LETTING YOUR MURDEROUS IMPULSES GET THE BETTER OF YOU.
YOU'LL MAKE A CERTAIN YOUNG LADY VERY SAD.
ONE MOVE, AND WE'LL HAVE TO FIGHT TO THE DEATH.
BUT BEFORE WE DO THAT, WHY DON'T WE TALK FOR A MOMENT?
YOU CAN GRANT US THAT MUCH, CAN'T YOU?

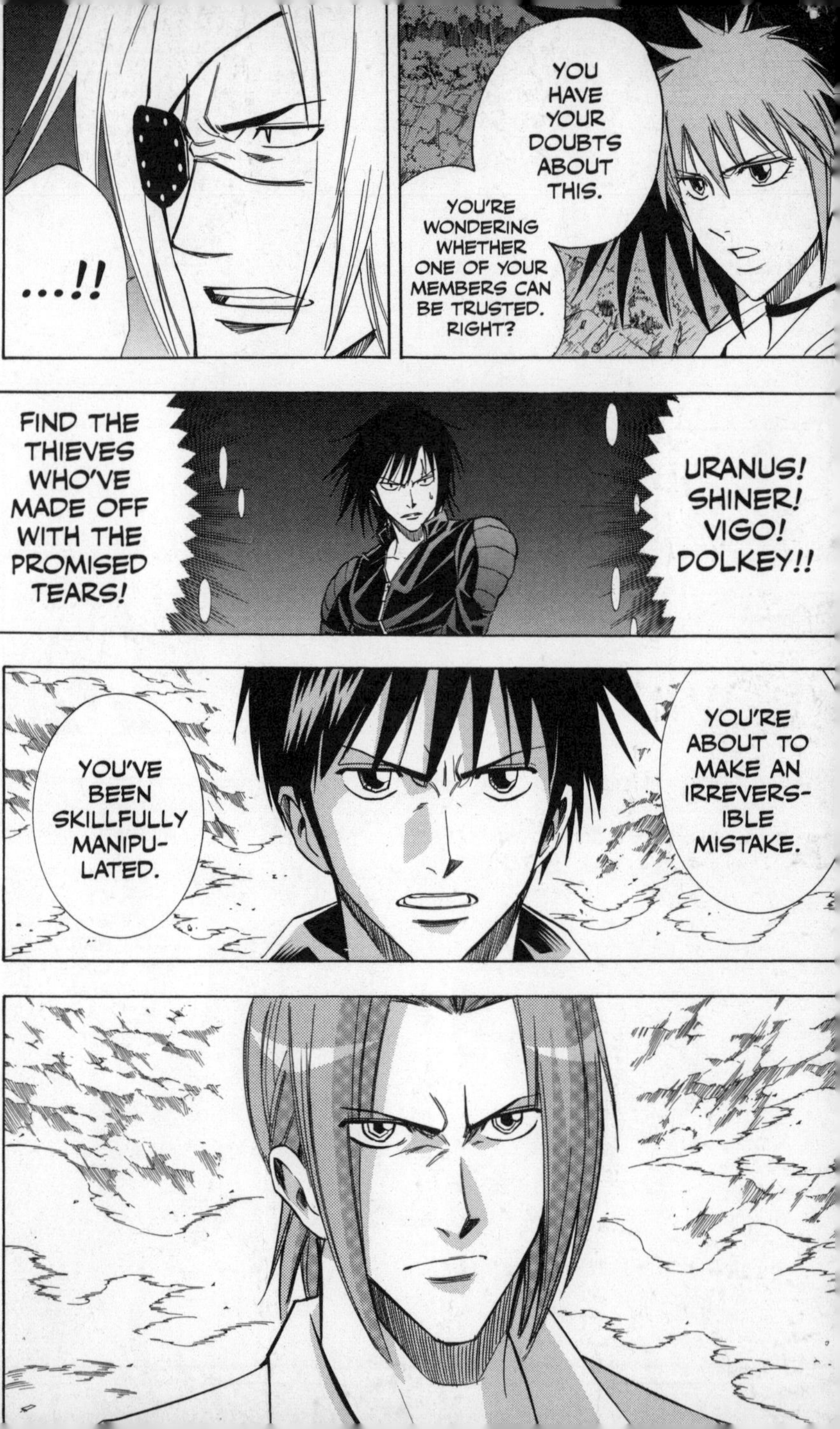
YOU HAVE YOUR DOUBTS ABOUT THIS.
YOU'RE WONDERING WHETHER ONE OF YOUR MEMBERS CAN BE TRUSTED. RIGHT?
...!!
URANUS! SHINER! VIGO! DOLKEY!!
FIND THE THIEVES WHO'VE MADE OFF WITH THE PROMISED TEARS!
YOU'RE ABOUT TO MAKE AN IRREVERS-IBLE MISTAKE.
YOU'VE BEEN SKILLFULLY MANIPU-LATED.

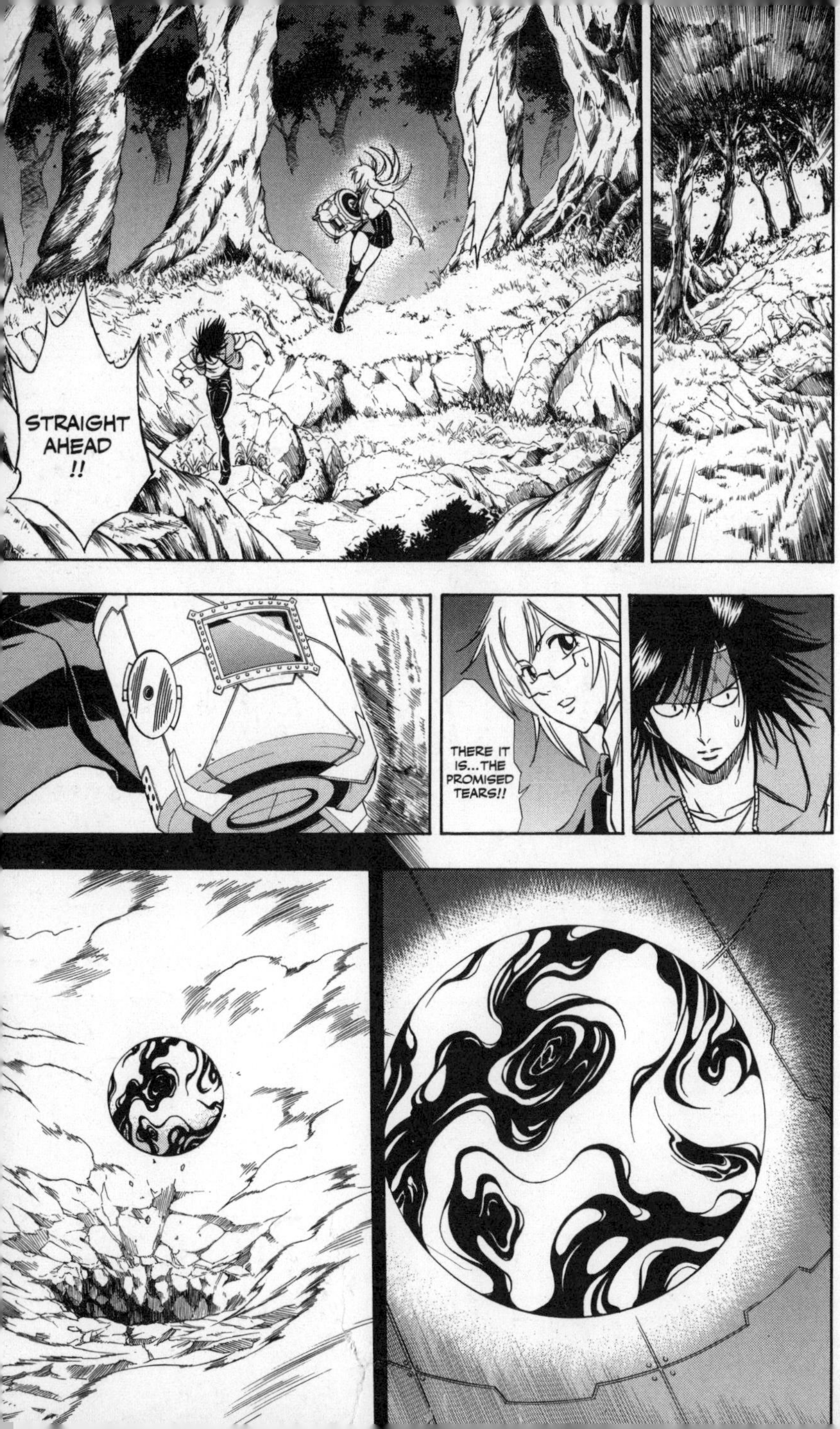
STRAIGHT AHEAD !!
THERE IT IS...THE PROMISED TEARS!!

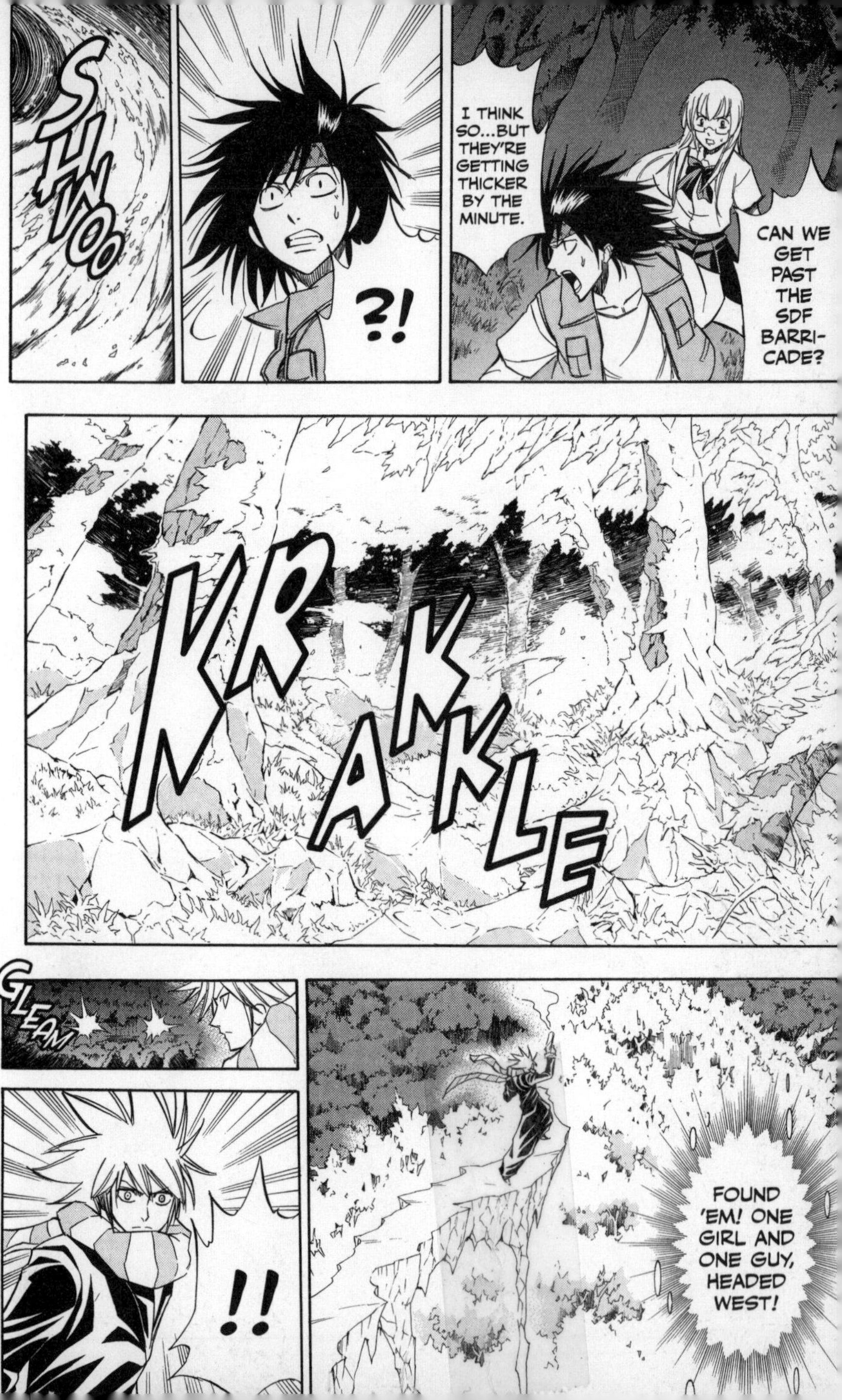
CAN WE GET PAST THE SDF BARRICADE?
I THINK SO...BUT THEY'RE GETTING THICKER BY THE MINUTE.
?!
SHVOO
KRAKKLE
FOUND 'EM! ONE GIRL AND ONE GUY, HEADED WEST!
GLEAM
!!

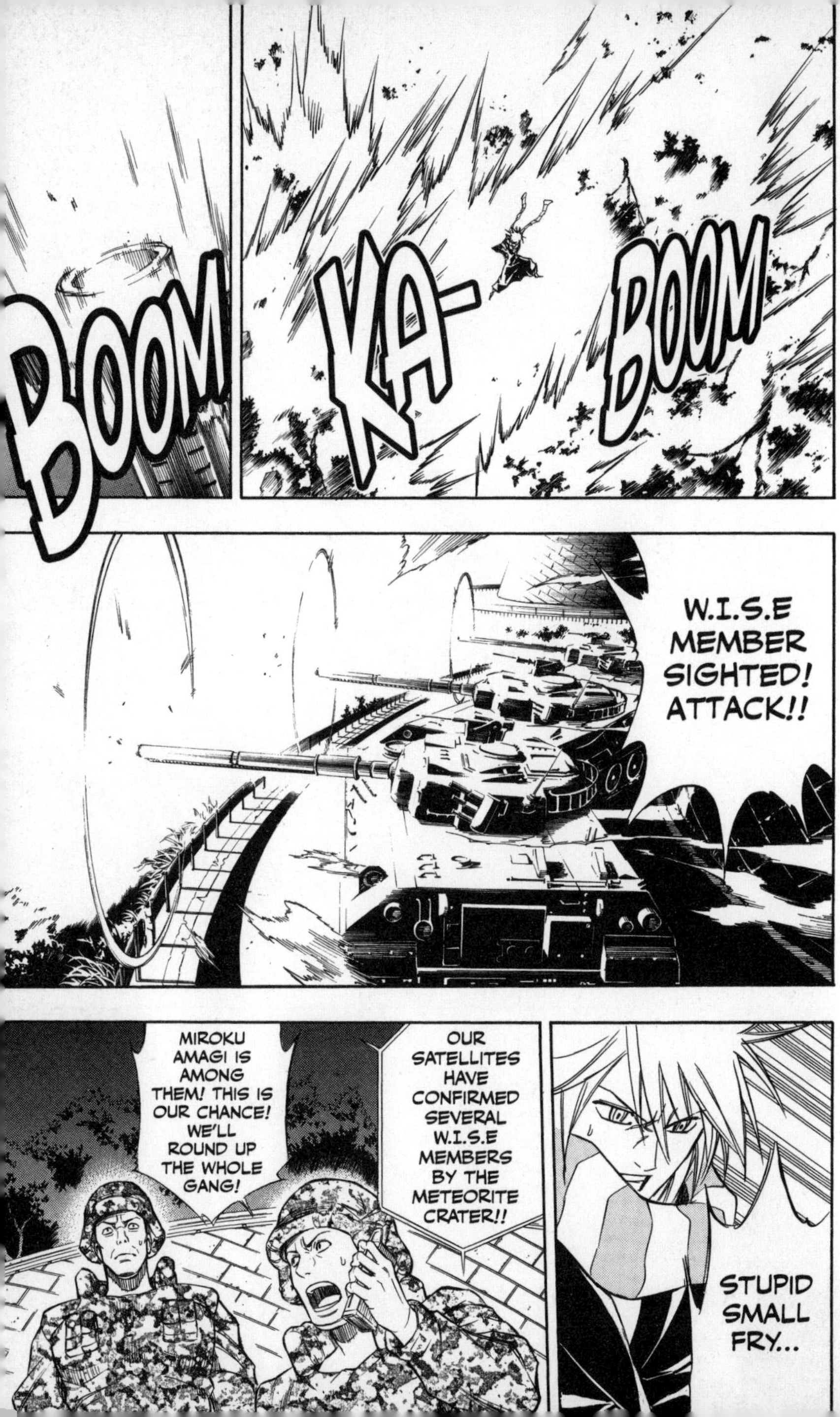
KA-BOOM
BOOM
W.I.S.E MEMBER SIGHTED! ATTACK!!
STUPID SMALL FRY...
OUR SATELLITES HAVE CONFIRMED SEVERAL W.I.S.E MEMBERS BY THE METEORITE CRATER!!
MIROKU AMAGI IS AMONG THEM! THIS IS OUR CHANCE! WE'LL ROUND UP THE WHOLE GANG!

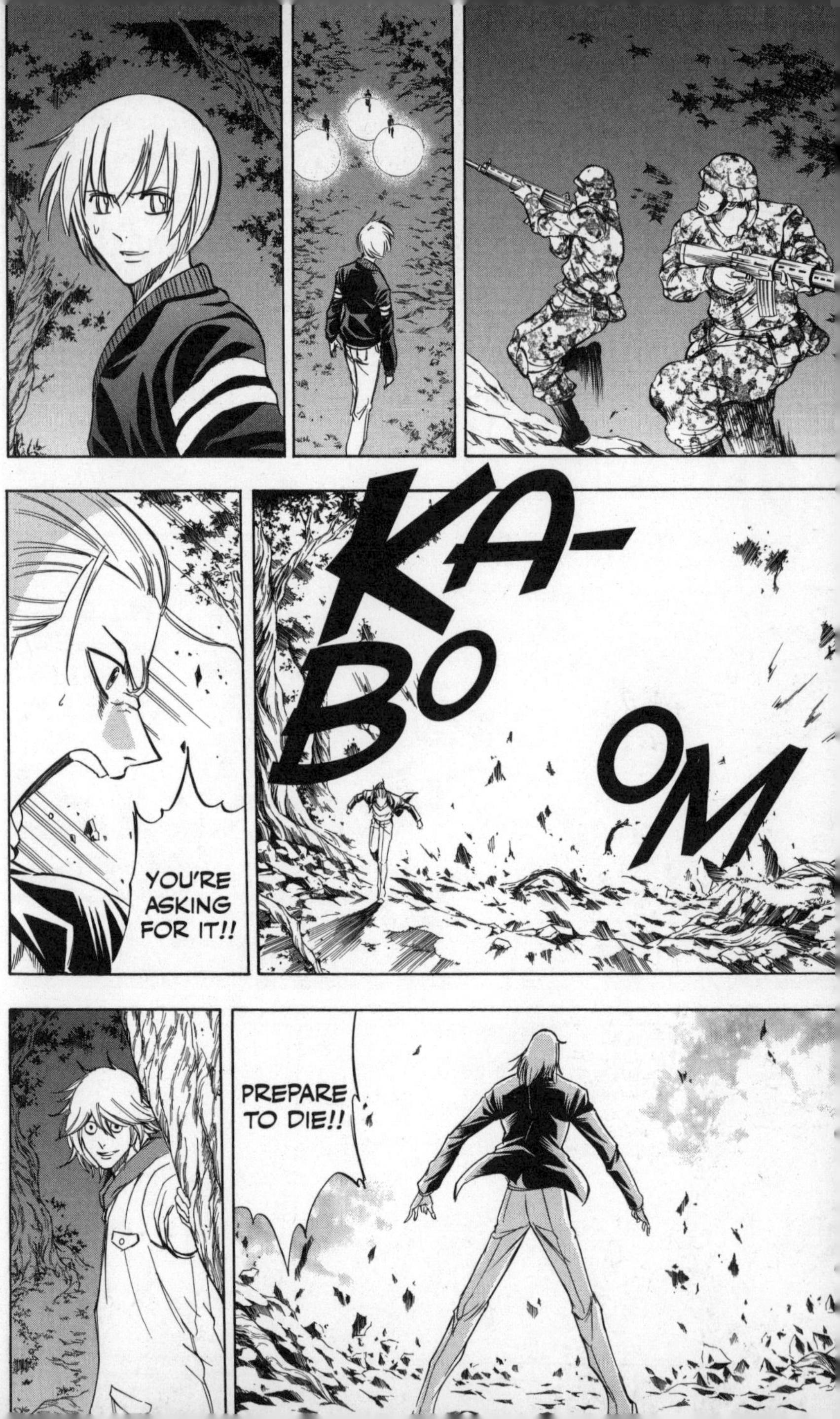
KA-BOOM
YOU'RE ASKING FOR IT!!
PREPARE TO DIE!!

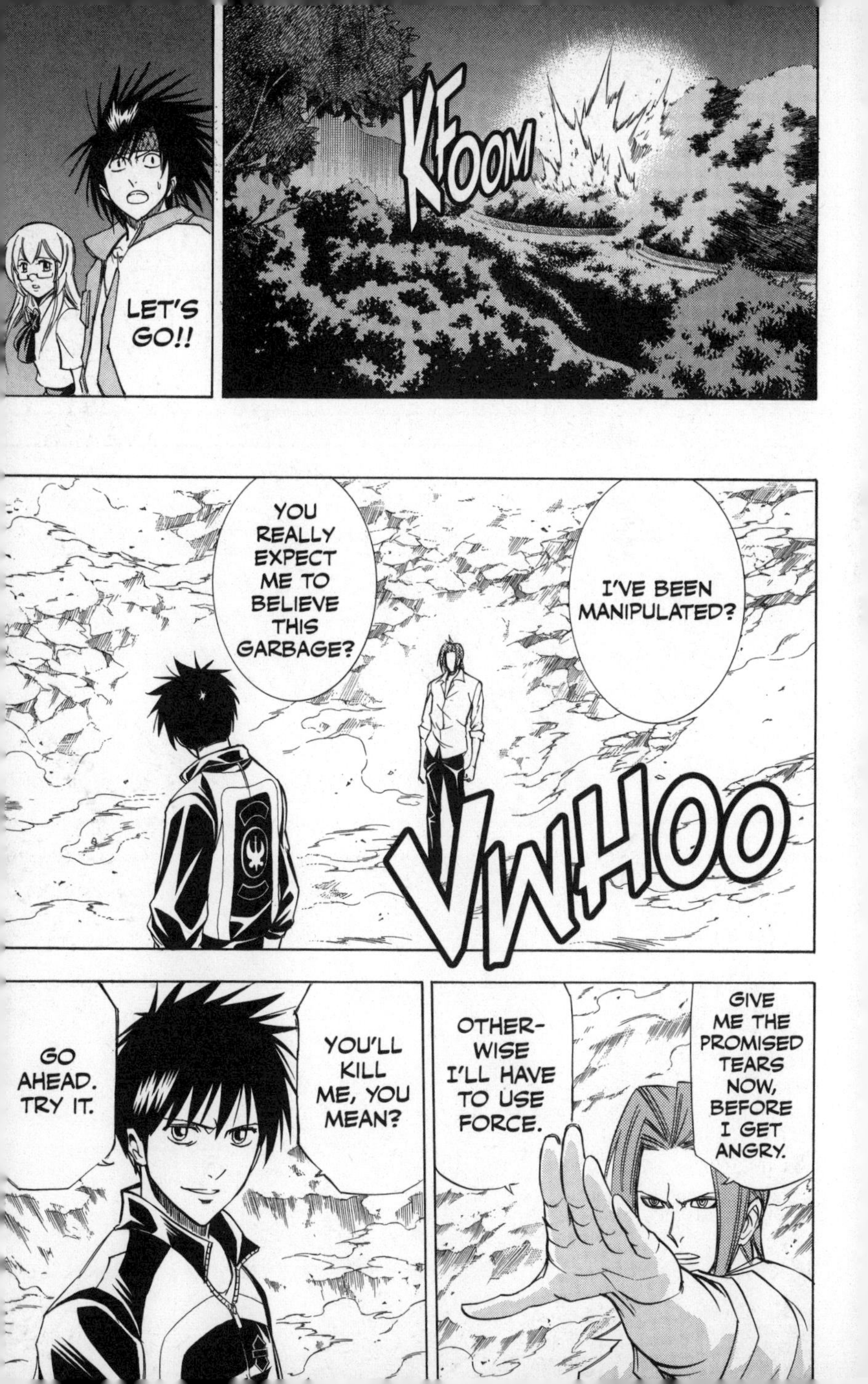
KFOOM
LET'S GO!!
I'VE BEEN MANIPULATED?
YOU REALLY EXPECT ME TO BELIEVE THIS GARBAGE?
VWHOO
GIVE ME THE PROMISED TEARS NOW, BEFORE I GET ANGRY.
OTHER-WISE I'LL HAVE TO USE FORCE.
YOU'LL KILL ME, YOU MEAN?
GO AHEAD. TRY IT.

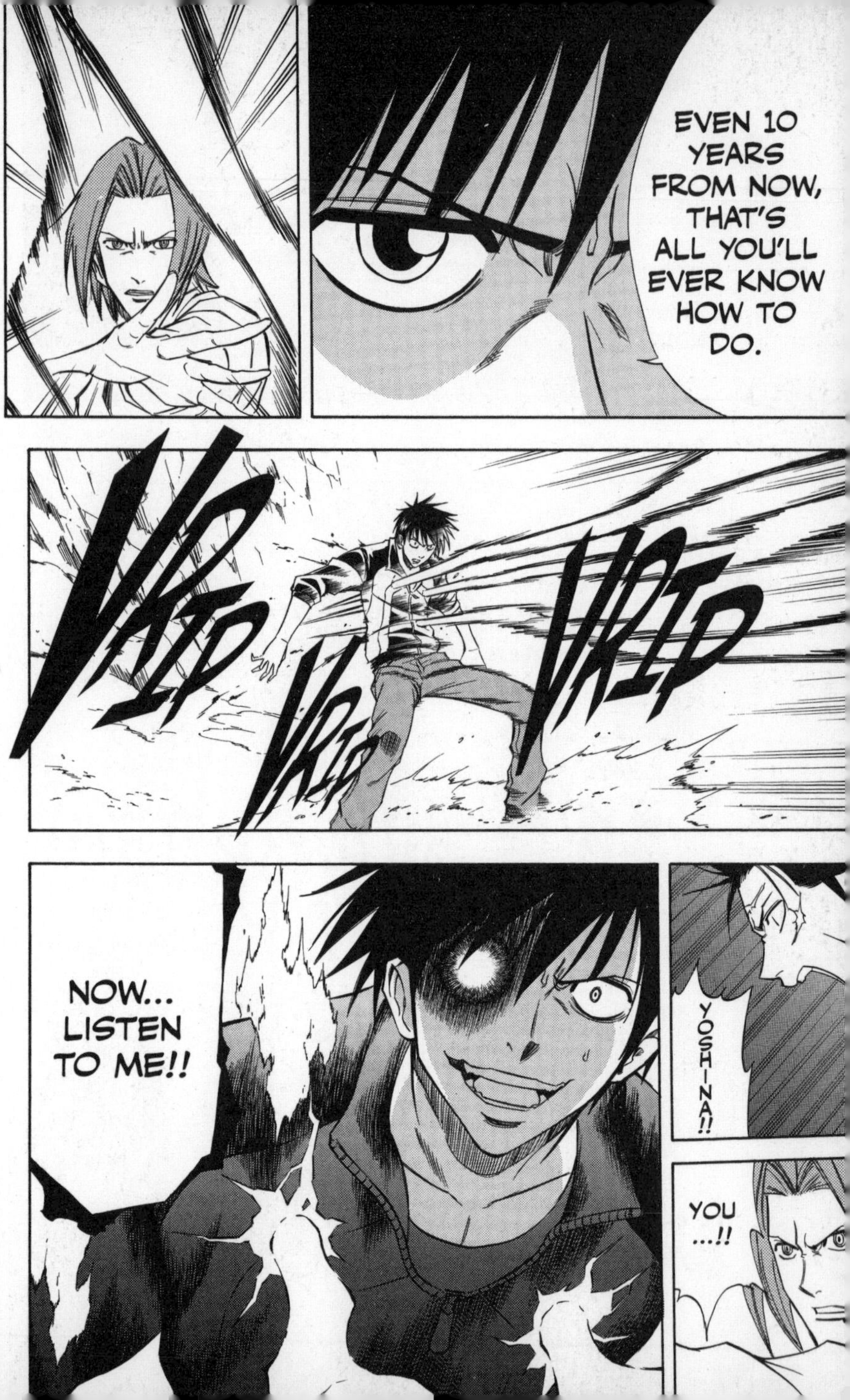
EVEN 10 YEARS FROM NOW, THAT'S ALL YOU'LL EVER KNOW HOW TO DO.
VRIP
VRIP
VRIP
YOSHINA!!
YOU ...!!
NOW... LISTEN TO ME!!

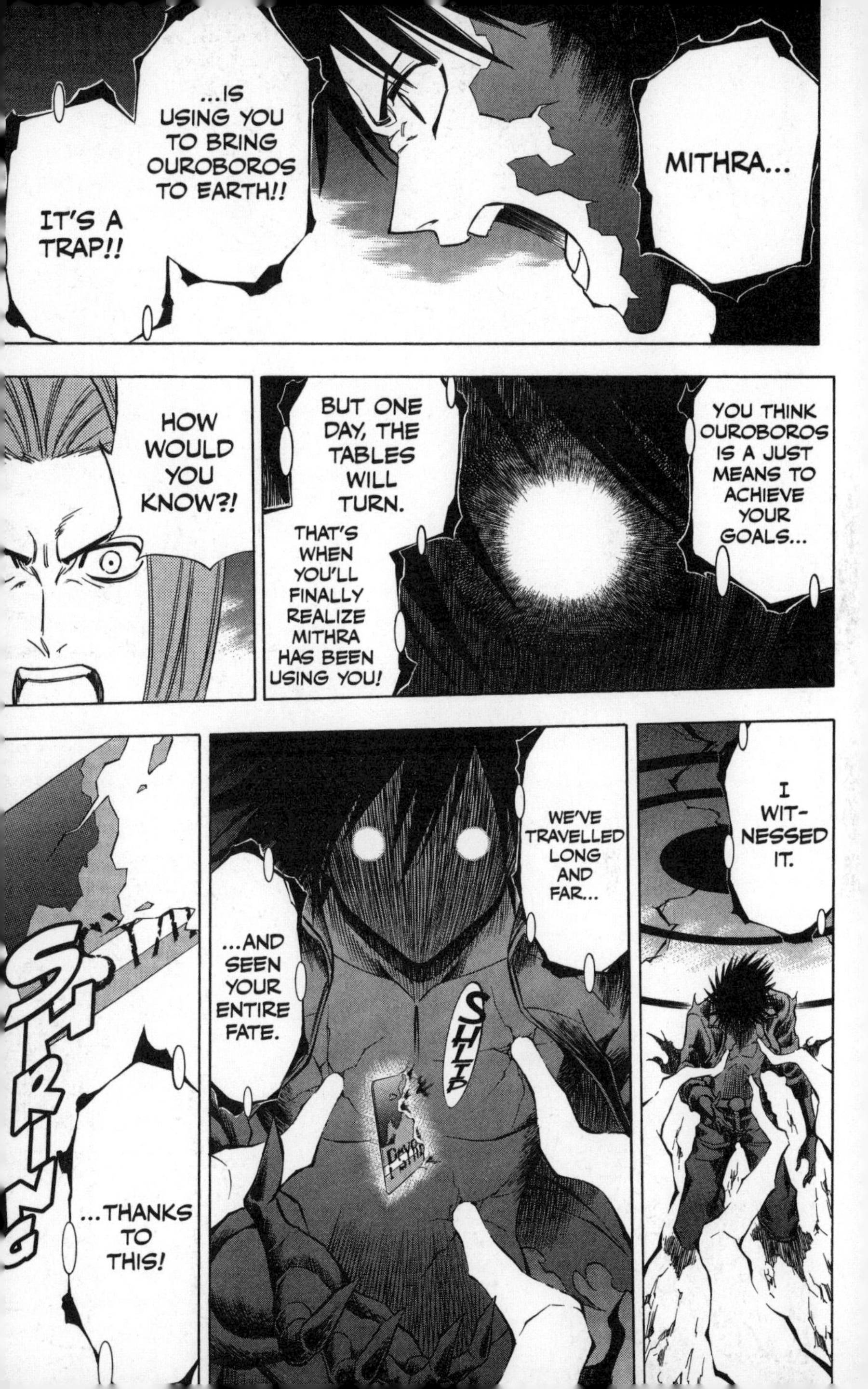
MITHRA...
...IS USING YOU TO BRING OUROBOROS TO EARTH!!
IT'S A TRAP!!
YOU THINK OUROBOROS IS A JUST MEANS TO ACHIEVE YOUR GOALS...
BUT ONE DAY, THE TABLES WILL TURN.
THAT'S WHEN YOU'LL FINALLY REALIZE MITHRA HAS BEEN USING YOU!
HOW WOULD YOU KNOW?!
I WIT-NESSED IT.
WE'VE TRAVELLED LONG AND FAR...
...AND SEEN YOUR ENTIRE FATE.
SHLIP
SHRING
...THANKS TO THIS!

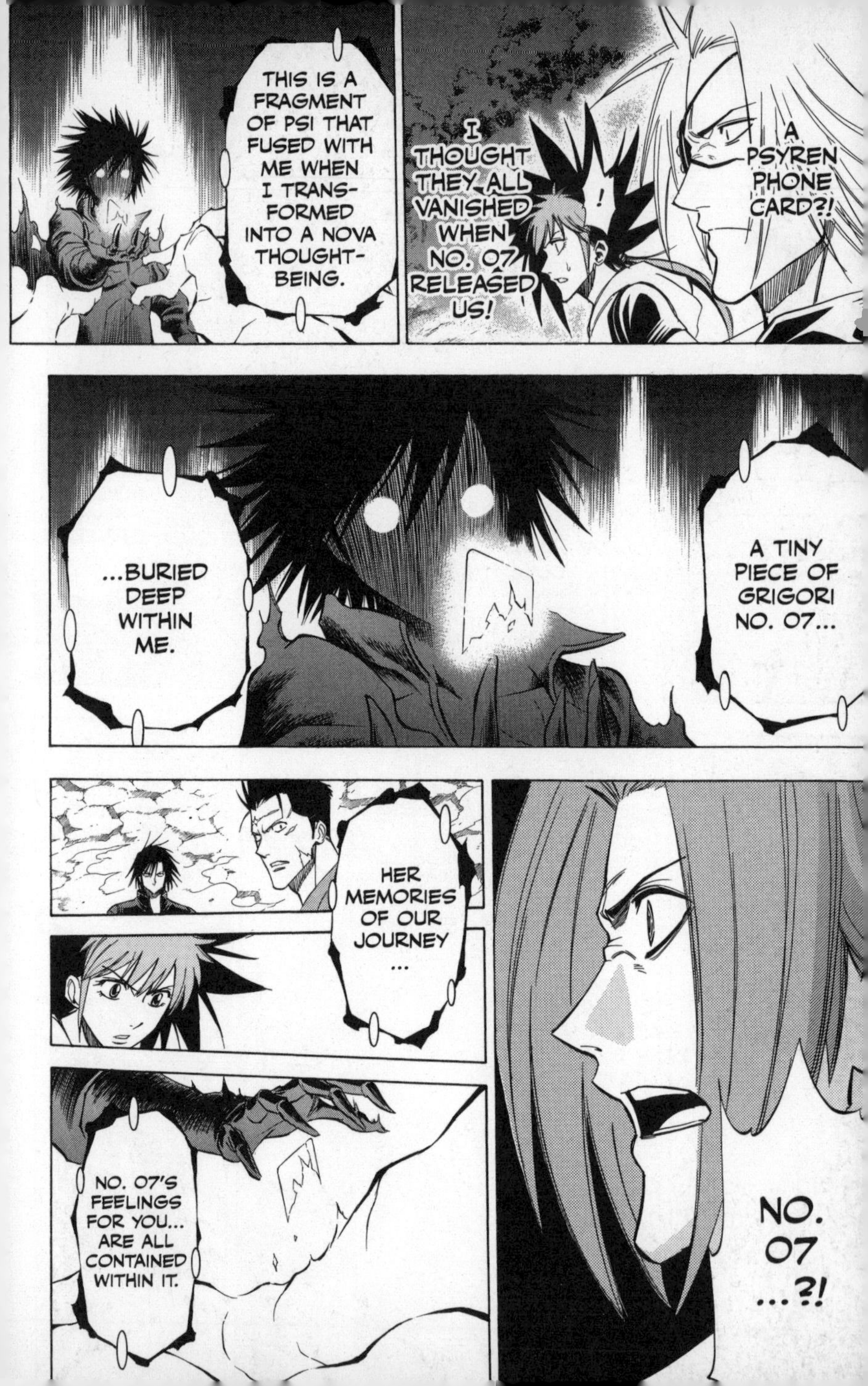
A PSYREN PHONE CARD?!
!
I THOUGHT THEY ALL VANISHED WHEN NO. 07 RELEASED US!
THIS IS A FRAGMENT OF PSI THAT FUSED WITH ME WHEN I TRANS-FORMED INTO A NOVA THOUGHT-BEING.
A TINY PIECE OF GRIGORI NO. 07...
...BURIED DEEP WITHIN ME.
NO. 07 ...?!
HER MEMORIES OF OUR JOURNEY ...
NO. 07'S FEELINGS FOR YOU... ARE ALL CONTAINED WITHIN IT.

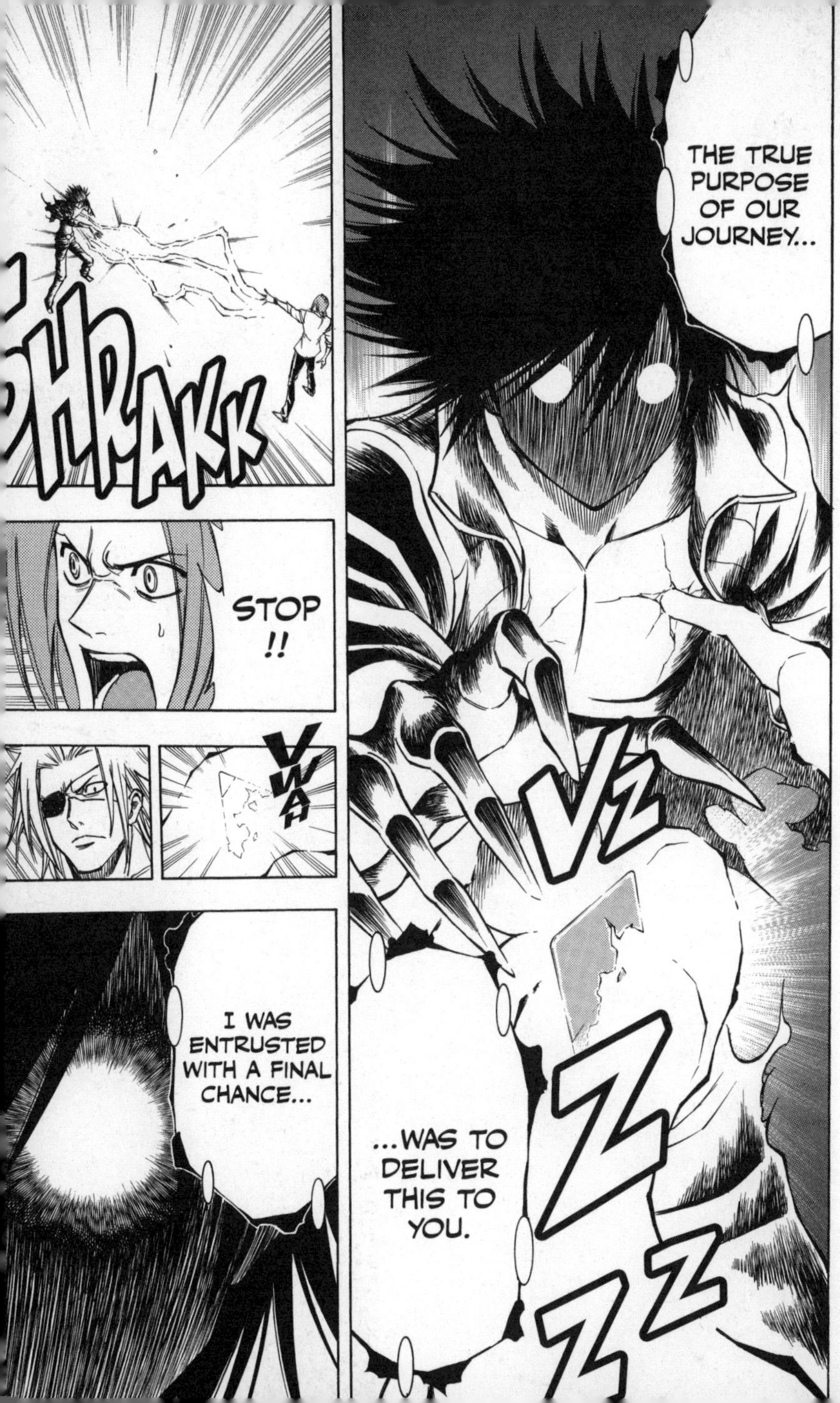
THE TRUE PURPOSE OF OUR JOURNEY...
VZZZZ
...WAS TO DELIVER THIS TO YOU.
PHRAKK
STOP!!
VWAH
I WAS ENTRUSTED WITH A FINAL CHANCE...

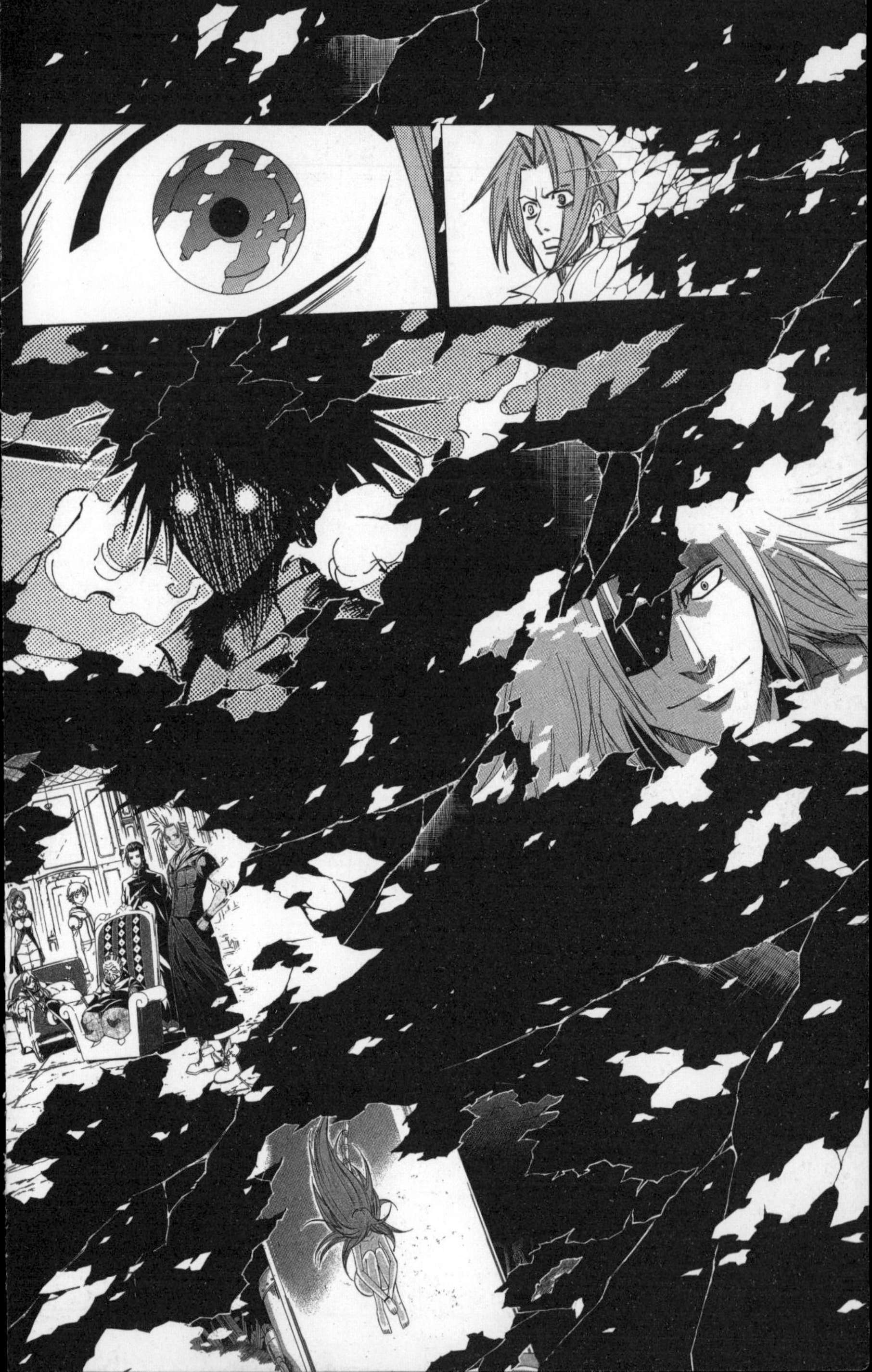

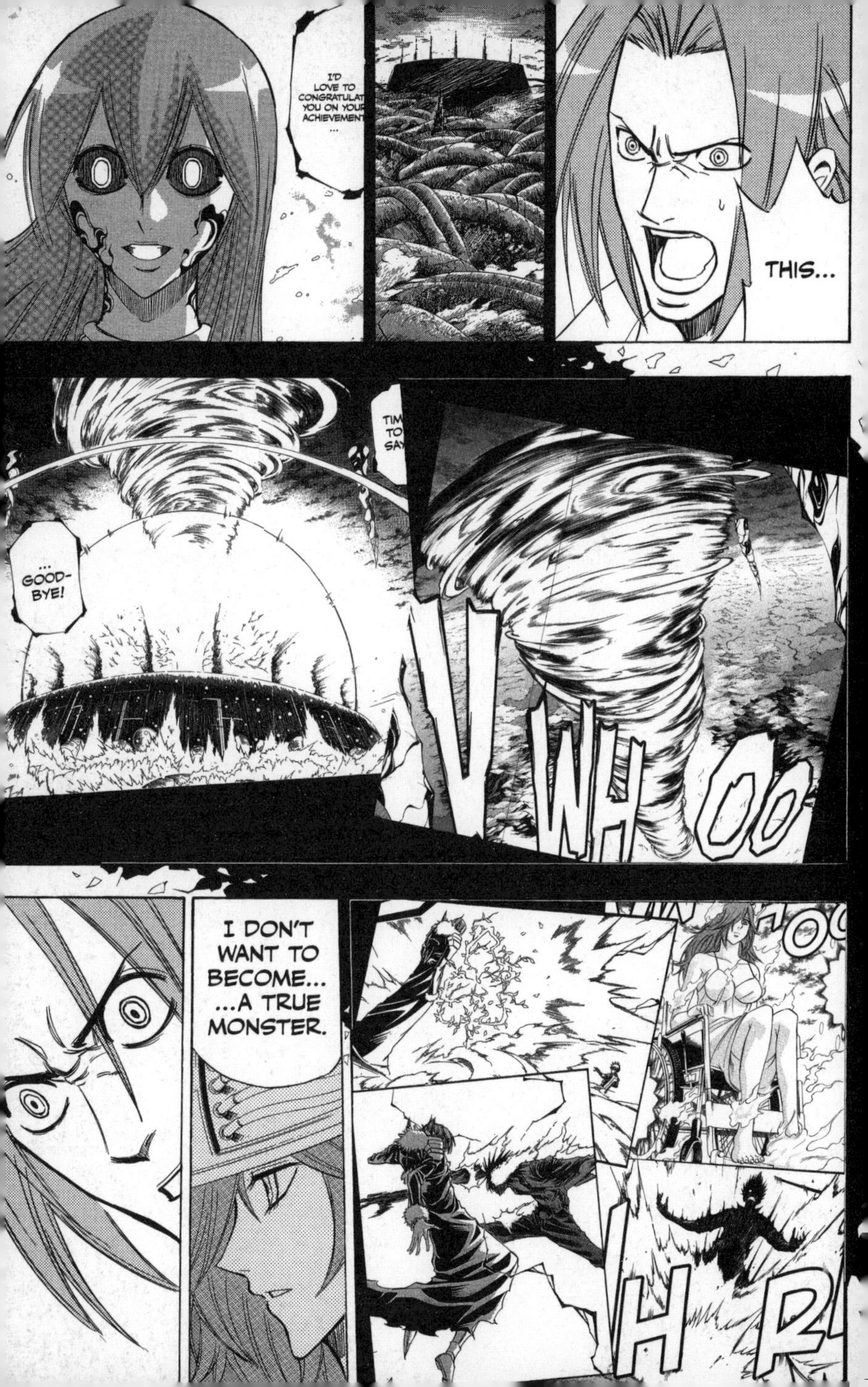
THIS...
I'D LOVE TO CONGRATULAT YOU ON YOUR ACHIEVEMENT ...
VWHOO-
...GOOD-BYE!
I DON'T WANT TO BECOME... ...A TRUE MONSTER.

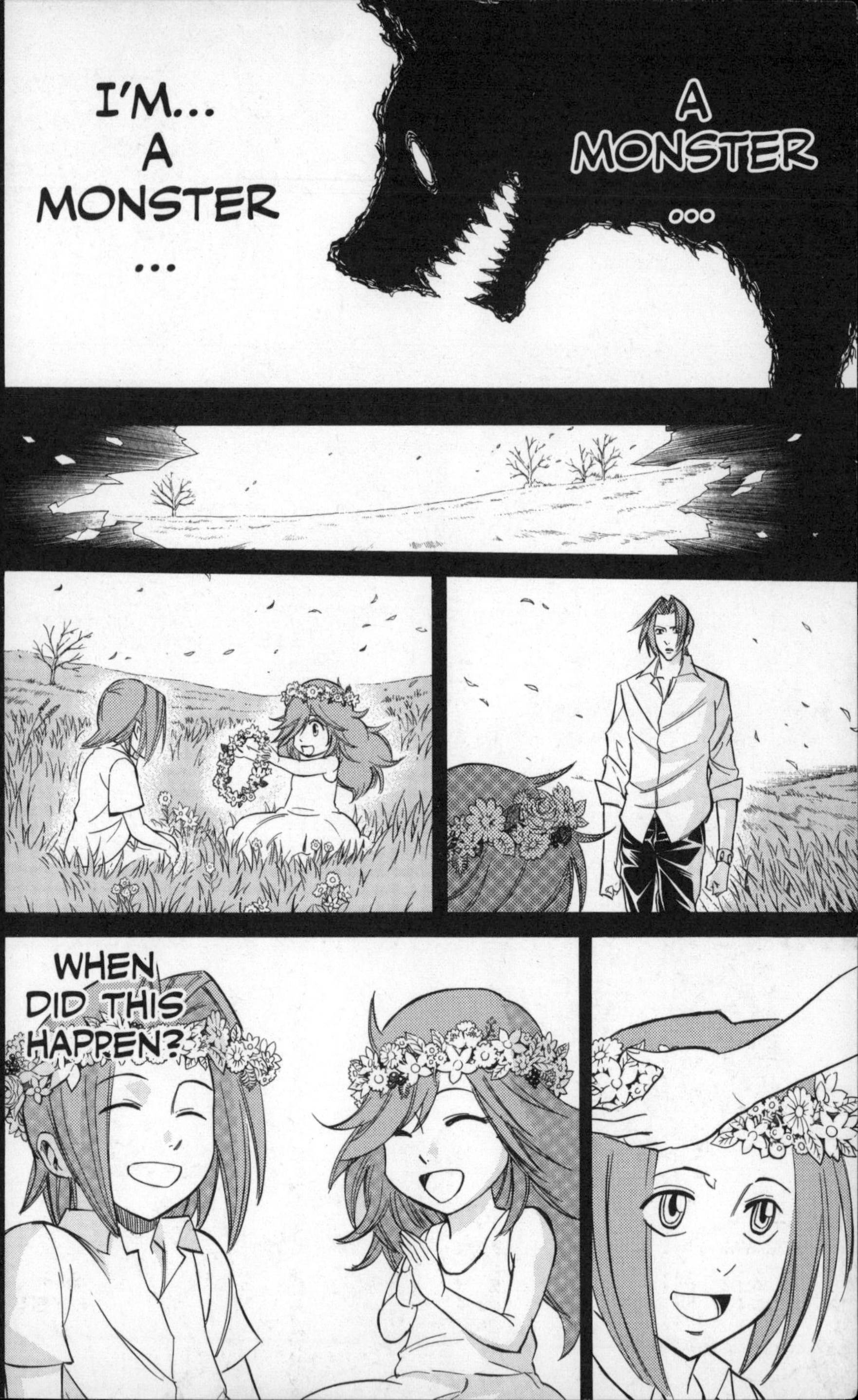
A MONSTER ...
I'M... A MONSTER ...
WHEN DID THIS HAPPEN?

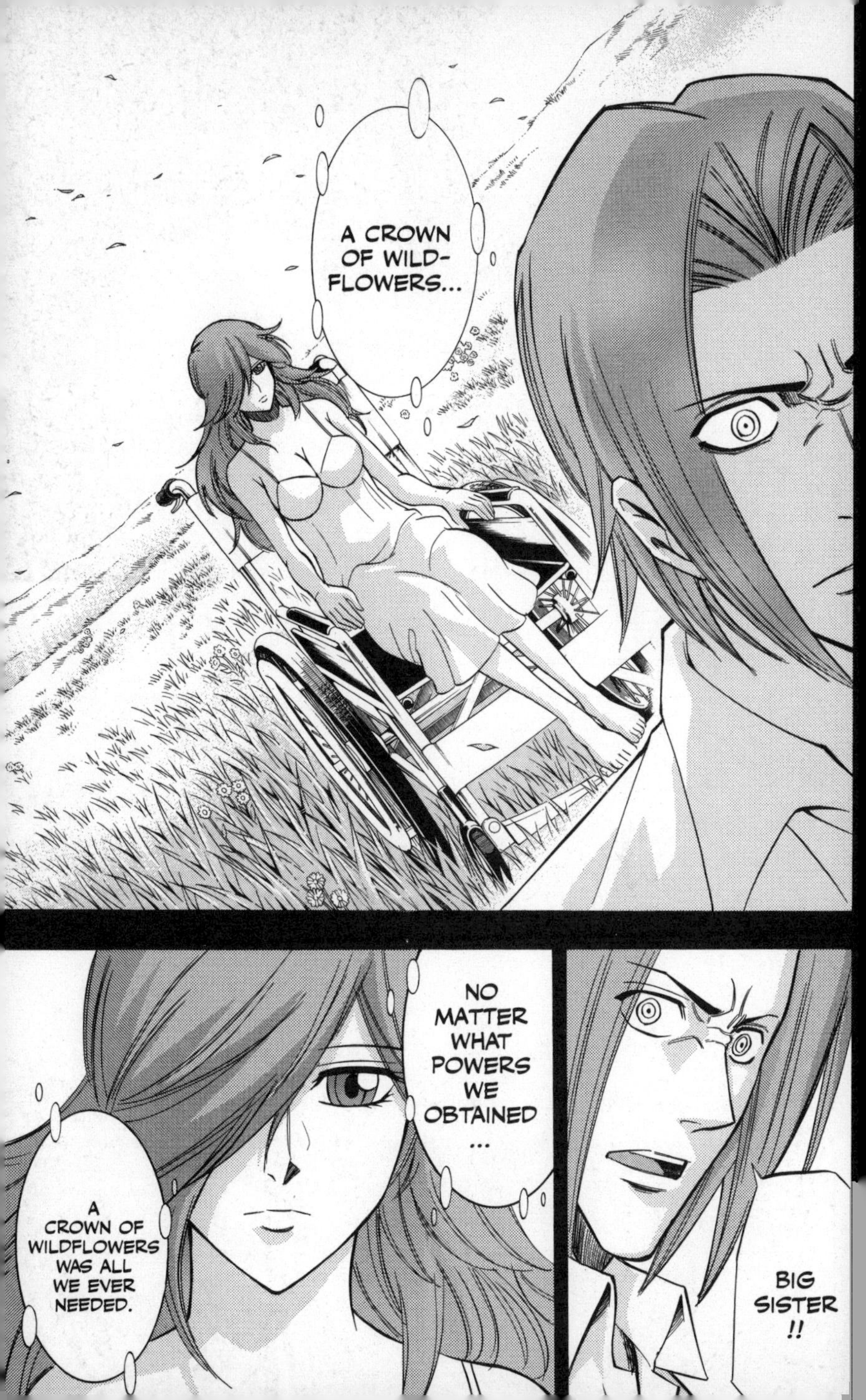
A CROWN OF WILD-FLOWERS...
BIG SISTER!!
NO MATTER WHAT POWERS WE OBTAINED...
A CROWN OF WILDFLOWERS WAS ALL WE EVER NEEDED.

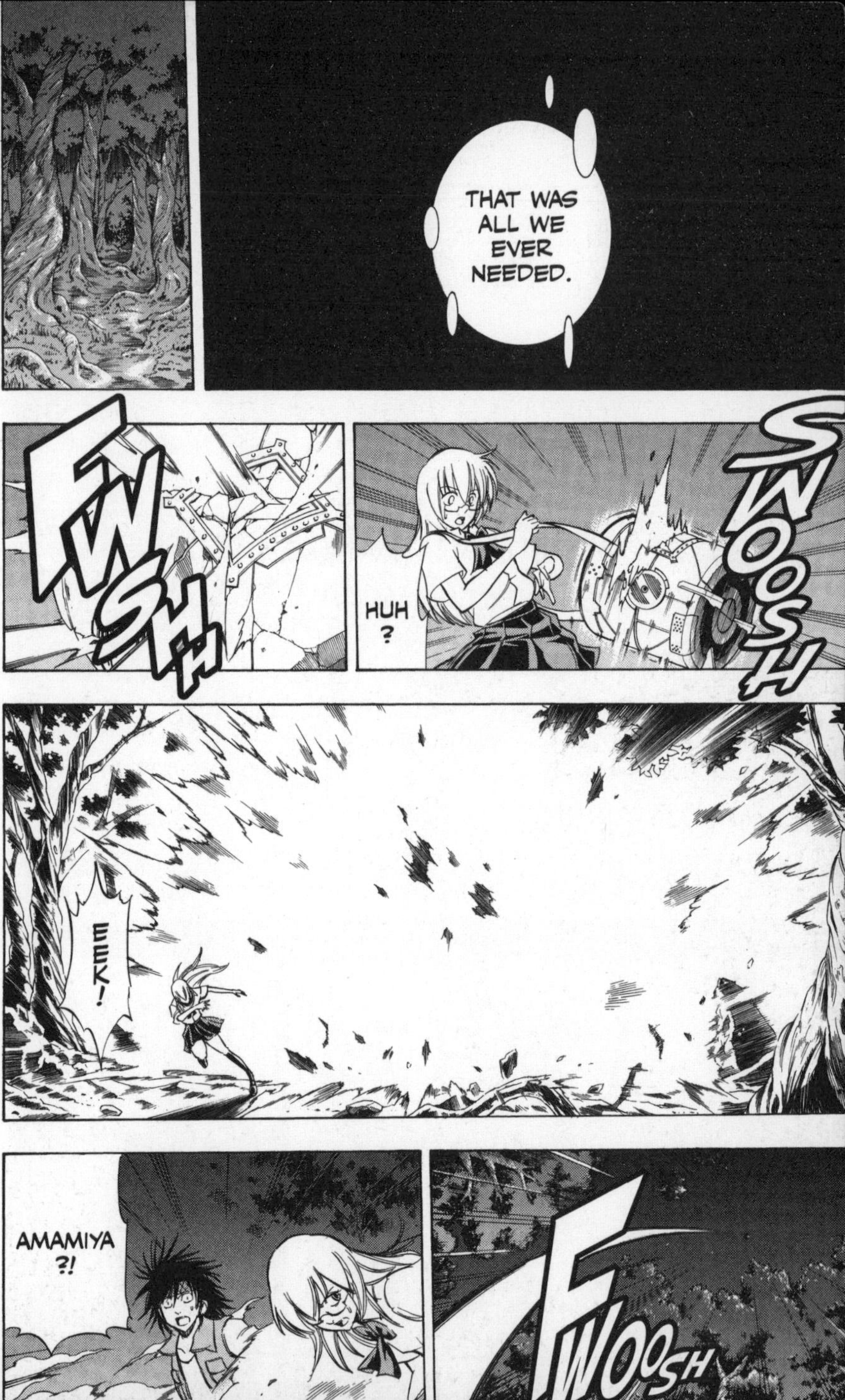
THAT WAS ALL WE EVER NEEDED.
SWOOSH
HUH?
FWSHH
EEK!
FWOOSH
AMAMIYA?!

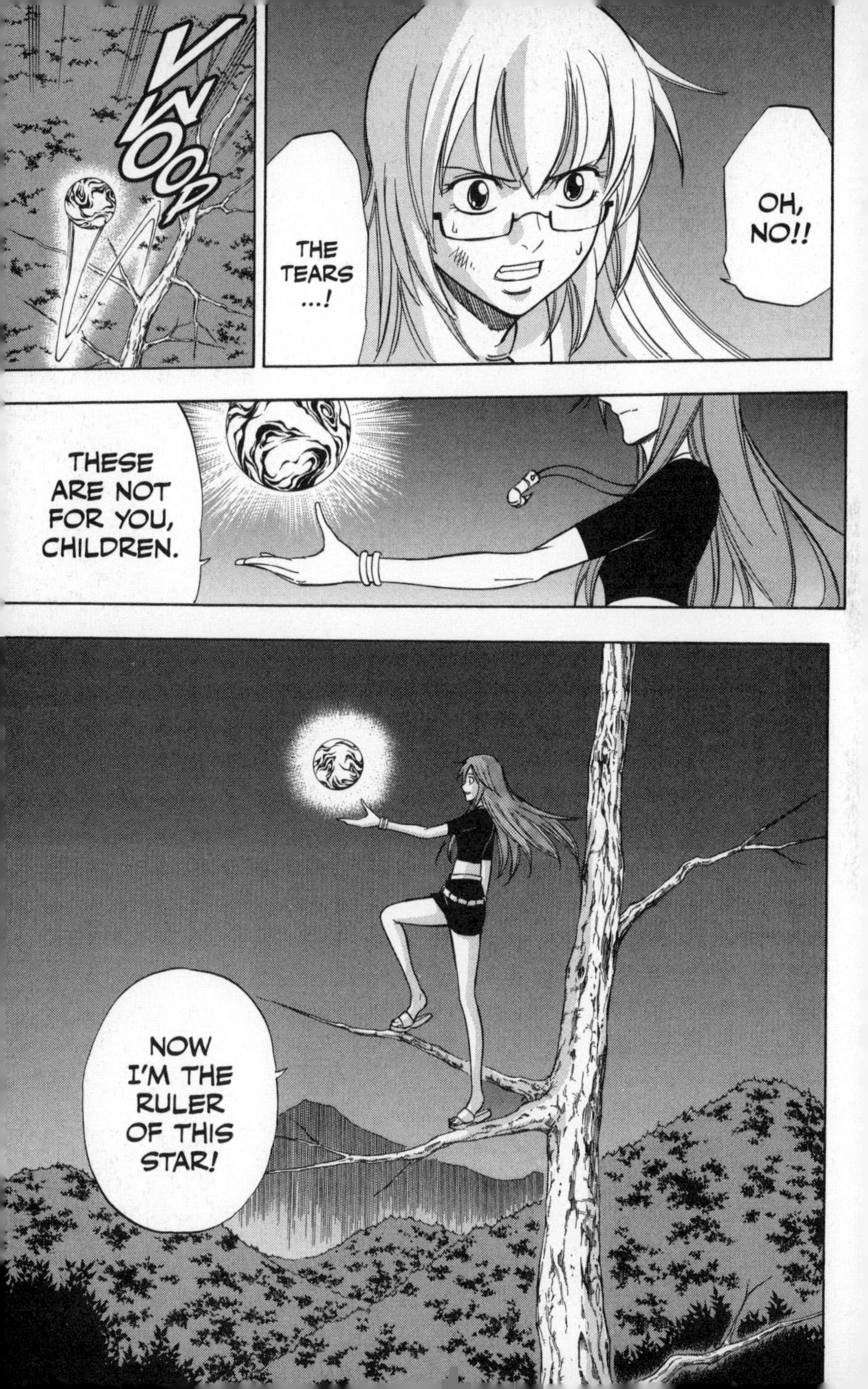
OH, NO!!
THE TEARS ...!
VNOOOP
THESE ARE NOT FOR YOU, CHILDREN.
NOW I'M THE RULER OF THIS STAR!

Mutters and mumblings...

NEXT TIME, I'D LIKE TO DO SOMETHING A BIT
MORE LIGHT AND FUN.

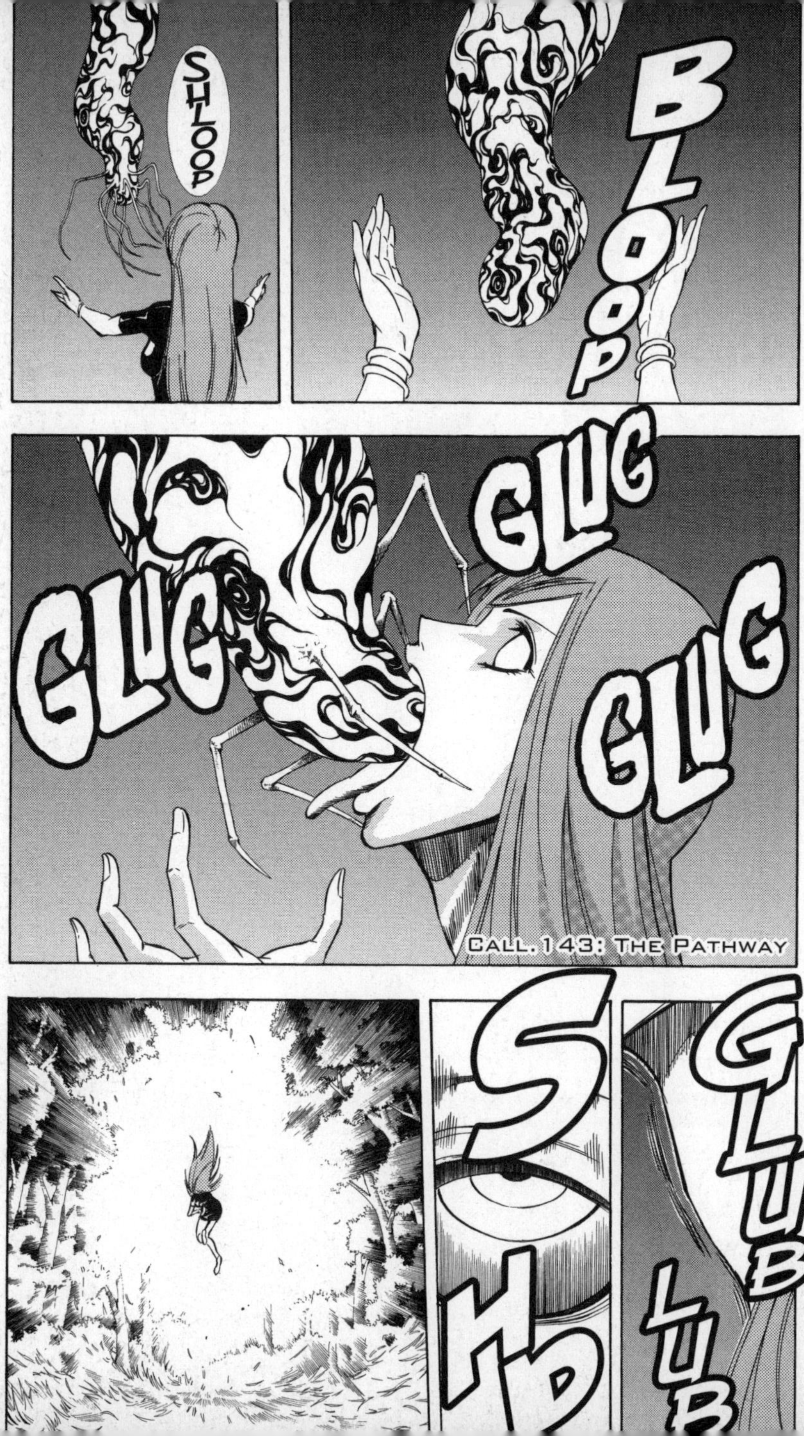
BLOOP
SHLOOP
GLUG
GLUG
GLUG
CALL. 143: THE PATHWAY
GLUB LUB
SHD

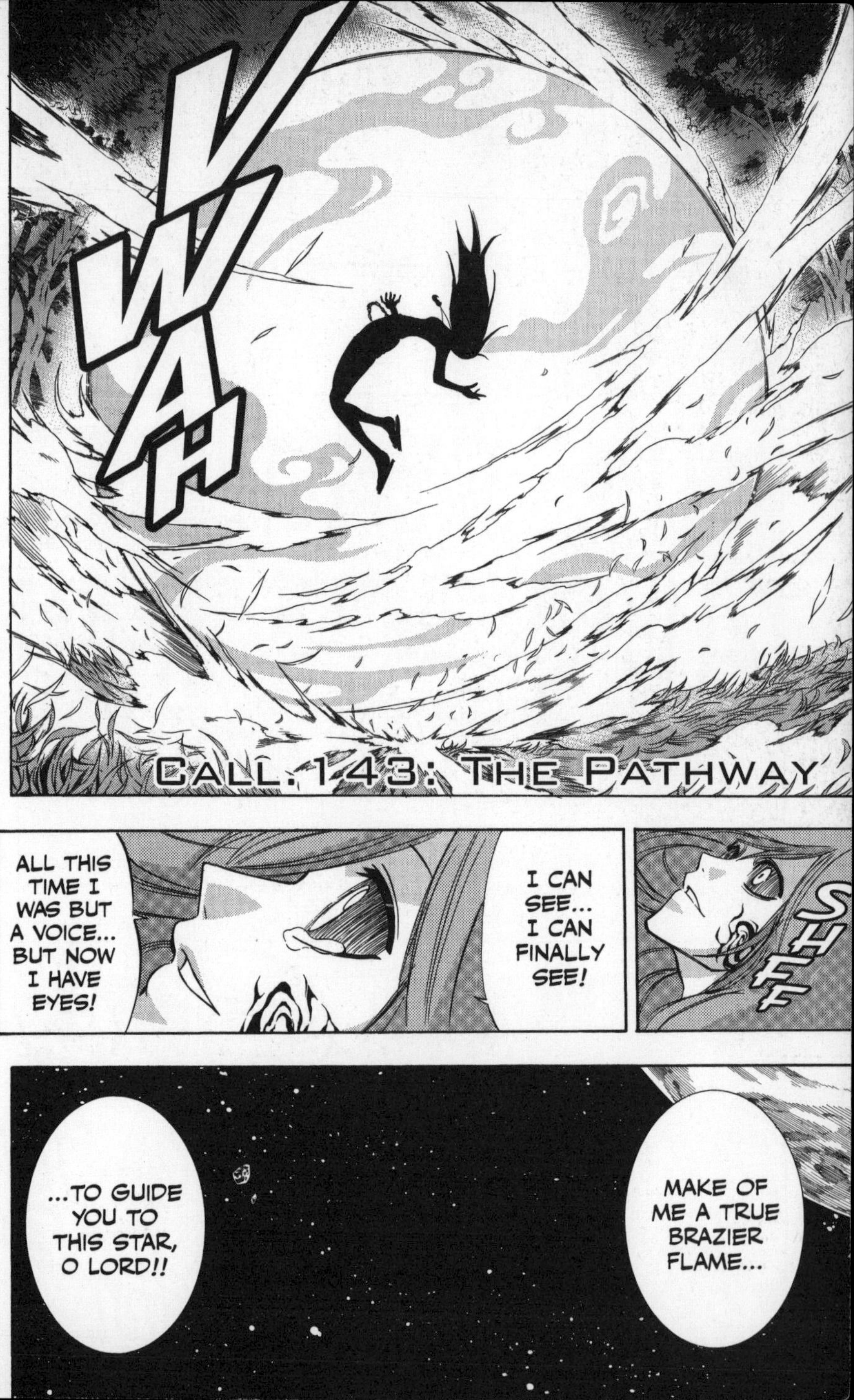
WAH
CALL.143: THE PATHWAY
SHFF
I CAN SEE... I CAN FINALLY SEE!
ALL THIS TIME I WAS BUT A VOICE... BUT NOW I HAVE EYES!
MAKE OF ME A TRUE BRAZIER FLAME...
...TO GUIDE YOU TO THIS STAR, O LORD!!

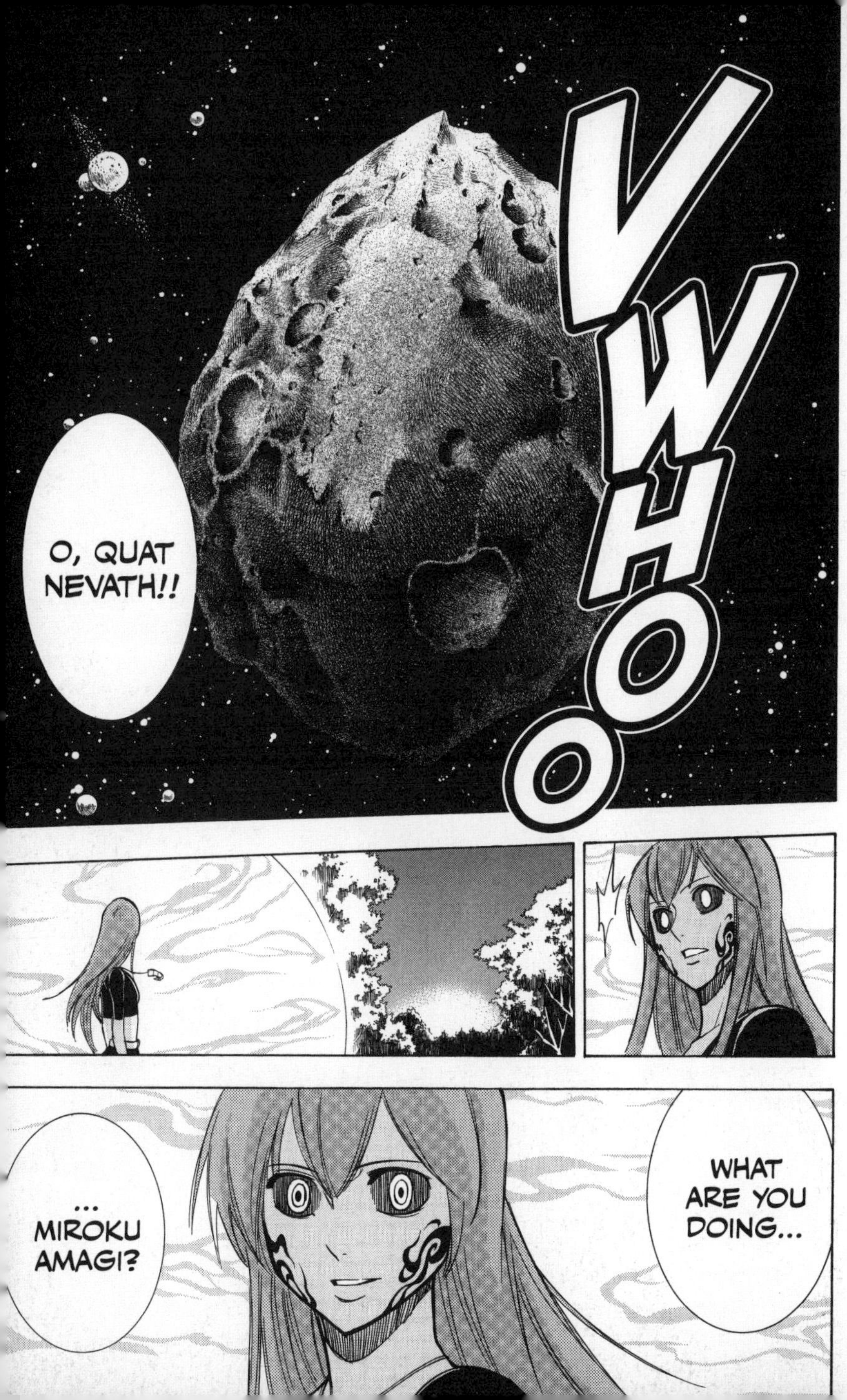
VWHOO
O, QUAT NEVATH!!
WHAT ARE YOU DOING...
...MIROKU AMAGI?

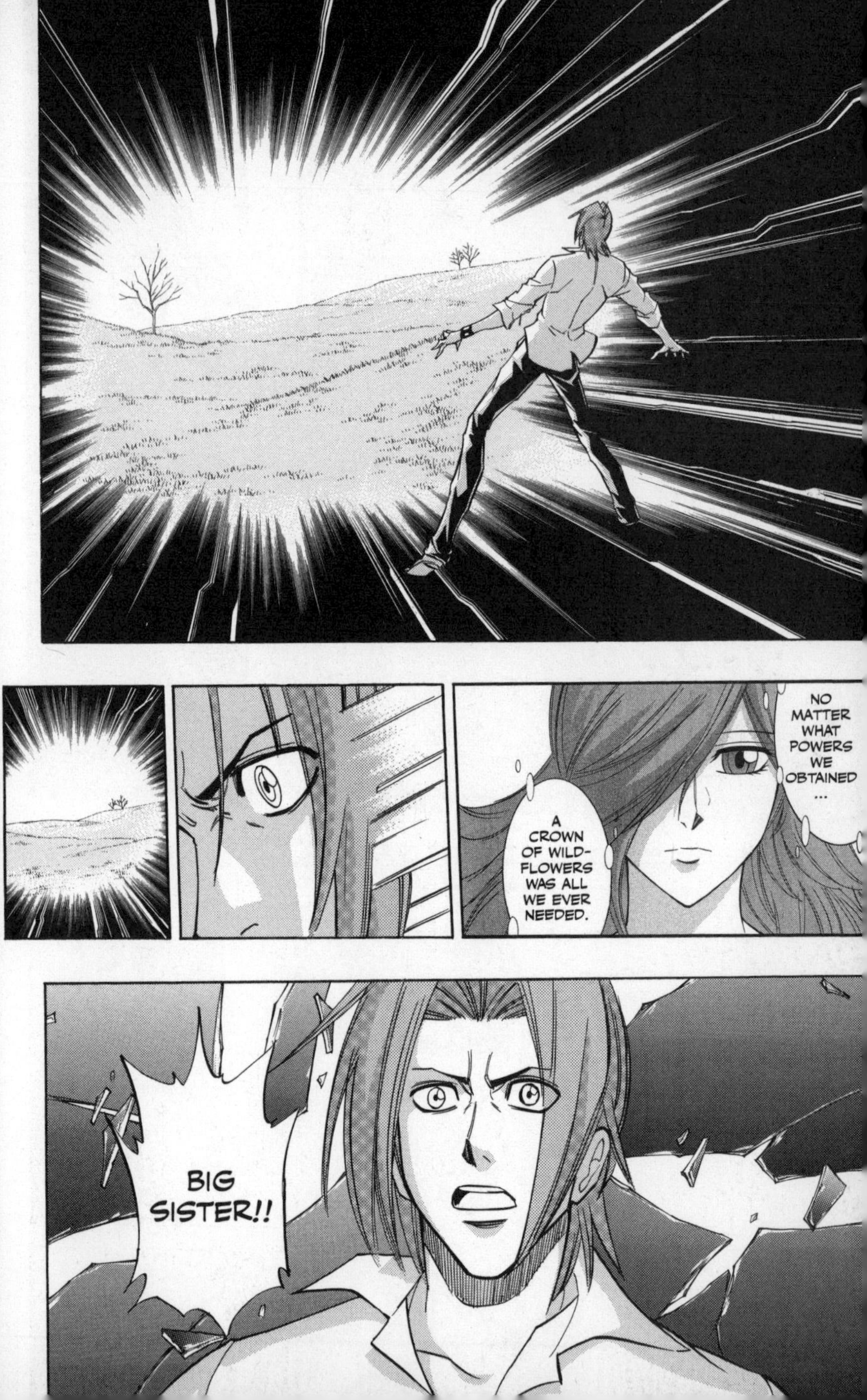
NO MATTER WHAT POWERS WE OBTAINED...
A CROWN OF WILD-FLOWERS WAS ALL WE EVER NEEDED.
BIG SISTER!!

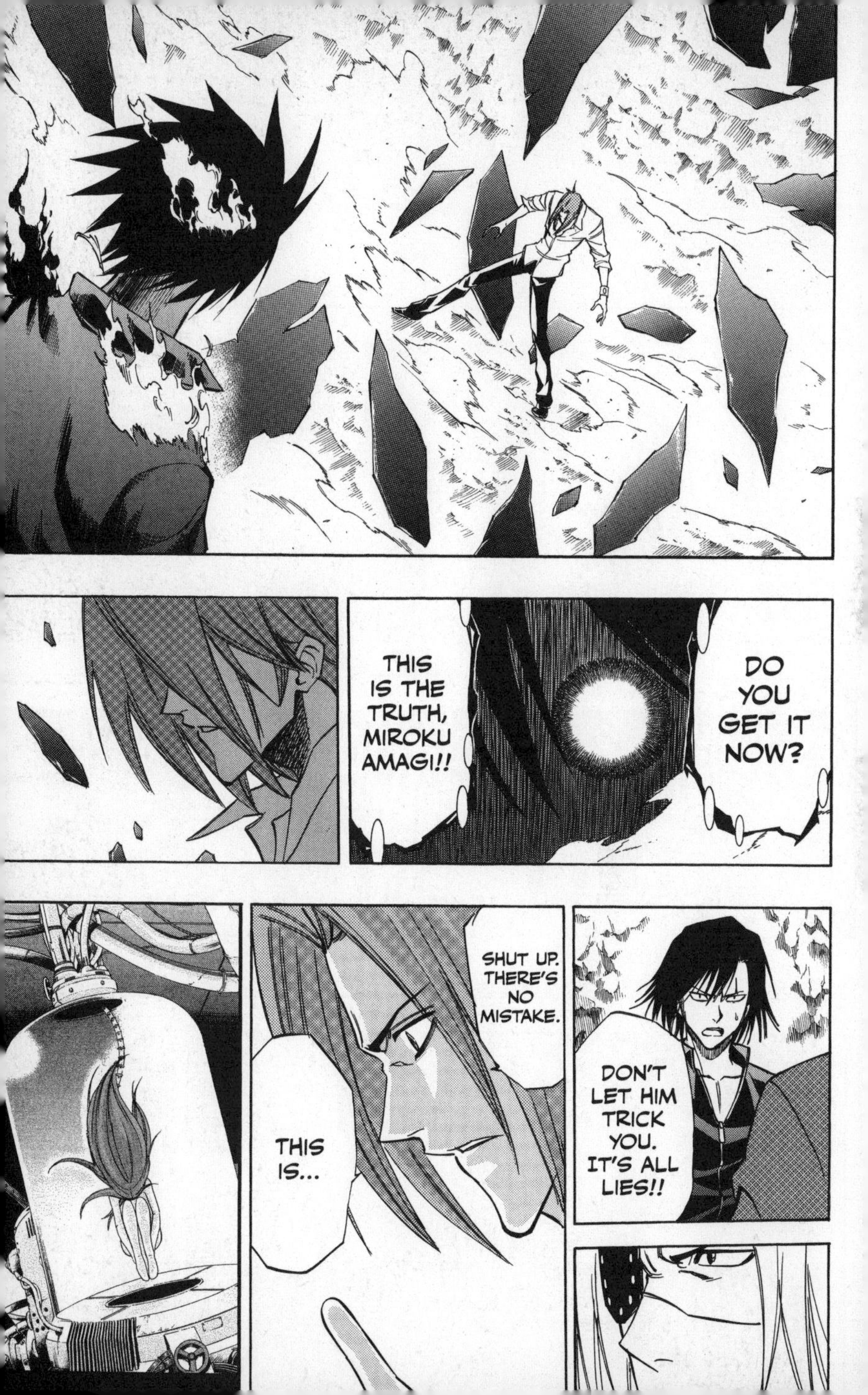
DO YOU GET IT NOW?
THIS IS THE TRUTH, MIROKU AMAGI!!
DON'T LET HIM TRICK YOU. IT'S ALL LIES!!
SHUT UP. THERE'S NO MISTAKE.
THIS IS...

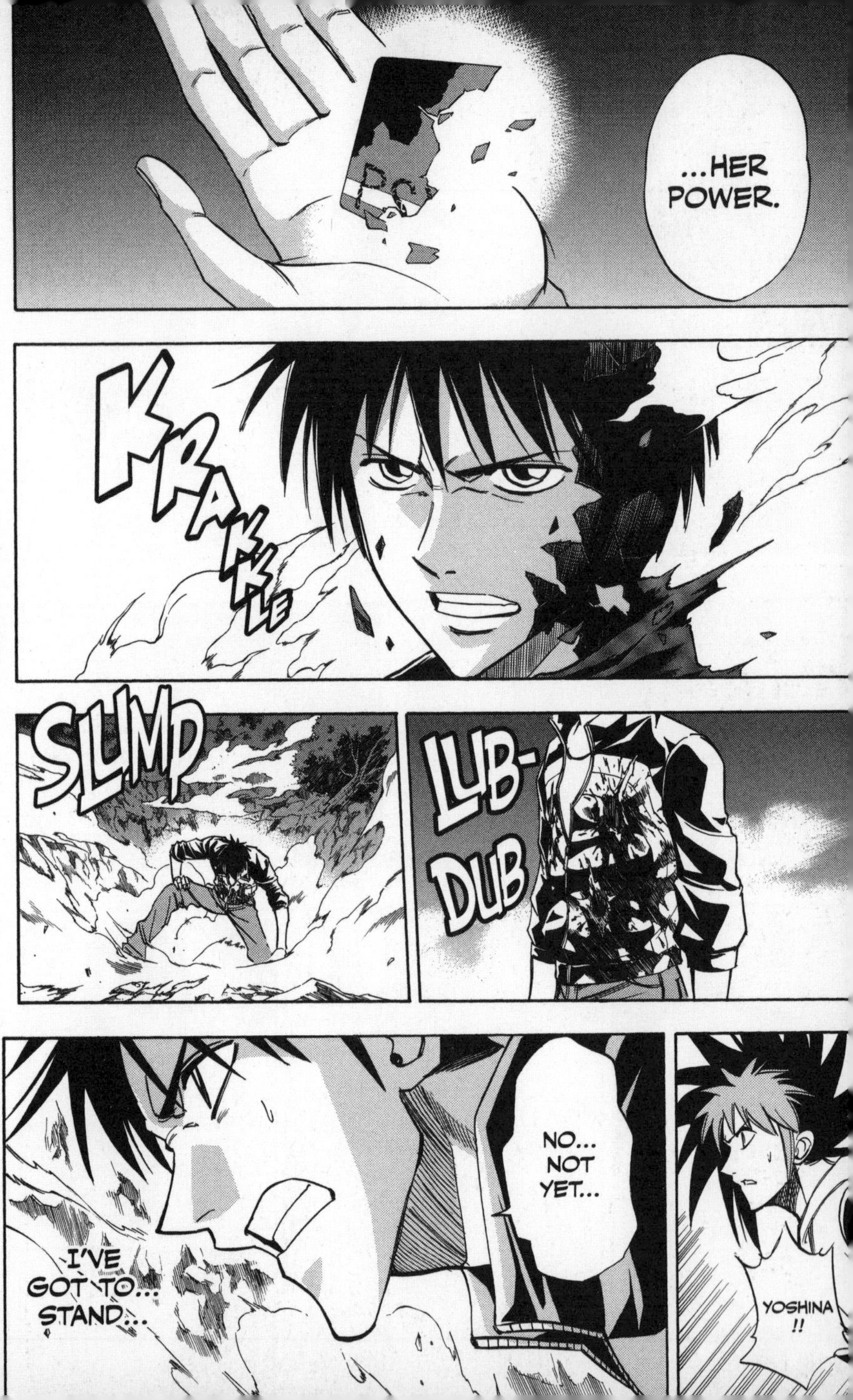
...HER POWER.
KRAKKLE
SLUMP
LUB-DUB
YOSHINA!!
NO... NOT YET...
I'VE GOT TO... STAND...

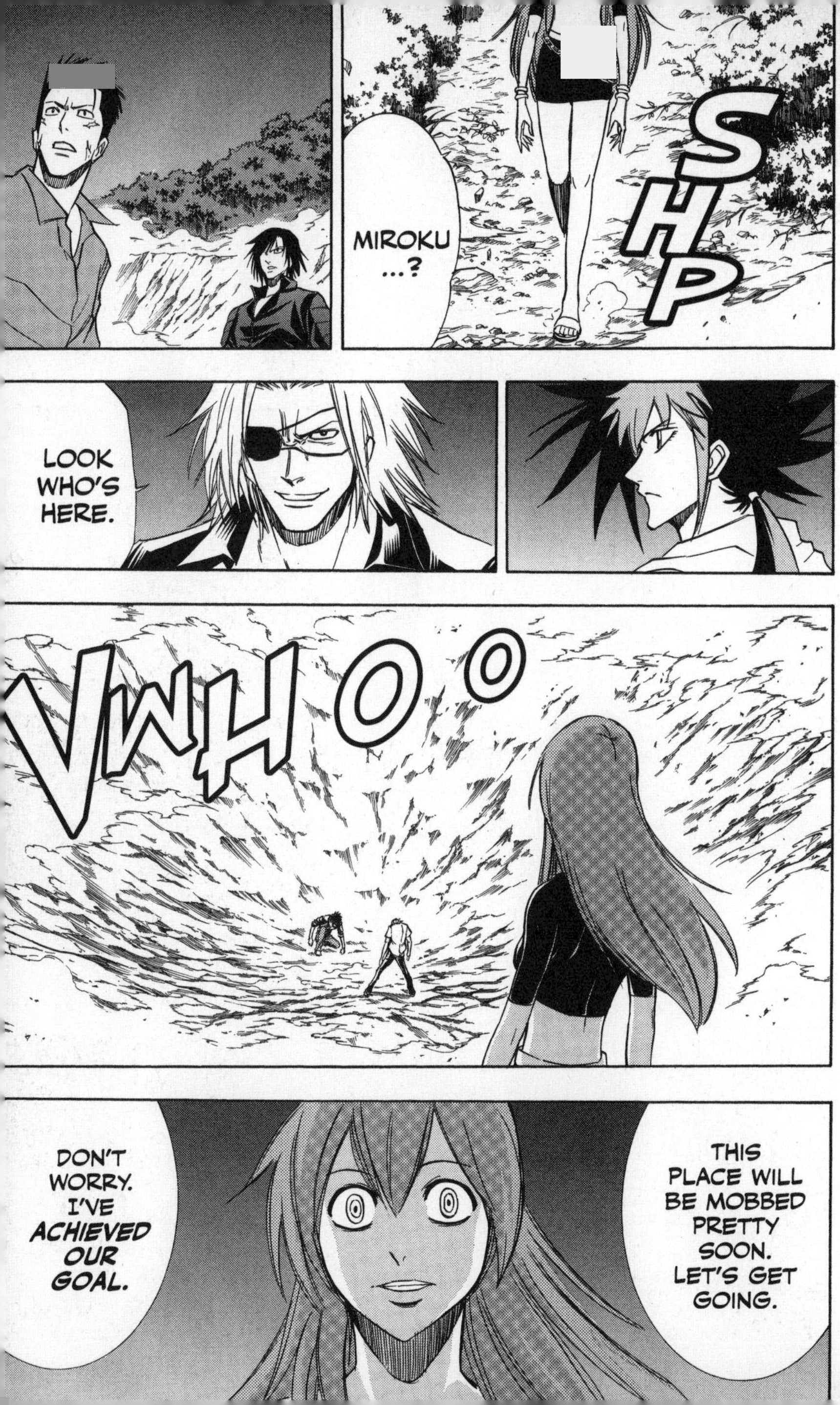
MIROKU ...?
SHP
LOOK WHO'S HERE.
VWHOOO
THIS PLACE WILL BE MOBBED PRETTY SOON. LET'S GET GOING.
DON'T WORRY. I'VE ACHIEVED OUR GOAL.

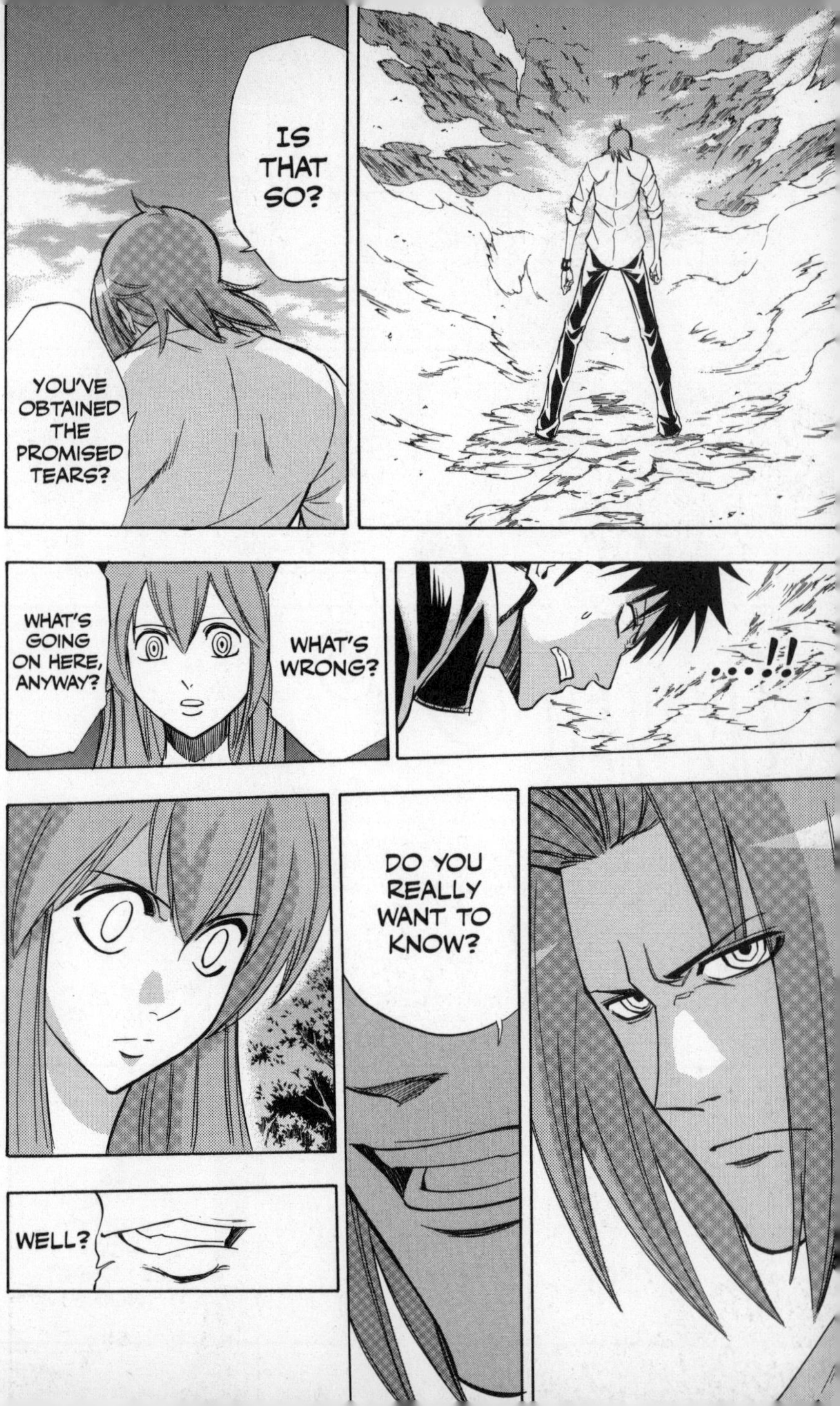
IS THAT SO?
YOU'VE OBTAINED THE PROMISED TEARS?
...!!
WHAT'S WRONG?
WHAT'S GOING ON HERE, ANYWAY?
DO YOU REALLY WANT TO KNOW?
WELL?

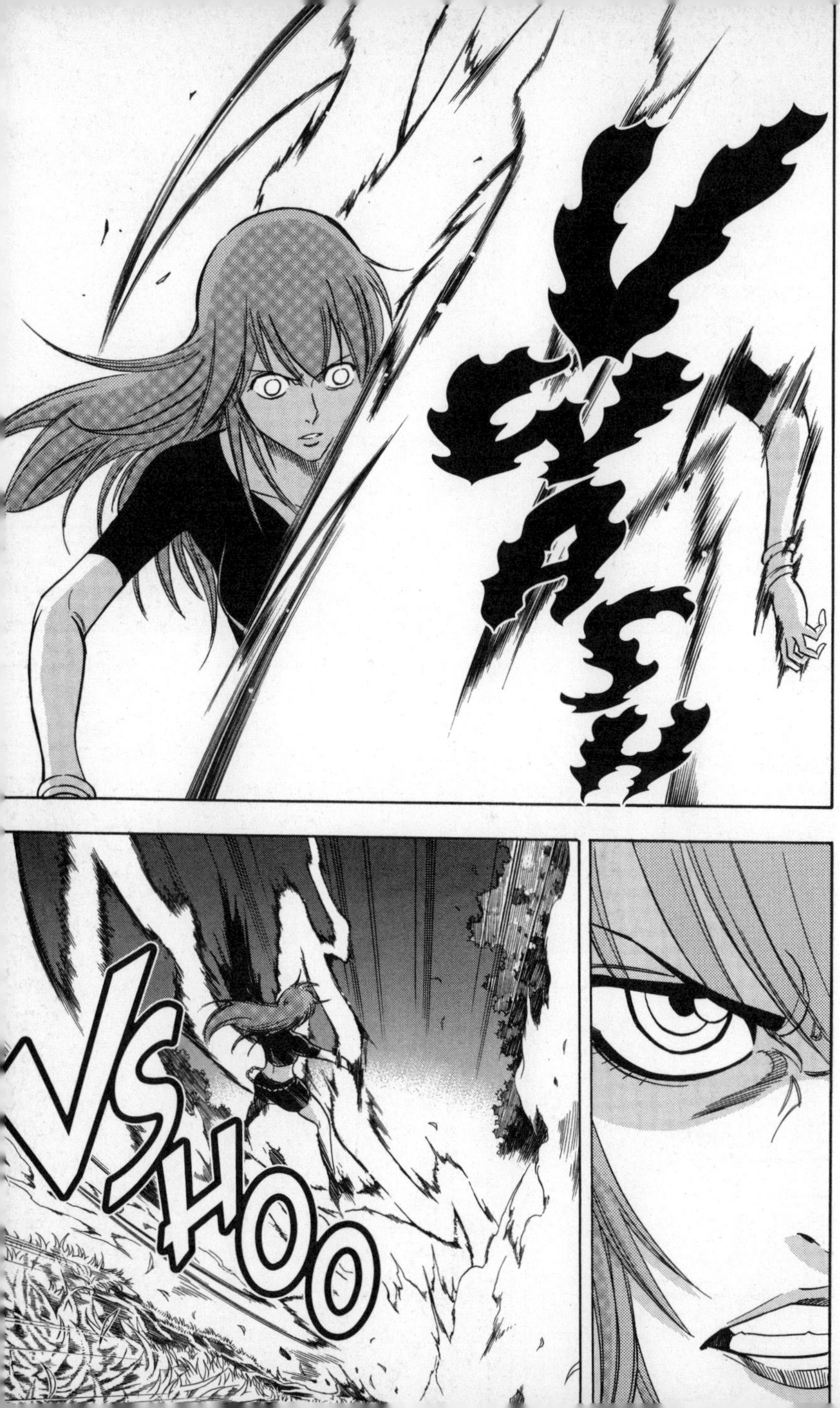
VSHOO

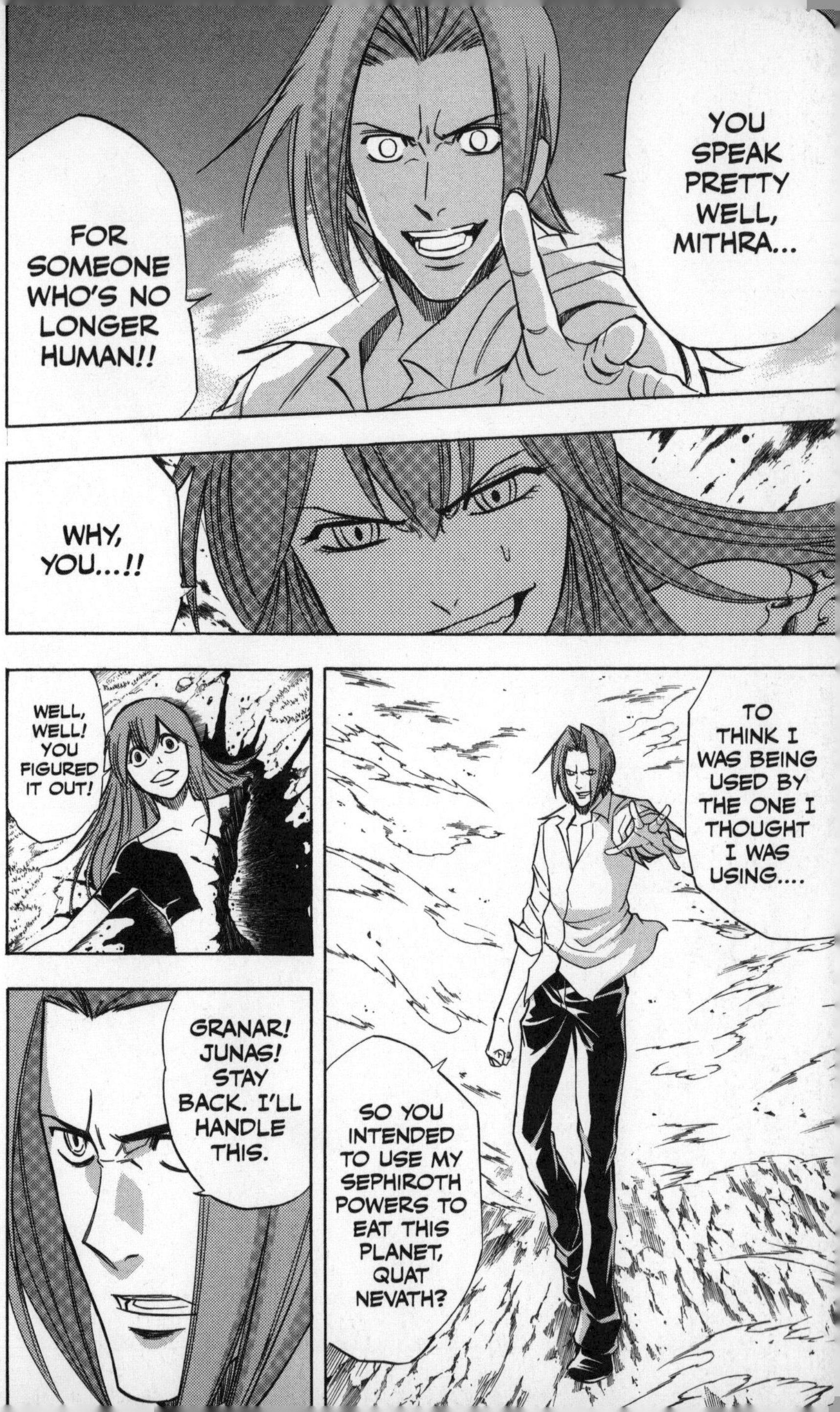
YOU SPEAK PRETTY WELL, MITHRA...
FOR SOMEONE WHO'S NO LONGER HUMAN!!
WHY, YOU...!!
TO THINK I WAS BEING USED BY THE ONE I THOUGHT I WAS USING....
SO YOU INTENDED TO USE MY SEPHIROTH POWERS TO EAT THIS PLANET, QUAT NEVATH?
WELL, WELL! YOU FIGURED IT OUT!
GRANAR! JUNAS! STAY BACK. I'LL HANDLE THIS.

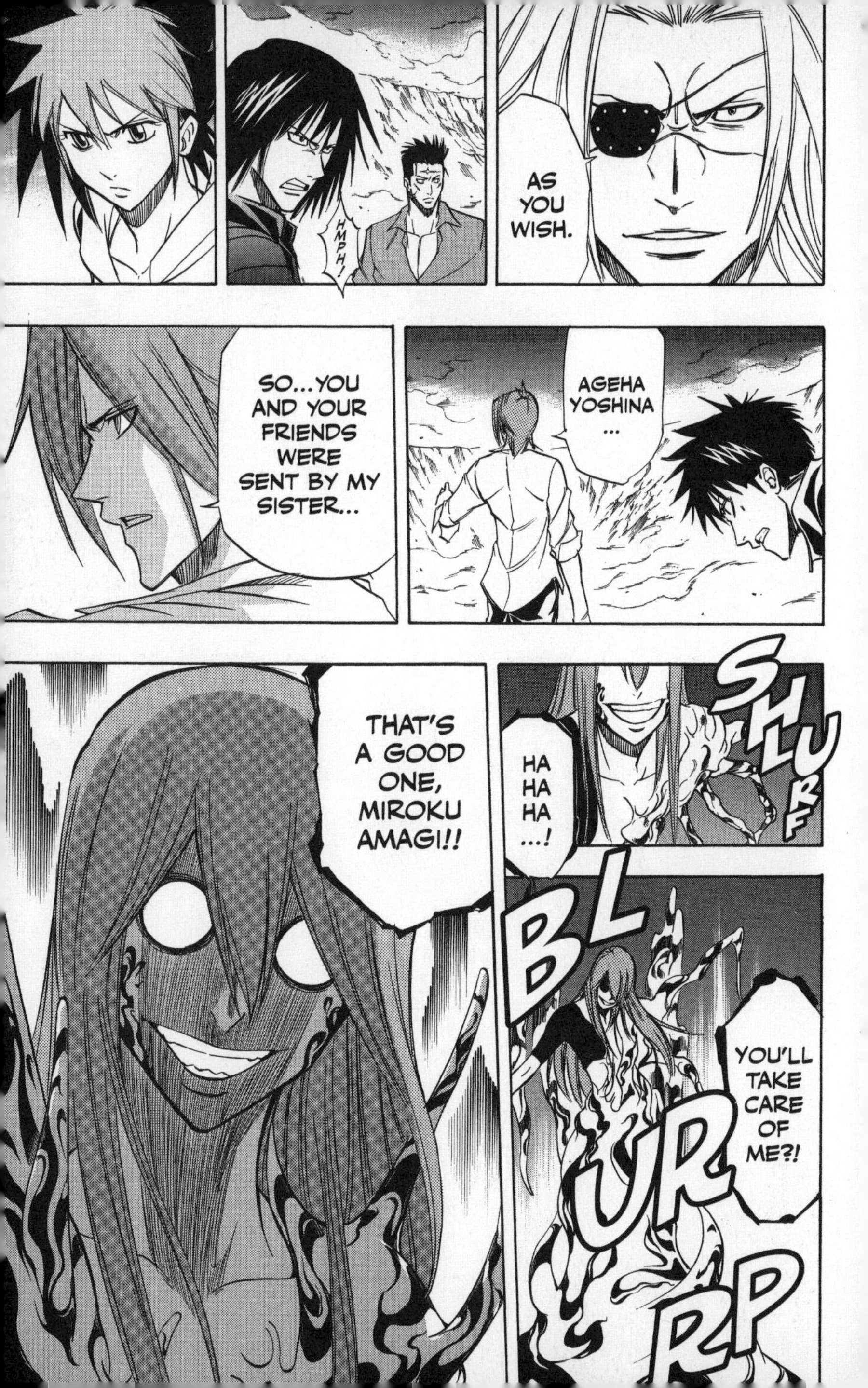
AS YOU WISH.
HMPH!
AGEHA YOSHINA ...
SO...YOU AND YOUR FRIENDS WERE SENT BY MY SISTER...
SHLURF
HA HA HA ...!
BLURRP
YOU'LL TAKE CARE OF ME?!
THAT'S A GOOD ONE, MIROKU AMAGI!!

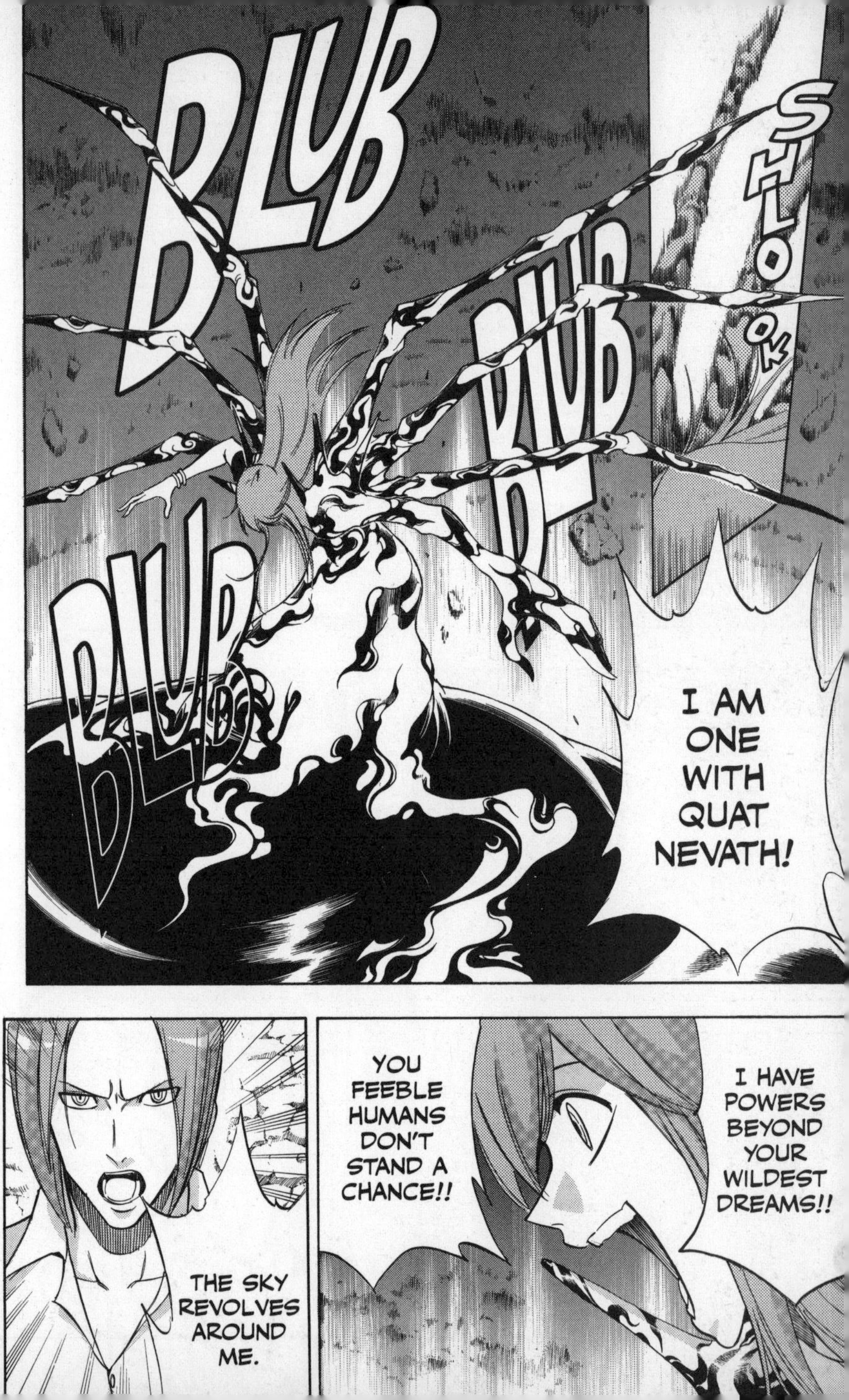
SHLOOK
BLUB
BLUB
BLUB
BLUB
I AM ONE WITH QUAT NEVATH!
I HAVE POWERS BEYOND YOUR WILDEST DREAMS!!
YOU FEEBLE HUMANS DON'T STAND A CHANCE!!
THE SKY REVOLVES AROUND ME.

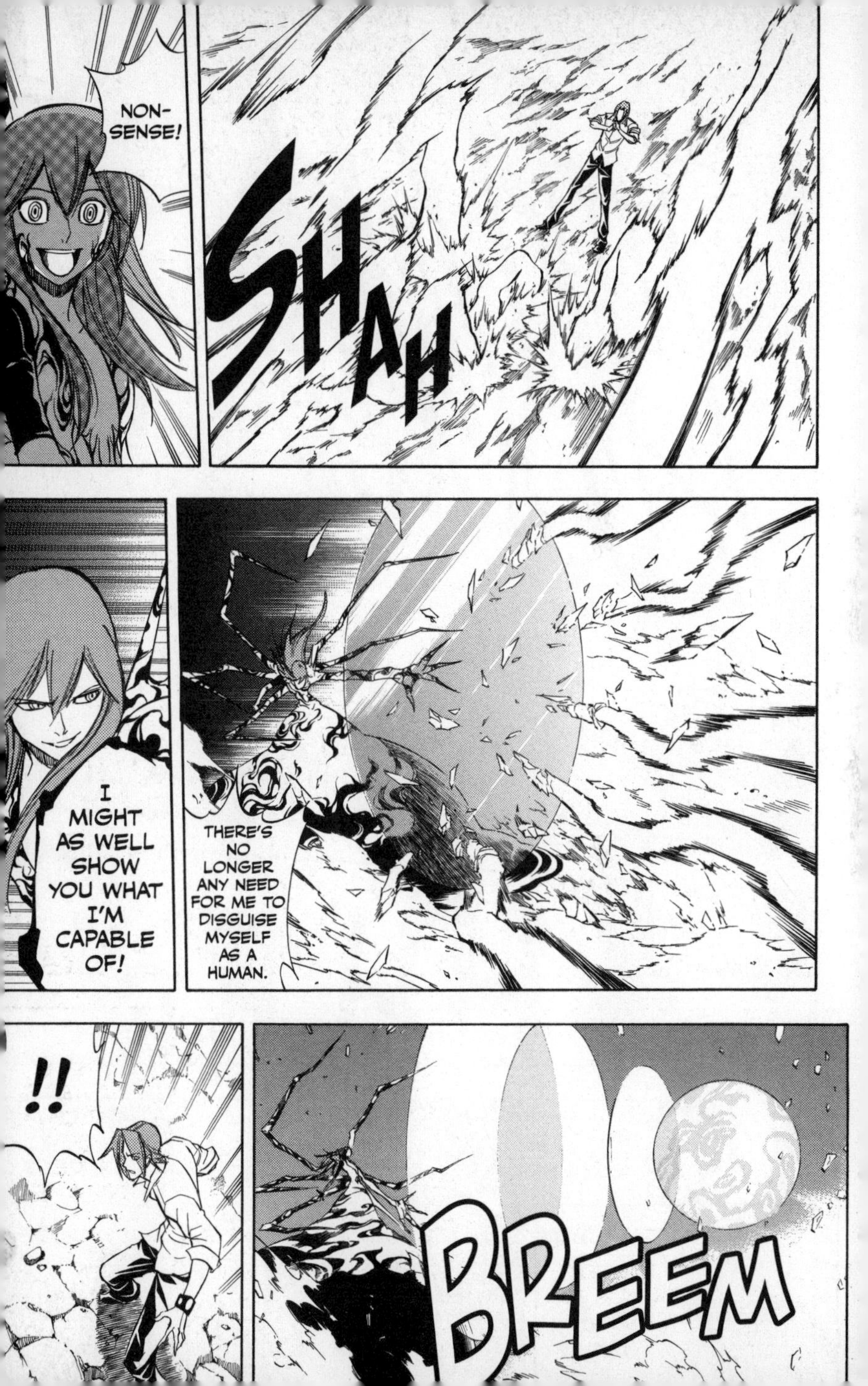
SHAH
NON-SENSE!
THERE'S NO LONGER ANY NEED FOR ME TO DISGUISE MYSELF AS A HUMAN.
I MIGHT AS WELL SHOW YOU WHAT I'M CAPABLE OF!
BREEM
!!

FWOOO

KHH Rr

INCRED-
IBLE
POWER...

YOSHINA
...!!

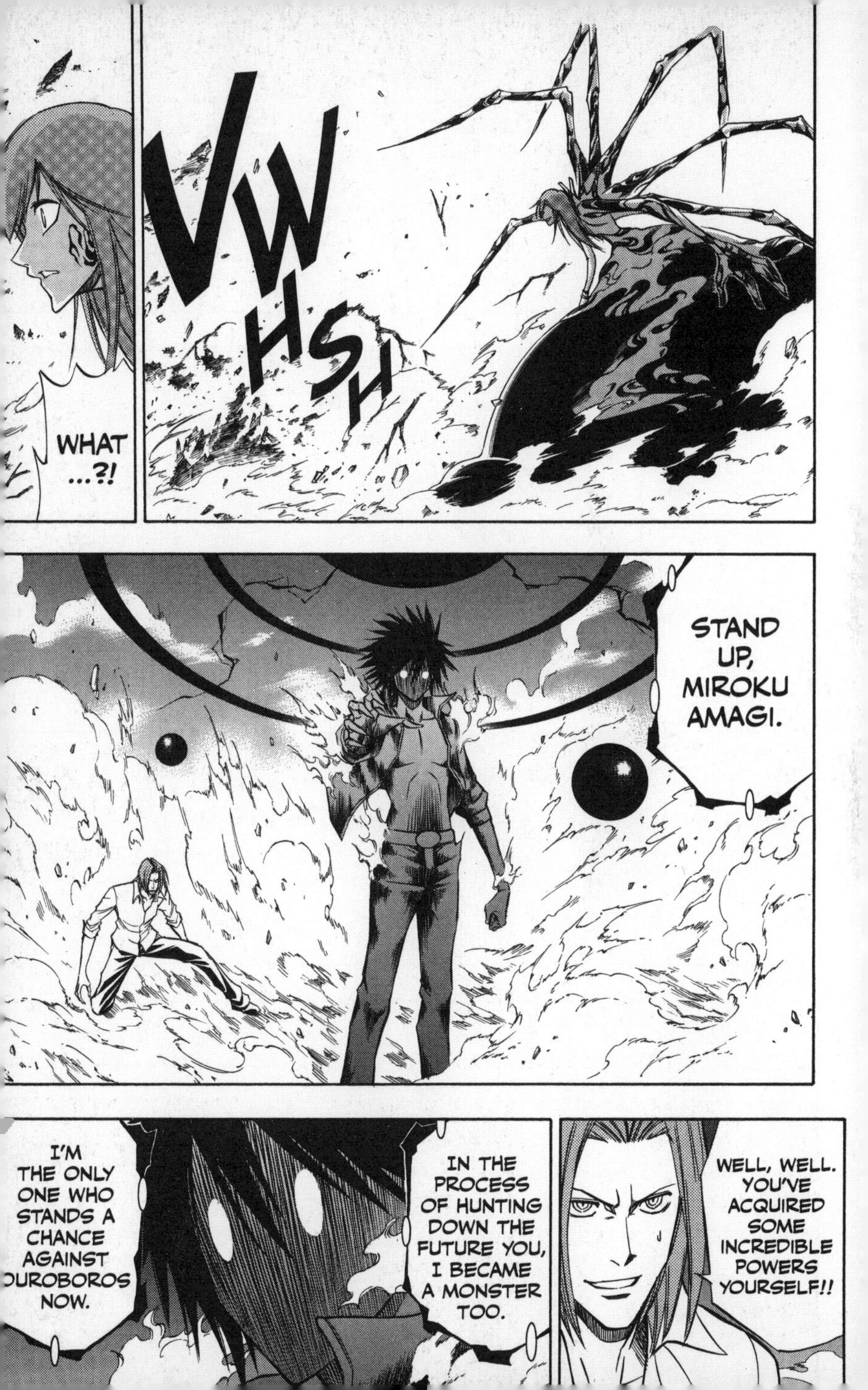
VWHSH
WHAT ...?!
STAND UP, MIROKU AMAGI.
WELL, WELL. YOU'VE ACQUIRED SOME INCREDIBLE POWERS YOURSELF!!
IN THE PROCESS OF HUNTING DOWN THE FUTURE YOU, I BECAME A MONSTER TOO.
I'M THE ONLY ONE WHO STANDS A CHANCE AGAINST OUROBOROS NOW.

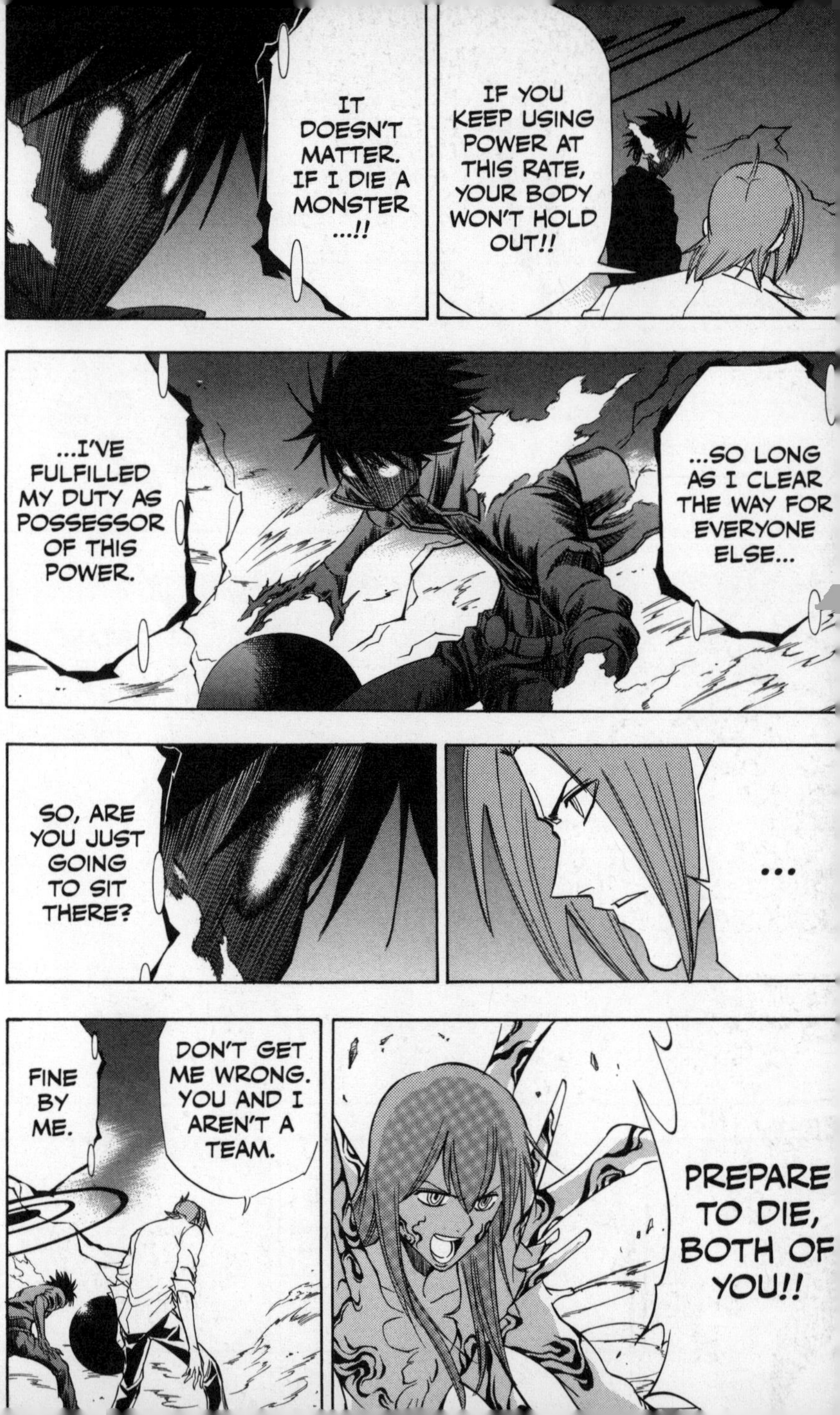
IF YOU KEEP USING POWER AT THIS RATE, YOUR BODY WON'T HOLD OUT!!
IT DOESN'T MATTER. IF I DIE A MONSTER ...!!
...SO LONG AS I CLEAR THE WAY FOR EVERYONE ELSE...
...I'VE FULFILLED MY DUTY AS POSSESSOR OF THIS POWER.
...
SO, ARE YOU JUST GOING TO SIT THERE?
PREPARE TO DIE, BOTH OF YOU!!
DON'T GET ME WRONG. YOU AND I AREN'T A TEAM.
FINE BY ME.

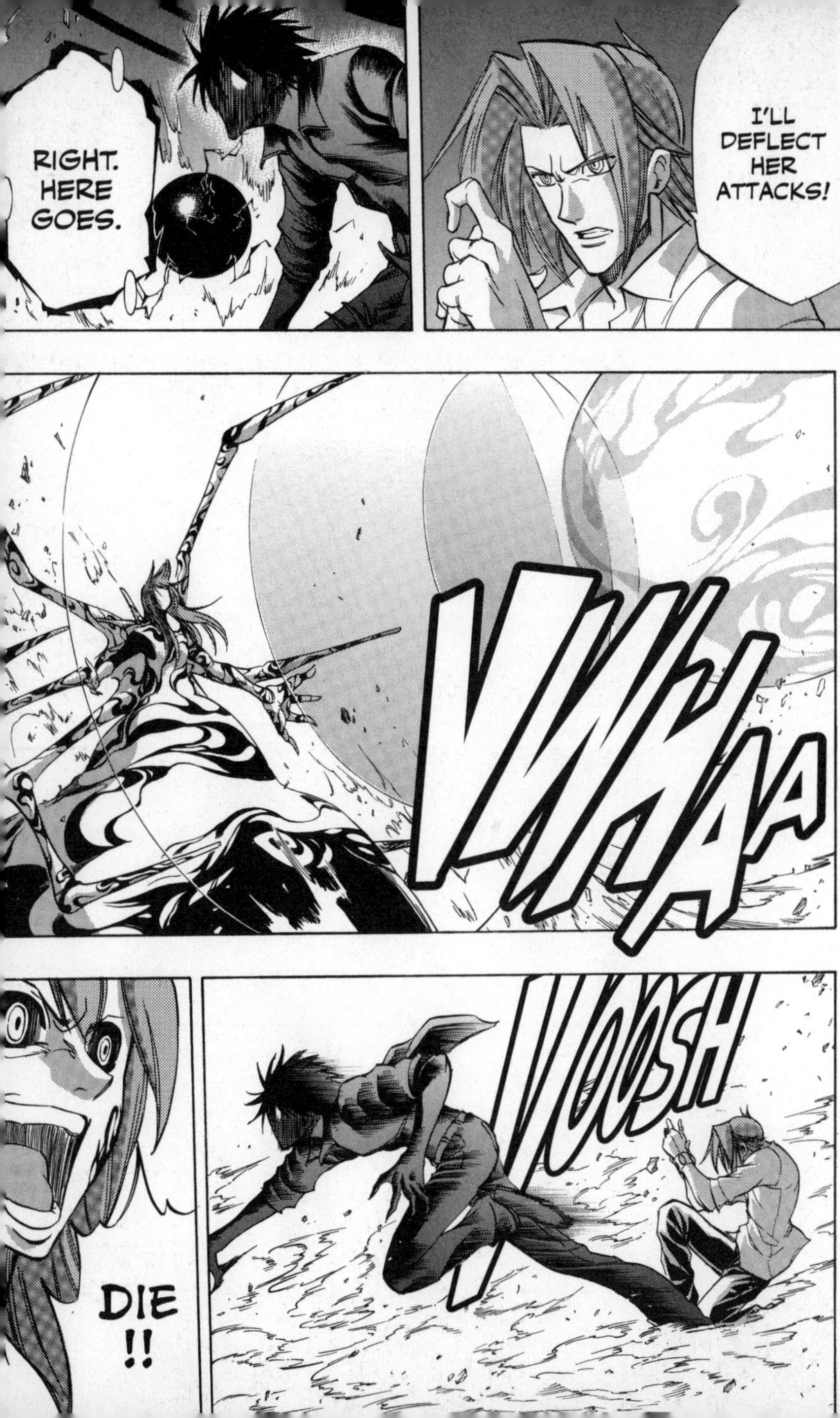
I'LL DEFLECT HER ATTACKS!
RIGHT. HERE GOES.
VWHAA
VOOSH
DIE !!

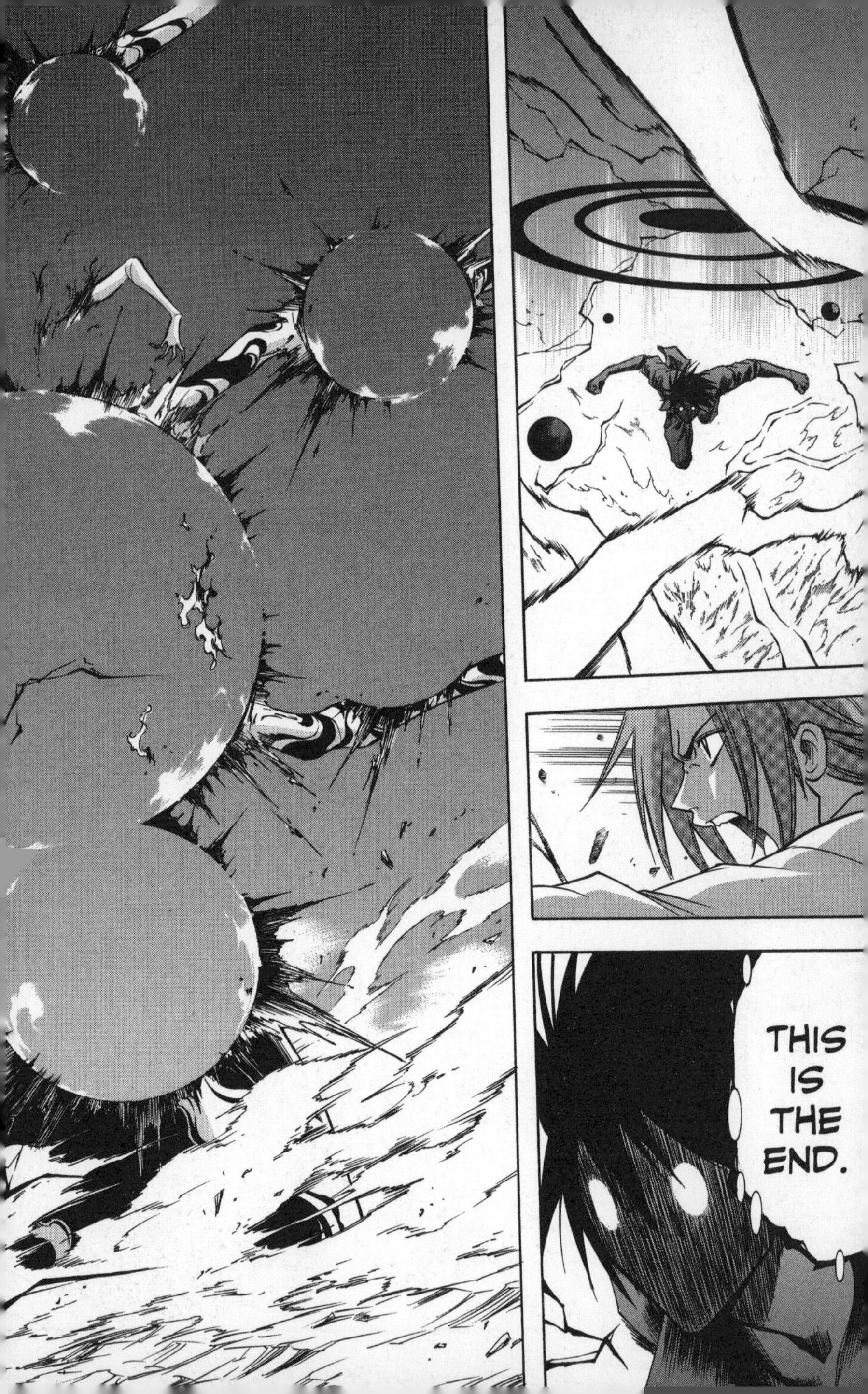
THIS IS THE END.

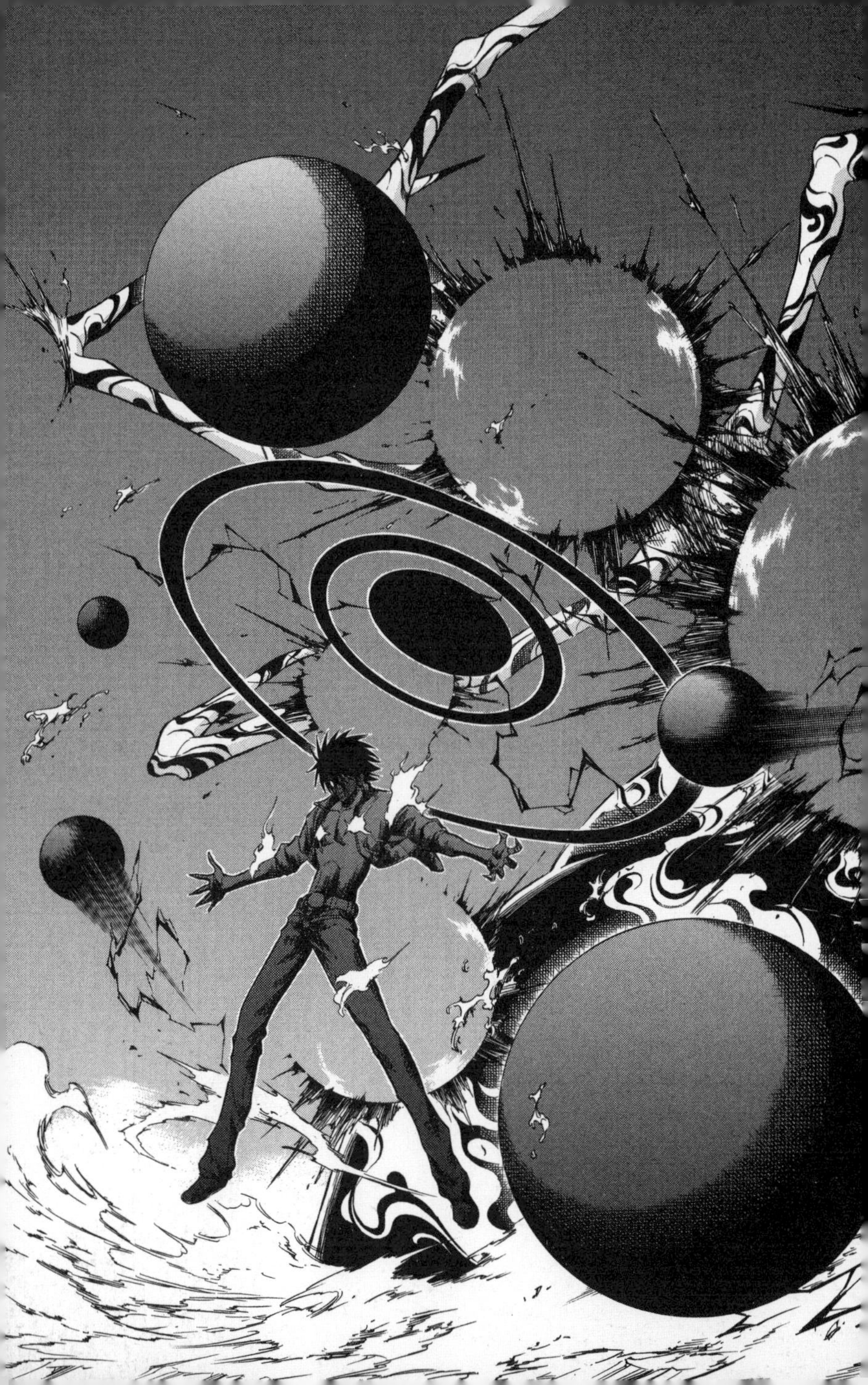

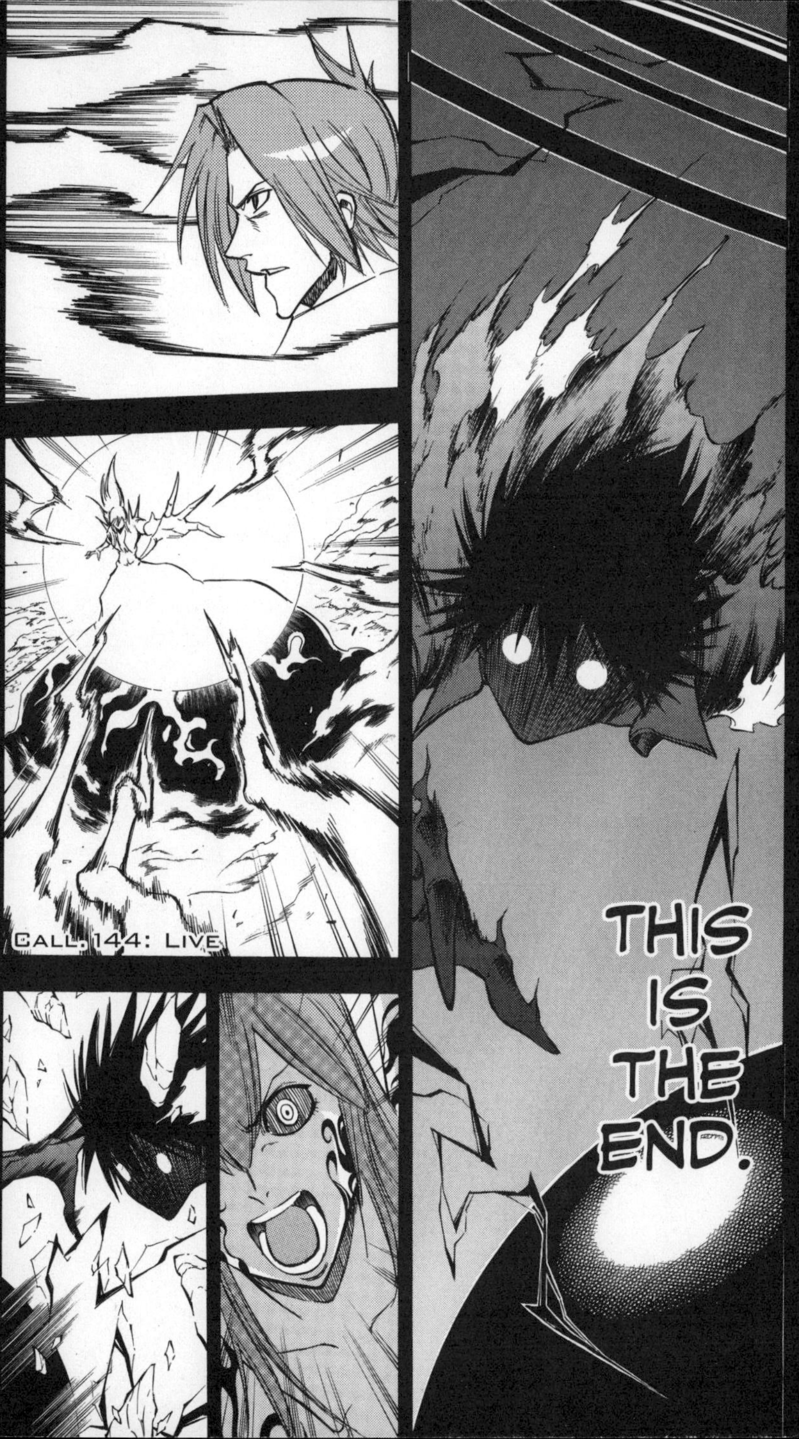
THIS IS THE END.
Call. 144: Live

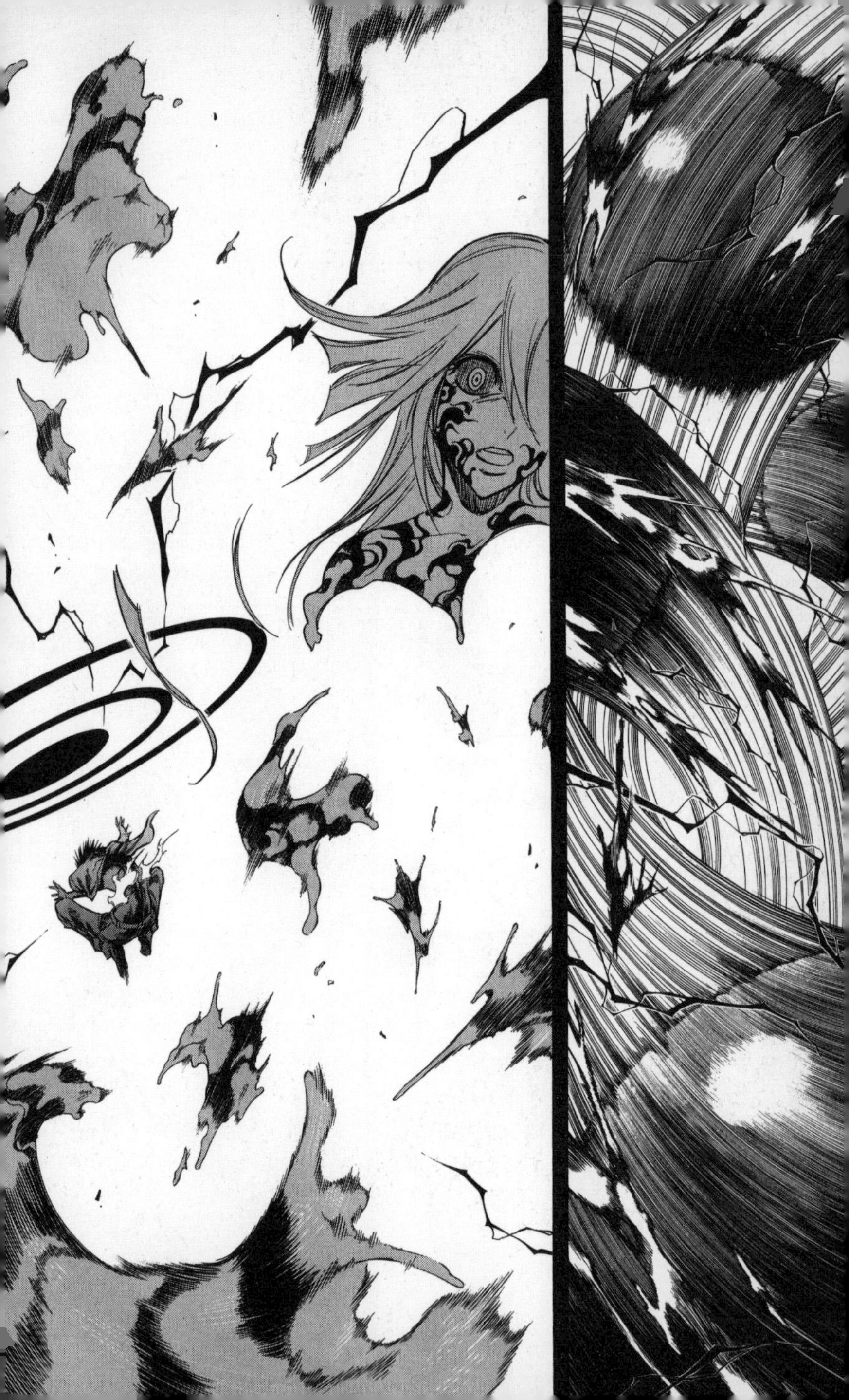

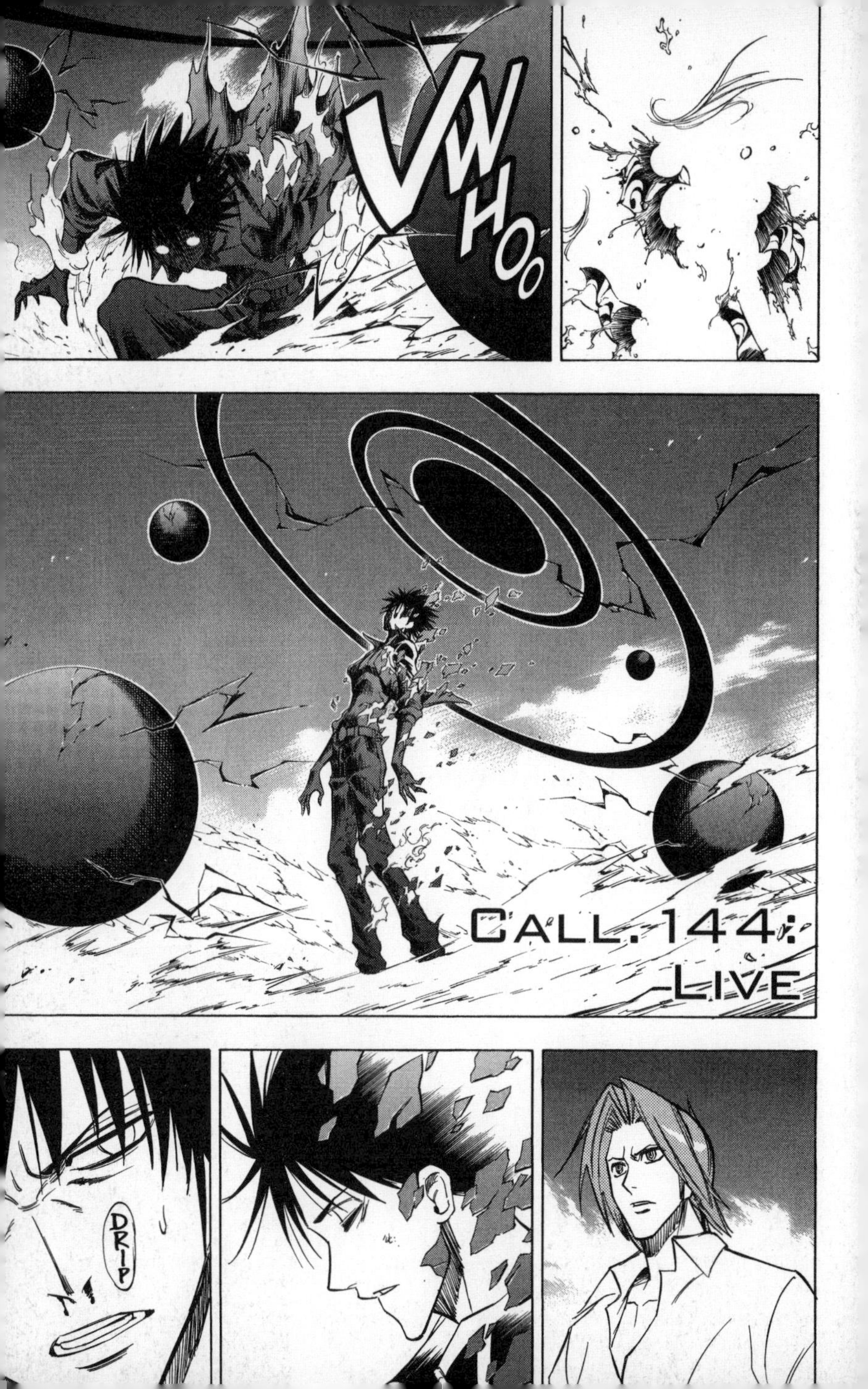
VWHOO
CALL. 144:
LIVE
DRIP

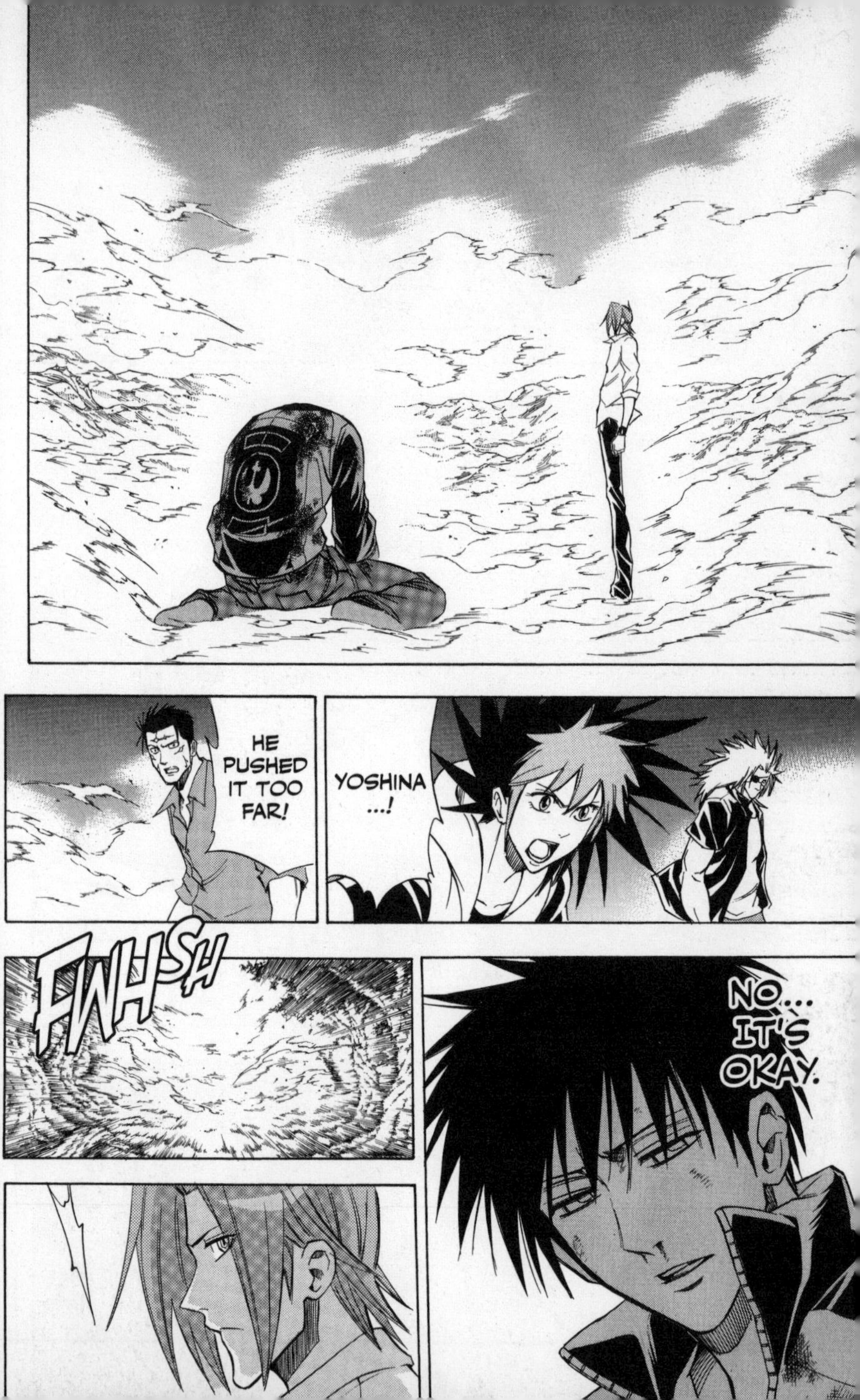
YOSHINA ...!
HE PUSHED IT TOO FAR!
NO... IT'S OKAY.
FWHSH

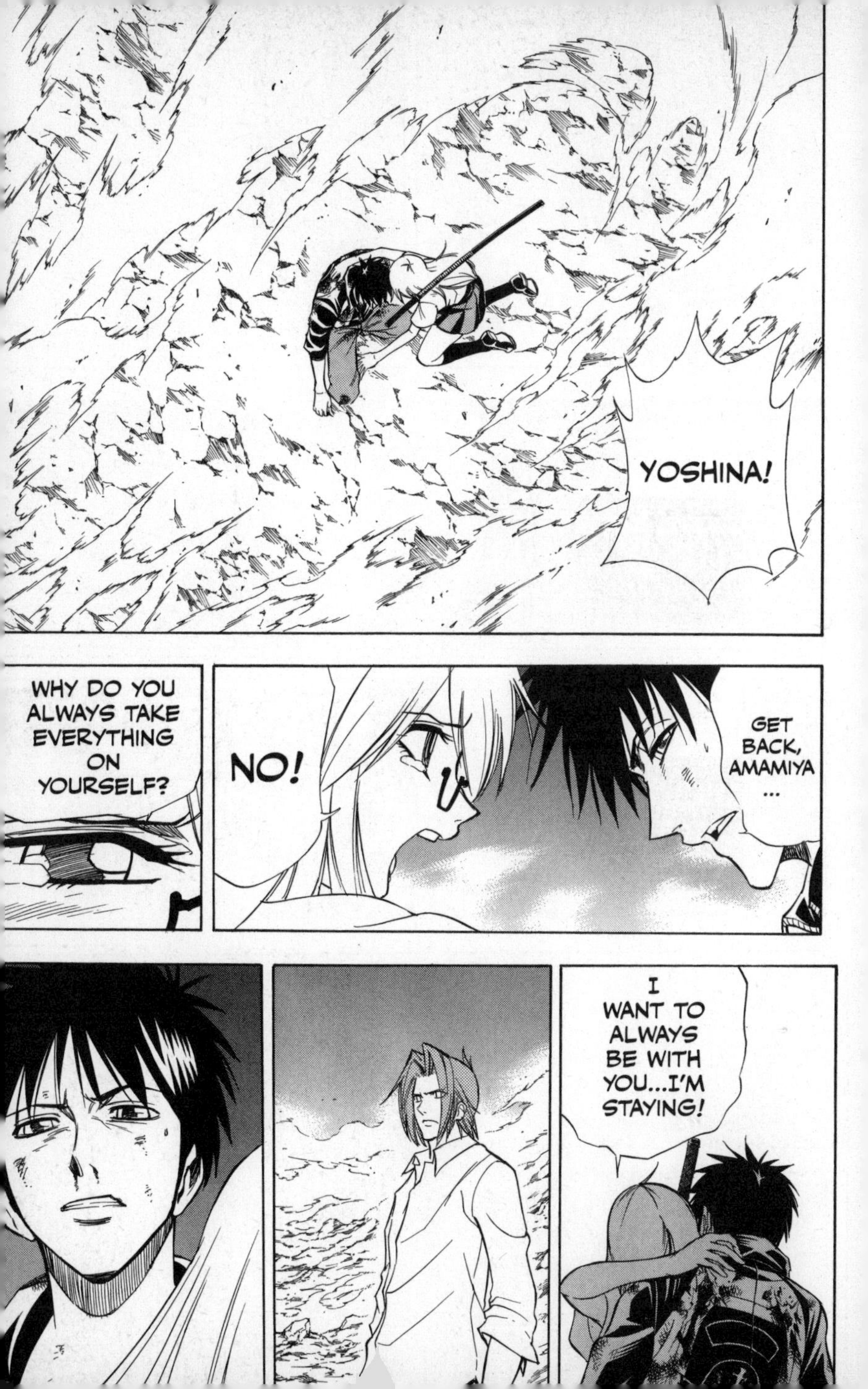
YOSHINA!
GET BACK, AMAMIYA ...
NO!
WHY DO YOU ALWAYS TAKE EVERYTHING ON YOURSELF?
I WANT TO ALWAYS BE WITH YOU...I'M STAYING!

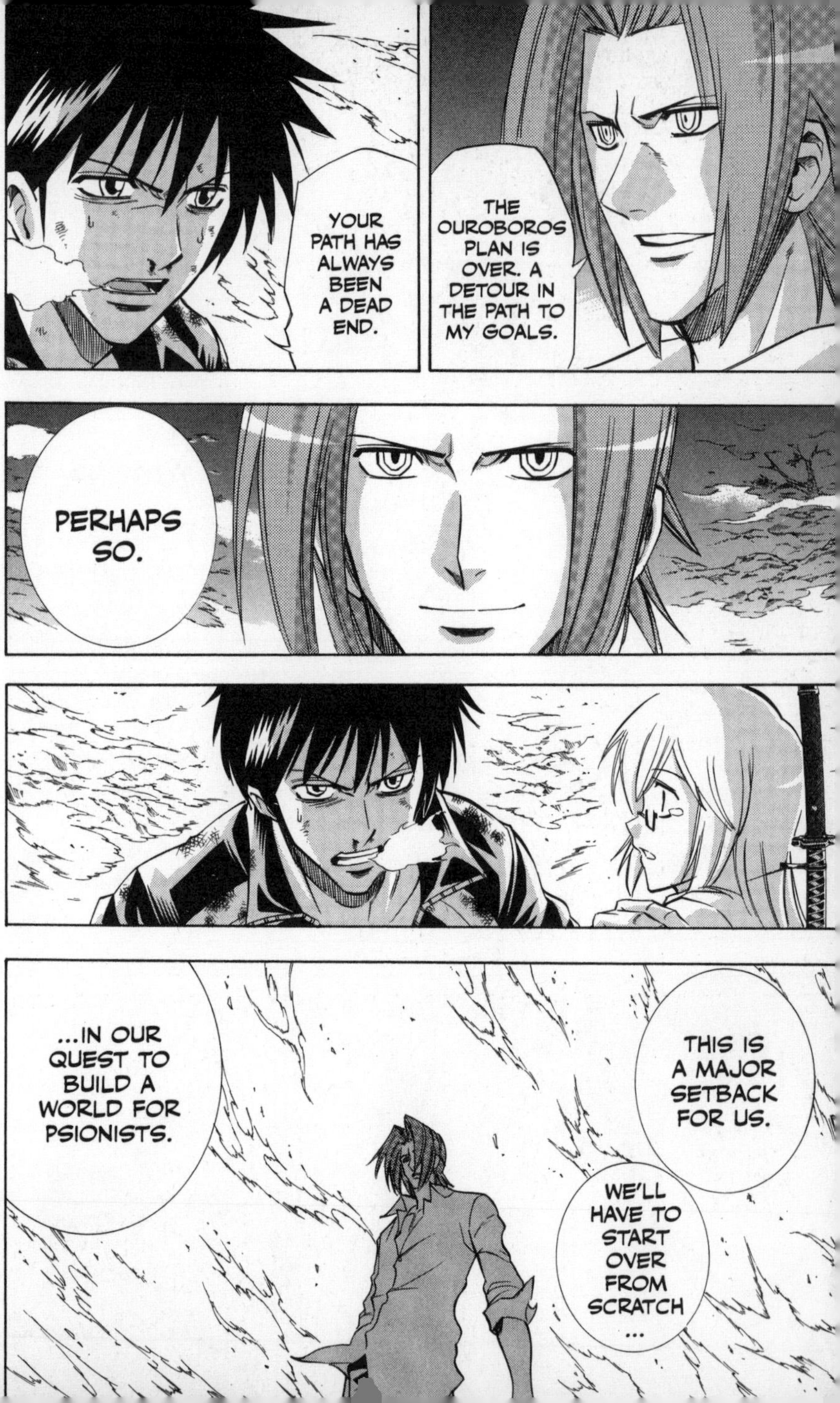
THE OUROBOROS PLAN IS OVER. A DETOUR IN THE PATH TO MY GOALS.
YOUR PATH HAS ALWAYS BEEN A DEAD END.
PERHAPS SO.
THIS IS A MAJOR SETBACK FOR US.
WE'LL HAVE TO START OVER FROM SCRATCH ...
...IN OUR QUEST TO BUILD A WORLD FOR PSIONISTS.

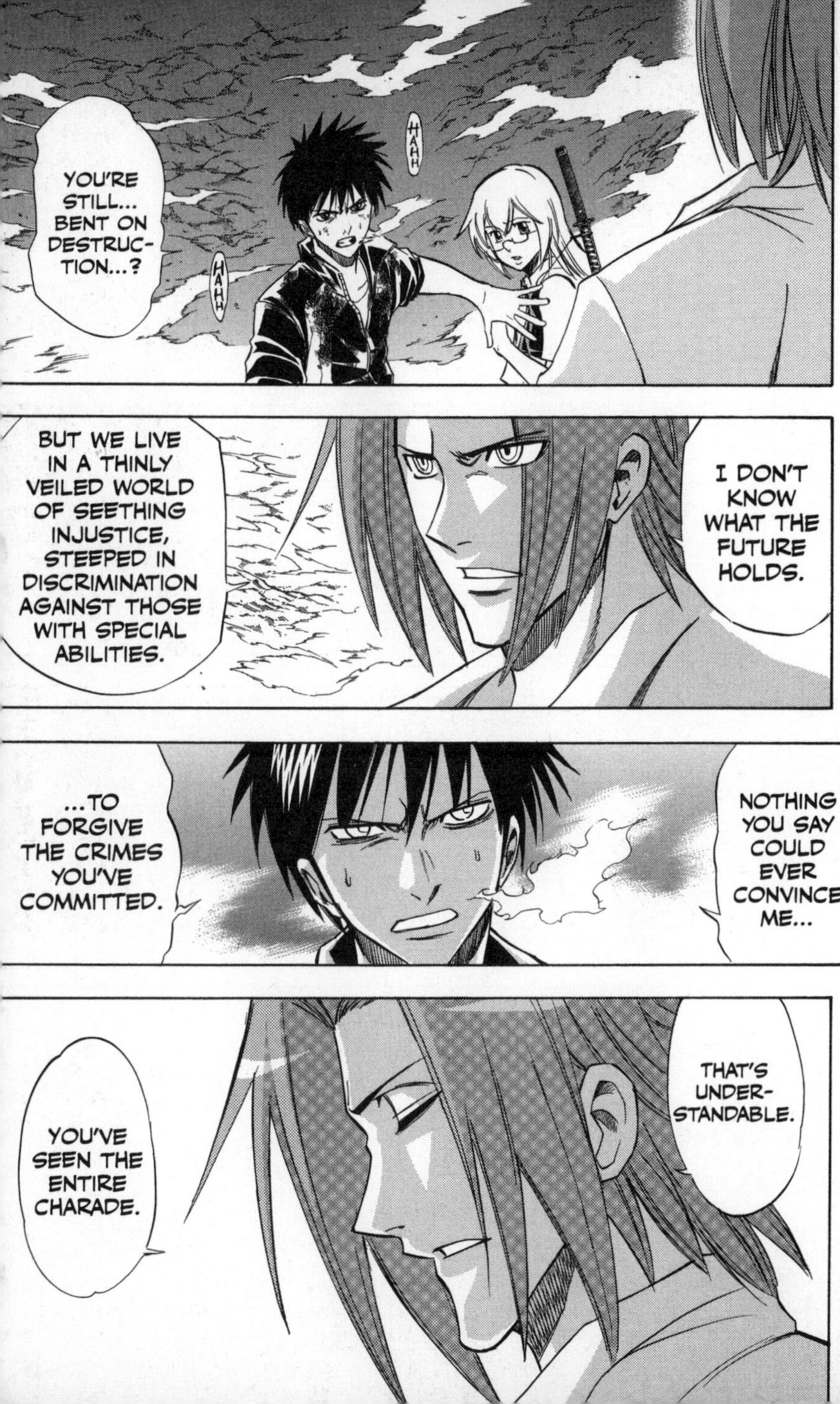
HAHH
YOU'RE STILL... BENT ON DESTRUCTION...?
HAHH
I DON'T KNOW WHAT THE FUTURE HOLDS.
BUT WE LIVE IN A THINLY VEILED WORLD OF SEETHING INJUSTICE, STEEPED IN DISCRIMINATION AGAINST THOSE WITH SPECIAL ABILITIES.
NOTHING YOU SAY COULD EVER CONVINCE ME...
...TO FORGIVE THE CRIMES YOU'VE COMMITTED.
THAT'S UNDER-STANDABLE.
YOU'VE SEEN THE ENTIRE CHARADE.

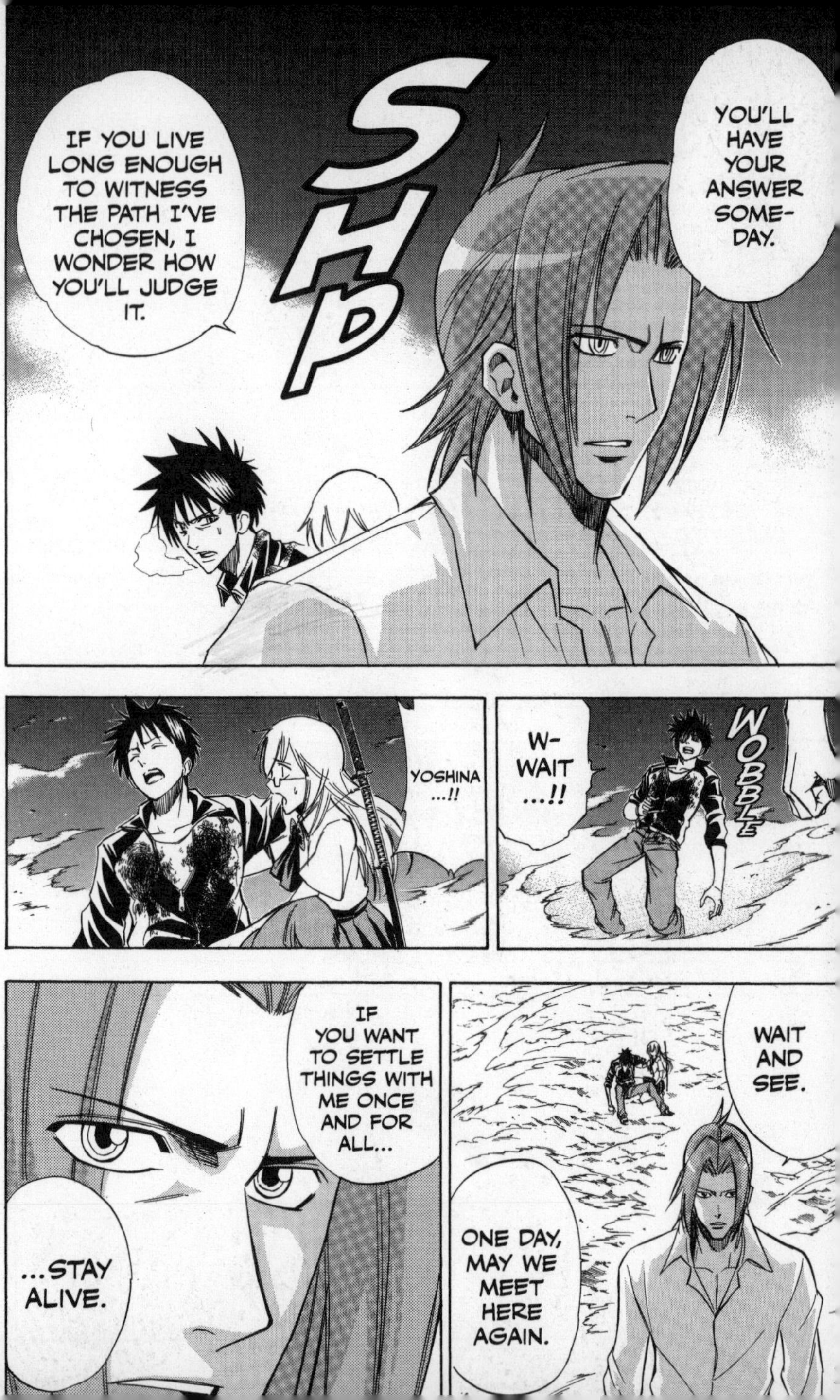
YOU'LL HAVE YOUR ANSWER SOME-DAY.
SHP
IF YOU LIVE LONG ENOUGH TO WITNESS THE PATH I'VE CHOSEN, I WONDER HOW YOU'LL JUDGE IT.
WOBBLE
W-WAIT ...!!
YOSHINA ...!!
WAIT AND SEE.
ONE DAY, MAY WE MEET HERE AGAIN.
IF YOU WANT TO SETTLE THINGS WITH ME ONCE AND FOR ALL...
...STAY ALIVE.

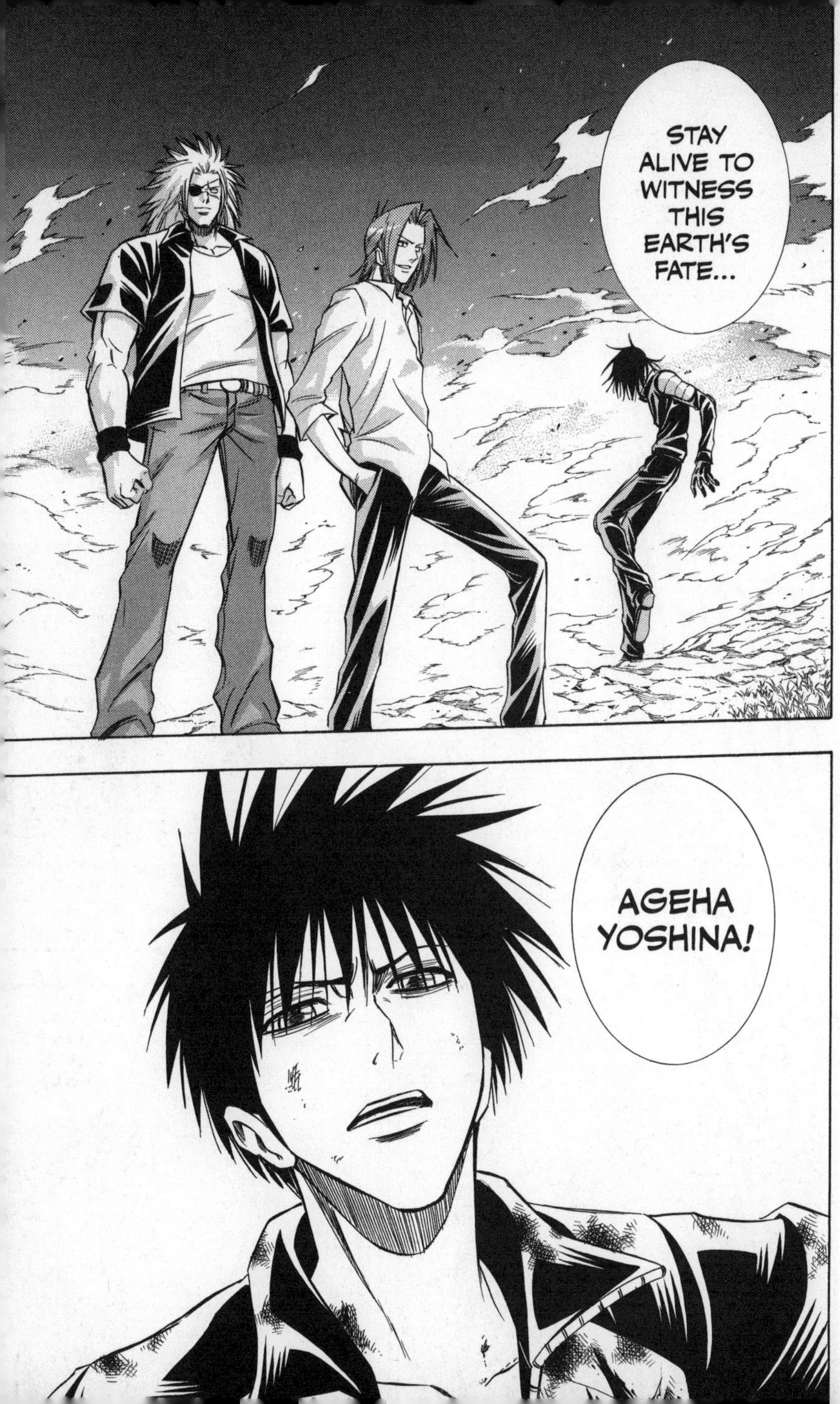
STAY ALIVE TO WITNESS THIS EARTH'S FATE...
AGEHA YOSHINA!

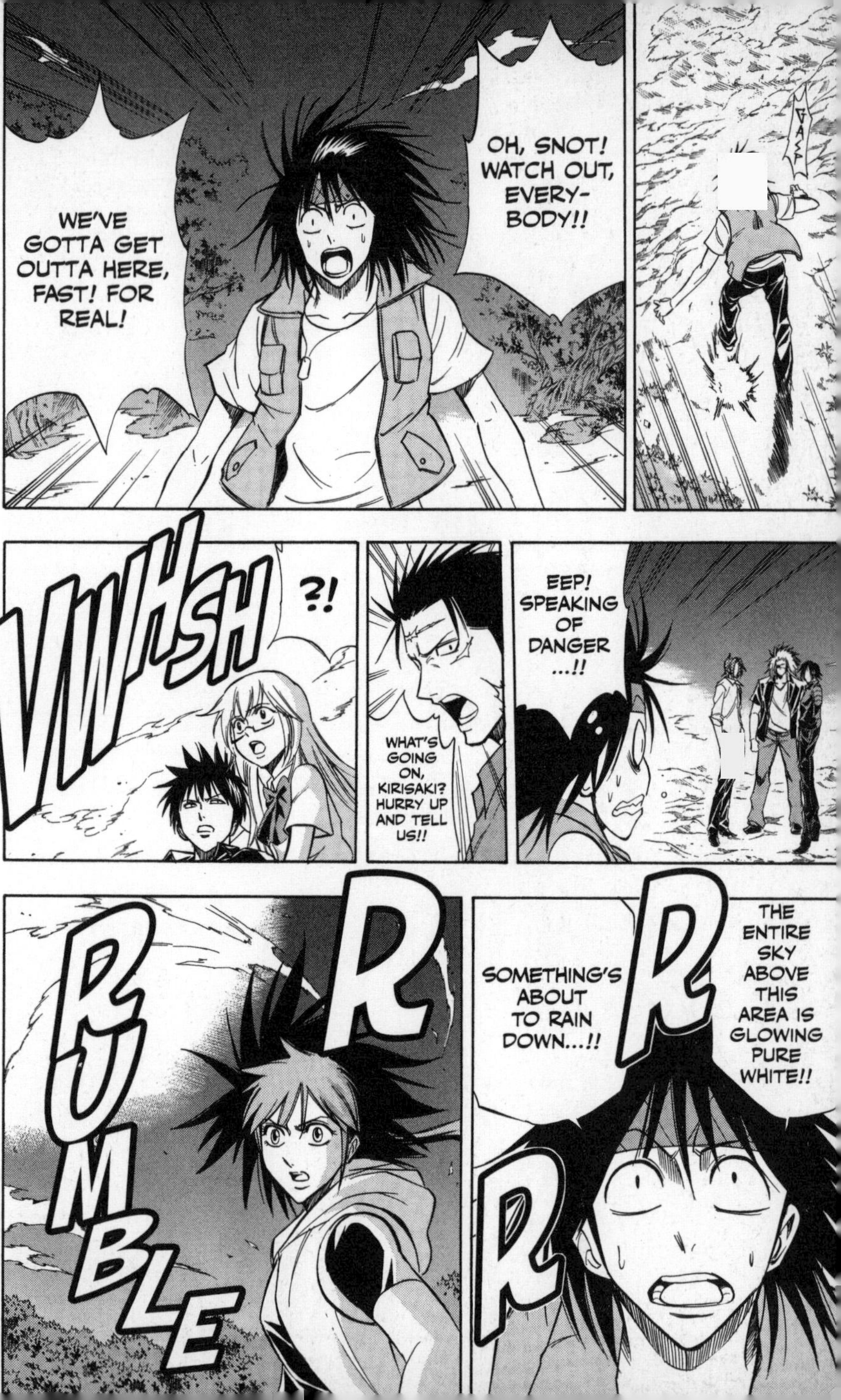
GASP
OH, SNOT! WATCH OUT, EVERY-BODY!!
WE'VE GOTTA GET OUTTA HERE, FAST! FOR REAL!
EEP! SPEAKING OF DANGER ...!!
WHAT'S GOING ON, KIRISAKI? HURRY UP AND TELL US!!
?!
VWHSH
THE ENTIRE SKY ABOVE THIS AREA IS GLOWING PURE WHITE!!
R
SOMETHING'S ABOUT TO RAIN DOWN...!!
R
R
R
RUMBLE

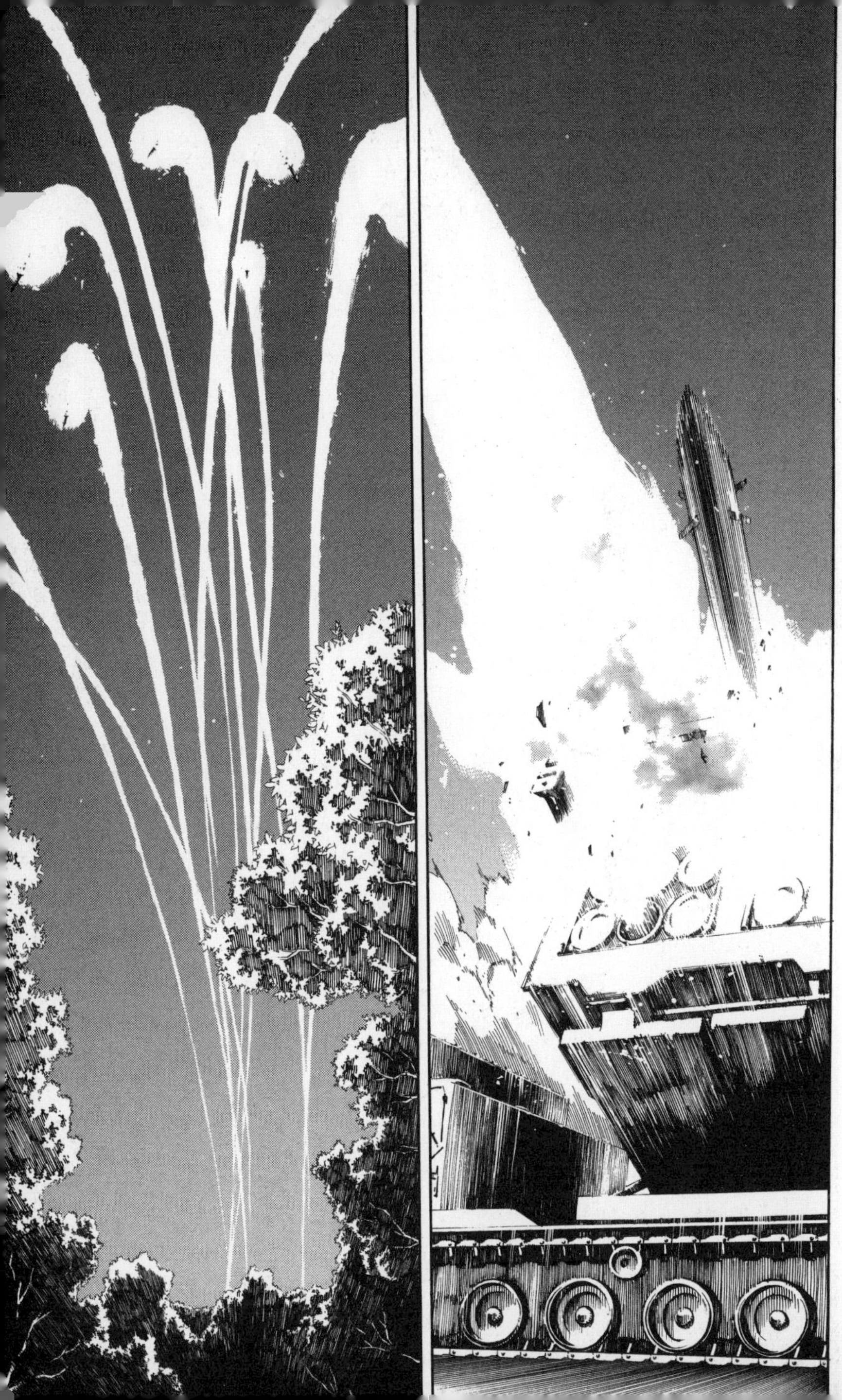

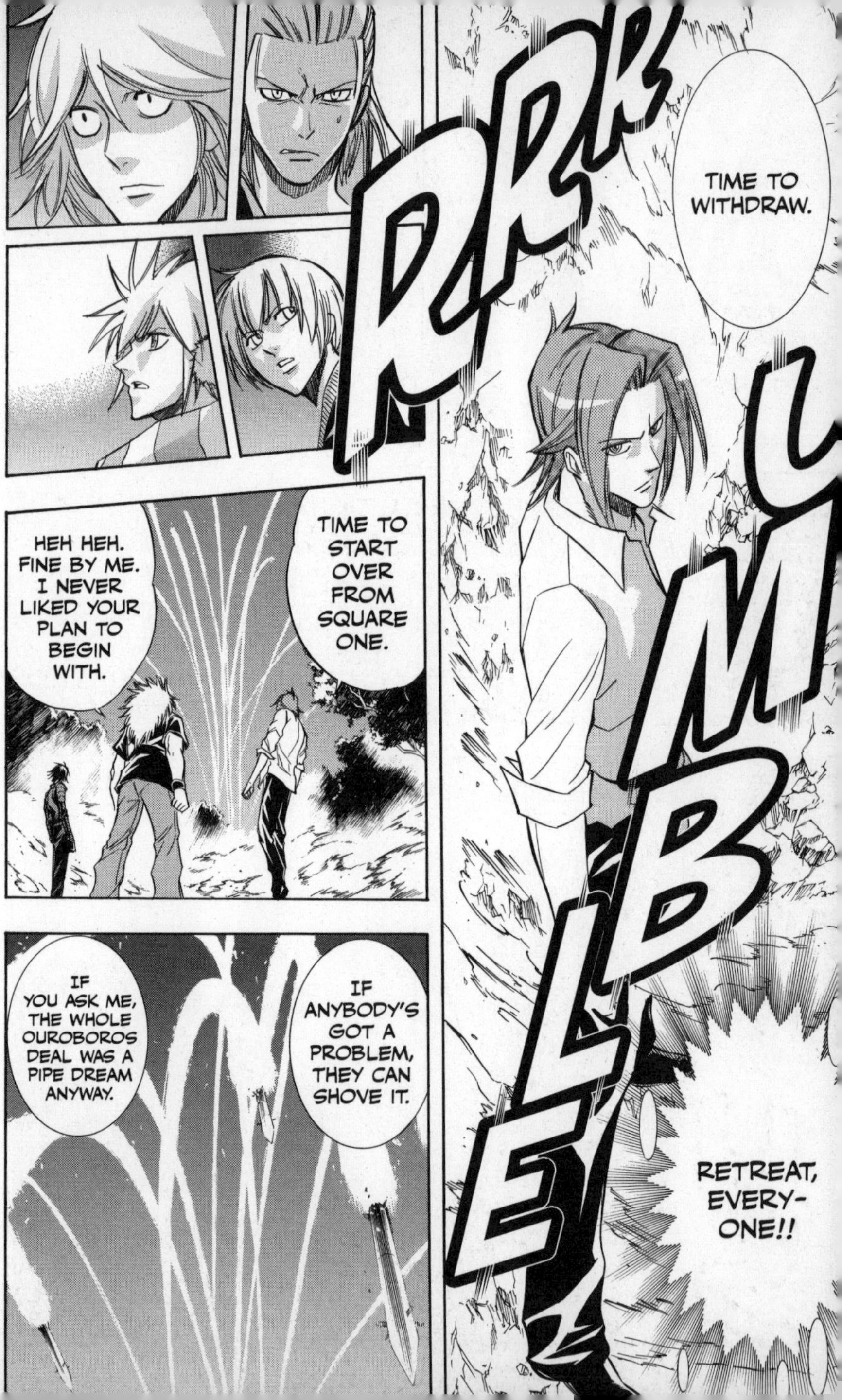
TIME TO WITHDRAW.
RRRUMBLE
RETREAT, EVERY-ONE!!
TIME TO START OVER FROM SQUARE ONE.
HEH HEH. FINE BY ME. I NEVER LIKED YOUR PLAN TO BEGIN WITH.
IF ANYBODY'S GOT A PROBLEM, THEY CAN SHOVE IT.
IF YOU ASK ME, THE WHOLE OUROBOROS DEAL WAS A PIPE DREAM ANYWAY.

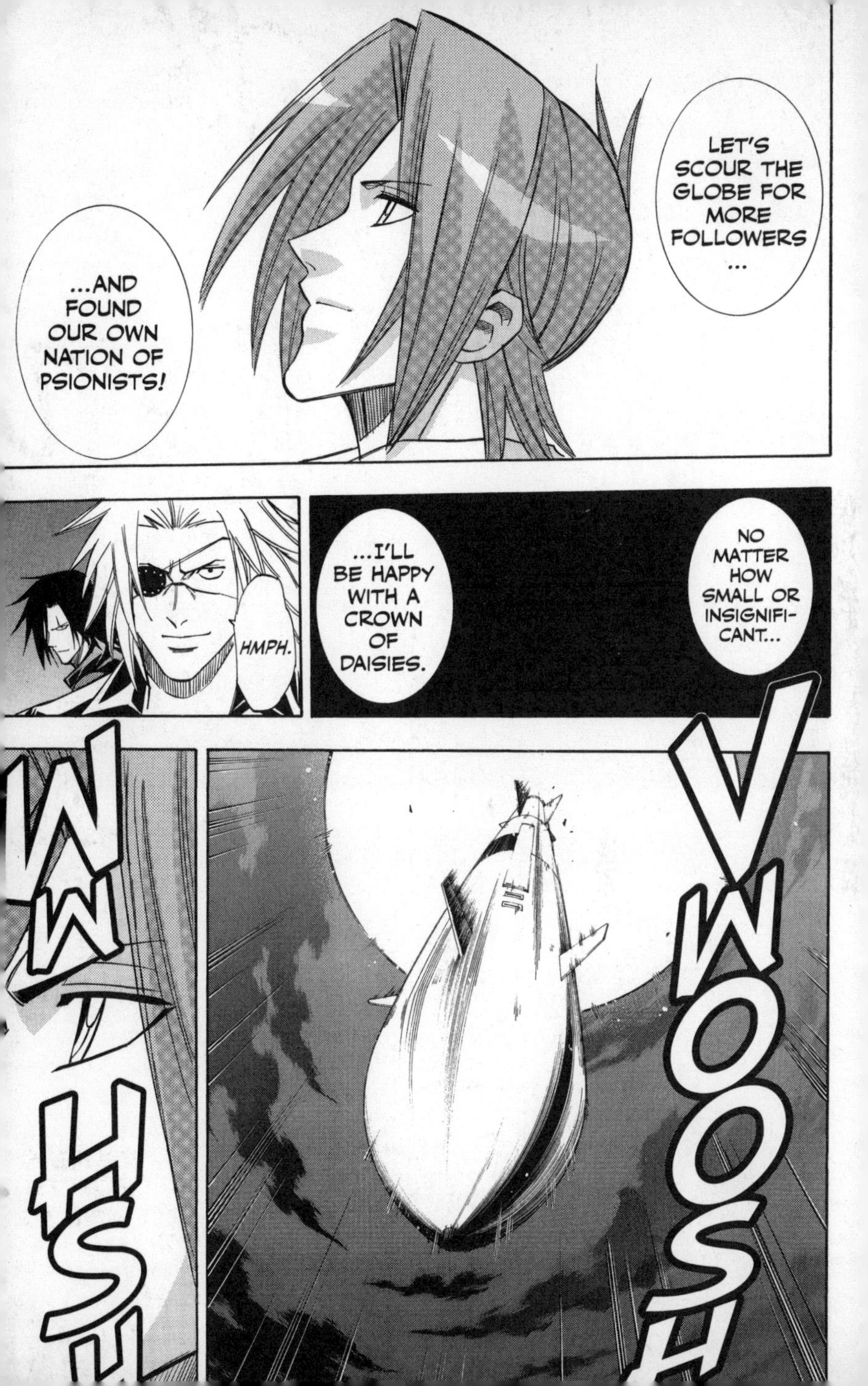
LET'S SCOUR THE GLOBE FOR MORE FOLLOWERS ...
...AND FOUND OUR OWN NATION OF PSIONISTS!
NO MATTER HOW SMALL OR INSIGNIFI-CANT...
...I'LL BE HAPPY WITH A CROWN OF DAISIES.
HMPH.
VWOOSH
WHSH

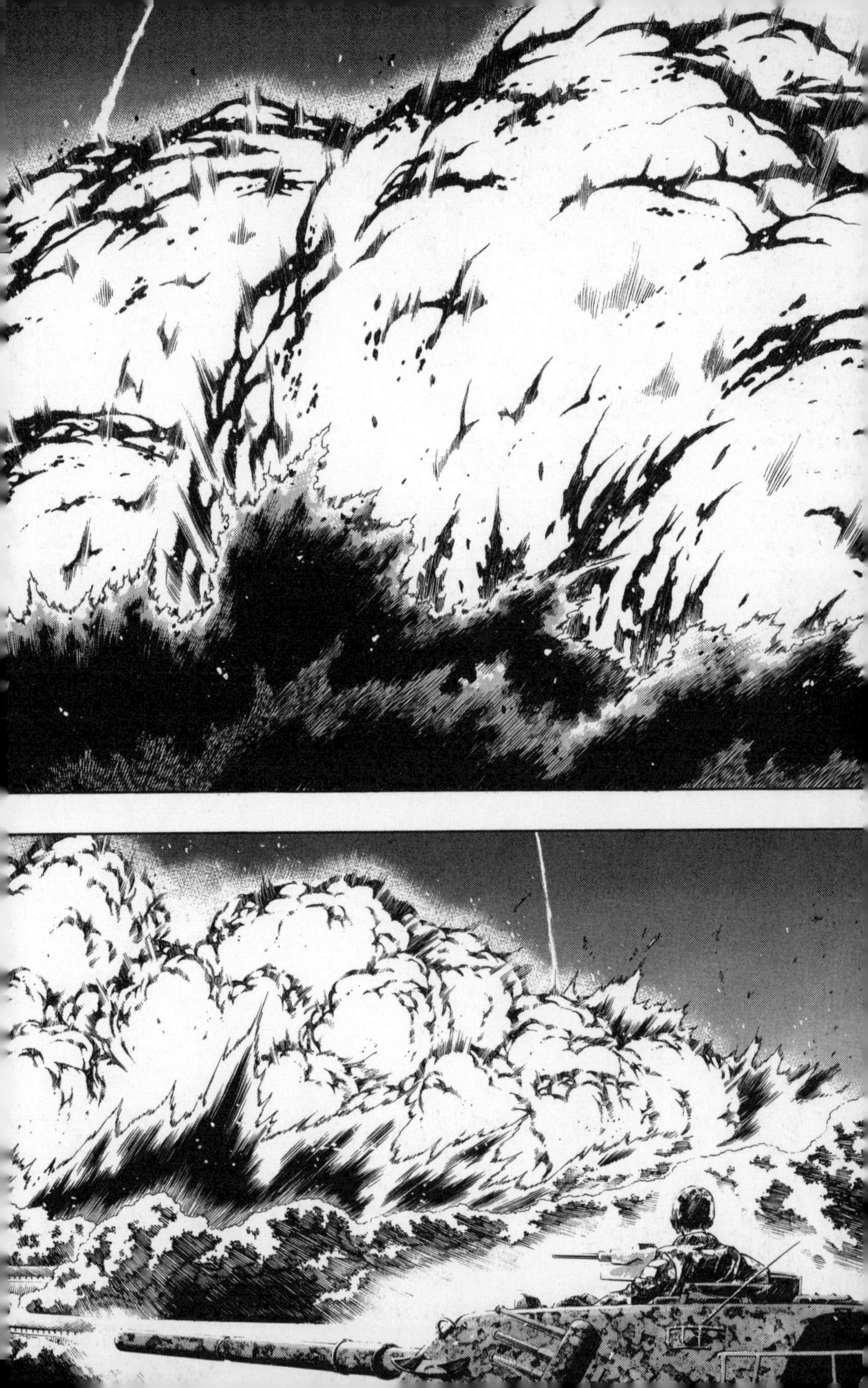

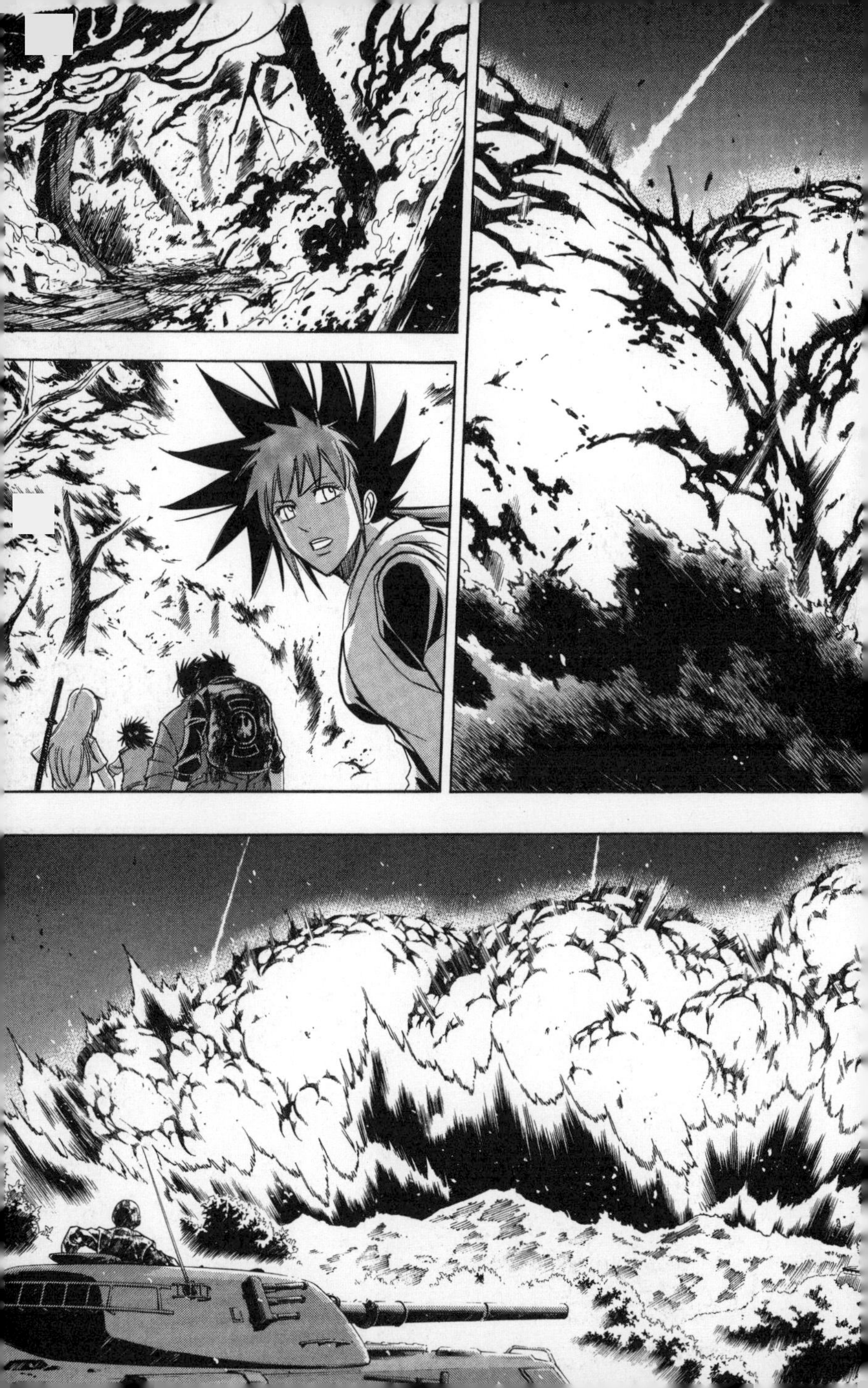

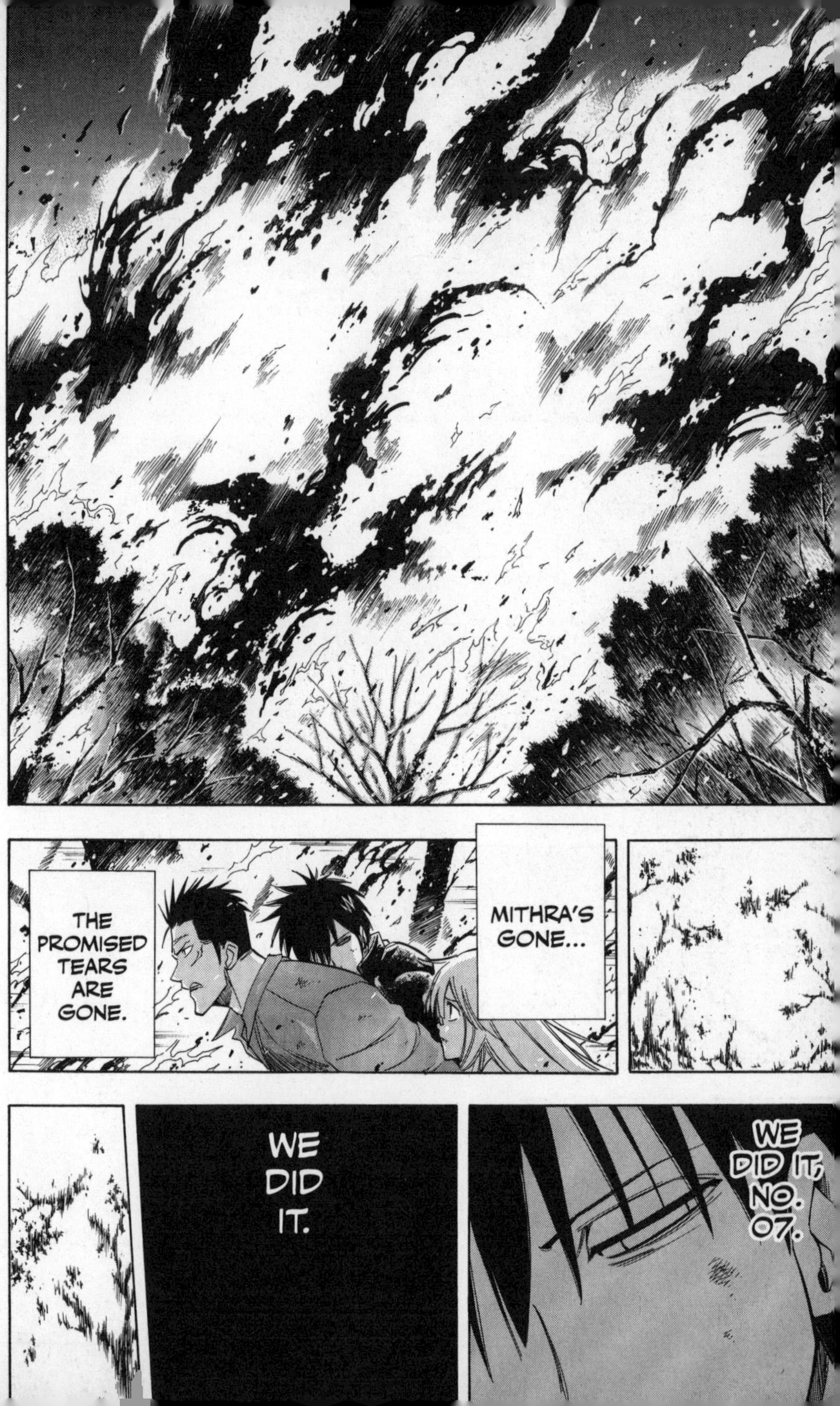
MITHRA'S GONE...
THE PROMISED TEARS ARE GONE.
WE DID IT, NO. 07.
WE DID IT.

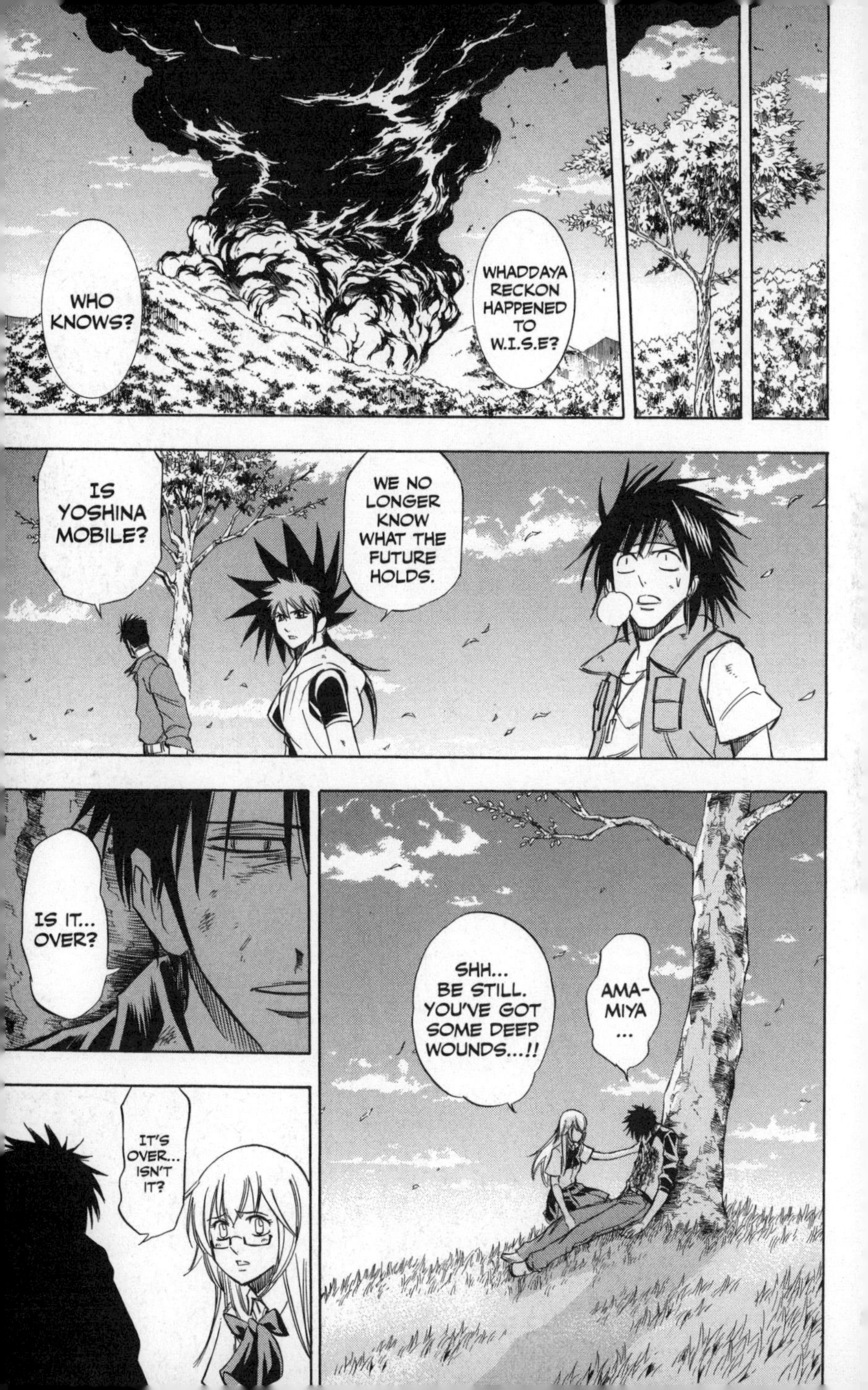
WHADDAYA RECKON HAPPENED TO W.I.S.E?
WHO KNOWS?
WE NO LONGER KNOW WHAT THE FUTURE HOLDS.
IS YOSHINA MOBILE?
AMA-MIYA...
SHH... BE STILL. YOU'VE GOT SOME DEEP WOUNDS...!!
IS IT... OVER?
IT'S OVER... ISN'T IT?

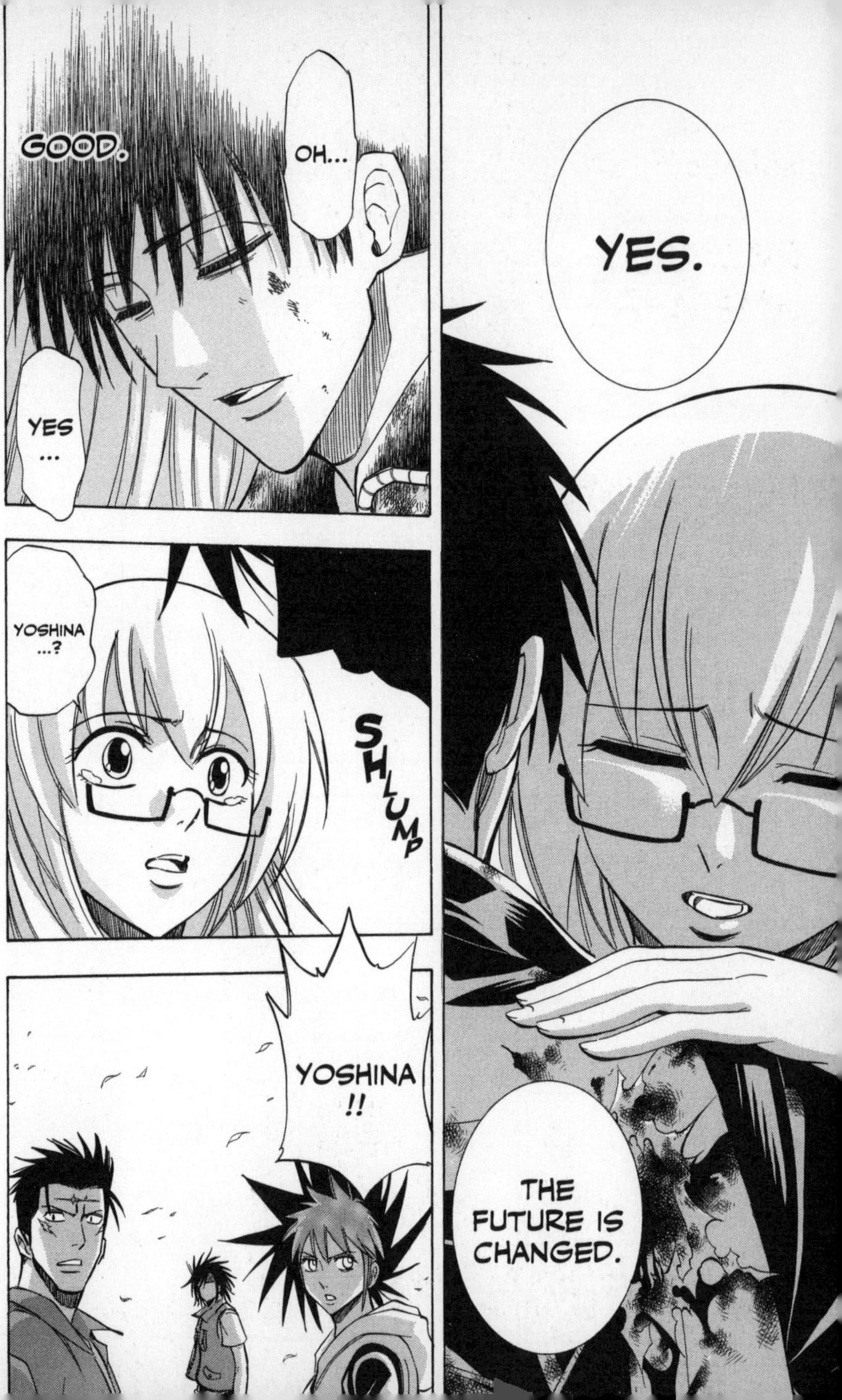
YES.
THE FUTURE IS CHANGED.
OH...
GOOD.
YES ...
YOSHINA ...?
SHLUMP
YOSHINA !!

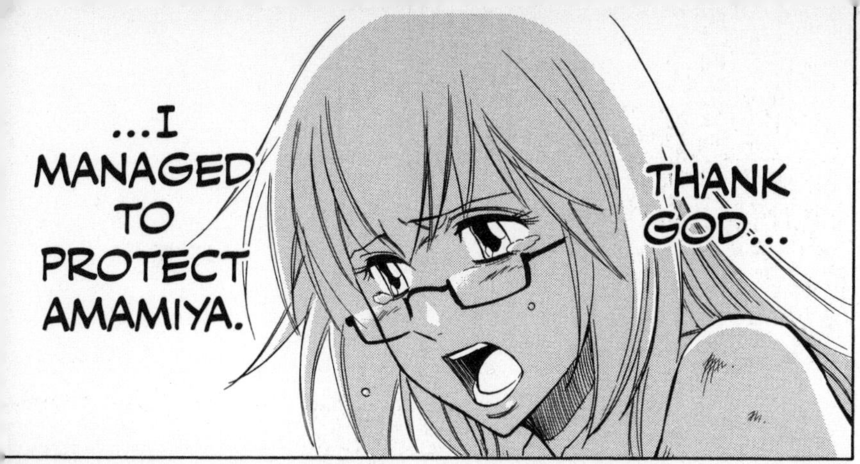
THANK GOD...
...I MANAGED TO PROTECT AMAMIYA.
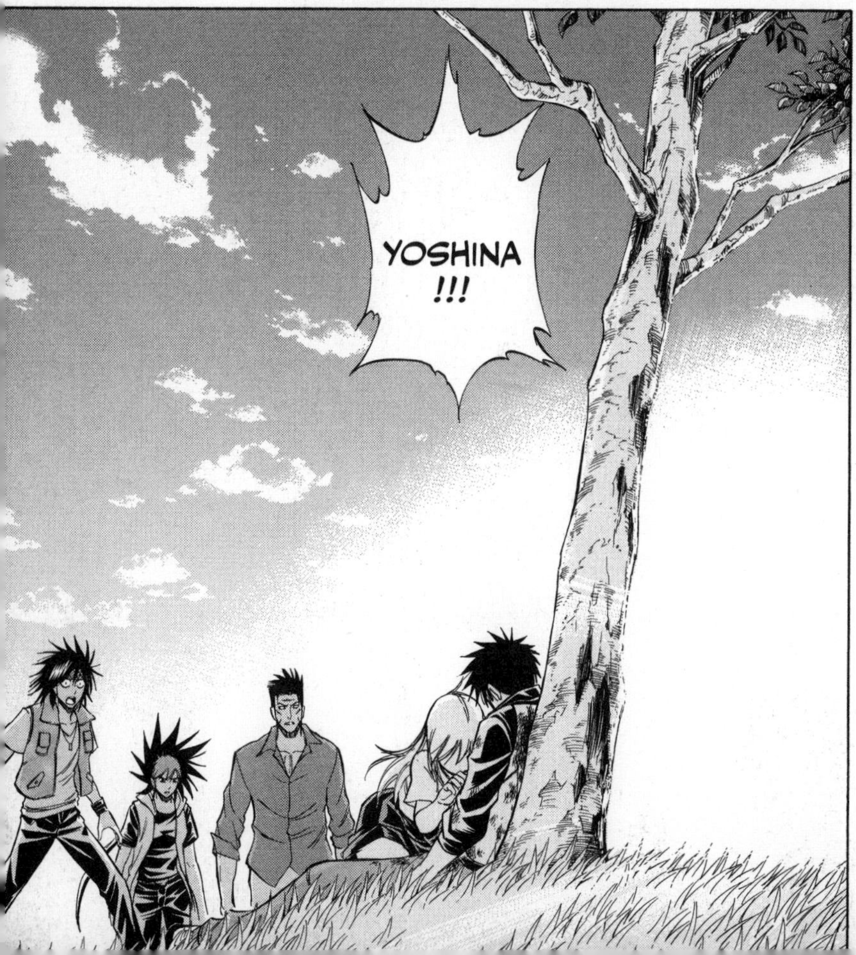
YOSHINA !!!

...and lastly, Ageha.

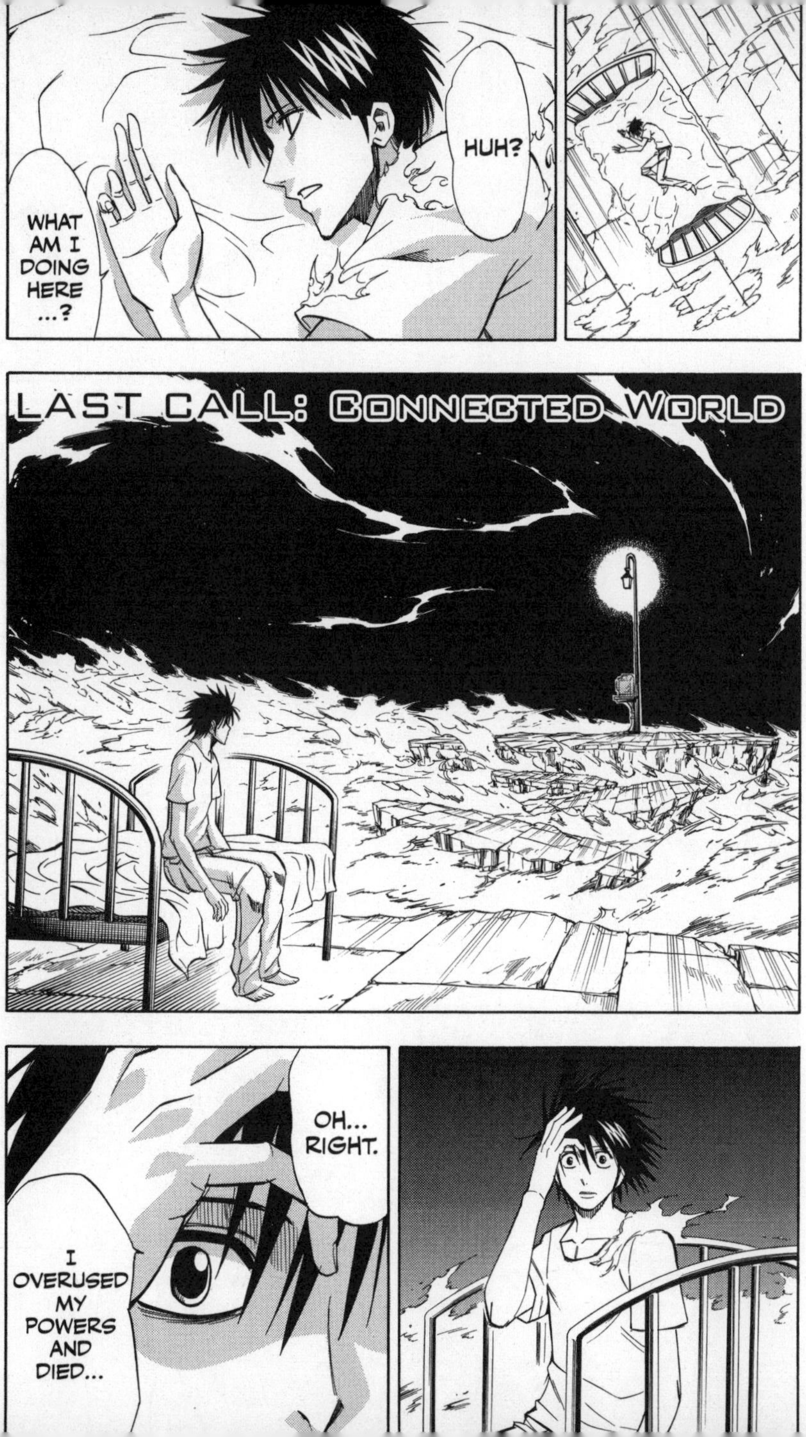
HUH?
WHAT AM I DOING HERE ...?
LAST CALL: CONNECTED WORLD
OH... RIGHT.
I OVERUSED MY POWERS AND DIED...

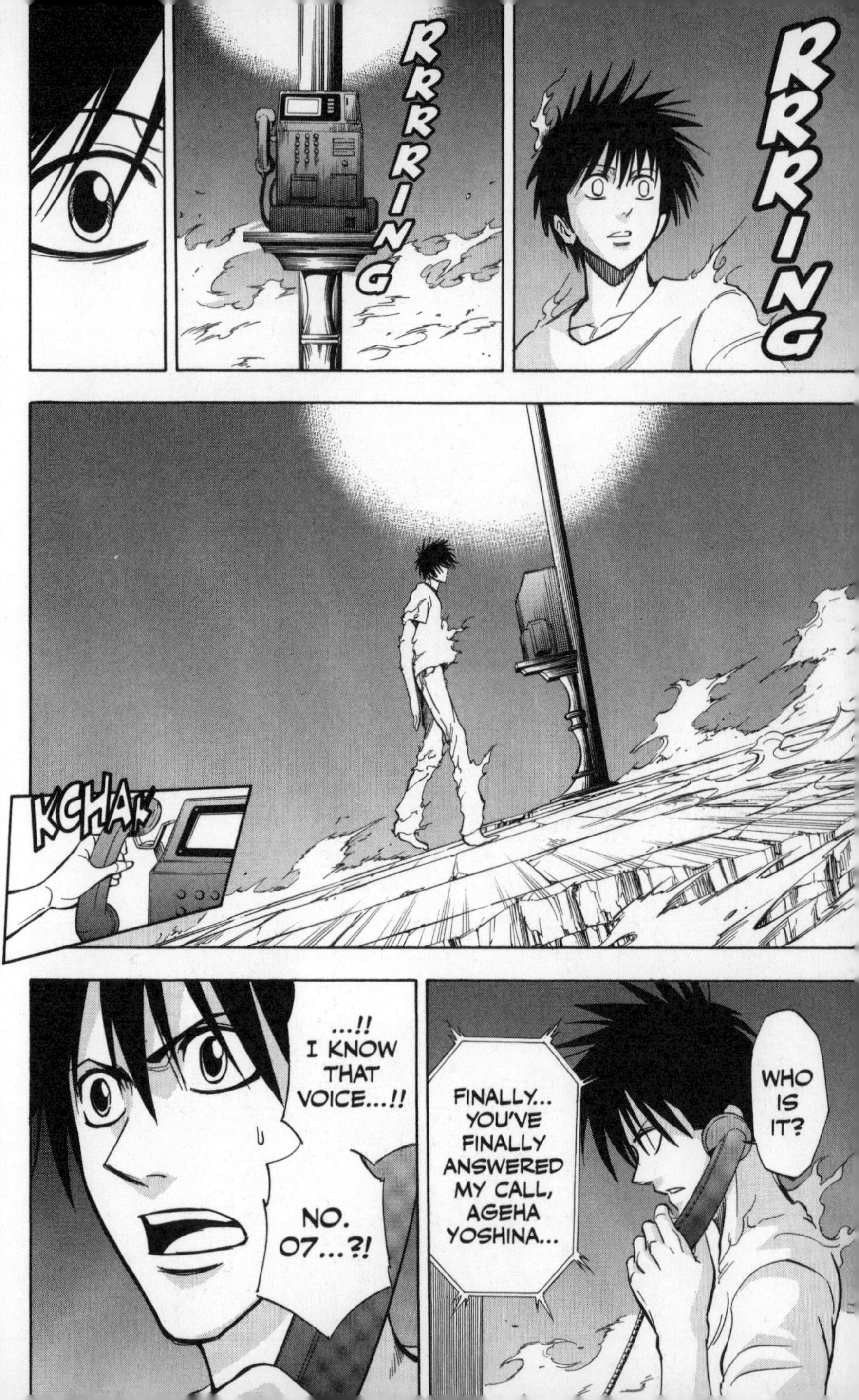
RRRING
RRRING
KCHAK
WHO IS IT?
FINALLY... YOU'VE FINALLY ANSWERED MY CALL, AGEHA YOSHINA...
...!! I KNOW THAT VOICE...!!
NO. 07...?!

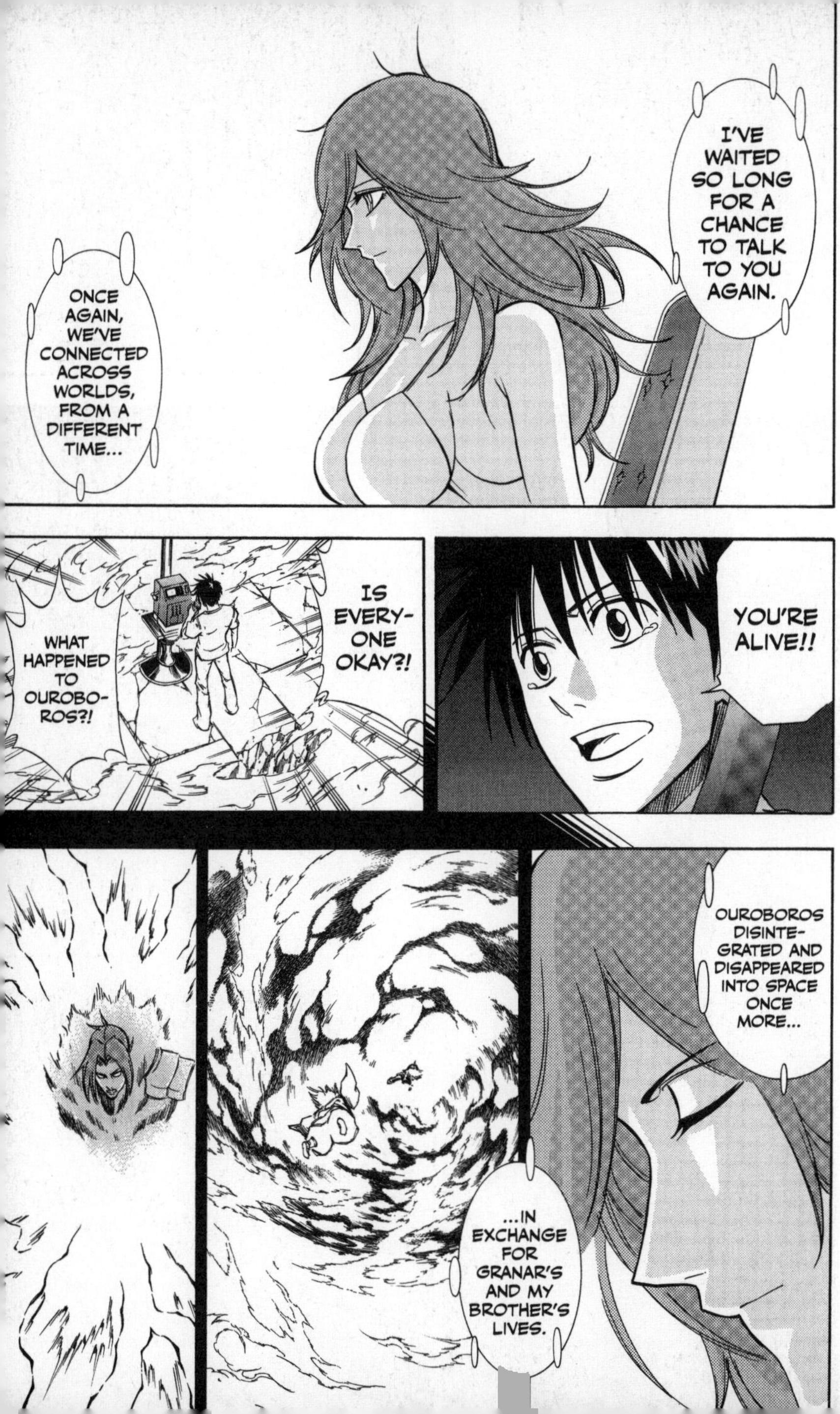
I'VE WAITED SO LONG FOR A CHANCE TO TALK TO YOU AGAIN.
ONCE AGAIN, WE'VE CONNECTED ACROSS WORLDS, FROM A DIFFERENT TIME...
YOU'RE ALIVE!!
IS EVERY-ONE OKAY?!
WHAT HAPPENED TO OUROBO-ROS?!
OUROBOROS DISINTE-GRATED AND DISAPPEARED INTO SPACE ONCE MORE...
...IN EXCHANGE FOR GRANAR'S AND MY BROTHER'S LIVES.

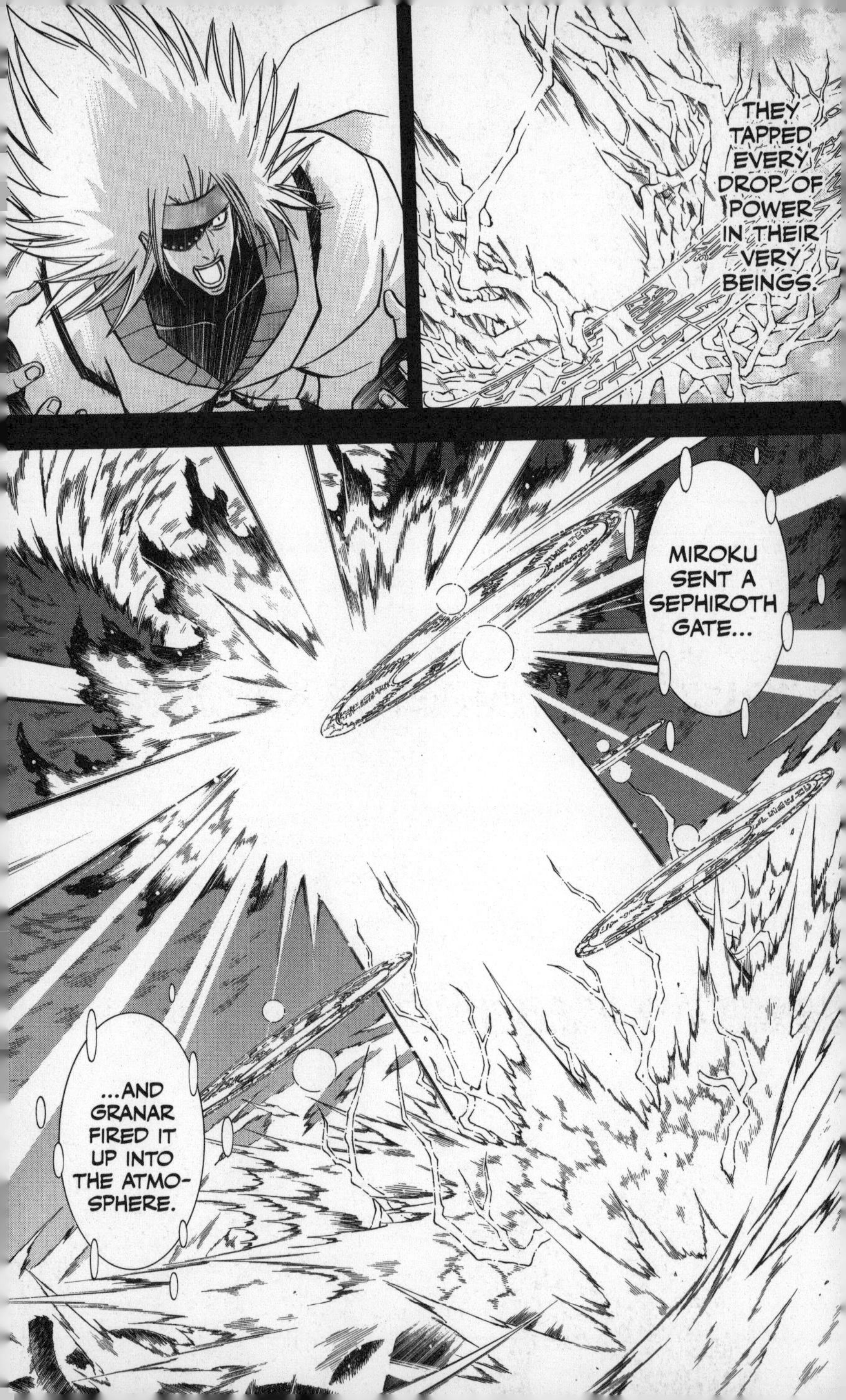
THEY TAPPED EVERY DROP OF POWER IN THEIR VERY BEINGS.
MIROKU SENT A SEPHIROTH GATE...
...AND GRANAR FIRED IT UP INTO THE ATMOSPHERE.

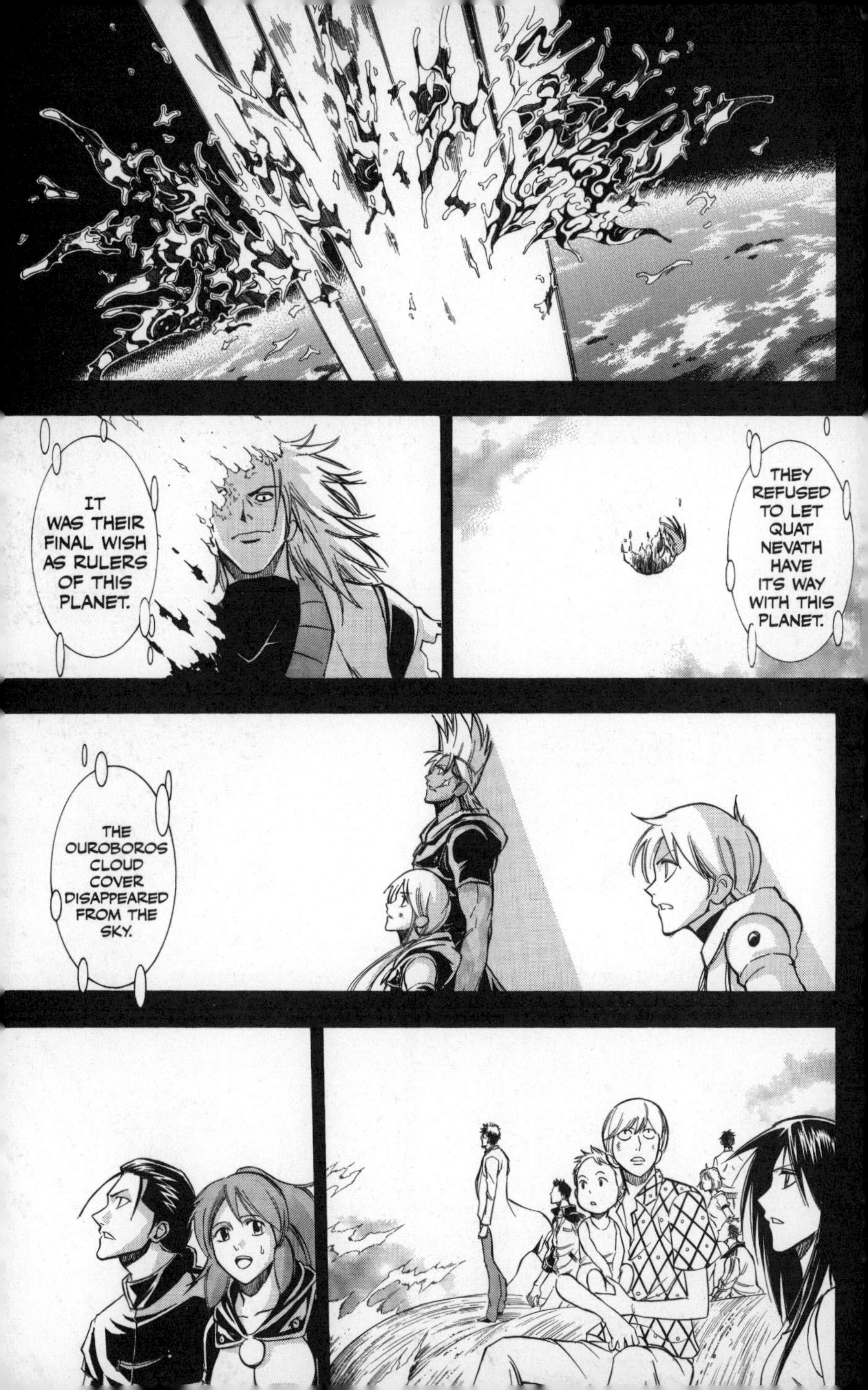
THEY REFUSED TO LET QUAT NEVATH HAVE ITS WAY WITH THIS PLANET.
IT WAS THEIR FINAL WISH AS RULERS OF THIS PLANET.
THE OUROBOROS CLOUD COVER DISAPPEARED FROM THE SKY.

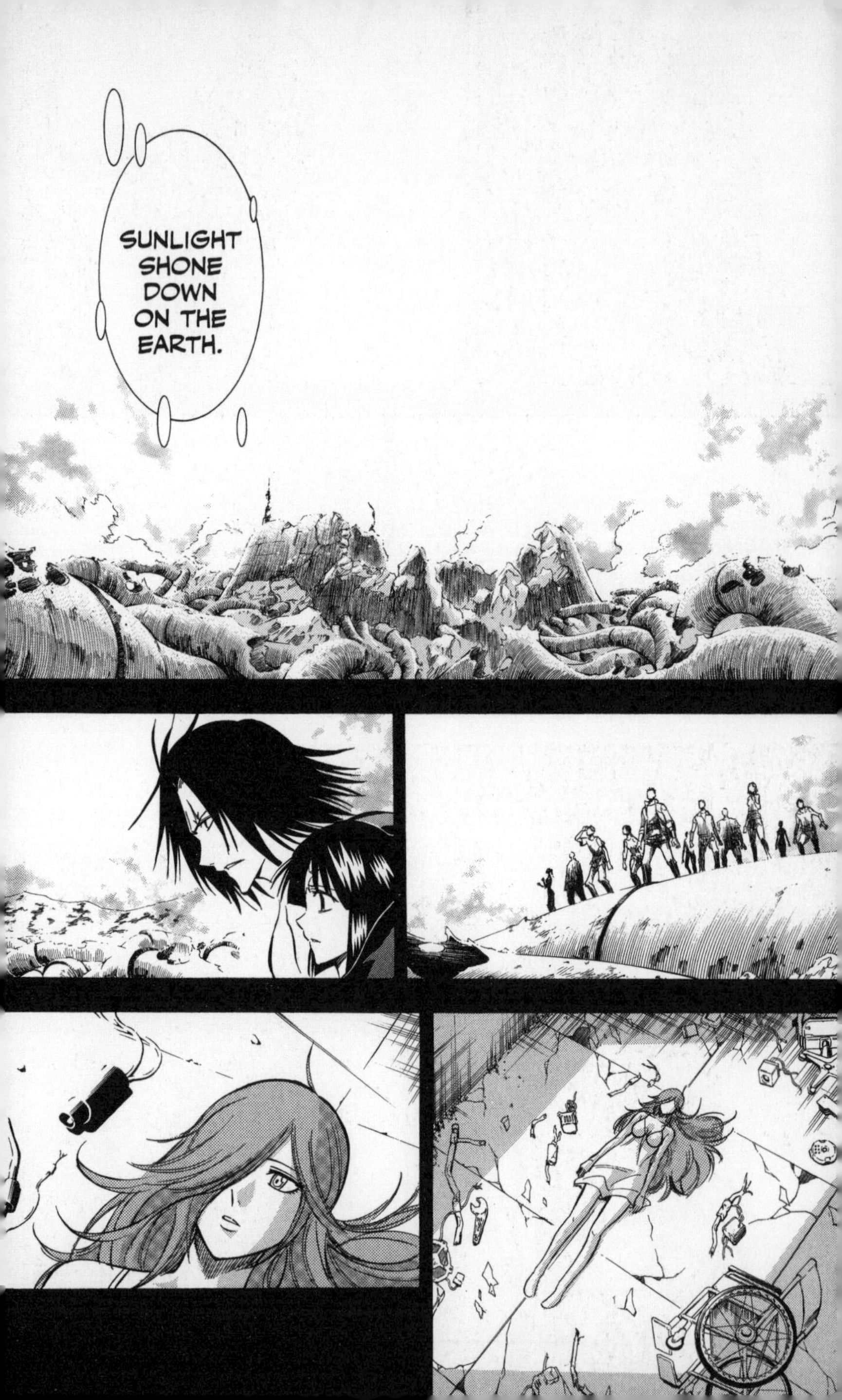
SUNLIGHT SHONE DOWN ON THE EARTH.

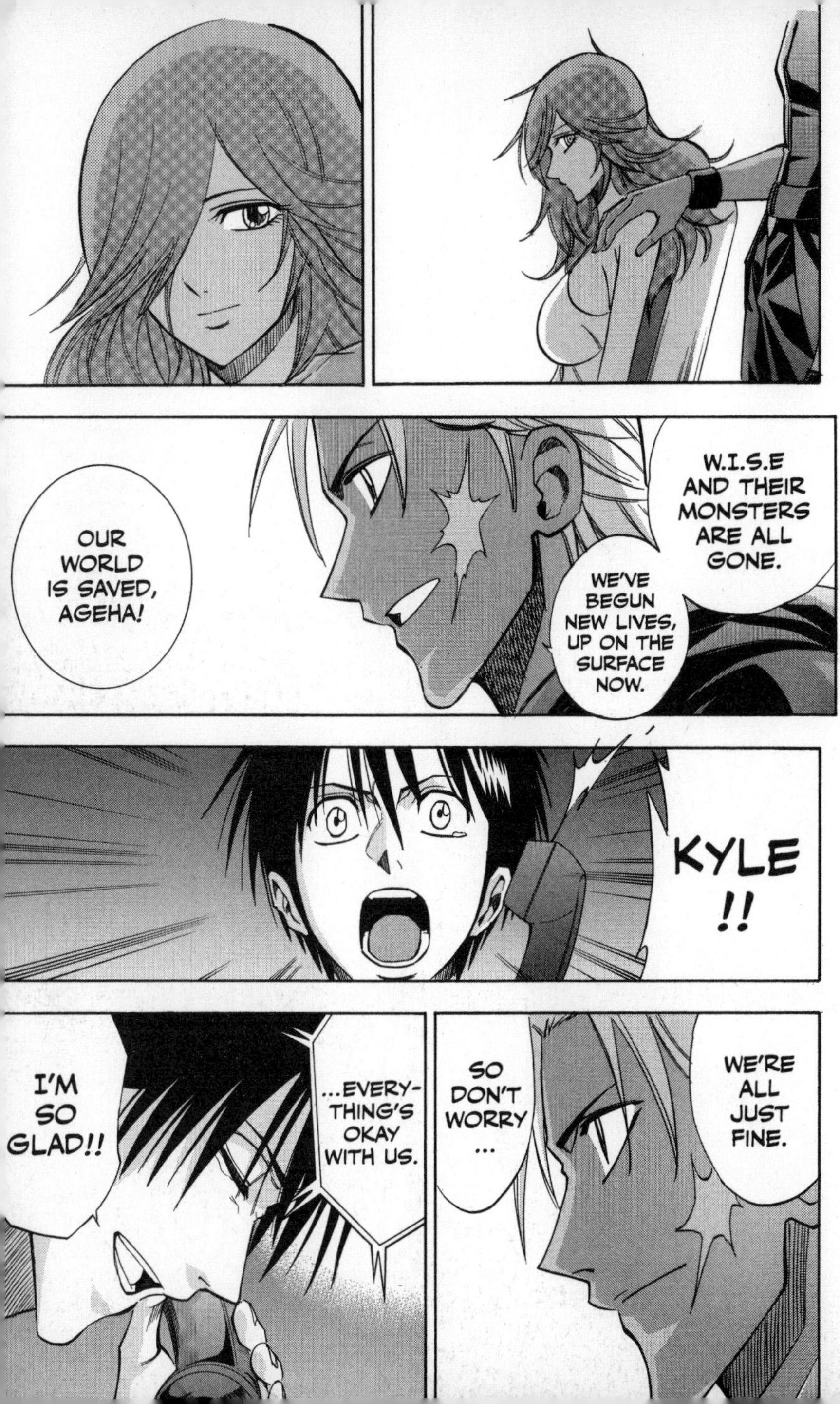
W.I.S.E AND THEIR MONSTERS ARE ALL GONE.
WE'VE BEGUN NEW LIVES, UP ON THE SURFACE NOW.
OUR WORLD IS SAVED, AGEHA!
KYLE !!
WE'RE ALL JUST FINE.
SO DON'T WORRY ...
...EVERY-THING'S OKAY WITH US.
I'M SO GLAD!!

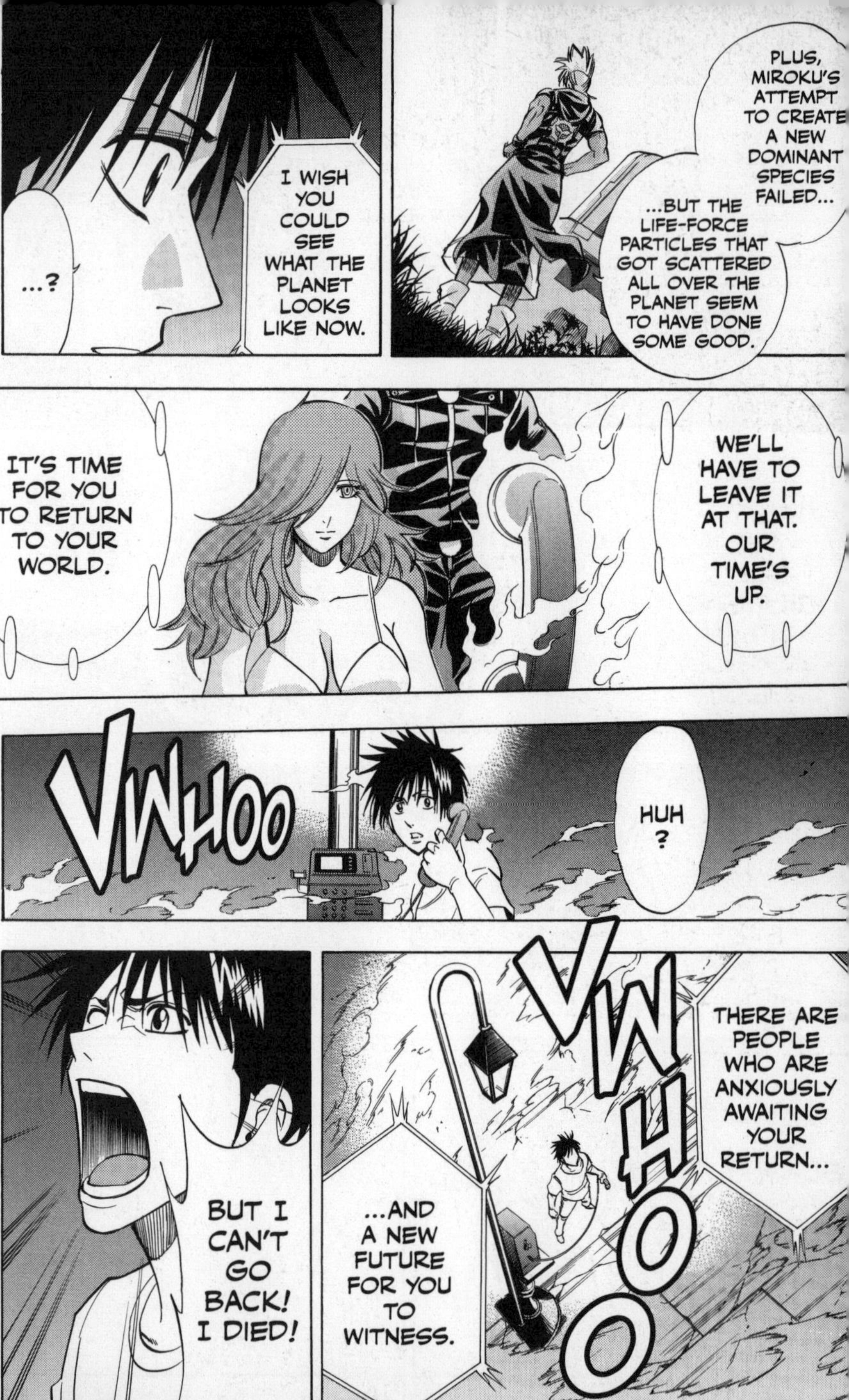
PLUS, MIROKU'S ATTEMPT TO CREATE A NEW DOMINANT SPECIES FAILED...
...BUT THE LIFE-FORCE PARTICLES THAT GOT SCATTERED ALL OVER THE PLANET SEEM TO HAVE DONE SOME GOOD.
I WISH YOU COULD SEE WHAT THE PLANET LOOKS LIKE NOW.
...?
WE'LL HAVE TO LEAVE IT AT THAT. OUR TIME'S UP.
IT'S TIME FOR YOU TO RETURN TO YOUR WORLD.
HUH?
VWHOO
VWHOOO
THERE ARE PEOPLE WHO ARE ANXIOUSLY AWAITING YOUR RETURN...
...AND A NEW FUTURE FOR YOU TO WITNESS.
BUT I CAN'T GO BACK! I DIED!

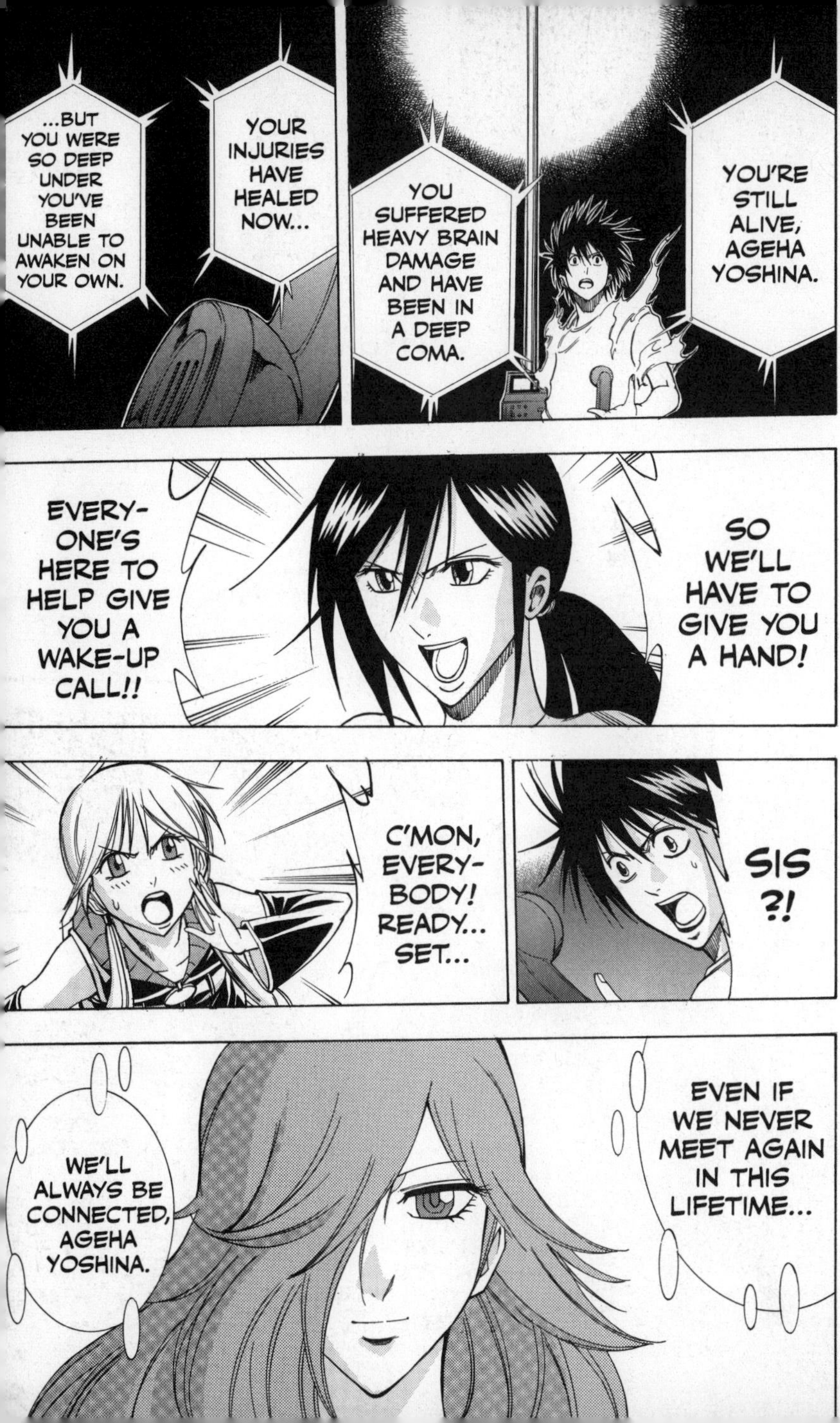

YOU'RE STILL ALIVE, AGEHA YOSHINA.
YOU SUFFERED HEAVY BRAIN DAMAGE AND HAVE BEEN IN A DEEP COMA.
YOUR INJURIES HAVE HEALED NOW...
...BUT YOU WERE SO DEEP UNDER YOU'VE BEEN UNABLE TO AWAKEN ON YOUR OWN.
SO WE'LL HAVE TO GIVE YOU A HAND!
EVERY-ONE'S HERE TO HELP GIVE YOU A WAKE-UP CALL!!
SIS ?!
C'MON, EVERY-BODY! READY... SET...
EVEN IF WE NEVER MEET AGAIN IN THIS LIFETIME...
WE'LL ALWAYS BE CONNECTED, AGEHA YOSHINA.

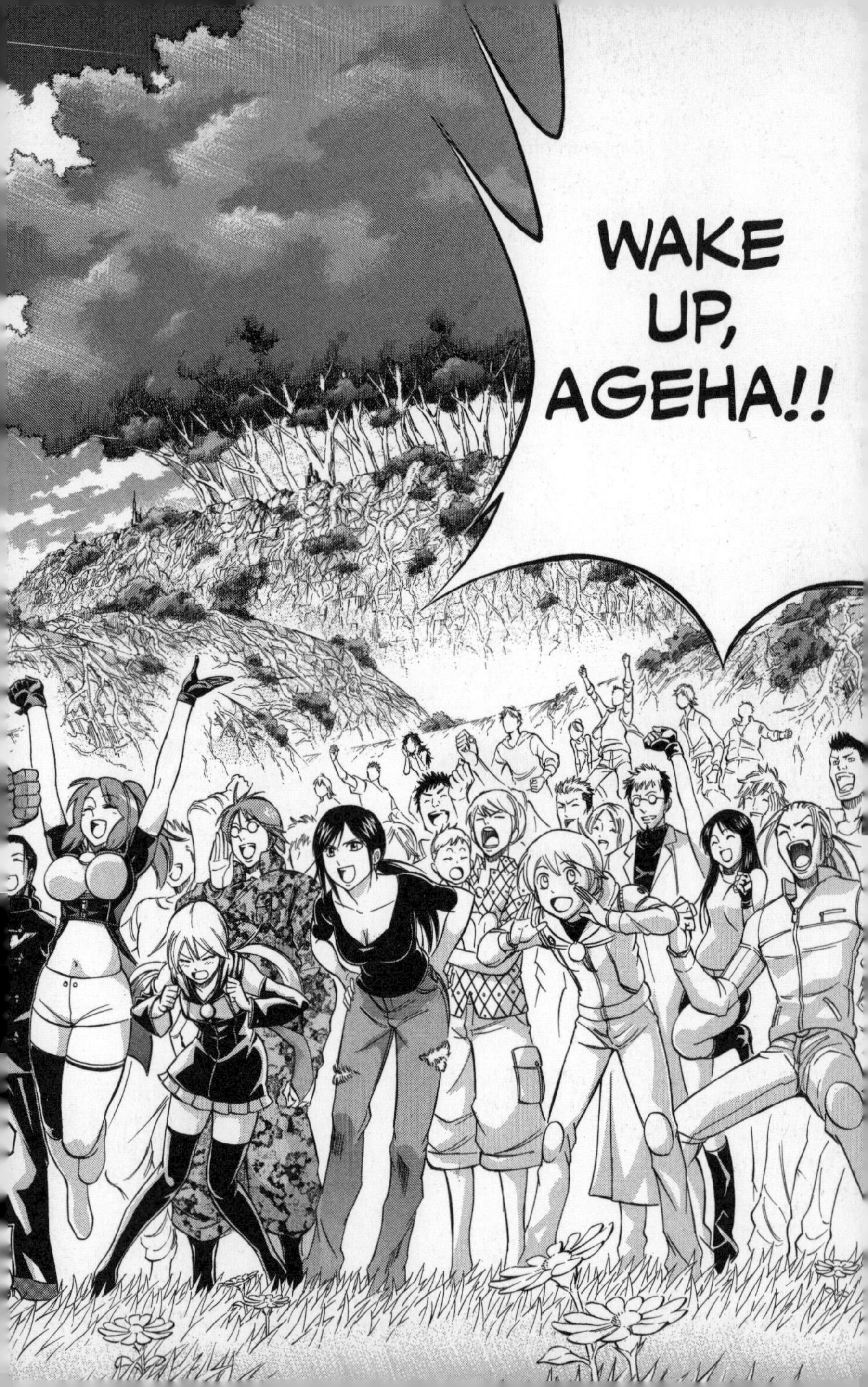
WAKE UP, AGEHA!!

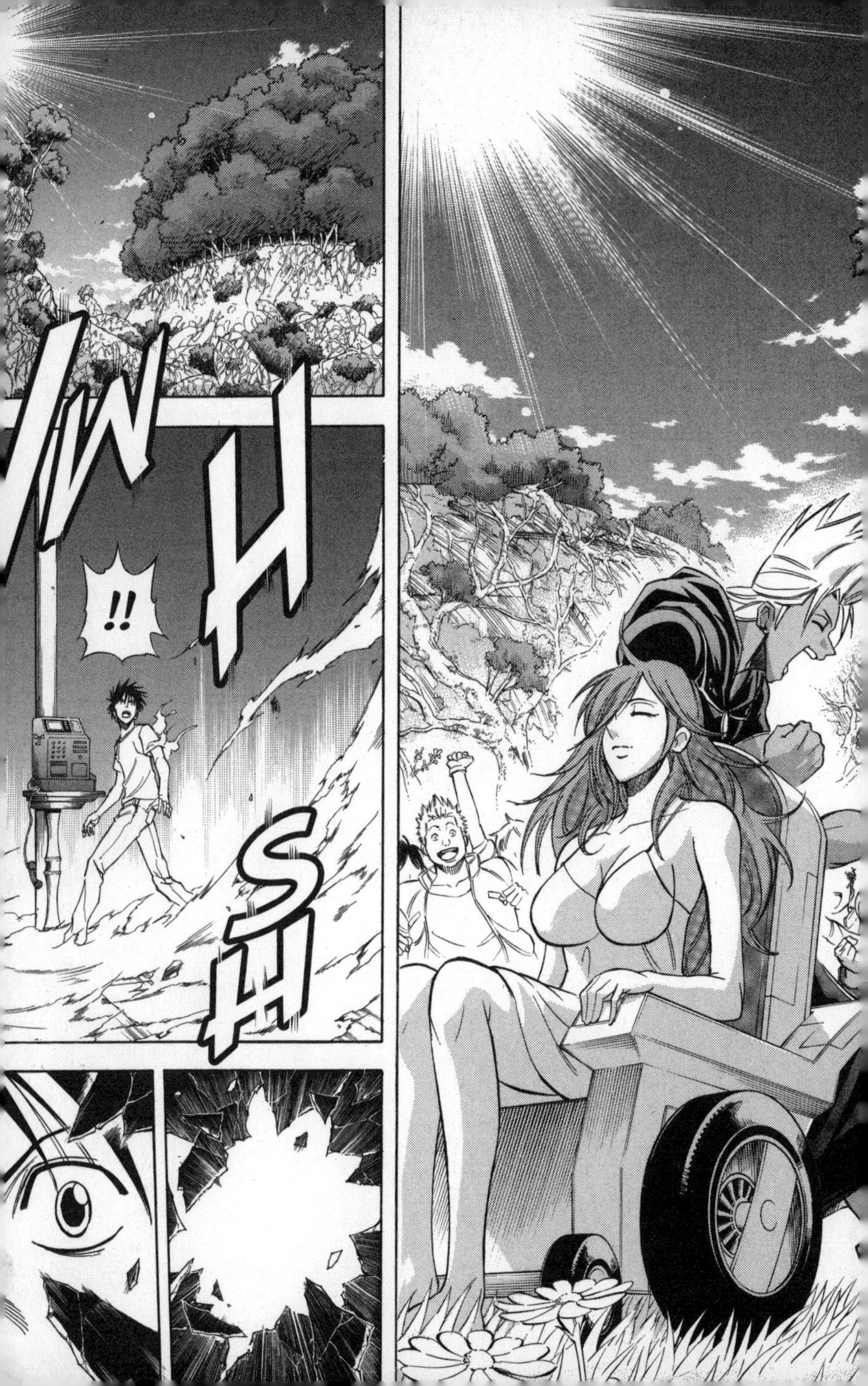
WHSH
!!

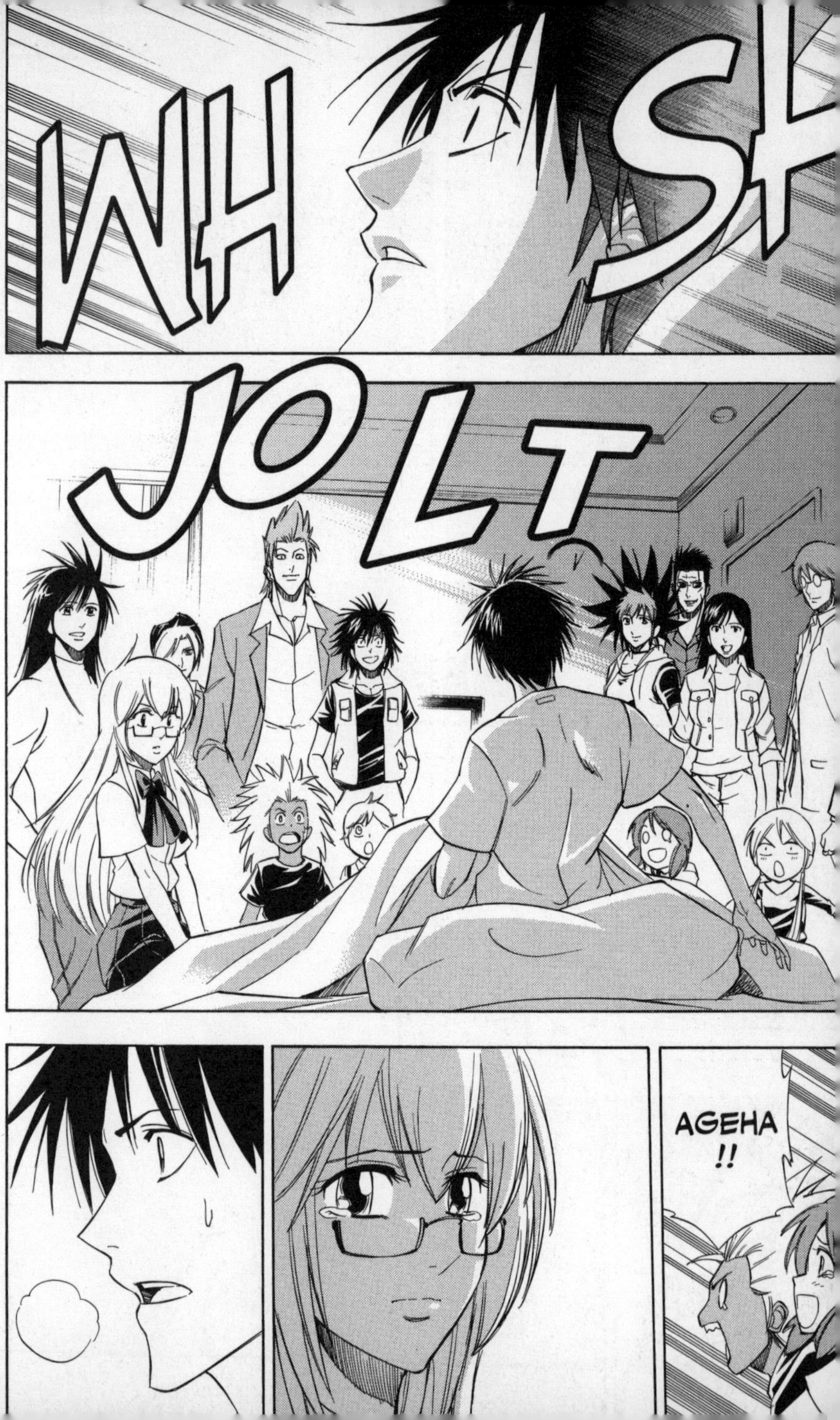
WHSH
JOLT
AGEHA !!

AGEHA!!

I PREDICTED YOU'D WAKE UP TODAY.

HOW COME...

...YOU'RE ALL HERE...?

OH, AGEHA! THANK GOODNESS!!

SQUEEZE

YOU OWE AMAMIYA A THANK-YOU. SHE'S BEEN BY YOUR SIDE FOR HALF A YEAR.

SORRY.

I'M BACK NOW.

I CAN'T LIVE WITHOUT YOU... PLEASE, DON'T EVER LEAVE ME AGAIN...!!

...THE WORLD HAD STARTED TO GET BACK ON TRACK.

IN THE SIX MONTHS I WAS UNCONSCIOUS...

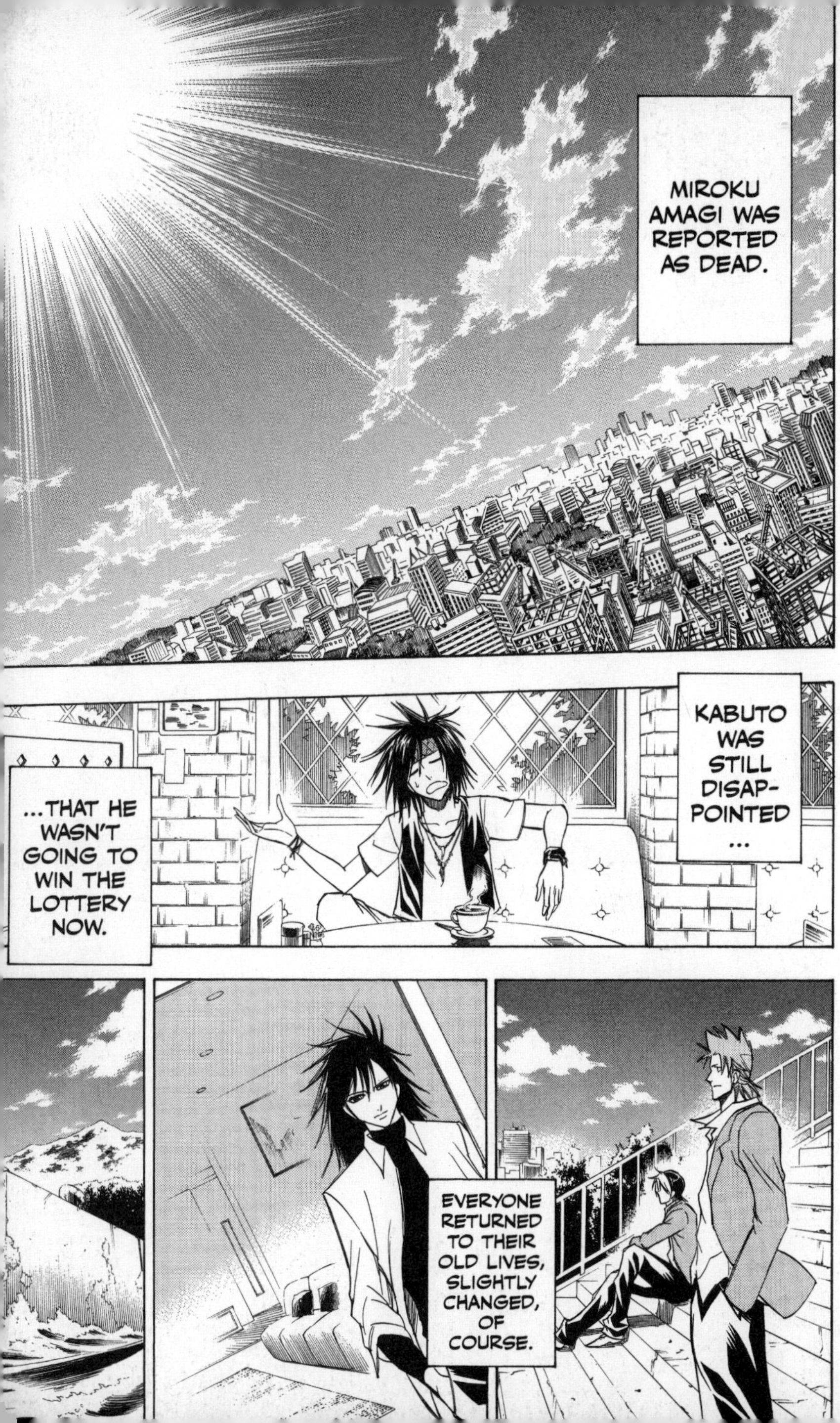
MIROKU AMAGI WAS REPORTED AS DEAD.
KABUTO WAS STILL DISAP-POINTED ...
...THAT HE WASN'T GOING TO WIN THE LOTTERY NOW.
EVERYONE RETURNED TO THEIR OLD LIVES, SLIGHTLY CHANGED, OF COURSE.

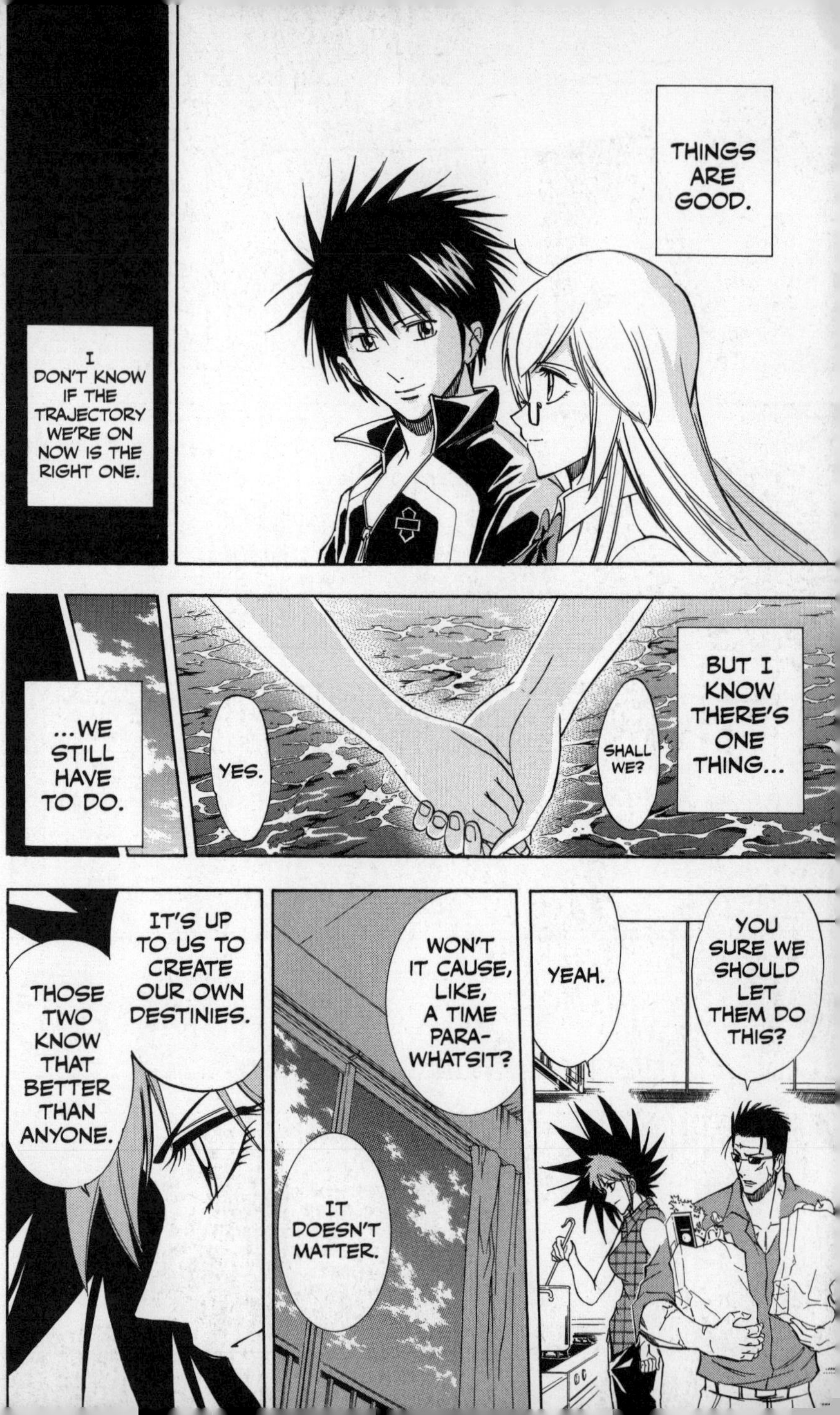
THINGS ARE GOOD.
I DON'T KNOW IF THE TRAJECTORY WE'RE ON NOW IS THE RIGHT ONE.
BUT I KNOW THERE'S ONE THING...
SHALL WE?
YES.
...WE STILL HAVE TO DO.
YOU SURE WE SHOULD LET THEM DO THIS?
YEAH.
WON'T IT CAUSE, LIKE, A TIME PARA-WHATSIT?
IT DOESN'T MATTER.
IT'S UP TO US TO CREATE OUR OWN DESTINIES.
THOSE TWO KNOW THAT BETTER THAN ANYONE.

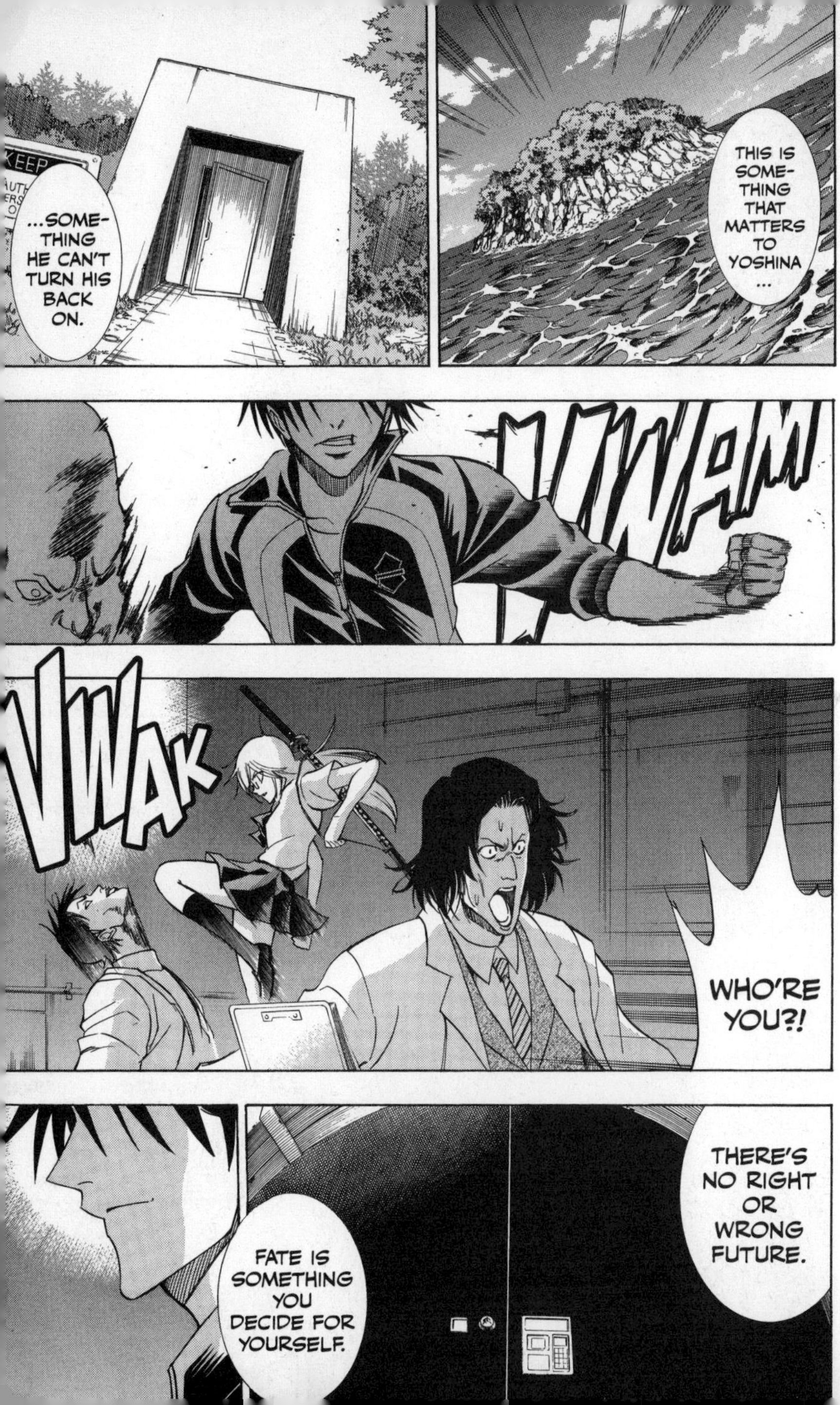
THIS IS SOMETHING THAT MATTERS TO YOSHINA ...
KEEP
...SOMETHING HE CAN'T TURN HIS BACK ON.
VWAM
VWAK
WHO'RE YOU?!
THERE'S NO RIGHT OR WRONG FUTURE.
FATE IS SOMETHING YOU DECIDE FOR YOURSELF.

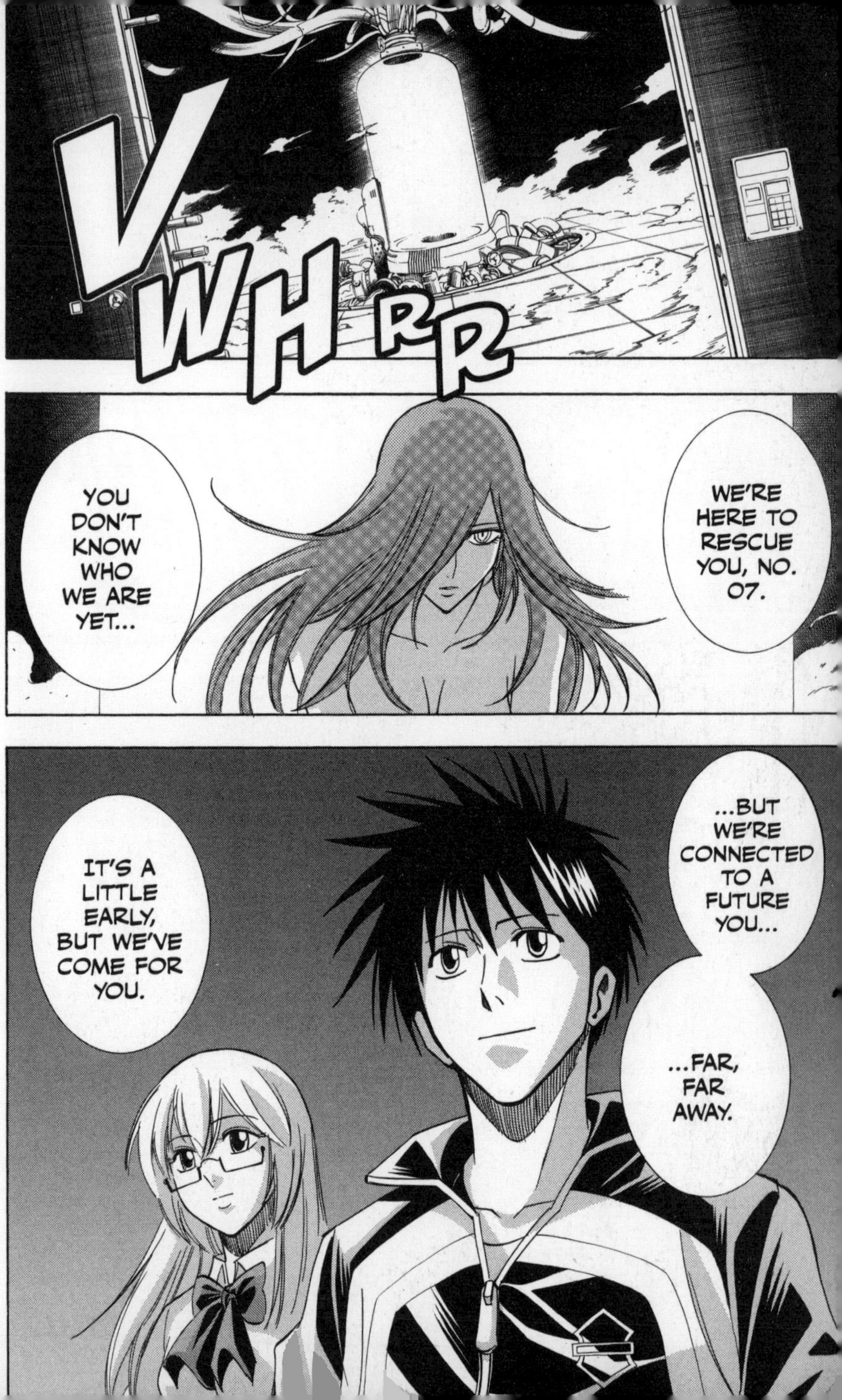
VWHRR
WE'RE HERE TO RESCUE YOU, NO. 07.
YOU DON'T KNOW WHO WE ARE YET...
...BUT WE'RE CONNECTED TO A FUTURE YOU...
...FAR, FAR AWAY.
IT'S A LITTLE EARLY, BUT WE'VE COME FOR YOU.

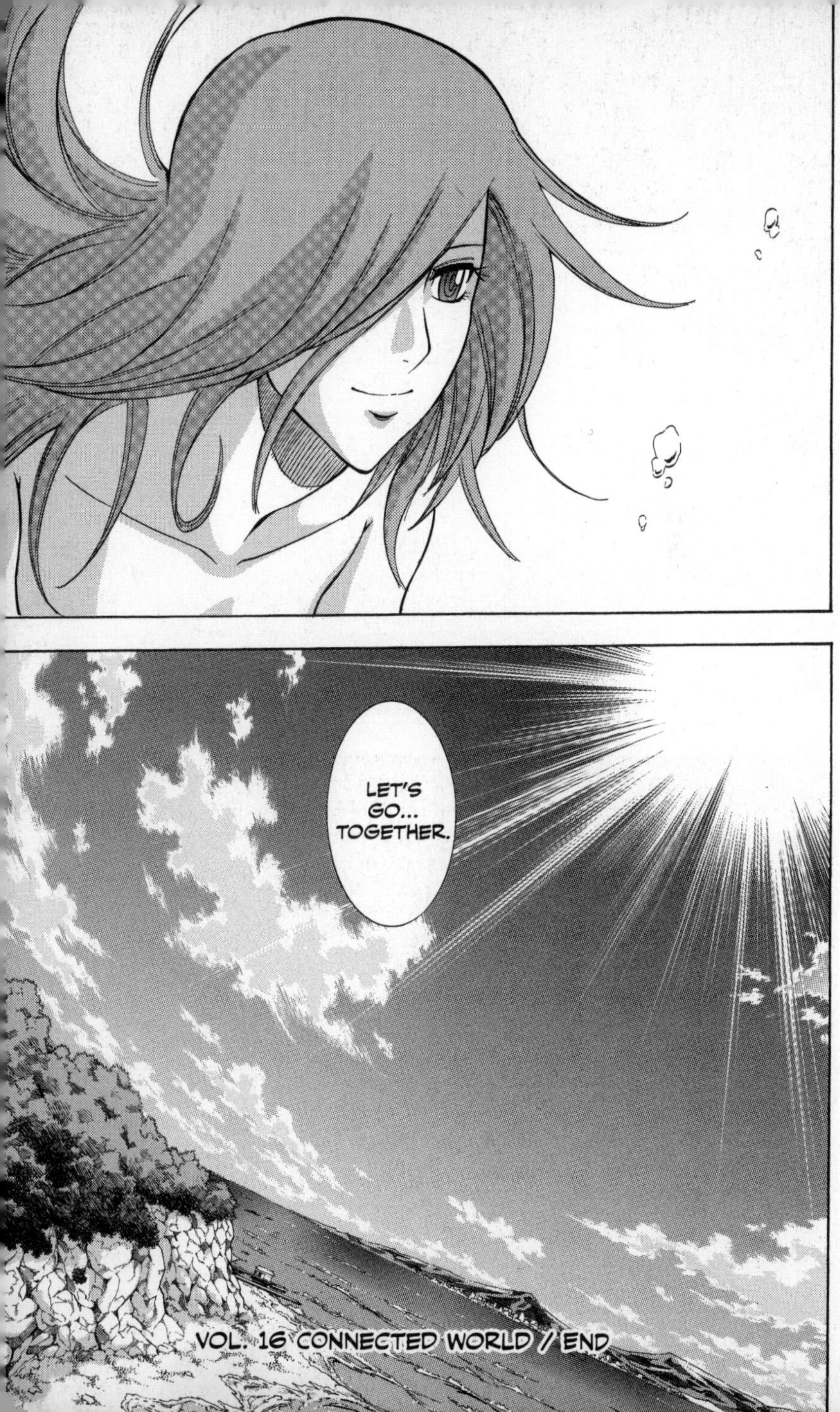
LET'S GO... TOGETHER.
VOL. 16 CONNECTED WORLD / END

PSYREN

Afterword 16

THANK YOU FOR BUYING VOLUME 16!!
I'M RELIEVED TO HAVE COMPLETED
THE SERIES WITHOUT MISHAP.
SOMETIMES A SHIVER RUNS DOWN MY
SPINE WHEN I THINK OF HOW WITLESSLY
I DELVED INTO A PLOT REVOLVING
AROUND CHARACTERS WHO TIME-TRAVEL
BACK AND FORTH BETWEEN THE PRESENT
AND THE FUTURE TO SAVE THE FATE OF
THE PLANET. I WAS IN A CONSTANT COLD
SWEAT, WORRYING THAT I WOULD GET
TRIPPED UP BY THE PITFALLS OF A
TIME-TRAVEL PIECE AND COMPLETELY
SCREW UP THE STORY. BUT IT WAS FUN.

I WANT TO THANK ALL OF MY STAFF
WHO HELPED OUT WITH *PSYREN*.
THANK YOU, SOW, FOR THE AMAZING
NOVELIZATION. AND ALL OF THE FANS
WHO HAVE SUPPORTED THE SERIES, YOU
HAVE BEEN FANTASTIC. THANK YOU SO
MUCH. I HOPE WE MEET AGAIN.

TOSHIAKI IWASHIRO
FEBRUARY, 2011

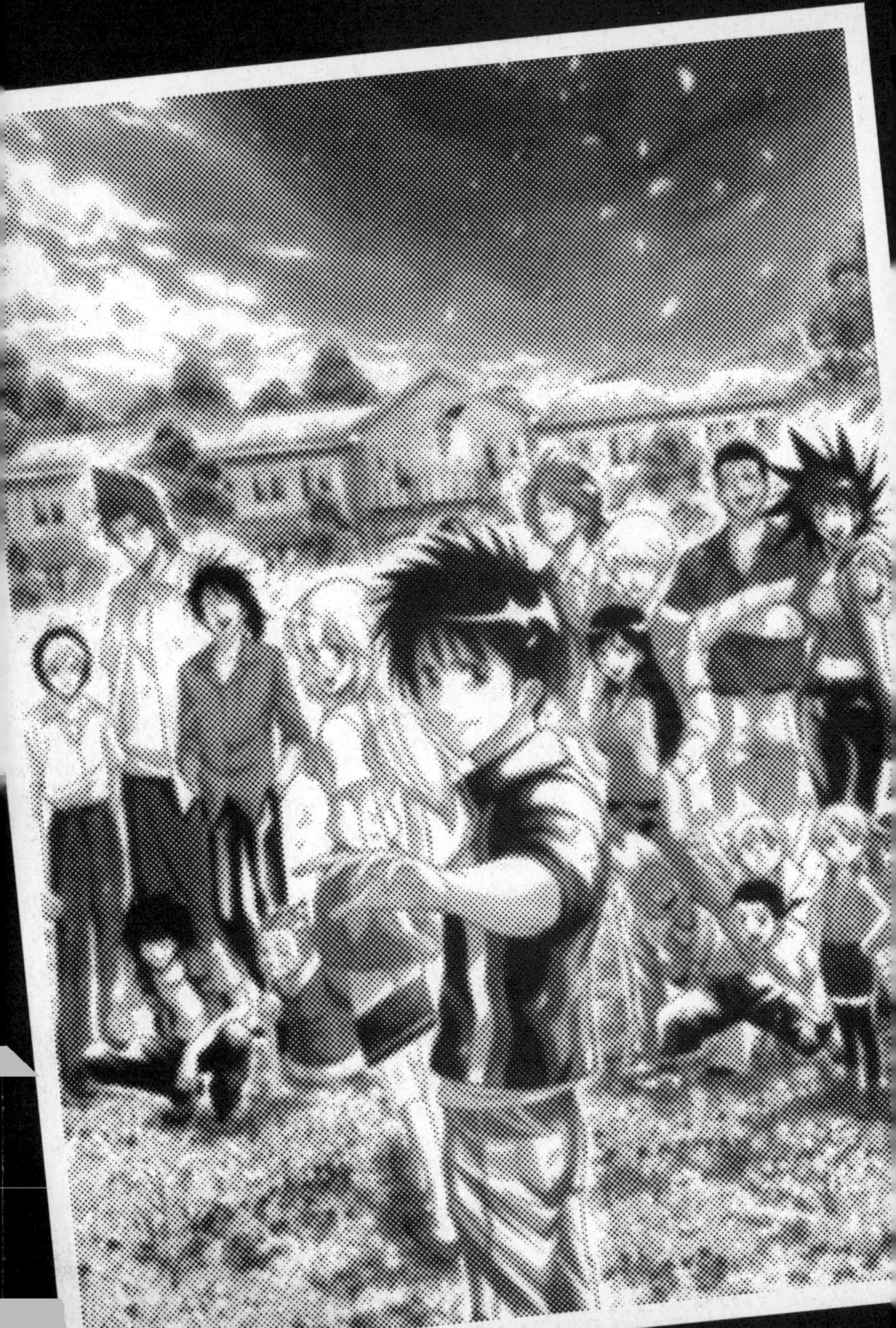

You're Reading in the Wrong Direction!!

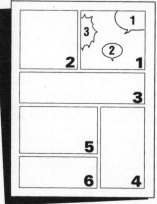

Whoops! Guess what? You're starting at the wrong end of the comic!

…It's true! In keeping with the original Japanese format, **Psyren** is meant to be read from right to left, starting in the upper-right corner.

Unlike English, which is read from left to right, Japanese is read from right to left, meaning that action, sound effects and word-balloon order are completely reversed—something which can make readers unfamiliar with Japanese feel pretty backwards themselves. For this reason, manga or Japanese comics published in the U.S. in English have sometimes been published "flopped"—that is, printed in exact reverse order, as though seen from the other side of a mirror.

By flopping pages, U.S. publishers can avoid confusing readers, but the compromise is not without its downside. For one thing, a character in a flopped manga series who once wore in the original Japanese version a T-shirt emblazoned with "M A Y" (as in "the merry month of") now wears one which reads "Y A M"! Additionally, many manga creators in Japan are themselves unhappy with the process, as some feel the mirror-imaging of their art changes their original intentions.

We are proud to bring you Toshiaki Iwashiro's **Psyren** in the original unflopped format. For now, though, turn to the other side of the book and let the fun begin…!

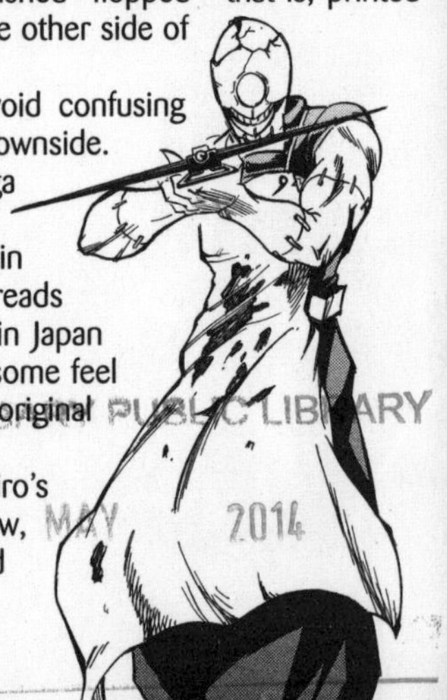

—Editor